Palgrave Studies in Economic History

Series Editor
Kent Deng, London School of Economics, London, UK

Palgrave Studies in Economic History is designed to illuminate and enrich our understanding of economies and economic phenomena of the past. The series covers a vast range of topics including financial history, labour history, development economics, commercialisation, urbanisation, industrialisation, modernisation, globalisation, and changes in world economic orders.

Tanja Skambraks · Martin Lutz
Editors

Reassessing the Moral Economy

Religion and Economic Ethics from Ancient Greece to the 20th Century

palgrave
macmillan

Editors
Tanja Skambraks
Karl-Franzens-Universität
Graz, Austria

Martin Lutz
Department of History
Humboldt-University of Berlin
Berlin, Germany

ISSN 2662-6497 ISSN 2662-6500 (electronic)
Palgrave Studies in Economic History
ISBN 978-3-031-29833-2 ISBN 978-3-031-29834-9 (eBook)
https://doi.org/10.1007/978-3-031-29834-9

Cover credit: Pusteflower9024/gettyimages

This Palgrave Macmillan imprint is published by the registered company Springer Nature Switzerland AG
The registered company address is: Gewerbestrasse 11, 6330 Cham, Switzerland

Contents

Notes on Contributors

E. Attila Aytekin obtained his Ph.D. from SUNY Binghamton University and is a professor of History at the Department of Political Science and Public Administration at Middle East Technical University, Ankara, Turkey. His research interests late Ottoman politics and society, the economic and social history of the Ottoman Empire, and Urban History. Among Aytekin's publications one prominent example is his article in the International Review of Social History titled "Peasant Protest in the Late Ottoman Empire: Moral Economy, Revolt, and the *Tanzimat* Reforms" (2012).

David Bete studied History and Hispanic Studies at the University of Göttingen from 2011 to 2016. Afterwards he continued his studies with a Master in History at the University of Granada, Spain until 2017. Since 2019 he is working as a research associate at the University of Göttingen, Germany while writing his PhD thesis.

Lorenzo Coccoli is a post-doc in the History of Political Thought at the University of Insubria. He is author of various articles on the history of political institutions, political thought and social history. He edited Genealogie del presente. Lessico politico per tempi interessanti (2014, with M. Tabacchini and F. Zappino), Ragion di Stato e ragioni della Chiesa (2019, with G. Borrelli), and I poveri possono parlare? Soggetti, problemi, alleanze (2021). In 2017, he published the monograph Il governo dei poveri all'inizio dell'età moderna. Riforma delle istituzioni assistenziali e dibattiti sulla povertà nell'Europa del Cinquecento.

Thomas Dorfner is a research fellow at the History Department of RWTH Aachen University. He attained his doctorate in 2015 at the University of Münster. His dissertation, which was published by Aschendorff Verlag, earned him the "Research prize for Legal History" for the year 2016. He is also currently working on a book about the economic activities of the Moravian Brethren in the Atlantic World.

Aviya Doron is completing her PhD at the Department of Jewish History at the Hebrew University of Jerusalem. Her research explores risk and trust in Jewish-Christian economic interactions in the German Empire, and the institutions that supported interreligious economic exchange. Combining legal and administrative archival sources in Latin and German with responsa literature, her research draws on institutional economic history, social-network analysis, and the history of daily life.

Paul Franke wrote his dissertation at the International Max-Planck Research School "Moral Economies of Modern Societies" at the Max-Planck Institute for Human Development and the Humboldt University Berlin. In 2016, he was awarded the Eadington Fellowship at the International Gaming Research Center at the University of Nevada Las Vegas. The same year, he spent the fall semester at the University of California Berkeley as a visiting researcher. Since September 2019, he is a postdoc at the Centre Marc Bloch in Berlin, an international research center in the social sciences and humanities.

Moritz Hinsch studied history and Greco-Roman archaeology at the Humboldt University, Berlin (2007–2012). He wrote his dissertational thesis on ancient Greek economic thought and household management as a doctoral fellow of the excellence cluster /Topoi/ (2013–2017). Since 2017, Hinsch has been a postdoctoral research assistant in Ancient history at the Humboldt University. His main field of research is the social and economic history of the Greco-Roman world from Archaic Greece to the beginning of the Roman imperial period.

Philip Knäble studied History and Social Sciences at the University of Bielefeld, Germany, and at the University Paris VII, France. Between 2009 and 2013 I was Ph.D. Candidate at the Bielefeld Graduate School in History and Sociology (BGHS). I received my Ph.D. in 2014 for a thesis on the ecclesiastical dance practices in later medieval France. Subsequently I was employed as research fellow in the Research Training Group "Expert Cultures from the Twelfth to the Eighteenth Century" at the University of Göttingen. At present I am teaching Early Modern History and Public History in Göttingen and I am guiding the research project "Reaping Souls and Yerba Maté: Franciscans and Jesuits as Economic Experts in Transatlantic Spaces of Entanglements (1535–1750)", funded by the Deutsche Forschungsgemeinschaft (DFG). This project investigates actors and practices in spaces of entanglement in the Atlantic world, most notably in Spain and its colonial cities and missions in the Jesuit and Franciscan provinces of Paraguay.

Giorgio Lizzul is Post-doctoral Junior Fellow on the Turin Humanities Programme, at the Fondazione 1563, Visiting Scholar at the Dipartimento di Studi Storici at the Università di Torino and Honorary Fellow of the Centre for the Study of the Renaissance, University of Warwick. He received his PhD in History from King's College London, and his BSc from LSE and MA from UCL and Queen Mary. He has been a fellow of the Italian Academy, Columbia University and I Tatti, The Harvard University Center for Italian Renaissance Studies.

Martin Lutz joined Humboldt University's Department of History in October 2012, where he is a postdoctoral researcher and lecturer of social and economic history. His research interests include the influence of religion in modern economic history, the history of globalization, business history and neo-institutional theory. Martin's current research project looks at religion and ethnicity's influence economic activity. In analyzing the history of Mennonite, Amish and Hutterite communities, he tackles the question of how these Anabaptist groups of German decent adjusted to the modern market economy in the United States and Canada in the nineteenth and twentieth centuries.

Benjamin Möckel is Assistant Professor at the Historical Institute of the University of Cologne. He received his PhD from the University of Göttingen in 2013 with a book on the post-war youth generations in East and West Germany after 1945. He is currently finishing a second book project, which is titled The Invention of the Ethical Consumer: Global Products and Political Activism in Britain and West Germany since the 1960s.

Franziska Quaas is Research Assistant in the Project "Gewalt-Zeiten. Temporalitäten von Gewaltunternehmungen" at the University of Hamburg. She is currently working on a Postdoc-Project on temporal dimension of military violence in medieval warfare. Previously, she was Research Assistant in the Project "Formulae – Litterae – Chartae. New edition of the early medieval formulae with an exploration and analysis of early medieval letters and charters in Western Europe (c. 500 – c. 1000)" at the Academy of Sciences and Humanities in Hamburg/University of Hamburg. Her PhD Thesis dealt with Formulaic Writing in early medieval private charters and formulae of the Eastern Franconian Empire. In addition to diplomatic issues, her research focuses on ideas of time and practices of violence in times of war.

Korinna Schönhärl is Heisenberg-Professor for Modern History at University Paderborn. She holds a PhD from Goethe-University Frankfurt. Her current research compares discourses on (honest) tax paying behaviour in Western Germany, Spain and the USA (1940s-1980s). Her habilitation thesis deals with European Investment in Greece in the nineteenth century. Further research foci are the history of economic thought, historiographic methodology, and financial history. Her particular expertise lies at the interface of economic, social and cultural history.

Tanja Skambraks is Professor of Medieval History at Karl-Franzens-University Graz, Austria. She studied Medieval History, English Literature and Communication Science at the Technical University Dresden and the University of Edinburgh. She got her Ph.D. in 2014 with a thesis on the history of medieval ritual, theatre and liturgy (The Boy bishop's Festival in Medieval Europe). From 2015 to 2023 she was assistant professor at the chair for Medieval History at the University of Mannheim. Her second book is about "Charitable Credit: the Monti di Pietà, Franciscan Economic Ethics and Poor Relief in late medieval Italy (fifteenth and sixteenth century)". Her research and publications focus on economic and social history, especially financial and banking history as well as methodology, material culture and the history of rituals.

List of Figures

CHAPTER 1

Introduction: Reassessing Moral Economy

Martin Lutz and Tanja Skambraks

Why Reassessing Moral Economy

Fifty years after E.P. Thompson's seminal article "The Moral Economy of the English Crowd in the Eighteenth Century," the historiographic debate on moral economies has vastly expanded and matured. Widening the focus on the eighteenth-century "English crowd" (Thompson 1971), scholars have addressed a plethora of themes, times and regions from a global perspective. Studies include the moral economy of gambling in Las Vegas, taxation in Germany, deindustrialization in Scotland and peasant protests in the Ottoman Empire and Southeast Asia (Franke 2023; Phillips 2021; Schönhärl 2019; Aytekın 2012; Scott 1976). As Norbert Götz claims in his intellectual history of moral economy, the concept is "capable of representing the workings of modern civil society"

M. Lutz
Humboldt University of Berlin, Berlin, Germany
e-mail: martin.lutz@hu-berlin.de

T. Skambraks (✉)
Karl-Franzens-Universität, Graz, Austria
e-mail: tanja.skambraks@uni-graz.at

T. Skambraks and M. Lutz (eds.), *Reassessing the Moral Economy*, Palgrave Studies in Economic History,
https://doi.org/10.1007/978-3-031-29834-9_1

(Götz 2015, 148). In connecting moral economy to modern civil society, he "detaches it from the value systems of the early modern period and reconfigures it as a mechanism central to economic choices of modern man and woman" (Götz 2015, 148). This focus on modern or modernizing society is also inherent in the earlier conceptualization of the three "moral economists" (Rogan 2018). R.H. Tawney, Karl Polanyi and E.P. Thompson all wrestled with the onslaught of modern capitalism and its detrimental impact on the laboring people.

This volume aims to widen the scope of "moral economy" as an analytical framework. It opens up new perspectives to employ the concept across epochal boundaries in different geographical settings in Europe, the Ottoman Empire and North America. In focusing on religion, the contributions to this volume focus on a prominent source of moral norms that has so far been neglected in the literature on moral economy. The case studies show how religion informed actors' perceptions of what they considered legitimate economic behavior.

Recent studies have shown the emergence of "moral economy" both as a term and as an analytical concept. Götz and Ute Frevert point to the end of the early modern period, when the older discourse on morality and economy changed direction. First cameralists and physiocrats, then liberal economists and philosophers such as Adam Smith, David Ricardo and John Stewart Mill began to think about the economy in a new way (Frevert 2019; Götz 2015). Götz pointedly states that "[t]he term 'moral economy' was created when morality was detached from the notion of economy in the middle of the eighteenth century, since its signification was no longer self-evident" (Götz 2015, 149). These developments allowed for a conceptualization of the moral and the economic as distinct spheres of social life. The rational, utility-maximizing and inherently egotistical *Homo economicus* emerged from this line of thought as an abstract model for human economic agency derived of moral values. This view has since shaped conceptualizations of the economy and economic action in classical and neoclassical theory. As Frevert states,

> [I]t expressed the desire of academics to prove, establish, and monopolize their professional expertise, it accompanied and enhanced the process of functional differentiation that characterized the advent of modernity. Moreover, it co-produced the illusion that human activity could be neatly divided into different segments, with each segment obeying different 'laws' and criteria. What Mill had called '*conscience*, or feeling of duty' was thus,

in theory, excluded from the economic sphere and might instead find its place in religious charity or welfare work. (Frevert 2019, 23)

At the same time, the presumption that moral values and economic action are somehow intertwined was never entirely lost. From the 1830s onward, social reformer Robert Owen and other British intellectuals employed the term "moral economy" to denounce the ongoing influence of values in the economic sphere (Götz 2015, 151). Owen tried to provide a socialist alternative to the political economy of liberal thinkers whom he staunchly criticized. As Gregory Claeys has shown, Owen thus took "moral economy" from its original Christian context to denote a socialist economic system governed by moral standards of fairness and justice. Crucially, Owen's socialist moral economy made due without divine intervention. As Claeys notes, "[w]ithout God the entire theoretical edifice of the moral economy was suddenly without any visible means of support [...] because the stewardship grounds for giving charity were absent, and the onerous burden which had encumbered private property since the Creation was thereby lifted" (Claeys 1987, 189–90). Owen's secularizing moral economy thus required a new legitimizing foundation grounded in emerging socialism.

By the turn of the twentieth century, R.H. Tawney further developed these intellectual strands under the impression of contemporary social destitution and Christian social teaching.[1] As an educator and social reformer, he was in the front line to study and mitigate the detrimental effects that industrialization had wrought upon the British working class. With Karl Polanyi and E.P. Thompson, Tawney stands as the first in line of three twentieth-century "moral economists" who inherently challenged the dominant view in economic thinking of a modern economic system bereft of moral foundations. Tawney also lamented the perceived loss of Christian virtues in an emerging capitalist order. In the foreword to the second edition of *Religion and the Rise of Capitalism* from 1936, he provided an extensive commentary of Max Weber's essays on "The

[1] It is not clear to what extent Tawney drew on Robert Owen's "moral economy." Rogan, Frevert and Götz do not explicitly refer to Owen as direct intellectual source for Tawney. In *Religion and the Rise of Capitalism*, Tawney only once mentions Robert Owen but it seems likely that the Owenite socialist tradition was familiar to him (Tawney 1936 [1926], 272).

Protestant Ethic and the Spirit of Capitalism," whose English translation by Talcott Parsons had been published six years earlier (Weber 2005 [1930]). Despite Tawney's criticism of Weber, he also contended that the emergence of modern capitalism was one of increasing secularization as

> Religion has been converted from the keystone which holds together the social edifice into one department within it, and the idea of a rule of right is replaced by economic expediency as the arbiter of policy and the criterion of conduct. From a spiritual being, who, in order to survive, must devote a reasonable attention to economic interests, man seems sometimes to have become an economic animal, who will be prudent, nevertheless, if he takes due precautions to assure his spiritual well-being. (Tawney 1936 [1926], 277)

Even Tawney, who in contrast to socialists Polanyi and Thompson was inspired by his own Christian convictions was convinced of the "'spiritual blindness' of the modern age" (Rogan 2018, 47).

Tawney's attributed secularization of economic life resonated in the later works by Karl Polanyi and E.P. Thompson. In *The Great Transformation*, Polanyi problematized the promise of economic liberalism as "a veritable faith in man's secular salvation through a self-regulating market" (Polanyi 2001 [1944], 141). In Thompson's work, religion is entirely absent in accounting for the moral impetus behind the food riots in eighteenth-century England. The English crowd emerges as a collective actor "defending traditional rights or customs" (Thompson 1971, 78). Thompson does not consider religious values as a source to account for perceptions of legitimate and illegitimate practices at the heart of the moral economy of the poor. Moral economy as devised by the three moral economists thus emerges as a conceptual framework confined to non-religious aspects of economic life as "the advent of commercial society outmoded religion" (Rogan 2018, 10).

The second limitation in Tawney, Polanyi and Thompson is temporal. All focused on the "great transformation" and its fundamental changes through individualization, commercialization, marketization and industrialization. The three moral economists were inherently preoccupied with the emergence of a modern economy as well as its legitimation and promotion in classical economic theory. Much less did they address the wider implications of "moral economy" as a conceptual framework to be employed outside a modernizing context.

We agree with Götz's presumption that there is "little reason to be content with the limitations of moral economy as defined by Thompson" (Götz 2015, 147–48) as confined so a specific historical time and space, i.e. the specific setting of peasant protest in eighteenth-century England. However, Götz's expansion of the analytical horizon in turn is limited to "[t]he potential of the term moral economy as a dynamic analytical tool that can illuminate the workings of civil society in the modern world" (Götz 2015, 158). In going even further, we consider the concept valuable beyond the confinements of modern society. We follow Andrew Sayer's contention that economies per se are moral economies. As a kind of inquiry, "moral economy" thus serves as a conceptual framework to the "study of how economic activities of all kinds are influenced and structured by moral dispositions and norms, and how in turn those norms may be compromised, overridden or reinforced by economic pressures" (Sayer 2006, 78). The volume's epoch-spanning agenda entails a long-term perspective to test the concept's analytical prowess from Ancient Greece to the twentieth century.

Research on premodern economic history, especially on the Middle Ages, can provide some inspiration and new insights here. Few researchers like Laurence Fontaine explicitly used the concept "moral economy"; some provided different termini to characterize premodern credit networks in rural areas, like Craig Muldrew's "economy of obligation," which seems not very far away from Thompson's moral economy. The role of theology for the evolution of a Christian economic ethics has been the most prominent focal point of medievalists in the last decades (Todeschini 2002, 2009; Langholm 1992; Noonan 1957).

The juxtaposition of economy and religion in medieval times is one main characteristic of economic theory, visible in the writings by theologians who were at the same time very often religious friars working as confessors and preachers in mercantile cities. Muldrew (1998) points out how late medieval and early modern rural credit was based on an economy of obligation, including mutual trust and reputation, and also Laurence Fontaine (Fontaine 2008, 2014) emphasizes the crucial role of these two elements for premodern economy. She furthermore shows the continuity of some elements of the medieval moral economy into the early modern period as well as how these moral values could be attributed to the market transactions and the definition of the market of the present day. Giacomo Todeschini's work (Todeschini 2002, 2009) on Franciscan theology and how it formed the economic semantics of the Middle Ages can be regarded as most valuable for the understanding of the highly entangled economic ethics and religious norms. These norms changed and evolved over time and especially as a reaction to new economic practices from the twelfth century on. The most important moral norms and values in the Middle Ages are connected to concepts like the just prize, the balance of contracts, work as well as the common good (*bonum commune*) and—of course—interest and usury which all evolved in the course of the commercial revolution (950–1350). This process of economic expansion brought about a series of new ethical questions to solve: for instance, how to deal with the potential loss of money spent in risky business or how to justify a fee for delayed repayment of credit. As mentioned before, the protagonists forming the discourse throughout the medieval period were theologians and legal scholars, who were not seldom involved in city politics due to family ties or simply because of their function as preachers and confessors. Thus, religious norms were influenced by economic practices and vice versa.

As this research on medieval Europe exemplifies, religion provides a useful lens to study moral economies across time and space. In contrast to Tawney, Polanyi and Thompson, we presume that the source was not entirely lost in the course of modernization, but continued to shape how actors perceived the good and the bad, the legitimate and the illegitimate, and hence employed a religious moral compass for economic action. The volume's diverse case studies suggest that in one way or another religion was an integral part in the moral embeddedness of economic life.

Aims of This Book

This book aims to address this twofold gap in the literature by reassessing the concept "moral economy," focusing on the impact of religious norms on economic practice in a long-term perspective. It provides twelve empirical case studies on the interrelation of economy and religion from antiquity to the twenty-first century by experts in their fields.

This epoch-spanning scope and the diverse thematic foci will be tied together by a joint reference to "moral economy" as an analytical framework. The volume will enable readers to gain insights concerning the similarities, parallels, continuities and discontinuities of economic thinking and practices in a very long historic perspective rarely found in the existing literature. In this sense, our volume aims to address the relevance of "moral economies" *avant la lettre*, with two third of the contributions covering premodern and early modern cases. Furthermore, this longue durée perspective will also enable the readers to connect historical cases with current questions about economical equality, wealth and today's approaches on financial, economic and ecological crises.

The authors draw on various theoretical and methodological strands in implementing the volume's analytical agenda, ranging from institutional theory, the social-cultural embeddedness of economic action to discourse analysis. The common denominator in all chapters is the question to what extent moral economy as a conceptual framework is applicable to study the relationship between religion and the economic sphere. The approach of all contributions will be micro-historical and mostly qualitative, thus also bridging a methodological gap: the one between cultural history and economic history. Readers from the spectrum of cultural history, history of religion and cultural studies will thus be enabled to get new and fresh perspectives on the topic of economy and those interested in economic history may gain profound and detailed insights into the anthropological prerequisites of economic discourse and practice. The book should also be of interest to readers in adjacent disciplines, in particular economic sociology and economic anthropology.

Based on this brief critique the volume pursues a twofold analytical agenda. First, we want to take moral economy out of its container of modernity to assess its applicability in an epoch-spanning perspective from Ancient Greece to the twentieth century. Second, we want to connect religion into the debate on moral economy as one prominent source of moral norms that has informed and shaped actors' perceptions of appropriateness, institutional development and practice in the economic sphere.

All articles in this book offer examples and case studies for the application of the concept moral economy. They also provide individual discussions of the advantages and drawbacks of this approach. In many ways, the book is thus a first step to an epoch-spanning discussion of moral economy as well as a fund of historical cases. The contributors tackled the following questions:

How are economic mentalities or ethics fostered by religion? Which parallels, continuities or ruptures concerning the ethical codes can be traced in a trans-epochal perspective? How do these ethics relate to and possibly develop into institutions in different epochs? Which new institutions emerged, which basic assumptions did they have, which strategies of survival and the balance between religious principles and commerce/economic growth become visible? Which impact did certain major developments like the Commercial Revolution of the Middle Ages or the Age of Exploration and the subsequent foundations of colonies have on these ethics? Do these developments incorporate local traditions and how do they adapt to temporal and environmental circumstances?

By looking at various collective and individual strategies and agendas of economic actors concerning their dealings with topics like provision, risk management or inequality we would like to contribute to a wider and better understanding of premodern, modern and maybe also contemporary economies. Conclusively, we aim at providing valuable insights into the hitherto underrated interplay between religion and economy.

Chapter Synopsis

The book is divided into three chronological parts. We chose this sequence of texts to enable readers to better undertake comparisons and see possible continuities and parallels as well as ruptures in the historical development of economic ethics and moral standards. Since most of the contributions deal with Christian religion, possible continuities might be particularly recognizable. Moreover, inter-religious comparisons, like the one between Jewish and Christian economic ethics in the Middle Ages or between the moral economy of Ottoman society in the nineteenth century and their Christian contemporaries become possible.

The book's first and longest part consists of five chapters. Covering the very long between the eighth century BCE and the late fifteenth century, it deals with the premodern epoch. The first chapter by Moritz Hinsch studies commerce in the Aegean world from ca. 700 to 150 BCE, analyzing the guiding role of the beliefs in divinely ordained justice for Greek rituals connected to economic activities. It is followed by Franziska Quaas' chapter on early medieval donations and land transfers to Bavarian cloisters (eighth and ninth century) as part of an economic strategy possibly motivated by religious motives. Aviya Doron offers insights into the evolvement of economic ethics in Jewish communities concerning inter-Jewish transactions as well as dealings with Christian business partners in the German lands. The fourth chapter by Tanja Skambraks deals with the interplay between economic ethics, economic practices and canon law and proposes three elements of characterization: embeddedness, innovations and feedback using source material from the Italian

Monti di Pietà. Giorgio Lizzul's chapter deals with the formation of a moral economy in late medieval Florentine chronicles.

The book's second part—covering the period between the sixteenth and the nineteenth century—starts with a chapter on Renaissance Italy, analyzing the "moral economy of pandemics" (Lorenzo Coccoli). The chapter by Philip Knäble and David Bete looks at the role of the Jesuit understanding of the concept of mission connected to the idea of perpetual economic growth in the Paraguayan province in the sixteenth and eighteenth century. Thomas Dorfner deals with the influence of religion on economic practice within a Christian community in the eighteenth century. Based on the presumption of commerce being a beneficial service to their fellow men, the members of the Moravian Church made sure to keep God's grace by regulating fair prices and establishing a reputation as reliable business partners.

The first chapter of the third part on the nineteenth century to the present day by E. Attila Aytekin's takes an approach closer to the original understanding of moral economy by E.P. Thompson, as he deals with the underlying values of the peasant economy in Ottoman Empire in the early nineteenth century. Contrary to the Ottoman intelligentsia frequently referring to Islam in their writings on economy, the peasants' economic values were less driven by (muslim and non-muslim) religious motives, but instead were characterized by subsistence ethics, the notion of justice and the valorization of labor. The chronology of the book ends with three chapters on the middle of the twentieth century. Martin Lutz's chapter follows a similar line as Dorfner's in analyzing the religious values as a driving force in the Mennonite moral economy of consumption. He shows how religious values concerning a "simple" way of life shaped the discourse and institutional evolution of Mennonites as this Anabaptist group gradually adjusted to American consumerism in a capitalist economy. Korinna Schönhärl focuses on the tax morale of members of the Catholic Church between in the 1940s and 1950s. By looking at three representatives of the Catholic clergy in Germany, Spain and the United States, she reveals that the seemingly centralized Catholic Church produced different opinions on tax morale that depended on the specific national contexts. Paul Franke provides the chronological endpoint of the empirical studies. In his chapter on gambling and morality in the casinos of Las Vegas (1945–1969), he points out that these were places where the visitors (mostly white middle class Americans) reconciled their conservative social views and their faith. At the same time, the entrepreneurs (mostly from marginalized religious and ethnic backgrounds) claimed their citizenship by running casinos businesses in accordance with moral standards.

In the book's final chapter, Benjamin Möckel synthesizes the conceptual strands offered by "moral economy" in this volume. Applying a praxeological perspective, he provides a systematic assessment of how economic practices in the empirical cases were linked to "moral claims, doubts, and narratives." He stresses the heterogeneity of morality concepts across time and space, a seemingly obvious observation, yet one that leads him to conceptualize of "moral economies" in the plural form even within one single societal context. Möckel further points out the complex nexus of religious moral and economy as a two-way process: while moral values can influence the economy, economic practice can also challenge and even change religious doctrine. In relating to E.P. Thompson's work, Möckel ends with an emphatic call for detailed and multifaceted description within this conceptual framework, an agenda that calls for further research in reassessing moral economy.

References

Aytekın, E. Attıla. 2012. Peasant Protest in the Late Ottoman Empire: Moral Economy, Revolt, and the Tanzimat Reforms. *International Review of Social History* 57 (2): 191–227. https://doi.org/10.1017/S0020859012000193.

Claeys, Gregory. 1987. *Machinery, Money and the Millennium: From Moral Economy to Socialism, 1815–1860*. Princeton, NJ: Princeton University Press. http://www.loc.gov/catdir/enhancements/fy1513/87002372-d.html.

Fontaine, Laurence. 2008. *L'économie morale: Pauvreté, crédit et confiance dans l' Europe preindustrielle*. Paris: Gallimard.

———. 2014. *Le marché. Histoire et usages d'une conquête sociale*. Paris: Gallimard.

Franke, Paul. 2023. *Feeling Lucky: The Production of Gambling Experiences in Monte Carlo and Las Vegas*. Worlds of Consumption. London: Palgrave Macmillan.

Frevert, Ute. 2019. Moral Economies, Present and Past: Social Practices and Intellectual Controversies. In *Moral Economies*, ed. Ute Frevert, 13–43. Geschichte und Gesellschaft Special Issue 26. Göttingen: Vandenhoeck & Ruprecht.

Götz, Norbert. 2015. Moral Economy: Its Conceptual History and Analytical Prospects. *Journal of Global Ethics* 11 (2): 147–62.

Langholm, Odd. 1992. *Economics in Medieval Schools: Wealth, Exchange, Value According to the Paris Theological Tradition, 1200–1350*. Leiden: Brill.

Muldrew, Craig. 1998. *The Economy of Obligation. The Culture of Credit and Social Relations in Early Modern England*. Hampshire: Palgrave Macmillan.

Noonan, John Thomas. 1957. *The Scholastic Analysis of Usury*. Cambridge, MA: Harvard University Press.

Phillips, Jim. 2021. *Deindustrialisation and the Moral Economy in Scotland Since 1955*. Edinburgh: Edinburgh University Press.

Polanyi, Karl. 2001 [1944]. *The Great Transformation: The Political and Economic Origins of Our Time*. Boston: Beacon Press.

Rogan, Tim. 2018. *The Moral Economists: R.H. Tawney, Karl Polanyi, E.P. Thompson, and the Critique of Capitalism*. Princeton, NJ: Princeton University Press.

Sayer, Andrew. 2006. Approaching Moral Economy. In *The Moralization of the Markets*, ed. Nico Stehr, Christoph Henning, and Bernd Weiler. First paperback printing, 77–97. New Brunswick, NJ and London: Transaction Publishers.

Schönhärl, Korinna. 2019. Steuermoral in Westdeutschland Nach Dem Zweiten Weltkrieg. Eine Diskursanalytische Rekonstruktion. *Leviathan* 47 (2): 169–91. https://doi.org/10.5771/0340-0425-2019-2-169.

Scott, James C. 1976. *The Moral Economy of the Peasant: Rebellion and Subsistence in Southeast Asia*. New Haven: Yale University Press.

Tawney, Richard. 1936 [1926]. *Religion and the Rise of Capitalism: A Historical Study*. London: John Murray. Holland Memorial Lectures, 1922.

Thompson, E.P. 1971. The Moral Economy of the English Crowd in the Eighteenth Century. *Past and Present* 50: 76–136.

Todeschini, Giacomo. 2002. *I mercanti e il Tempio. La società cristiana e il circolo virtuoso della ricchezza fra Medioevo ed età moderna*. Bologna: Il Mulino.

———. 2009. *Franciscan Wealth: From Voluntary Poverty to Market Society*. New York: Franciscan Institute Publications.

Weber, Max. 2005 [1930]. *The Protestant Ethic and the Spirit of Capitalism*. Reprint. Routledge classics. London: Routledge; Taylor and Francis. Translated by Talcott Parsons.

PART I

Antiquity and Middle Ages

CHAPTER 2

The Popular Morality of Ancient Greek Commerce

Moritz Hinsch

Introduction[1]

The concept of moral economy is both absent and present in the study of Greco-Roman antiquity. On the one hand, the embeddedness of economic behaviour has been the most-debated topic ever since the ancient economy became a major subject of research at the end of the nineteenth century. Participants in the debate, on the other hand, did not use the catchphrase 'moral economy'. The term denotes,

[1] Epigraphical corpora cited in abbreviation are *DVC* = S. I. Dakaris / I. Vokotopoulou / A.-Ph. Christidis 2013. Τα χρηστήρια ελάσματα της Δωδώνης. Athen; *IG* = Inscriptiones Graecae. 1877 ff. Published by the Berliner Akademie der Wissenschaften. Berlin; *LOD* = É. Lhôte 2006. Les lamelles oraculaires de Dodone. Geneva. *SEG* = Supplementum Epigraphicum Graecum. 1923 ff. Edited by Jacob E. Hondius et al. Leiden.

M. Hinsch (✉)
Historisches Seminar, Ludwig-Maximilians-Universität München, München, Germany
e-mail: M.Hinsch@lmu.de

T. Skambraks and M. Lutz (eds.), *Reassessing the Moral Economy*, Palgrave Studies in Economic History,
https://doi.org/10.1007/978-3-031-29834-9_2

in E. P. Thompson's words, 'the *mentalité*, [...] the political culture, the expectations, traditions, and, indeed, superstitions of the working population most frequently involved in actions in the market' (E. P. Thompson 1991, 260). This absence might be explained by institutional divisions between disciplines rather than differences in outlook. Thompson and most of the authors applying his concept of moral economy focused on the early modern and modern periods (e.g. Fontaine 2008; Zak 2008; Frevert 2019). Like Karl Polanyi, who coined the termed 'embeddedness', Thompson stressed that the 'economization' of society, i.e. the dominance of the idea of autonomous markets as a prevalent (and superior) form of social organisation, was a historically recent development brought about by the Industrial Revolution and the rise of Western capitalism (Polanyi 2001 [1944]; E. P. Thompson 1977). Polanyi, however, took a universalist approach, and studied not only the 'great transformation' of the modern era but also premodern empires and the economic thought of Aristotle (cf. his chapters in Polanyi et al. 1957). Hence, Polanyi's 'embeddedness' was within easy reach of ancient historians, while Thompson's 'moral economy' was not.[2] In this sense, the theoretical debate about the ancient economy had been a discussion about moral economy *avant la lettre*.

Ancient historians nonetheless have something to learn from the debates about the moral economies of later periods. As Marc Bloch noted long ago (1928), a comparative perspective helps the specialised historian to identify blind spots within her own field of research. Such a blind spot is the religious aspect of the ancient economy. The economic aspect of ancient religion, in turn, has received growing scholarly attention in recent years. Greek sanctuaries were economic organisations that collected fees, retained deposits, leased land, and handed out monetary loans; festivals and pilgrimage created opportunities for periodic markets and local commerce.[3] What has received less attention is one of the central questions of the economic history of the Middle Ages and Early Modern

[2] An exemption is Gallant (1991, 7–10), who employs the concept only indirectly through reception of Scott (1976). Discussions and applications of Polanyi's concept are too numerous to reference; for overviews, the reader is referred to Eich (2006, 1–104 (30–42 on Polanyi), Wagner-Hasel (2009), and Reden (2015, 91–105).

[3] On the economic organisation of sanctuaries, see Davies (2001), Horster (2004), Chankowski (2011) and Sassu (2014); on the economic impact of pilgrimage and festivals, see the chapters in Collar and Myrup Kristensen (2020).

Period: how did religious beliefs and practices shape institutions and economic behaviour?

In his attempt to map the economic effects of worldviews, Max Weber studied religion in Europe, ancient Israel, China, and India, but switched to political organisation and civic ideology once he came to ancient Greece and Rome (M. Weber 1999 [1921]). Many of the recent studies applying institutional analysis to the ancient economy, if often only indirectly, challenge Weber's conclusions, who argued that civic ideology and institutions had limiting effects on economic development. Like Weber, however, they continue to focus on governance and politics rather than religion (e.g. Bresson 2015). Ancient political culture is certainly more historically special in a comparative perspective than the fact that Greeks and Romans, like the majority of traditional worshippers around the world, prayed for personal welfare and believed in divine justice. Yet, the most remarkable phenomena of a period do not necessarily provide the best explanations for every aspect of everyday life and popular mentality. In this chapter, I will argue that religious beliefs and their expression in institutions and rituals are a key to better understand the moral economy of ancient Greek commerce.

I will focus on commerce, because it is the most controversial topic in the debate about the embeddedness of the ancient Greek economy. Both 'primitivists' and 'modernists' attributed a largely negative economic effect to norms and values. The 'primitivists' argued that moral norms inhibited the development of monetized commerce. 'Modernists' did not question the premise that ethics hinder economic action. They argued instead that the moral norms described by the 'primitivists' were restricted to the elite or altogether defunct.[4] In a forthcoming chapter on the culture of ancient Greek business, Mirko Canevaro and David Lewis offer a pertinent criticism of such a purely negative understanding of embeddedness and collect many examples for the juxtaposition of commercial profit-seeking with concerns for piety and honesty in ancient Greek business. Traders and moneylenders were especially concerned to signal their trustworthiness and enforce fairness in others, because monetized business more than anything else relied on trust (Hinsch 2021, 539–47). In this perspective, the embeddedness of commerce in religious and other

[4] Balanced accounts of the older debates are cited above, n. 2. A recent monograph strongly arguing in favour of profit-maximisation overriding any normative concerns is Leese (2021).

moral norms and institutions was not a hindrance to commerce, but a precondition for its flourishment.

The sources primarily used for ancient economic thought is another reason for the relative neglect of the religious aspect of the ancient Greek economy. A primary source for the ethics of ancient economic behaviour have been the fourth-century philosophical writings of Plato, Xenophon, and Aristotle. These writers discussed the social and moral limits to profit-seeking and the market in mostly secular terms. In different ways, each of them exhibited an upper-class contempt for traders (especially small traders), artisans, and menial labourers. They considered the acquisition of material wealth a threat to virtue, only justified to the extent that the acquired wealth supported a leisured life as citizen or philosopher (Helmer 2021; Hinsch 2021). The elitist and intellectualist nature of these texts does not exclude them *per se* as sources of popular morality. Their criticism of widespread assumptions often reveals popular attitudes *ex negativo*. As often, they present popular beliefs in a rationalised way and dressed up in fancy language. As I will argue in this chapter, the absence of religion in the philosopher's writings on the moral economy should not be explained by the erosion of religiosity, but rather the polycentric nature of Greek religion. Greek polytheism reflected the political fragmentation of the Greek world. The innumerable city-states and tribal federations did not have a single dogmatic tradition. Instead, they shared a bundle of myths and ritual practices that could be adapted to local or personal needs. There was no organised clergy with a monopoly on interpretation or ritual (for introductions to Greek polytheism, see Vegetti (1993), Price (1999), and Bremmer (2021)). As we will see, the fading of references to divine justice from the late fifth century onwards was a matter of cultural development in rhetoric and literature. The popular morality of ancient Greek commerce remained embedded in religious beliefs and practices.

Private Welfare and Divine Intervention

To the Greeks, the world was densely populated by deities. Wherever one stayed or whatever one did there was some superhuman agent one should not give offence to or could appeal to for help (Vegetti 1993, 319–20; Gager 1999, 12). The twelve Olympic gods residing on Mount Olympus were, quite literally, on top of a large and untidy hierarchy, which reached down to the chthonic gods of the underworld and countless nature deities, daemons, and heroes (deified humans). In

Theophrastus' *Characters*, a late fourth-century collection of entertaining sketches of personified moral faults, the 'superstitious man' (*deisidaimōn*) is characterised by performing rituals of purification or thanksgiving with every step he takes (*Characters* 16). Theophrastus ridicules not the belief in the omnipresence of divine forces in general, only excessive fear of such forces. Greek *deisidaimōn*, 'god-fearing', in difference to its modern rendering 'superstitious', does not denote a character trait that is negative *per se*. Consultants of Greek oracles often asked for specific lists of all the gods, daemons, and sometimes heroes, they needed to worship to be successful in their undertakings (cf. Carbon 2015).

Like relations among humans, relations with superhuman agents were governed by the principle of reciprocity. Worshippers offered prayer, sacrifice, or dedications as gifts and tokens of respect, and hoped for favours in return. Gift-giving, unlike contract-writing, creates moral, not legal obligations and leaves the nature and timing of retribution unspecified. Greek writers stressed that divine favours could not be secured through sacrifice or prayer against the gods' will or in support of crime.[5] This rule gave a moral dimension to the reciprocal relationship with the gods. The gods depended on human worship *and* protected divine law, so they were expected to discriminate between legitimate and illegitimate offers, rewarding the just and punishing evildoers (Dover 1974, 249–53).

Judging from the point of view of an eschatological religion like Christianity, Greek popular religion appears decidedly inner-worldly. Most worshippers were concerned with personal well-being rather than the salvation of their soul or the propagation of true faith. It should be added, though, that even in religious traditions more concerned with salvation, like Catholicism or Buddhism, popular religion tends to focus on inner-worldly well-being rather than salvation(Sharot 2001). At the same time, as the following survey seeks to show, even practices that sought to ensure personal welfare were informed by ideas of divine justice, including often vague, but nonetheless relevant beliefs in punishment and reward in the afterlife.

For 'ordinary' Greeks, the principal expression of divine favour was material wealth. Athenian comedy is a good source for such views, since it was written for large, socially mixed audiences. In Aristophanes' play *Birds*, staged in 414, an Athenian exile named Peisetairos advises the birds

[5] E.g. Aeschylus, *Supplicants* 363–4; Menander, frg. 1001 Kassel-Austin; *Homeric Hymn to Hermes* 546–9; Euripides, *Ion* 373–80; Herodotus, *Histories* 6.86.

on how to win back human worship from the Olympic gods. The task is easy, Peisetairos explains. Humans will worship the birds if the bird gives them what humans 'love most'—wealth. The birds can do so by exploiting their own role in divination. Since bird omens are consulted before any important affair, the birds could ingratiate themselves with humans by ensuring economic success: simply indicate the right spots for silver mining, the right time to start a maritime trading voyage, the location of a hidden treasure within the house (*Birds* 592–625). Aristophanes' later play *Plutos—'Wealth'—*, was built on the same premise. Humans venerate Zeus because he gives them wealth in return for sacrifices and dedications. If Plutos, the god of wealth, is healed from his blindness, people will stop worshipping Zeus (*Wealth* 87–142). Behind the carnivalesque phantasies lurks the popular belief in Zeus and other gods as dispensers of material wealth.

One of the best sources for the general belief in the gods as dispensers of wealth is the oracular tablets from the sanctuary of Zeus at Dodona in north-western Greece. These tablets, several thousands dated into the time from ca. 550 to 167 BCE, were inscribed with questions answered with the help of a lot-oracle.[6] 98 per cent of these enquiries were made by private individuals concerning their own affairs. Among these, economic matters are the single biggest topic. Property and acquisition constitute 39 per cent of topics in a selection of 1,393 private enquiries with identifiable topic. Within this subgroup, trade, ship-ownership, and sea-travel, which in many cases were linked to trade, together make up 21 per cent of questions (Hinsch 2022). This finding illustrates the remarkable level of mobility and commerce in the Greek world even in a rather remote area. At the same time, it serves as a reminder of how the severe uncertainties of premodern maritime trade fuelled the demand for divine guidance and protection (Eidinow 2007, 72–73; Carbon 2017). In the Dodona tablets, this hope is signalled by the recurring use of the word *sōteria*, 'rescue/safety'. An anonymous enquirer from c. 375 asked (*DVC* 1363A):

> Will I succeed [in going] to Carthage, and will it be better to sail there and trade in Koan wine for the rescue/safety (*sōteria*) of myself, my ship, and the merchandise/capital (*chrēmata*)?

[6] On Dodona as a sanctuary, see Chapinal-Heras (2021); on the oracle tablets, see the chapters in Soueref (2017).

Some enquiries expressed their hope for profit even more directly. They asked for 'a fair amount of monetary profit' (*LOD* 107A), whether a maritime trading venture would bring success and 'monetary profit' (*chrēmatōn onasis*) (*DVC* 3030A), whether sheep-raising would be 'useful and profitable' (*LOD* 80), or, as a married couple did, hoped for 'safety of their wealth/money as well as future utility/profit' (*DVC* 313A).

These blunt statements of profit-seeking at first look seem to support the idea that profit-maximisation superseded all other motives among ordinary Greeks. To avoid such a misperception, we need to consider the context of the oracular enquiries. It was common knowledge that oracles needed to be approached with a pure heart; immoral requests would evoke divine wrath (Bonnechère 2018; cf. Parker 2016, 72–74). That consultants openly expressed their hope for economic success, therefore, shows that commercial profit-seeking was not in itself considered improper. Let me push the implications of the oracle tablets for our understanding of the role of ethics in economic activity even further. Zeus, the oracle god of Dodona, was the founder and protector of justice among gods and humans. Apollo, the other major oracle god, was believed to have received the gift of divination either from Zeus or from Themis. Themis, in turn, was the personification of divinely ordained custom and a wife of Zeus and was also worshipped in Dodona.[7] Whatever mythological version we prefer, the message remains the same. Oracles were a device to implement divine justice among humans. One consulted them not because they guaranteed success, but to realign one's plans with divine will.[8] By asking Zeus about commercial prospects, consultants expressed their intention to seek profit in accordance with divinely ordained custom.

Relations between humans and gods were conceptualised as reciprocal exchanges. This exposed humans to the criticism of turning worship

[7] Zeus: *Homeric Hymn to Hermes* 533–549; Themis: Diodorus, *Library of History* 5.67.4; Themis was also considered an earlier patroness or co-founder of the oracle in Delphi: Aeschylus, *Eumenides* 1–19; Ephorus frg. 31b (FGrH 70); Euripides, *Iphigenia among the Taurians* 1259–83; *Orphic Hymns* 79, 3–5; for worship of Themis in Dodona, see Chapinal-Heras (2021, 109–10). A certain Archephon, who hoped to get rid of his debts through work as a ship owner (and, likely, maritime trader) addressed Zeus together with Themis; *LOD* 94.

[8] This included the dark belief that oracles might deliberately mislead consultants to punish them for an immoral request or earlier crime; cf. Trampedach (2015, 410–18).

into a business. In such a criticism of popular attitudes, Plato sarcastically called praying and sacrificing a 'commercial skill', i.e. the art of striking a bargain with the gods (*Euthyphro* 14b–15a). Modern scholarship has likewise commented on the 'commercial' flavour of dedications of 'first fruits' (*aparchai*) and tithes (*dekatai*) by artisans and traders and their advertising effects vis-à-vis future partners, both human and divine (Straten 1981, 68–72; Hurwit 1999, 62; for overviews of the material, see Boardman et al. (2004, 308–10) and Jim (2014, 133–75)). There can be no doubt that dedicants hoped for a tit-for-tat. A dedicatory inscription of an Athenian cobbler, set up in the fourth century, calls the stele to which it belongs a 'gift' and asks the deity 'to give wealth and good health in return' (*antididou plouton te kai euaiōn hugieian*) (*SEG* 55.307, 8–10). Sometimes, dedications were vowed on condition of economic success (e.g. *IG* I^3 872; IV^2 1, 123, 21–29), creating a further incentive for the gods to lend their help.

Nonetheless, an interpretation of offerings as purely instrumental would be misguided. Hopes of further divine assistance do not exclude genuine feelings of gratitude. Furthermore, dedicants did not think of their gifts as substitutes for piety and justice, but as manifestations of these virtues (cf. Jim 2014, 60–89). A hellenistic dedicatory inscription from Halicarnassus in Western Anatolia (*SEG* 28.838) identifies the dedication as a gift to Aphrodite, who, besides being the goddess of love and desire, was also protectress of seafarers and maritime traders (Demetriou 2010; Eckert 2011):

> Phaeinos [gave] you this, Kypris (= Aphrodite), a beautiful and noble statue, sharing with full hands the first fruits of his works, since ever you send him out as a great merchant (*megan emporon*) onto the sea, this pious man with pious deeds (*ex hosiōn hosios*) kept his house (*dōma*) together.

Phaeinos credited the goddess not only with his economic success but also with his choice of business, another indication that there was no categorical conflict between piety, justice, and commercial profit-seeking.[9] At the same time, the inscription shows that dedications not only advertised

[9] Compare *SEG* 54.1568, the autobiographical epitaph of a certain Sophytos found in modern-day Kandahar, describing how he re-established through trade his 'ancestral house', which had been wrecked long ago by the goddesses of fate, the Moirai. In the many years in which Sophytos visited many towns 'for the sake of trade', he always acquired 'wealth without reproach' *(olbon alōbētōs)*.

business success but also conveyed a moral tale. It would pay off to abstain from the short-term profits of opportunism, because the immortal gods would reward piety and justice in the long run.

Belief in the universality of reciprocity encouraged people to trust in deferred rewards for moral integrity. It also made them uneasy about deferred punishment for crookedness. Book one of Plato's *Republic* is set in Athens' port Piraeus, in the house of Kephalos, where Socrates and his friends meet to have a conversation on justice. We know from various sources that Kephalos was a metic in Athens, i.e. non-citizen resident, with various business interests (cf. Davies 1971, 587–90), and Plato himself makes sure to characterise Kephalos as a business man. Kephalos describes himself as a 'money-maker', who wishes to leave an enlarged estate to his sons (*Republic* 1.330b). Asked what he considers the 'greatest good' brought to him by wealth, Kephalos answers peace of conscience. When a man reaches old age, Kephalos explains, he begins to grow uncomfortable about the tales of punishment for wrongs in the underworld, about which he used to laugh when was young. Now he lies awake at night, 'reckoning up' (*analogizetai*—an accounting expression) and 'examining' whether he has wronged anybody. But the man who has a clear conscience because he has always been 'just and pious' *(dikaiōs kai hosiōs)*, lives out his days in sweet calm (330e–331a). Wealth is valuable, Kephalos concludes, because it allows one to avoid cheating and never to owe any sacrifice to the gods or money to humans (331a–b). Socrates summarises this definition of justice as 'to speak the truth and return what is owed' (331c). Plato finds the definition insufficient, but makes clear that it is a conventional definition, entertained by a respectable and pious man like Kephalos.[10] His choice of dramatic setting and illustrative examples further locate this religiously grounded concept of justice in a world of commerce. The just man, it turns out, is 'useful' with regard to 'contractual dealings' *(symbolaia)* and 'partnerships', that is, the 'joint use of gold and silver', as in the case of giving and guarding a deposit (331d–333c). A pious man is a just man is a good business partner.

Plato's prime example for justice as honesty is guarding and returning a deposit. Indeed, returning a deposit was considered the epitome

[10] Socrates and the other interlocutors enter Kephalos' house when he has just finished a sacrifice, *Republic* 1.327c. On Plato's evaluation of Kephalos' understanding of justice, see Lycos (1987, 26–39).

of honesty throughout the classical period and beyond (e.g. Pseudo-Aristotle, *Problems* 29.3; cf. Millett 1991, 204–5). The religious dimension of deposits becomes evident in a legend related by the fifth-century historian Herodotus (*Histories* 6.86). The Spartan Glaukos accepted a cash deposit from a guest friend but hesitated to return it when a long time after the depositor's children demanded its deliverance. He asked the oracle in Delphi whether he should acquire the deposit through oath, i.e. to falsely swear that he had never received the money. The oracle uttered a threat:

> 'Glaukos son of Epikydes, it is more profitable now
> To prevail by your oath and seize the money
> Swear, for death awaits even the man who swears true.
> But Oath has a son, nameless; he is without hands
> Or feet, but he pursues swiftly, until he catches
> And destroys all the family and the entire house.
> The line of a man who swears true is better later on.'
> (*trans. A. D. Goodley*)

Terror-stricken, Glaukos asked for forgiveness and returned the deposit, but it was too late. Glaukos' house was rooted out and his name fell to oblivion among the Spartans. Glaukos is the opposite of the pious businessman Kephalos. Avarice has let him to consider the abuse of four divinely sanctioned institutions: guest-friendship, deposits, oaths, and oracles. But like Kephalos, Glaukos fears divine punishment for unjust gains.

This concern over punishment in the afterlife strikingly resembles similar concerns among Christian moneylenders and merchants in the Middle Ages (Le Goff 2008 [1986]). But is it representative of ancient Greek attitudes? In a study of Athenian popular religion, Jon Mikalson has argued that Kephalos' concerns were exceptional. Most Athenians 'took little interest in the bleak and uncertain prospect of the afterlife' (Mikalson 1983, 80–82). It is certainly true that our literary sources do not mention divine punishment where we might expect it, while they also convey statements of the belief that death is the end to all hopes and pains (Dover 1974, 266–67). Nonetheless, Mikalson overstates his case. Judgement in the underworld was described or alluded to as something known and believed in from our earliest literary sources onward. In Homer and Hesiod, around 700 BCE, we find the Erinyes, the goddesses of revenge, haunting perjurers, both in this world and the next; Homer describes how in the underworld Minos, son of Zeus, judges the dead and evil-doers suffer torments. Also from Homer and Hesiod onwards we find the complementary idea that persons of exceptional excellence will enjoy afterlife in some desirable place like the Island (sometimes Islands) of the Blessed or the Elysian Fields. In the course of the centuries, the representation of beliefs in the transmigration of the soul became more detailed in literary discourse as well as burial customs and iconography (Sourvinou-Inwood 1995; Nesselrath 2020). From the sixth century onwards, a set of mystic beliefs in the transmigration and reincarnation of souls, labelled 'Orphism' in modern scholarship, developed. The heterogeneity of these beliefs is illustrated by Plato, who alone presents three different variations in his dialogues (Edmonds 2013; Nesselrath 2020, 192–206). Parallel to such ideas about punishment in the afterlife existed widespread ideas about deferred divine retribution that would target either the perpetrator later in life or his offspring.[11]

Evidently, a characteristic of Greek religion was not the absence of ideas of judgement in the afterlife but rather the thriving plurality of such ideas. It is certainly true that 'speculation about rewards and punishment in accordance with supernatural judgment after death no doubt appealed more to some moods and temperaments than to others' (Dover 1974, 268). But references in public oratory and in drama—genres with broad audiences—confirm that knowledge of such ideas was widespread and taken seriously by most people to some degree.[12] What mattered in everyday life was not a elaborate theory on how exactly divine punishment worked, but the diffuse belief in its existence.

A belief in divine punishment, even after death, was a logical inference from the overarching belief in reciprocity as a universal mechanism. If injustice gave offence to the gods for which they would reciprocate, and if the gods were both immortal and omniscient, then divine retribution would sooner or later, in this life or another, follow, rewarding the good and punishing the wicked. As in the case of revenge among humans, the

[11] E.g. Solon, frg. 13 West, Theognis, *Elegiac Poems* 345–50, and Herodotus' story about Glaukos, cited above; the Moirai, goddesses of fate, and Dikē, deified Justice, work slowly, but unerringly: e.g. Aeschylus, *Libation-Bearers* 306–14; Lysias, *Against Alcibiades* 20; Aristophanes, *Clouds* 1242.

[12] Oratory: Hyperides, *Funeral Speech* 43; Demosthenes, *Against Timocrates* 104; *Against Aristogeiton* 53–4; Drama: Aeschylus, *Eumenides* 264–75; *Suppliants* 230–1; Aristophanes, *Frogs* 146–50; 168–79; 354–70; Herodas, *Mimes* 2.90–1.

uncertainty about the specific timing and of retribution heightened the terror: Zeus may hit 'anyone anytime', as Solon put it (frg. 13 West). In this perspective, justice in business became a matter of personal safety.

The Contingencies of Commerce

Solon and others grounded their warnings about divine justice in the experience of contingency: the gods give and they take away. In modern times, religion has often been described as a mechanism to cope with contingency, a way to remain hopeful in the face of the severe limits to human planning. Whether this is the principal function of religion or not, contingency was certainly prominent in Greek popular thought on moneymaking and wealth. Windfalls—positive contingencies—were celebrated by lavish dedications of tithes or 'first fruits'.[13] Given the limits of ancient technology negative contingencies loomed larger on a Greek's mind. The local markets of the Mediterranean world were only loosely integrated. The success of a maritime trader hinged on many incalculable factors: fluctuations in local production, the outbreak or end of hostilities, or whether other traders had reached the same harbour earlier. Piracy and seizure were endemic, property rights difficult to enforce beyond one's own city-state, and storms unpredictable. The many questions on maritime trade and travel in the oracle tablets of Dodona remind us of the acute awareness of these risks (see above, p. 4).

A wealth of rituals existed to protect the ship and the people on board (Wachsmuth 1967; Eckert 2011; Fenet 2012). Greek travellers made offerings to the gods at the start of a voyage and at its conclusion, as well as during the voyage, sometimes in dramatic circumstances. The *Homeric Hymn to the Dioscuri*, for example, describes the epiphany of the Dioscuri, sons of Zeus, who come to the rescue of a ship already overwhelmed by winds and waves in the very last moment.

In such dangers, the gods were vowed gifts and honours in case of rescue. The hellenistic antiquarian Polycharmos (*FGrH* 640, frg. 1) preserved a legend about a trader who was rescued by a figurine of Aphrodite which he had taken on board as a souvenir. He dedicated the figurine to the goddess after his safe return, made a sacrifice to the gods, and held a banquet with relatives and friends. In a fragment from

[13] E.g. Herodotus' story about the Samian trader Kolaios, *Histories* 4.152; cf. *ibid.* 3.57.2 and Pausanias, *Description of Greece* 10.9.3-4.

comedy (Diphilos, frg. 42 Kassel-Austin), a cook for hire ranks different types of clients according to liberality. A ship patron who fulfils a vow made when he feared shipwreck is not a good choice: 'He's not doing anything because he enjoys it, but only what the rules require. As the libations are being poured, he's calculating how much of the cost he can pass on to the other people on board, and each of them feels his stomach churning'. A trader who has returned safely with big and easy profit is a good choice: 'He's delighted because he's made ten or 12 percent, and he's yapping about fares, and belching up loans, and using gay pimps to arrange liaisons. The minute he's off the boat I bow down before him, / take his right hand, invoke Zeus / the Saviour, and fixate on working for him' (trans. D.S. Olson). This satire of attitudes to thanksgiving suggests two things. First, vows were not a private affair. It was a matter of pious obligation, not personal enthusiasm to fulfil them. Fellow travellers or acquaintances in port were witnesses to vows taken and fulfilled and participated in the accompanying feasting. Second, thanksgiving was a religiously sanctioned occasion to promote one's business success. The successful trader who returned from Byzantion probably enjoyed wine and women, but he also reminded people that his business had divine blessing.

Shipwreck was also considered the result of divine intervention, the gods' punishment for serious crime (Wachsmuth 1967, 265–76). In Euripides' *Electra*, the Dioscuri appear on stage to announce that they will never help the polluted and only save those who are friends of 'piety and justice in their life'. Therefore, no one should act unjustly or set sail in company with perjurers (1349–53; cf. Aeschylus, *Eumenides* 538–65). This belief was so well-established that it could be used as an argument in court. In 400 or 399, the Athenian politician Andocides, who stood accused of sacrilege, cited his successes in maritime trade as proof that the gods did not bear him a grudge (*On the Mysteries* 137; cf. Antiphon, *On the Murder of Herodes* 81–84). The strength of this argument is indicated by the lengths to which his opponents went to refute it. If the gods did not punish Andocides through shipwreck, one of them argued, they did so to punish him, or his descendants more severely later (Lysias, *Against Andocides* 19–32).

These speeches evince a widely held belief in divine intervention. At the same, they help to explain why arguments built addressing such beliefs become rare in fourth-century forensic speeches. The problem was not that claims of divine intervention lacked plausibility, but rather that there were too many plausible explanations based on divine intervention. With no clerical authority to decide the matter, such reasoning did not provide steady rhetorical grounds to win an argument. In everyday business, however, a widespread, if diffuse, belief in divine retribution transformed the experience of uncertainty into another argument for fairness.

Artisans and other specialists also faced the risks of travel and insecure contract enforcement when they moved about in search of employment opportunities. But even when they stayed at home they faced hazards. Wartime preparations or public building projects would create additional demand for their goods and services, but at an unsteady rate, and, in case of war, with more losers than winners. Apart from the big events that left traces in the written record, we should assume many small crises of 'unsalability' *(aprasia)* of products (e.g. Demosthenes, *Against Aphobus I* 19–21).

In the absence of accumulated wealth or formal insurance, workplace accidents posed an existential risk for craftsmen and the families they had to feed. Smiths and potters, who worked with open fire, faced the constant danger of house fires. Less dramatic, but still severe damage could be caused by aberrations in the production process, as when a fully stacked pottery kiln was lost due to temperature irregularities. Depictions of workshops in vase painting show protective apotropaic amulets *(baskania)* on top of kilns and forges.[14] Alison Burford has argued that such evidence should not be overestimated. Ancient craftsmen relied on their skill and ingenuity, not magic (Burford 1972, 121–23, 196–98). Putting it like this, however, creates a false dichotomy between religion and technology (and religion and magic). No ancient observer expected divine help to work as a substitute for skill or forethought. The support of the gods was needed to deal with contingencies that lay beyond human control (e.g. Xenophon, *Memorabilia* 1.1.6–9; *The Cavalry Commander* 9.8–9). Additional evidence for the apotropaic rituals of artisans is provided by deposits of drinking and eating vessels, so-called 'saucer pyres', which were found under the floors of many Athenian workshops and private households, especially around the *agora*, the central meeting place and marketplace of the city. According to Susan

[14] cf. Rotroff (2013, 83–84). Such amulets were considered a common feature in workshops by ancient lexicographers; cf. Pollux, *Onomasticon* 7.108 and Phrynichos, *Lexicon* s.v. *baskanion*.

Rotroff's detailed analysis (2013), these vessels, once filled with foodstuffs, were burned and then buried as an offering to chthonic deities in response to recent misfortunes or as protection against future misfortunes. The large numbers of excavated pyres and their wide chronological spread indicate that artisans made sure to combine human skill with divine protection.

From the perspective of popular morality, it is interesting to see that workshop accidents could be given a normative interpretation similar to shipwrecks. The best evidence for this is the so-called 'potter's prayer' or 'kiln song' (*Homeric Epigram* 13), a cursing song which was probably composed in fifth-century Athens as a literary pastiche of older oral texts (Faraone 2001). The song describes a kind of bargain between poet and potter:

> If you will pay me for my song, o potters,
> then come, Athena, and lay thy hand above the kiln!
> May the cups and all the dishes turn a good black,
> may they be well fired and fetch the price asked,
> many being sold in the marketplace and many in the roads,
> and bring in much money, and may my song be pleasing.
> But if you (sc. Potters) turn shameless and deceitful,
> then do I summon the ravagers of kilns,
> both Syntrips ('Smasher') and Smaragos ('Crasher') and
> Asbetos ('Unquenchable') too, and Sabaktes ('Shake-to-Pieces')
> and Omodamos ('Conqueror of the Unbaked'), who makes
> much trouble for this craft.
> Destroy the stoking tunnel and chambers,
> and may the whole kiln
> be thrown into confusion, while the potters loudly wail.
> As grinds the horse's jaw, so may the kiln grind
> to powder all the pots within it.
>
> (*trans. Ch. Faraone*)

The poet recruits the demonic personifications of misproduction to enforce the rules of the moral economy of the marketplace. Profit is legitimate, even considered just; but it should derive from quality merchandise, not fraud.

Justice and Trust in the Marketplace

Economic misfortune as divine punishment was the flipside of wealth as a divine gift. To ensure material welfare, it was not enough to worship the gods; one also had to follow the rules they had established for transactions among humans (e.g. Xenophon, *Memorabilia* 4.4.16–25; cf. Dover 1974, 256–57). Themis, 'divinely ordained custom', was considered Zeus's second or even first wife (Hesiod, *Theogony* 901; Pindar, frg. 30 Maehler). Either way, her prominent position in the Greek pantheon emphasises the sacredness of justice. In Hesiod's divine genealogy, Zeus and Themis have several children: *Eunomia*, 'Good Order', *Dikē*, 'Justice', *Eirēnē*, 'Peace'—these three sisters 'watch the deeds of mortal humans'—and the *Moirai*, the goddesses of fate, who give 'good and evil things' to humans (*Theogony* 902–6). This genealogy shows how religious personification helped to understand the notions of commutative and distributive justice as subtypes of the familiar principle of reciprocity. Whoever committed a crime or took more than his due among humans simultaneously gave offence to the gods by disrespecting their rules (Dover 1974, 256–58).

Myth also helped to discern the links between divine order, human trust, and prosperity. From Homer onwards (*Odyssey* 24.482–6), public order, peace, and wealth—personified as the god Plutos—went together. In early poetry, the wealth brought by peace was mostly associated with agriculture. Hesiod described Eirēnē as 'sprouting' *(tetaluia)*, a metaphor suggesting agricultural prosperity. The association is reiterated by Hesiod's description of Plutos as the son of Demeter, 'born in a thrice-ploughed field' on Crete (*Theogony* 969–70). In Aristophanes' play *Peace*, staged in 422 during the Peloponnesian war, the Athenian winegrower Trygaeus travels to the Olympus to free the goddess Peace in order to save his fields from war-time devastation.[15] But the blessings of peace are not confined to farmers. Trygaeus prays for better supplies in the marketplace (*Pax* 999–1015; 1198–1202) and calls on everybody to help him free Peace: 'farmers, and traders, and builders, and craftsmen and metics and foreigners and islanders,[16] all folks get together now!' (296–8). Fourth-century orators arguing for peace likewise pointed out how peace would further commerce and thereby enhance a city's prosperity (Isocrates, *On*

[15] Aristophanes' *Farmers* had a similar plot; see also *Carmina Popularia* frg. 1 Diehl; Euripides, frg. 453 Nauck and *Supplicants* 486–91.

[16] Athenian hegemony extended over the cities of the Aegean islands.

the Peace 19; cf. Xenophon, *Ways and Means* 5.1–5). Such arguments made sense on their own, but they also resonated with contemporary religious beliefs, as the goddess Peace received its own cult in Athens around the same time. A famous public votive statue set up in the *agora* in the 370s represented the goddess as holding an infant Plutos on her arms like a nurse (Stafford 2000, 173–93). Peace nurtured Wealth for everyone.

The genealogy set out in Hesiod's *Theogony* suggests that wealth was a consequence of peace, and peace a consequence—'child'—of divine rule, and syndrome—'sibling'—of good order and justice (Rudhardt 1999; Pironti 2009). In the *Work and Days*, Hesiod elaborated on this correlation. He exhorts his brother Perses to 'listen to Dikē' and avoid *hubris*. Ill-gotten gains will sooner or later fall back on the perpetrator and destroy him (213–8). A just man, in contrast, will receive 'blessed wealth' (*olbos*), while the family of the man who keeps his oaths will live on (280–5). Hesiod when widens the perspective to make justice the cornerstone of collective welfare. Dikē, helped by her father Zeus, will bring hunger, plague, and infertility over cities where corrupt judges give 'crooked judgements'. Cities where straight judgements are given to both citizens and foreigners will blossom and enjoy peace and wealth (225–37).

Hesiod imagined wealth mainly as agricultural. In subsequent centuries, commercial wealth was included in imaginations of the good community. In the fifth century, the epinician poet Pindar reiterated the familiar association of divine custom, public justice, and wealth, and used it as praise for the two outstanding trade entrepots of his time, Corinth and Aegina. 'Wealth-blessed Corinth' is described as 'a servant to foreign guests (*xenoi*)' and 'Poseidon's doorway', an allegorical description of the city's favourable position at the isthmus between the Greek mainland and the Peloponnesian peninsula. Eunomia, Pindar goes on, dwells in Corinth, together with her sisters Dikē and Eirēnē, 'a steward (*tamias*) of man's wealth', while *hubris* is kept at bay (*Olympian Odes* 13.1–10). Similar associations between seafaring, hospitality, justice, good order, and wealth are evoked in Pindar's praise of Aegina, 'home of Themis' and 'City of Justice' (*dikaiopolis*) (*Pythian Odes* 8.1–28; *Olympian Odes* 8.21–29; *Isthmian Odes* 5.22; *Nemean Odes* 3.2–3; 5.8; 4.11–13). That these are virtues of an emporium becomes clear when we compare Pindar's praise of Corinth with Corinth's later blame of Corcyra, a Corinthian colony which became an important emporium in its own right. According to Thucydides (*Histories* 1.37), the Corinthians blamed the Corcyreans for having grown insolent and unjust because their favourable position in the Ionian Sea allowed them to control maritime trade. Instead of accepting mutual agreements, they seek shameful profits as judges of the foreigners frequenting their port. Whether these accusations were true or not, they attest the existence of a concept of moral economy of commerce: the good emporium grows wealthy by administering fair justice to citizens and foreigners alike.

In Thucydides' account, the Corinthians allude to the same model of the good emporium as Pindar but without any reference to the gods. The growth of intellectual discourse and prose literature, what has been called 'the fifth-century enlightenment' (e.g. Guthrie 1993), brought about a literary discourse that for the first time in Greek history avoided direct reference to divine agency. There is, however, continuity in sentiment and semantics. In the writings of the so-called Anonymus Iamblichi, for example, *eunomia* is once again described as the foundation of prosperity (frg. 7.1–3 Diels-Kranz 89). Good order (*eunomia*) creates trust (*pistis*) which induces people to share money/resources (*chrēmata*). As a result, scare goods 'circulate' (*kukloumena*) to everybody's profit. Those who base themselves on *eunomia* will enjoy prosperity because they will not have to waste their time with legal disputes, devoting it instead to productive works (*erga*). The Anonymus excels in the praise of *eunomia* just like Hesiod but now with a focus on a monetary economy built on trust and credit (the 'sharing' of resources). Such ideas became a commonplace in the fourth century. The rhetorician Isocrates imagined how in Athens' glorious past the trust in the lawcourts to enforce the repayment of debts had resulted in prosperity and social peace (*Areopagiticus* 29–34). Aristotle likewise suggested that the rich should advance capital to the poor and abstain from exploitation and corruption to uphold social peace (*Politics* 5.1308^{b}32–1309^{a}15; 6.1320^{a}32–^{b}11; 6.1321^{a}35–42). Isocrates and Aristotle addressed a small, well-educated upper class, but their line of reasoning resonated with larger audiences. In a maritime case of the year 322, the plaintiff claimed that in judging his case, more was at stake than just the recovery of his loan. The judges would set a precedent 'for the whole *emporium*', since many people engaged in maritime trade were watching: 'if you hold that contracts and agreements made between man and man are to be binding, and show no leniency towards those who transgress them, lenders will be more ready to risk their money, and the business of your port will be increased' (Pseudo-Demosthenes, *Against Dionysodorus* 48; trans. N. J. DeWitt).

This and similar statements (cf. Pseudo-Demosthenes, *Against Chrysippus* 51–52; Xenophon, *Ways and Means* 3.3) suggest that Athenians were concerned for preserving a reputation of impartial justice, quite like the citizens of the medieval trading entrepots of Genoa and Venice. Fourth-century orators avoided arguments built on assumptions about divine intervention, but not because they thought their audiences had lost faith. In speeches concerning disputes about private loans and property rights, they used informal oaths ('By Zeus!') to stress the sincerity of their statements, reminded the audience of oaths taken regarding deposits, contracts, or arbitration in financial matters; cited reluctance to take such oaths as admissions of guilt, mentioned sanctuaries as go-to meeting places to settle financial disputes, attributed salvation at sea to divine help, and referred to punishment in the underworld as a shared belief.[17] In 325, Demosthenes could still remind the judges of Eunomia, the divinity that 'loves just deeds', and Dikē, who sits at Zeus' side and watches over the deeds of men (*Against Aristogeiton I* 11; cf. 35).

Because prosperity did not rest on individual worship alone, it was a sacred duty of lawgivers and magistrates to ensure that divine custom would materialise through human institutions. Prayers, sacrifices, and oaths framed any public undertaking and reminded officeholders of their duties (Busolt and Swoboda 1926, 514–27). In Thebes, the temples for Themis, the Moirai, and Zeus Agoraios ('Protector of the Agora') were set right next to each other. A city's *agora* was marked off by boundary stones as a sacred space reserved to the unpolluted (H. A. Thompson and Wycherley 1972, 117–19). Just as many different gods were charged with the protection of seafarers, there were many gods protecting the marketplace. Across the Greek world we find Hermes Agoraios, Zeus Agoraios, Athena Agoraia, Themis Agoraia, and Aphrodite Agoraia (Kuhle 2020, 297–98; cf. Robert 1969, 118–19). Of these gods, Hermes was most

[17] Informal oaths as marker of sincerity: Demosthenes, *Against Zenothemis* 10, 29, 31; *For Phormio* 55, 61; *Against Pantaenetus* 51, 53; *Against Nausimachus* 11; Pseudo-Demosthenes, *Against Apaturius* 25, 37; *Against Callippus* 9; *Against Dionysodorus* 38; oaths: *Against Apaturius* 13–14; *Against Olympiodorus* 11, 30, 32; Isaeus, *On the Property of Menecles* 31–33; rejection of oath as admission of guilt: *Against Callippus* 15–19, 26–30; *Against Phormio* 21; sanctuaries as meeting places: Isocrates, *Trapeziticus* 17–20; salvation from shipwreck: *Against Zenothemis* 8; cf. *Against Phormio* 10; judgement in the underworld: Demosthenes, *Against Timocrates* 104; *Against Aristogeiton* 52–53 (these last two speeches were written for public cases).

closely associated with the marketplace. Next to his cult statue in the Athenian *agora* stood an altar on which the market overseers performed their sacrifices (Kuhle 2020, 301–5). In Erythrai, where priesthoods were sold by auction, the priesthood of Hermes Agoraios fetched by far the highest price (*Inschriften von Erythrai*, no. 201). Since the auction price indicates a cult's expected income from sacrifices and temple fees, the high price indicates the high number of offerings to Hermes by both magistrates and individuals transacting business in the marketplace (Robert 1969, 462, n. 1).

One of the ways the gods protected market exchange was to act as divine witnesses through the swearing of oaths. Whoever violated a sworn agreement would commit the evil of perjury (e.g. Aristophanes, *Clouds* 1227–55, 1277–8; Pseudo-Demosthenes, *Against Olympiodorus* 48.9–11). Oaths were therefore omnipresent in business (Dover 1974, 248–49; Graf 2005). In Athens, small vendors swore by Hermes to vouch for the quality of their merchandise (Kuhle 2020, 328–32). In Ainos, buyers of real estate had to perform a sacrifice and swear an oath at the altars of Apollo or Zeus Agoraios (Theophrastus, frg. 650 Fortenbaugh). In Delos, market overseers had to swear an oath if they had been unable to collect a fine before the end of their term of office (*Inscriptions de Délos*, no. 509, 27–31).

The omnipresence of oaths was marked by ambivalence. Hermes, the god of oath, is a trickster who knows how to deceive with words (Brown 1947). Herodotus makes the Persian King Cyrus declare his contempt for a people that has established places in the middle of their cities to defraud each other by swearing oaths. Cyrus said so, Herodotus explains, because the Greeks, unlike the Persians, have established *agorai* to buy and sell (*Histories* 1.153.1). Plato went so far as to suggest abolishing oaths altogether. In earlier times, he argues, oaths worked because people feared the gods. In his time, people have either stopped to believe in divine intervention or think they can bribe the gods with sacrifices and flattery. Under such conditions, it is a matter of piety to abolish juridical oaths since they would by design turn half the citizenry, i.e. the guilty parties in lawsuits, into perjurers (*Laws* 11.948b–e; cf. Föllinger 2016, 151–56). For similar reasons, Plato proposes to outlaw the use of oaths to affirm the quality of merchandise in the marketplace (11.916d–918a). Incidentally, Plato's rejection of oaths is one of the best pieces of evidence for the continued use of religious ritual in everyday business. His narrative of moral decay, on the other hand, leads us to the question on how to describe the longer-term development of the religious embeddedness of Greek commerce.

The Religious Embeddedness of Commerce: Continuity and Change

Plato's pessimistic view on contemporary religion has lent support to the idea of religious decline during the fourth century. According to a once influential scholarly view, traditional religiosity took lasting damage from the new scepticism established by sophists and philosophers in the second half of the fifth century (Nilsson 1940, 120–39; Dodds 1951, 188–244). The chronological distribution of literary references to divine intervention seemingly supports this model. References are plenty in poetry and early prose until the end of the fifth century but become rare in (surviving) fourth-century oratory, historiography, and philosophical treatises. In Aristophanes' *Clouds*, staged in 423, the rustic old-timer Strepsiades, seeking to evade his debt obligations, is persuaded by sophistic arguments that perjurers having nothing to fear from Zeus (*Clouds* 395–402). There can be little doubt that the scepticism of fifth-century intellectuals seemed as shocking to some as it seemed attractive to others (Dodds 1951, 188–89). But to interpret the *Clouds* as evidence for the erosion of traditional religiosity is to misunderstand Aristophanes' jokes. Attitudes to oaths are another reiteration of the main theme of the play, the clash of rustic simpleton with urban trickster (cf. Aristophanes, *Knights* 316–21). Ultimately, the poet and his audience sided with religious conformity. Strepsiades' creditors offer a counterpoint to the topsy-turvy jokes of the main characters when they express their astonishment about Strepsiades new-learned disregard for oaths and gods (*Clouds* 1227–78). In the end, Strepsiades seeks forgiveness from Hermes for his temporary fall from faith and burns down the sophists' school (1476–85). Rather than serving as evidence for the decay of popular belief, Aristophanes' *Clouds* indicates its continuation (Brulé 2009a, 2009b).

Doubts and disagreements had always been part of the discourse on divine justice. From the start, those exhorting divine punishment had warned that delay might be mistaken for absence (see above, p. 7). Oaths had always been described as tools of deceit. Since they create trust, they create the opportunity to abuse trust (Homer, *Odyssey* 394–6; Hesiod, *Theogony* 226–32). In Athens, at least, oaths mostly served an assertory rather than promissory function, that is, they were sworn in cases of distrust or dispute (Carawan 2007; Carter 2007). In such a case, the oath did not produce trust but forced the swearing party to make a commitment that was difficult to deny, this way ensuring both divine and human punishment in case of perjury. In this perspective, the function of human institutions was not to substitute for divine justice, but to supplement it.

Going back to Plato, we find that he takes a similar view in the *Laws*. The philosopher wants to abolish oaths because they systematically create perjurers, not because he has lost faith in divine justice. Instead of letting market sellers swear oaths, he declares it a pious duty of every citizen to supervise their honesty. A citizen who fails to indict a trader for selling faked merchandise should be declared 'an evil person' (*kakos*), because he deprives the gods of their share—the merchandise which in case of confiscation would be dedicated to 'the gods of the marketplace' (*Laws* 11.917d). Plato worries not that the gods will not eventually punish transgressors. He worries that in the meantime people will give yet more offence in the mistaken belief that they are able to ignore or manipulate the gods. Regarding craftsmen, who are 'sacred to Hephaistos and Athena', Plato determined that they should not only pay a fine to the buyer if they fail to execute their work in time, but also to their own patron god for dishonouring him. A buyer who does not pay a craftsman according to agreement is committing an evil deed as well. He 'dishonours Zeus, Patron of the city, and Athena, who are partners in the constitution, – thereby dissolving great partnerships through love of a little gain' (11.920d–921d). Like Hesiod, Plato still believed that peace and prosperity rested on the human implementation of divine law.

This view prevailed throughout later times. Hellenistic city-states both set up laws regulating commerce and began to prescribe sacrifices for gods that protected the livelihood of the community. The city of Cos, a much-frequented emporium, decreed mandatory sacrifices to Poseidon, Aphrodite Pandamos ('of the people'), and Aphrodite Pontia ('of the sea') from those who live off the sea, like fishermen, traders, shipowners, or collectors of harbour taxes (*IG* XII 4, 1293; 319, 4–13, 25–29; 302, 22–24). Such regulations were a convenient way to raise revenues. Their acceptance, however, rested on an intact belief that it was a civic duty to ensure the worship of a city's patron deities. Nor can such demonstrations of civic piety be dismissed as hollow posturing. More secretive ways to seek divine help survived into hellenistic times as well: magic spells to bind competition, apotropaic sacrifices to protect the workplace, and oracles to enquire about business plans. Whenever such material disappears from our record, the best explanation is one of changed economic circumstances or religious topography rather than a general decline in religiosity.[18]

My interpretation of the religious embeddedness of Greek commerce is in line with the now current understanding of religious change during the late classical and hellenistic period as a limited and gradual change of fashion focus (Hornblower 2011, 213–16; Chaniotis 2007). As suggested above, cultural rather than religious changes might explain the absence of references to divine justice in public speeches and philosophical debate after c. 400. The change initiated by the fifth-century Greek enlightenment was not a decline in religiosity, but greater sophistication in rhetorical argument and theological speculation.

The competitiveness and inclusiveness characteristic of Greek politics was mirrored in Greek polytheism. Without a corpus of canonical texts or a clerical authority monopolising its interpretation, anyone arguing his case in court or assembly could find an interpretation of shared beliefs that supported his particular version of events.[19] The same holds true for philosophical debate, where everyone was free to make his (very rarely her) own cosmological speculations.[20] The problems created by religious plurality for the use of arguments of authority were been even more pronounced in literary discourse, since historians and philosophers addressed a panhellenic audience, and every city and region had its local cults, myths, and deities. Philosophers were well-advised to concentrate on general speculation rather than 'applied' religious ethics.

Such theological speculation, however, did not help traders and artisans navigating a Mediterranean world full of local deities demanding gifts

[18] See, for example Chapinal-Heras (2021, 192–96, 225, and 233) on possible explanations for the decline in the numbers of oracle enquiries in Dodona during the hellenistic period; compare Rotroff (2013, 89) on the disappearance of artisans' offerings to chthonic deities in Athens during the third century BCE.

[19] Compare the case of Andocides and his accusers, discussed above, p. 27; on the open nature of debates about the interpretation of oracles in Greek politics, see Vernant (1974) and Trampedach (2015).

[20] There were trials for impiety *(asebeia)*, the most famous of which resulted in Socrates' execution, and popular thought remained hostile to philosophical speculation until hellenistic times; but the overall number of trials was low, and those we know of were politically motivated; no permanent institution existed to fight heresies; private idiosyncrasies were mocked rather than prosecuted.

and honours. These men and women needed specific rites and places of worship to avert evil and seek good fortune. They therefore became familiar with the local gods or built their own sanctuaries in the places they went to make business.[21]

The world of Greek commerce was a polycentric and polytheistic world, interconnected and yet fragmented. To construct a model of a single Greek popular morality of commerce is therefore only justified in analytical terms. It is a conceptual framework to describe what was in reality an everchanging kaleidoscope of local rites and customs. What remained constant, however, was the religious embeddedness of the moral economy of ancient Greek commerce.

Bibliography

Bloch, Marc. 1928. Pour une histoire comparée des sociétés européennes. *Revue De Synthèse Historique* 46: 15–50.

Boardman, John, Thomas Mannack, Claudia Wagner, Robert Parker, and Evgenia Vikela. 2004. "Greek Dedications." In *Thesaurus Cultus Et Rituum Antiquorum (ThesCRA). Vol. 1: Processions, Sacrifices, Libations, Fumigations, Dedications*, 269–318. Los Angeles: J. Paul Getty Museum.

Bonnechère, Pierre. 2018. Pureté, justice, 'piété' et leurs contraires: l'apport des sources oraculaires. In *Purity and Purification in the Ancient Greek World: Texts, Rituals, and Norms*, ed. Jan-Mathieu Carbon and Saskia Peels, 49–91 Kernos Supplement 32. Liège: Presses universitaires de Liège.

Bremmer, Jan N. 2021. *Greek Religion*, 2nd ed. Greece & Rome. New Surveys in the Classics 46. Cambridge: Cambridge University Press.

Bresson, Alain. 2015. *The Making of the Ancient Greek Economy: Institutions, Markets, and Growth in the City-States.* Princeton, NJ: Princeton University Press.

Brown, Norman O. 1947. *Hermes the Thief: The Evolution of a Myth.* Madison: University of Wisconsin Press.

Brulé, Pierre, ed. 2009a. *La norme en matière religieuse en Grèce ancienne.* Kernos 21. Liège: Centre International d'Étude de la Religion Grecque Antique. Actes du XIe colloque international du CIERGA (Rennes,

[21] In the late seventh century, the Egyptian pharaoh Psammetichos I. established Naukratis in the Nile delta as a port-of-trade for Greek traders; one of the first things he did, according to Herodotus, was to allocate to them places to set up altars and a temple precinct; cf. *Histories* 2.178; In the same vein, the Athenians in 333/2 BCE granted the right to own land *(enktēsis)* to a group of traders from Kition on Cyprus so that they could build a sanctuary for Aphrodite; cf. *IG* II^3 337.

septembre 2007). http://bvbr.bib-bvb.de:8991/F?func=service&doc_library=BVB01&local_base=BVB01&doc_number=017594094&sequence=000001&line_number=0001&func_code=DB_RECORDS&service_type=MEDIA

Brulé, Pierre. 2009b. Les *Nuées* et le problème de l'incroyance au Ve siècle. In Brulé 2009a, 49–67.

Burford, Alison. 1972. *Craftsmen in Greek and Roman Society.* Aspects of Greek and Roman Life. London: Thomas & Hudson.

Busolt, Georg, and Heinrich Swoboda. 1926. *Griechische Staatskunde. Vol. 2: Darstellung Einzelner Staaten und der zwischenstaatlichen Beziehungen*, 3rd ed. Handbuch der Altertumswissenschaft 4.1, 1. München: C.H. Beck.

Canevaro, Mirko, and David Martin Lewis. Forthcoming. The Rites, Rituals, and Sites of Business. In *A Cultural History of Business in Antiquity*, ed. John K. Davies and Colin E.P. Adams. London: Bloomsbury.

Carawan, Edwin M. 2007. Oath and Contract. In Sommerstein and Fletcher 2007, 73–80.

Carbon, Jan-Mathieu. 2015. "Five Answers Prescribing Rituals in the Oracular Tablets from Dodona." *Γραμματεῖον* 4: 73–87.

Carbon, Jan-Mathieu. 2017. Sailing to Dodona: On the Naa, the Aktia, and Times of Consultation at the Oracle. In Soueref 2017, 95–111.

Carter, David M. 2007. Could a Greek Oath Guarantee a Claim Right? Oaths, Contracts and the Structure of Obligation in Classical Athens. In Sommerstein and Fletcher 2007, 60–72.

Chaniotis, Angelos. 2007. "Religion und Mythos." In *Kulturgeschichte des Hellenismus. Von Alexander dem Großen bis Kleopatra*, ed. Gregor Weber, 139–157. Stuttgart.

Chankowski, Véronique. 2011. Divine Financiers: Cults as Consumers and Generators of Value. In *The Economies of Hellenistic Societies, Third to First Centuries BC*, ed. Zosia H. Archibald, John K. Davies, and Vincent Gabrielsen, 142–65. Oxford: Oxford University Press.

Chapinal-Heras, Diego. 2021. *Experiencing Dodona: The Development of the Epirote Sanctuary from Archaic to Hellenistic Times.* Berlin and Boston: de Gruyter.

Collar, Anna, and Troels Myrup Kristensen, eds. 2020. *Pilgrimage and Economy in the Ancient Mediterranean.* Religions in the Graeco-Roman world volume 192. Leiden and Boston: Brill.

Davies, John K. 1971. *Athenian Propertied Families, 600–300 B.C.* Oxford: Clarendon Press.

———. 2001. Temples, Credit, and the Circulation of Money. In *Money and Its Uses in the Ancient Greek World*, ed. Andrew Meadows and Kirsty M.W. Shipton, 117–28. Oxford: Oxford University Press.

Demetriou, Denise. 2010. Τῆς Πάσης Ναυτιλίης Φύλαξ: Aphrodite and the Sea. *Kernos* 23: 67–89.

Dodds, Eric R. 1951. *The Greeks and the Irrational*. Sather Classical Lecture 25. Berkeley: University of California Press.

Dover, Kenneth James. 1974. *Greek Popular Morality in the Time of Plato and Aristotle*. Oxford: Blackwell.

Eckert, Martin. 2011. Die Aphrodite der Seefahrer. *Hephaistos* 28: 99–124.

Edmonds, Radcliffe G. 2013. *Redefining Ancient Orphism: A Study in Greek Religion*. Cambridge: Cambridge University Press.

Eich, Armin. 2006. *Die Politische Ökonomie des antiken Griechenland (6.–3. Jahrhundert V. Chr.)*. Köln: Böhlau.

Eidinow, Esther. 2007. *Oracles, Curses, and Risk among the Ancient Greeks*. Oxford: Oxford University Press.

Faraone, Christopher A. 2001. A Collection of Curses Against Kilns (Homeric Epigram 13.7–23). In *Antiquity and Humanity: Essays on Ancient Religion and Philosophy Presented to Hans Dieter Betz on His 70th Birthday*, ed. Adela Y. Collins and M.M. Mitchell, 435–49. Tübingen: Mohr Siebeck.

Fenet, Annick. 2012. Voyages en mer dans le mond Grec et Roman. In *Thesaurus Cultus Et Rituum Antiquorum (ThesCRA). Vol. 6: Stages and Circumstances of Life, Work, Hunting, Travel and Addendum to Vol. II Music*, 405–414. Los Angeles: J. Paul Getty Museum.

Föllinger, Sabine. 2016. *Ökonomie bei Platon*. Berlin: de Gruyter.

Fontaine, Laurence. 2008. *L'économie morale: Pauvreté, crédit et confiance dans l'Europe préindustrielle*. NRF Essais. Paris: Gallimard.

Frevert, Ute, ed. 2019. *Moral Economies*. Geschichte und Gesellschaft Special Issue 26. Göttingen: Vandenhoeck & Ruprecht.

Gager, John G. 1999. *Curse Tablets and Binding Spells from the Ancient World*. New York: Oxford University Press.

Gallant, Thomas W. 1991. *Risk and Survival in Ancient Greece: Reconstructing the Rural Domestic Economy*. Cambridge.

Graf, Fritz. 2005. Eid. In *Thesaurus Cultus Et Rituum Antiquorum (ThesCRA). Vol. 3: Divination, Prayer, Veneration, Hikesia, Asylia, Oath, Malediction, Profanation, Magic Rituals and Addendum to Vol. II, Consecration*, 237–246. Los Angeles: J. Paul Getty Museum.

Guthrie, William K. C. 1993. *The Fifth-Century Enlightenment: A History of Greek Philosophy. Vol. 3.2*. Cambridge: Cambridge University Press.

Helmer, Étienne. 2021. *Oikonomia: Philosophie grecque de L'économie*. Kaïnon - anthropologie de la pensée ancienne 18. Paris: Classiques Garnier.

Hinsch, Moritz. 2021. *Ökonomik Und Hauswirtschaft Im Klassischen Griechenland*. Historia Einzelschriften. Stuttgart: Steiner.

———. 2022. Zeus' Herrschaft Über Reichtum Und Glück: Antikes Wirtschaften Im Spiegel Der Orakelanfragen Von Dodona. *Klio* 104.

Hornblower, Simon. 2011. *The Greek World, 479–323 B.C.*, 4th ed. Routledge History of the Ancient World. London: Routledge.
Horster, Marietta. 2004. *Landbesitz griechischer Heiligtümer in archaischer und klassischer Zeit.* Religionsgeschichtliche Versuche und Vorarbeiten 53. Berlin: de Gruyter.
Hurwit, Jeffrey M. 1999. *The Athenian Acropolis: History, Mythology, and Archaeology from the Neolithic Era to the Present.* Cambridge: Cambridge University Press.
Jim, Theodora Suk Fong. 2014. *Sharing with the Gods: Aparchai and Dekatai in Ancient Greece.* Oxford: Oxford University Press.
Kuhle, Antje. 2020. *Hermes und die Bürger: Der Hermeskult in den griechischen Poleis.* Hermes–Einzelschrift 119. Stuttgart.
Le Goff, Jacques. 2008 [1986]. *Wucherzins und Höllenqualen: Ökonomie und Religion im Mittelalter*, 2nd ed. Stuttgart: Klett-Cotta.
Leese, Michael. 2021. *Making Money in Ancient Athens.* Ann Arbor: University of Michigan Press.
Lycos, Kimon. 1987. *Plato on Justice and Power: Reading Book I of Plato's Republic.* Basingstoke and London: Macmillan Press.
Mikalson, Jon D. 1983. *Athenian Popular Religion.* Chapel Hill: University of North Carolina Press.
Millett, Paul C. 1991. *Lending and Borrowing in Ancient Athens.* Cambridge.
Nesselrath, Heinz-Günther. 2020. Zum Hades und darüber hinaus: Mythische griechische Vorstellungen zum Weg des Menschen über den Tod ins Jenseits von Homer bis Platon. In *Mythische Sphärenwechsel: Methodisch neue Zugänge zu antiken Mythen in Orient und Okzident*, ed. Annette Zgoll and Christian Zgoll, 161–212. Berlin and Boston: de Gruyter.
Nilsson, Martin Persson. 1940. *Greek Popular Religion.* Lectures on the History of Religions, New Series 1. New York: Columbia University Press.
Parker, Robert. 2016. Seeking Advice from Zeus at Dodona. *G&R* 63: 69–90.
Pironti, Gabriella. 2009. Dans l'entourage de Thémis: Les Moires et les normes panthéoniques. In Brulé 2009, 13–27.
Polanyi, Karl. 2001 [1944]. *The Great Transformation: The Political and Economic Origins of Our Time.* Boston: Beacon Press.
Polanyi, Karl, Conrad M. Arensberg, and Harry W. Pearson, eds. 1957. *Trade and Market in the Early Empires, Economies in History and Theory.* Glenco: Free Press.
Price, Simon R.F. 1999. *Religions of the Ancient Greeks.* Key Themes in Ancient History. Cambridge: Cambridge University Press.
Reden, Sitta von. 2015. *Antike Wirtschaft.* Enzyklopädie der griechisch-römischen Antike 10. Berlin: De Gruyter Oldenbourg.
Robert, Louis. 1969. *Opera minora selecta, Bd. 1: Épigraphie et antiquités grecques.* Amsterdam: Hakkert.

Rotroff, Susan I. 2013. *Industrial Religion: The Saucer Pyres of the Athenian Agora*. Hesperia Supplement 47. Princeton: American School of Classical Studies at Athens.
Rudhardt, Jean. 1999. *Thémis et les Hôrai: Recherche sur les divinités grecques de la justice et de la paix*. Recherches et rencontres Littérature 14. Genf: Droz.
Sassu, Rita. 2014. *Hiera chremata: Il ruolo del santuario nell'economia della polis*. Studi umanistici Serie Antichistica 20. Rome: Sapienza Università editrice.
Scott, James C. 1976. *The Moral Economy of the Peasant: Rebellion and Subsistence in Southeast Asia*. New Haven: Yale University Press.
Sharot, Stephen. 2001. *A Comparative Sociology of World Religions: Virtuosos, Priests, and Popular Religion*. New York: New York University Press.
Sommerstein, Alan Herbert, and Judith Fletcher, eds. 2007. *Horkos: The Oath in Greek Society*. Bristol: Bristol Phoenix Press.
Soueref, Konstantinos, ed. 2017. *Δωδώνη. Οι Ερωτήσεις Των Χρησμών. Dodona. The Omen's Questions*. Ioannina.
Sourvinou-Inwood, Christiane. 1995. *'Reading' Greek Death: To the End of the Classical Period*. Clarendon Paperbacks. Oxford: Clarendon.
Stafford, Emma. 2000. *Worshipping Virtues: Personification and the Divine in Ancient Greece*. London: Duckworth.
Thompson, Edward Pett. 1977. Folklore, Anthropology and Social History. *The Indian Historical Review* 3: 247–266.
———. 1991. The Moral Economy Reviewed. In *Customs in Common*, 259–351. New York: New Press.
Thompson, Homer A., and Richard Ernest Wycherley. 1972. *The Agora of Athens: The History, Shape, and Uses of an Ancient City Center*. Athenian Agora XIV. Princeton: American School of Classical Studies at Athens.
Trampedach, Kai. 2015. *Politische Mantik: Die Kommunikation über Götterzeichen und Orakel im klassischen Griechenland*. Studien zur Alten Geschichte 21. Heidelberg: Verlag Antike.
van Straten, Folkert T. 1981. Gifts for the Gods. In *Faith, Hope and Worship: Aspects of Religious Mentality in the Ancient World*, ed. Hendrik S. Versnel, 65–151. Studies in Greek and Roman Religion 2. Leiden: Brill.
Vegetti, Mario. 1993. L'homme et les dieux. In *L' homme grec*, ed. Jean-Pierre Vernant, 319–55. L' univers historique. Paris: Éditions du Seuil.
Vernant, Jean-Pierre. 1974. "Parole Et Signes Muets." In *Divination Et Rationalité*, ed. Jean-Pierre Vernant, 9–25. Recherches Anthropologiques. Paris: Éd. du Seuil.
Wachsmuth, Dietrich. 1967. *Pompimos ho daimon: Untersuchung zu den antiken Sakralhandlungen bei Seereisen*. Berlin: Berlin.
Wagner-Hasel, Beate. 2009. Hundert Jahre Gelehrtenstreit über den Charakter der antiken Wirtschaft: Zur Aktualität von Karl Büchers Wirtschaftsanthropologie. *Historische Anthropologie* 17: 178–201.

Weber, Max. 1999 [1921]. *Die Stadt: Max-Weber-Gesamtausgabe. Vol. 22,1.* Tübingen: Mohr Siebeck.

Zak, Paul J., ed. 2008. *Moral Markets: The Critical Role of Values in the Economy.* Princeton: Princeton University Press.

CHAPTER 3

Early Medieval Property Transfers in Favour of the Church Between Religion and Economy

Franziska Quaas

Transferring the Concept of "Moral Economy" to the Early Middle Ages

Conceptions of the character of medieval economy have long been shaped by the idea that, like other pre-modern economies, it was primarily characterised by a special embeddedness of economic, social and ethical-religious spheres. According to this idea pre-modern economies differed fundamentally from the modern liberal market economy, which would have dissolved itself from its former social embedding in the process of modernisation and thus established itself as an independent, autonomous sphere (Polanyi 1944; Polanyi 1957; see furthermore Simmel 1900; Sombart 1902; Weber 1920; Mauss 1923/1924). In Marxist economic history in particular, the differentiation between embedded and allegedly

F. Quaas (✉)
University of Hamburg, Hamburg, Germany
e-mail: franziska.quaas@uni-hamburg.de

T. Skambraks and M. Lutz (eds.), *Reassessing the Moral Economy*, Palgrave Studies in Economic History,
https://doi.org/10.1007/978-3-031-29834-9_3

dis-embedded economies was used to demonstrate that morality could only play a role in pre-capitalist societies, whereas it would be destroyed in capitalist economic systems (Rogan 2018). In this sense, E. P. Thompson, with his concept of "moral economy", was referring to economic forms that would have been inherent in traditional, pre-capitalist societies of the past (Thompson 1963, 1971).

This concept has come under criticism in research on economic history. Thus, doubts have been raised as to whether the phenomenon of embeddedness as one signifier of moral economy can really be understood as a signum solely characteristic to pre-modern economies.

Based on the assumption that every economic phenomenon is shaped by morals in one way or another (von Schmoller 1893; Granovetter 1985; 482, 506), a whole series of attempts have been made in order to prove that the phenomenon of a close interweaving of economic and moral spheres is not only observable for pre-modern societies, but also for the modern market economy (Beckert 2002, 2006; Fourcade and Healy 2007). Based on these studies, a broad consensus has been established that the phenomenon of embeddedness is not a suitable criterion for emphasising differences between pre-modern and capitalist economies and societies (Booth 1993a, b, 1994, 653–54; Davis 2012, 410–12; Hahn 2014; Knäble 2017, 117–18). Since economic activities in all societies are shaped by morality and embedded correspondingly, it could be stated instead that in fact "all economies – not merely pre- or non-capitalist ones – are moral economies" (Sayer 2006, 78). Hence, the concept of "moral economy"[1] is meanwhile ascribed the status of an epistemologically helpful tool that is predestined to shed more light on the complex relationship between economy and morality in general (Frevert 2019a, 9; Frevert 2019b, 38; Götz 2015, 147–48; Knäble 2017, 117–18).

Consequently, the concept of "moral economy" has also been applied to diverse fields in the context of the study of pre-modern epochs such as the Middle Ages (see for example Faith 2020; Fouracre 2020; Salzmann 2010; Signori 2003). Despite the variety of issues that have been examined in these studies with regard to "moral economy", it is striking that

[1] About the history of the concept brought in to play by Thompson, see Arnold (2001, 86), Götz (2015) and Knäble (2019, 58–59).

the question of the influence of religion in general as well as of the significance of religious institutions and communities in particular on economic practices[2] have been largely ignored.[3]

The lack of studies that specifically ask about the significance of religion and religious institutions for economic and social practices within the framework of research into moral economies is conspicuous for several reasons. First of all, ecclesiastical institutions unquestionably functioned as very important "economic players" in medieval society insofar as they were among the largest landowners and agricultural producers of their time and accordingly not only preserved, developed, exchanged and sold their products and property, but also administered them in several ways (Devroey 2020, 469). For these reasons alone, the institution of the church can be characterised as one of the most significant elements in early medieval economy (Wood 2018, 110–11; 2019). But for another, even more important reason, a closer look at ecclesiastical institutions proves fruitful for the study of moral economy in the Middle Ages: Since behind the transfers of property carried out by the devout laity in favour of saints and the sacred sites representing them, there were rarely only economic, but also social and above all religious motives. A more detailed analysis of the transfers of property between ecclesiastical institutions and lay people is thus particularly suitable for coming closer to answering the question of what exactly the embeddedness between religion and economy might have been shaped in the Middle Ages.

The starting point for analyses of property transfers in favour of the Church in the Middle Ages is relatively favourable due to the availability of a large number of sources. From early medieval Bavaria alone, which will be the focus of this article, a total of almost 2.000 charters from the bishoprics of Freising, Regensburg, Passau and Salzburg as well as the monasteries of St. Emmeram, Mondsee and Schäftlarn[4] have been

[2] On the state of research, see Lutz (2018, especially 716–17, 728 and 724).

[3] Exceptions are Knäble (2019), Skambraks (2017) and Skambraks (2018).

[4] Editions: *Die Traditionen des Hochstifts Freising*, ed. Theodor Bitterauf, , 2 vols. Munich: Rieger, 1905 and 1909; *Die Traditionen des Hochstifts Regensburg und des Klosters St. Emmeram*, ed. Josef Widemann. Munich: Beck, 1943; Edition: *Die Traditionen des Hochstifts Passau*, ed. Max Heuwieser. Munich: Verlag der Kommission für Bayerische Landesgeschichte, 1930; *Salzburger Urkundenbuch*, ed. Willibald Hauthaler, 3 vols. Salzburg: Selbstverlag der Gesellschaft für Salzburger Landeskunde, 1910, 1916 and 1918; *Die Traditionen des Hochstifts Regensburg und des Klosters St. Emmeram*, ed. Josef Widemann. Munich: Beck, 1943; *Das älteste Traditionsbuch des Klosters Mondsee*,

preserved dating from the period from the eighth to the tenth centuries, in which diverse forms of property transfers between these institutions and individuals or groups of persons have been documented. These charters include donations, *precariae* and exchanges of property. The Bavarian private charters have only been preserved as copies in mostly fragmentary and incomplete cartularies. Therefore, they cover at best shorter chronological phases of the history of these institutions.[5] Thus, it is not possible to reconstruct neither their property situations nor the legal transactions in any way undistorted or even complete form. However, both the information contained in the cartularies about the individual transfers of property and the way the texts of the charters in question are formulated make it possible to gain insights into the way the embeddedness of religion and economy was actually shaped.

In contrast to studies that focus primarily on the reconstruction of the property and economic history of individual monasteries and bishoprics (Caro 1901, 1902; Freudenberg 2013; Goetz 1989, 2006; Rädlinger-Prömper 1987; Störmer 1989), local societies (Hummer 2005; Innes 2000; Kohl 2010; Störmer 1994) and individual families (Bührer-Thierry 1999; Goetz 1999; Staab 1999) or that take a closer look at the social networks that emerge through the reciprocal exchange processes between lay people and ecclesiastical institutions (Davies 2007; Rosenwein 1989) this article will examine the complex interrelationship of economic and religious motives involved in the transfers of property between the laity and the church. In a first step, the early medieval Bavarian private charters documenting the donations performed by the laity in favour of ecclesiastical institutions will be examined to determine whether they are able to shed light on the significance of various economic and religious motives for such transfers of property. Secondly, it is to be asked whether it is possible to trace the importance individual people attached to the various economic and religious motives for their strategies in dealing with property. Finally, this chapter will pursue the question to what extent the decreasing number of donations and growing number of transactions of exchange, observable from the middle of the ninth century onwards, can really be understood as a manifestation of a decrease in religious motives

ed. Gebhard Rath and Erich Reiter. Linz: Oberösterreichisches Landesarchiv, 1989; *Die Traditionen des Klosters Schäftlarn 760–1305*, ed. Alois Weisthanner. Munich: Beck, 1953.

[5] On the transmission of the cartularies and the quantitative and chronological distribution of the early medieval Bavarian private charters, see Quaas (2020).

of the laity in carrying out property transfers in favour of the church, and to what extent this points to an increasing importance of property-strategic and, in some respects, purely economic backgrounds of these legal transactions. Thus, a better understanding of the early medieval moral economy and the contemporary conceptions of the embeddedness between religion and economy can be gained.

The Relevance of Religious and Economic Motives in Making Donations to the Church

Even a cursory look at the legal content of the surviving Bavarian private charters from the eighth to tenth centuries reveals that a very specific form of property transfer between the laity and the church is particularly dominant: namely donations in favour of saints and their sacred sites. Since donations of almost all Bavarian monasteries and bishoprics account for a share of just over half to well over three quarters of the total transmission of the respective corpora, they can undoubtedly be characterised as the most important form of property transfer carried out between laymen and ecclesiastical institutions.

The importance of donations in favour of the church is due not least on the religious functions that contemporaries attributed with them. This is based on the idea that the remission of sins, the acquisition of salvation and the chance of redemption can be increased by performing certain good deeds. These good works included various forms of exchanging earthly for heavenly goods (Herz 1958; Quaas 2021a, b; Todeschini 1994), as well as almsgiving as a way of obtaining the treasure in heaven and thus acquiring eternity.[6] Accordingly, it was anything but far-fetched to understand donations to churches as alms (Czock 2021, 15; Innes 2000, 32–33) that thus lead to salvation.

Several legal texts show this idea of a close connection between salvation and the giving of alms, which also included *donationes pro anima* (on these, see Angenendt 2008; Brown 2015; Czock 2021, 13–16; Davies 2007; Innes 2000, 13–50; Magnani Soares-Christen 2003; Silber 1995), was not merely confined to theological discourse in the Carolingian period, but had a broader social and political impact. Thus, in various

[6] See Lk 12, 33–34; likewise see Caesarius of Arles: Sermo 158, 6; Leo the Great: Sermo 17, col. 181; Augustine: Sermo 177, 10.

capitularies as well as in the "Admonitio generalis", almsgiving is defined as an effective measure of attaining eternal life.[7] In accordance with the high religious significance attributed to donations of property in favour of the church, the right of every devout Christian to undertake such a donation for the salvation of the soul, which was actually already guaranteed in the "Codex Theodosianus",[8] was repeatedly attributed special importance in the Carolingian period. Not only several *leges* like the "Lex Alamannorum" or the "Lex Baiuvariorum", but also the Bavarian Council of Dingolfing (770) and capitularies of Charlemagne (803) and Louis the Pious (818/819)[9] explicitly refer to this. Corresponding to this, all individuals, including the actual heirs of the property transferred, who strove to detract these from the church were to be subject to both financial and spiritual penalties such as excommunication or even eternal damnation.[10]

Beyond these records initiated at the highest political level to legally justify donations in favour of the church, the texts of the surviving early medieval Bavarian private charters documenting such *donationes pro anima* also provide information about the importance that was actually attributed to the religious functions of donations at the level of local societies as well. In fact, about half of the surviving charters mention that the respective donations were made *pro remedium animae* or *pro redemptione animae*, but in particular the *arengae* of some of these charters indicate the specific motives for the transfers of property to the church. These

[7] See Theodulf of Orleans: Capitula 2, 10 (MGH Capitula Episcoporum 1, p. 174); Admonitio generalis (MGH Capitula regum Francorum I No. 22), p. 53; Admonitio generalis c. 80.

[8] See Codex Theodosianus XVI, 2, 4 (in: Theodosiani libri XVI cum constitutionibus Sirmondianis et leges novellae ad Theodosianum pertinentes I, 2, p. 836): "Habeat unusquisque licentiam sanctissimo catholicae venerabilique concilio decedes bonorum quod optavit relinquere."

[9] See Lex Alamannorum 1, 1; Lex Baiuvariorum I, 1; Council of Dingolfing (770), c. 6 (MGH Conc. 2, 1), c. 6; Capitulare legibus additum (803), c. 6 (MGH Capitularia regum francorum I, No. 39); Capitula legibus addenda (818/819), c. 9 (MGH Capitularia regum francorum I, No. 139): "Ut omnis homo liber potestatem habeat, ubicumque voluerit, res suas dare pro salute animae suae."

[10] See Lex Alamannorum 1, 2: "Et si aliqua persona aut ipse, qui dedit, vel aliquis de heredibus eius post haec de ipsas res de illa ecclesia abstrahere voluerit, vel aliquis homo, qualiscumque persona hoc praesumpserit facere, incurrat in Dei iudicio et excommunicationem sanctae ecclesiae et effectum, quod inchoavit, non obtineat, et multa illa, quae carta contenit, prosolvat et res illas ex integro redat et fredo in publico solvat, sicut lex habet."

arengae focus not only on the brevity of earthly life,[11] the *fragilitas humana*,[12] the transience of the world[13] and the imminent threat of its end,[14] but in particular on the demand to despise transient, earthly goods[15] and exchange them for heavenly ones[16] so that a treasure in heaven may be acquired.[17] In a few individual cases, the texts of the respective charters contained even more substantial statements about the actual external occasions of the donations: Thus, some of them were made in the light of a serious illness and the associated expectation of imminent death,[18] while others were undertaken in the advance of a long and

[11] See for example Trad. Mondsee No. 111: "Vita brevis haec est nimium, sed longa futura. Ideoque unicuique necesse est cum caducis et transitoriis rebus festinare, ut adquiret ea, quae non sunt transitoria sed eterna, quae numquam veterescunt et deficiunt, sed permanent in aeternum."

[12] See for example Trad. Passau No. 28a: "Dum fragilitas humani generis pertimescit ultimum vitae temporis subitaneam transpositionem esse venturam, oportet, ut non inveniat unumquemque hominem in utroque sexu inparatum, ne sine aliquid boni operis refectione migraret de seculo, sed dum in iure suo et potestate consistit preparet sibi viam salutis per quam ad eternam vitam valeat pervenire, sacra scriptura testante: Qui hic domino largiturus erit parva, accipiet centupla in eterna vita."

[13] See for example Trad. Freising No. 29: "Dum dominus Jesus Christus numerare precem caelestia iuxta lectione: Perit mundus et ea quae in mundo sunt, illud vero quod in ecclesiis aut pauperibus rogatur numquam periit, sed in memoria aeterna pro iustitia reputatur, igitur ego […] dono […]."

[14] See for example Trad. Freising No. 170: "Mundi terminum adpropinquantem ruinis crebrescentibus iam certa signa manifestantur."

[15] See for example Trad. Schäftlarn No. 10: "Preceptum evangelicum tonat per orbem terrarum, in quo fideles ammonet, ut caduca discipiant et ad aeternam patriam tendant, ut lucrum sibi in perventione faciant sicut ab ore veritatis evangelista conclamat: Thesaurizate vobis thesauros in caelo."

[16] See for example Trad. Mondsee No. 19/1: "Latores legum sanxerunt, ut, qui de iure suo proprio alicui aliquid tradere voluerit hoc coram plures testibus per scripturarum seriem firmiter facit oblicari: ut in evum atque inconvulsum valeat perdurare, sicut dominus dixit in evangelio: date et dabitur vobis, multum accipiat, qui sibi de terrenis et caducis rebus comparat premia sempiterna."

[17] See for example Trad. Freising No. 700: "Divina inspiratione evangelisque verbis ego indignus Cozbertus diaconus ammonitus quibus dicitur: Therausizate vobis thesauros in caelo ubi neque erugo neque tinea demolitur et ubi fures non effodiunt nec furantur."

[18] See for example Trad. Freising No. 213a: "Nunc quoque postquam Hadumar infirmitate depressus […] tradidit […] ut deus omnipotens illum liberaro dignaretur de ac peste quam patiebatur vel si deo volenta vitam fragile finiret, intercessionibus sanctae Mariae […] ibidem celebrarentur vel nominantur, ut aliquantulum indulgentiae animabus eorum in mansionibus sempiternis mereantur accipere per magnam misericoridam omnipotentis

perilous pilgrimage[19] or the participation in a military campaign.[20] In addition to the counter-gifts of remission of the sins and acquisition of a place in heaven, the donations were sometimes also tied to the fulfilment of very specific liturgical rewards on the part of the church. These included the performance of prayer services, the reading of psalms, the celebration of masses[21] or even the granting of entry into the monastic community[22] or the obtainment of an ecclesiastical burial place.[23] Statements like that of the scribe Cozroh, who was concerned to preserve the names of the donors,[24] testify to the fact that the ecclesiastical institutions were committed to preserving the memory of their donors in the long term by securing their names in written records. Notably, this happened independently of explicit requests to be entered in ecclesiastical books of remembrance.

Despite such indications pointing to religious motives behind the donations serving the acquisition of otherworldly rewards, doubts have been expressed as to whether spiritual motives alone provide sufficient explanation for the high quantity of such transfers of property in the early Middle Ages (Hartung 1988, 417–18). In fact, a closer look at the texts

dei [...]."; see Trad. Freising No. 260b: "Nunc enim ego Tiso presbiter magna egritudine depressus etiam ad ulimum vitae deductus eadem supradictam ecclesiam cum tota integritate tradedi [...] ut iure legitime usque in perpetuum pro remedium animae meae ibidem firmiter permansisset. Iam enim graviter dolore conpulsus ambulare non potui, cum adductus ad domum sanctae Mariae fui."

19 See for example Trad. Freising No. 410: "Brevem commemoratorii, quid quidam homo nominee Ratkis, dum iter deo gubernante ad Romam carpebat [...] tradidit [...]"; likewise, see Trad. Freising No. 557a; see Trad. Regensburg/St. Emmeram No. 256.

20 See for example Trad. Freising No. 415: "[...] quidam homo nominee Uo, antequem se moveret in ostes, tradidit [...] ea ratione traditionem fecit, si in illo comitatu vitam finiret, eodem die tenetur ad iam dicto domo, si autem inde venire, tunc fuissiet in sua potestate"; likewise, see Trad. Freising No. 419.

21 See for example Trad. Freising Nos. 888, 1036; Trad. Mondsee No. 19/1.

22 See for example Trad. Freising No. 104; Trad. Mondsee Nos. 19/1 and 27/1.

23 See for example Trad. Freising Nos. 171, 1036; Trad. Mondsee No. 19/1; Trad. Regensburg/St. Emmeram No. 208, 258, 260.

24 See Trad. Freising, praefatio: "Tandem enim divina inspiratione tam almivolo animo inhesit, ut in perpetuum permaneret eorum memoria, qui hanc domum suis rebus ditaverunt et herediaverunt; seu quicquid pro remedio animarum suarum ad ipsam domum tradiderunt et condonaverunt."

of the surviving charters shows that a large part of the donations was tied to conditions that provided the donors with financial, economic or even strategic advantages in respect to the property, primarily in their earthly lifetime. This is by no means limited to the terms contained in some of these documents to ensure lifelong provisions of care and welfare for the donors, which could include the guarantee of a lifelong right to accommodation and alimentation to be secured by the church.[25]

After all, the donors were able to secure far-reaching and often long-during rights to the transferred property for themselves, their relatives or other individuals. Apart from granting themselves rights to repurchase or prohibit the respective ecclesiastical institutions to alienate the property transferred or to hand it over to third parties as *beneficium*,[26] the donors also might retain power of disposal over the goods for themselves or selected individuals despite the transfer to the church. This could be achieved, for example, by postponing the validity of the transfer until after the donor's death,[27] by reserving the right of lifelong usufruct, by stipulating that the property be granted as *beneficium* to the donor himself,

[25] See Trad. Freising Nos. 39, 95, 171, 304, 404, 725, 888; Trad. Mondsee Nos. 16a, 16b, 1971, 130, 136; see Trad. Passau No. 76; Trad. Regensburg/St. Emmeram No. 253.

[26] See Trad. Freising Nos. 460, 520, 653, 693; Trad. Regensburg/St. Emmeram No. 14.

[27] See Trad. Freising Nos. 1, 8, 18, 24c, 28, 33, 47, 50, 64, 66, 67, 68, 69, 76, 80, 82, 89, 92, 93, 96, 97a, 98, 101, 102a, 102b, 103, 105a, 105b, 109a, 109b, 119, 131, 134, 140, 152, 153, 160, 170, 173, 174, 181, 192, 199, 200g, 222, 243, 264b, 278a, 301, 302, 303, 306, 312, 349, 356, 359, 381, 389, 411, 415, 425, 428, 429, 452, 467, 468, 469, 480, 485, 502, 504, 505, 510, 512, 516b, 517, 518, 521, 523a, 523c, 546, 550b, 551, 552, 568, 576a, 586, 589, 593, 611, 617, 648, 659, 664, 700, 711, 728, 734, 735, 809, 858, 1031, 1287; see Trad. Mondsee Nos. 2, 9, 11, 12, 13, 17, 18, 31, 33, 37, 41, 43, 45, 61, 64, 69, 72, 75, 77, 83, 86, 87, 89, 96, 97, 103, 105, 109, 110, 112, 15, 119, 125, 127, 135; Trad. Passau Nos. 4, 8, 16, 19, 20, 26, 32, 35, 42, 44b, 47, 52, 53, 57b, 62, 77, 89 Trad. Regensburg/St. Emmeram Nos. 2, 7, 14; Trad. Schäftlarn No. 25, 26.

his heirs or other individuals designated by him[28] or even by securing the right to buy back the respective property.[29]

In most cases, such conditions did not entail any disadvantage for the ecclesiastical institutions concerned. On the contrary, the practice of granting properties as *beneficia* not only possessed the advantage of the borrowers staying responsible for their economic management and exploitation but also on the fact that the bestowal of these rights could in turn depend on conditions that were beneficial for the church itself. In addition to the borrower's obligation not to deteriorate or alienate the goods,[30] he could, for example, be obliged to pay regular interest[31] or to improve and extend the property.[32] Simultaneously, for the donors, transfers of property in favour of the church did not always necessarily mean an actual renunciation of possession or of certain rights to it, due to the

[28] See Trad. Freising Nos. 11, 23, 24, 29, 31, 36, 37, 38, 39, 42, 48, 77, 100, 122, 124, 125, 139, 143, 154, 170, 182, 195, 198, 218, 200a, 200c, 200d, 209, 213, 214, 224, 236, 255, 257, 264a, 273, 280, 293, 294, 296, 300, 305, 311, 313, 314, 315, 316, 317, 320, 321, 328, 329, 330, 333b, 336, 338, 341, 343, 345, 346, 347, 348, 351, 352, 354, 358, 363, 365, 371, 372, 373, 374, 375, 382, 391, 392, 394, 397a, 400a, 402, 414, 421, 422, 426, 427, 431, 433, 434a, 435a, 435b, 436, 439, 441, 442, 445, 450, 457, 459, 460, 461, 470, 472, 474, 479, 486, 487, 488, 489, 494, 499b, 500, 501, 506, 509, 511, 513, 520, 522, 530, 535, 536, 540a, 541, 542, 550, 556, 569, 574a, 576b, 588a, 594, 595, 601, 606, 607a, 608, 612, 614, 620b, 623, 624, 627, 630, 634, 636, 637, 646, 647, 655a, 656a, 660, 662, 665, 667a, 669, 675, 676, 679a, 682, 683, 685, 690, 694, 696a, 696b, 701, 709, 714, 716, 732, 740, 741, 743, 759, 785, 854, 857, 859, 866, 1183, 1257; Trad. Mondsee Nos. 10, 12, 16, 19/2, 20, 60, 61, 76, 80, 88, 103, 111, 113, 120, 121, 128, 134; Trad. Passau Nos. 31, 39, 41, 45, 46, 50, 56, 59, 60, 63, 64, 71 Trad. Regensburg/St. Emmeram Nos. 8, 9, 12, 13, 17, 18, 19, 26, 27, 32, 36, 48, 86, 160, 166, 195, 204, 212, 220, 251, 253, 257, 259; Trad. Schäftlarn No. 28.

[29] See Trad. Freising Nos. 190, 226; Trad. Regensburg/St. Emmeram Nos. 29, 253.

[30] See Trad. Freising Nos. 124, 177, 333b, 338, 345, 472, 522, 550, 601, 740; Trad. Mondsee Nos. 61, 80, 88; Trad. Regensburg/St. Emmeram No. 19.

[31] See Trad. Freising Nos. 77, 100, 139, 154, 179, 195, 255, 273, 300, 320, 343, 345, 351, 392, 421, 426, 435a, 439, 441, 457, 459, 460, 461, 486, 522, 535, 569, 608, 614, 620, 647, 682, 684, 685, 694, 696b, 701, 714, 716, 785; Trad. Mondsee Nos. 10, 80b; Trad. Passau Nos. 31, 41, 46.

[32] See Trad. Freising Nos. 11, 23, 31, 37, 38, 92, 93, 177, 213, 214, 218, 236, 264a, 293, 300, 320, 336, 338, 341, 345, 353, 357, 365, 371, 372, 373, 375, 390, 436, 460, 465, 472, 488, 492, 509, 511, 520, 522, 540a, 541, 542, 550a, 556, 574a, 594, 595, 601, 607a, 613, 614, 634, 636, 672, 678, 685, 690, 701, 706, 714, 740, 856; Trad. Mondsee Nos. 60, 61, 76, 80, 88, 103, 121, 128, 134; Trad. Passau Nos. 55, 69; Trad. Regensburg/St. Emmeram Nos. 7, 12, 19, 27, 29, 32, 73, 86, 164.

possibility of linking the transfer to conditions that granted them further power of disposal and use. Therefore, donations in favour of the church did not necessarily have to be connected to the deterioration of the donor's economic and financial circumstances. Donations to ecclesiastical institutions were not only remunerative from the perspective of securing the salvation of the soul. But the economic value of the donations went far beyond the mere preservation of control in many respects. Because of the prohibition of alienation of ecclesiastical property, donations to the church had the additional advantage of long-term securement of the transferred property, the preservation of which was otherwise exposed to several potential external threats.

One of these threats in early medieval Bavaria was an extensive right of inheritance, which identified a whole series of individuals as potentially entitled to inherit[33] and thus could result in a fragmentation of the property. Although the "Lex Baiuvariorum" prescribed for the protection of potential heirs that they had to have been provided with their respective *portiones* before transferring property to the church,[34] donations to ecclesiastical institutions contributed to preserve the respective property in its entirety and, by specifying various modalities of transfer, allowed the donors greater control and power concerning the decision who was to be granted rights such as repurchase, borrowing or usufruct of the property. The circumvention of hereditary rights leading to a multitude of conflicts between the favoured ecclesiastical institutions and the heirs of the donors who claimed ownership or certain rights[35] in early medieval Bavaria, could thus also represent a further, quite pragmatic economic motive for carrying out a transfer of property (Hartung 1988, 422; Jahn 1988, 412–14).

In addition, it cannot be ruled out that the donations made to the church in Bavaria at the end of the eighth century were undertaken by the Bavarian elites in view of the political fall of Duke Tassilo and the successive integration of Bavaria into the Carolingian Empire. These elites sought to secure their possessions, some of which had been donated,

[33] See Lex Baiuvariorum XV, 10.

[34] See Lex Baiuvariorum I, 1: "Ut si quis liber persona voluerit et dederit res suas ad ecclesiam pro redemptione animae suae, licentiam habeat de portione sua, postquam cum filiis suis partivit".

[35] See for example Trad. Freising Nos. 142, 143a, 143b, 145, 147, 166, 183, 184, 186.

acquired or lent by the duke. One possible indication of such fears for the property caused by political change can be identified in the *arengae* of the donation charters (Esders and Mierau 2006, 287–94; Freund 2004, 156–59; Kohl 2010, 87–88).[36]

Apart from hereditary and political threats to the preservation of property, which might have moved Bavarian donors to transfer their properties to the church, some capitularies and council decisions such like those of the Councils of Reisbach, Freising and Salzburg (800) testify to the fact that donations often were made rather involuntarily. Ecclesiastical institutions were repeatedly inculcated with the canonical prohibition of enforcing donations.[37] In particular, the donation of churches founded by noble families was repeatedly extorted in the course of the act of their consecration by the responsible bishop.[38] The background of these

[36] Freund (2004, 156–59) and Esders and Mierau (2006, 291) for example cite (among others) the following arengae of donation charters from the time after 788 as evidence: Trad. Freising No. 132 ("Cogitante vel tractante me de anima mea seu de vita futura, ut in quantitate apud pio domino veniam merear accipere") and Trad. Freising No. 170 ("Mundi terminum adpropinquantem ruinis crebrescentibus iam certa signa manifestantur"). However, it must be taken into account that these arengae are either already to be found in the "Formulae Marculfi" (Formulae Marculfi II, 3) or in a series of Bavarian private charters from the beginning of the eighth century and are thus of an older date. The arengae cited thus follow an older tradition and were not formulated specifically against the current political background (for more details, see Quaas 2020, forthcoming).

[37] See (for example) the "Capitula de causis cum episcopis et abbatibus tractandis" (811) (MGH Capit. I No. 72), c. 5: "Inquirendum etiam, si ille seculum dimissum habeat, qui cotidie possessiones suas augere quolibet modo, qualibet arte non cessat, suadendo de coelestis regni beatitudine, communando de aeterno supplicio inferni, et sub nomine Dei aut cuiuslibet sancti tam divitem quam pauperem, qui simpliciores natura sunt et minus docit atque cauti inveniuntur, sic rebus suis expoliant et legitimos heredes eorem exerceant cui paternarum hereditas, ne ad eum perveniret, ab alio praerepta est"; see "Concilia Rispacense, Frisingense, Salisburgense" (800) (MGH Conc. II, 1), c. 11: "Ut nullus episcopus vel abbas atrahere audeat res nobilium causa ambitionis [...]".

[38] See for example Trad. Freising No. 328: "Construxit praedictus Sigibaldus oratorium in curte sua. Deinde veniens supplicando ad venerabilem Hittonem episcopum, ut ibidem venire dingaretur, et sic fecit, et venerabilis episcopus ibidem veniens et alii plerique nobiles viri cum eo adfuissent. Tunc venerabilis episcopus querens, quomodo praedictum oratorium hereditare voluisset, et ille statim prumptus adesset et fatebat se cum tribus mancipiis supradictam ecclesiam hereditare. Tunc venerabilis episcopus consecravit ecclesiam necnon et altarem insuper et reliquias additit [...] Sigibaldus [...] tradidit omnia iura propria hereditatis [...] in ea vero ratione, ut ille ipse, quousque in hac fragili vita degeret, ad illius usum et potestatem haberet, et post obitum illius firmiter teneatur ad domo sanctae Mariae absque ulla contradictione". See similarly, Trad. Freising Nos. 7, 11,

practices constituted the idea that the disposal over ecclesiastical property should lie solely with the bishop.[39]

Beyond the fact that donations could thus also be motivated by external circumstances such as the active effort of church representatives or acute threats to the property, it can be observed that many of these donations were tied to the granting of various rights of repurchase, usufruct or loan to the donor or persons designated by him, associated with very concrete economic advantages for the actors concerned. This raises justified doubts as to whether the donations were really always based primarily on the aforementioned spiritual motivations. In this light, the economic advantages associated with making donations to the church seem to have a greater importance, leading researchers like Hartung (1988, 429–30 and 436) or Jahn (1988, 412–14) to fundamentally question the religious focus of the transfers of property towards the salvation of the soul. Hence, they at best attribute secondary importance to spiritual motives for the decision of the donors to undertake transfers of property to ecclesiastical institutions. This view has repeatedly been criticised (Kohl 2010, 96) and although there is now a broad consensus that both, religious as well as pragmatic and economic considerations were behind the transfers of property (Goetz 1999, 873), the question of the exact relationship between these two motives has so far received only minor attention.

Possibilities and Limits of Determining Motives for Property Transfers in Favour of the Church

An approach to the aforementioned question proves to be not too easy an undertaking for several reasons. For both the charters documenting the transfers of property and various indications in their texts, which could potentially provide insight into the specific significance of religious and

13b, 15, 30, 51, 52, 54, 68, 80, 85, 88, 91, 92, 101, 143, 144, 260, 262, 266, 270, 274, 316, 324, 327, 336, 349, 394, 427, 442, 470, 476, 591. On such cases, see Esders and Mierau (2000, esp. 101–44).

[39] See Concilium Ascheihmense (MGH Conc. II, 1 No. 10), c. 3: "De potestate episcoporum, qui claves polique ligandi atque solvendi deveuntur et curam pastoralem exerceunt in pleve, unde et sine dubio rationem reddituri sunt, ut ecclesiasticis rebus dominentur atque spensando provideant. Unde synodus Nicenensis ait, ut omnes res ecclesiasticas in potestate epicoporum sint."

economic motives for the transfer, are to be treated with caution in several respects.

At first glance, it might seem obvious to examine the quantitative relation between the references to religious and economic motives behind the transfers. In fact, religious or liturgical counter-gifts are only rarely specified as a condition for the donations.[40] Generally, references to spiritual motives for the donations are limited to the brief mention that the property in question was transferred for the salvation of the soul of the donors or other individuals. More comprehensive theological explanations of the donations in the form of *arengae* can only be verified for 5–15% of the preserved donations in Bavarian corpora. Hence, the evidence for actual religious motives behind them is mainly concentrated on the *pro remedium animae*-references, while more wide-ranging religious contexts can only be proven for a vanishingly small proportion of donations.

However, the hypothesis that spiritual reasons were of only secondary importance compared to strategic and economic considerations seems questionable. In fact, there are several reasons to doubt such a conclusion. Some indications suggest that—at best—only limited significance can be attributed to the mention of conditions under which donations may have been made. Notably only a part of the surviving Bavarian private charters concerning donations contain conditions to which the respective transfer was linked,[41] including some that provided economic advantages on the

[40] Less than one per cent of the Bavarian charters documenting donations in favour of the church contain such conditions.

[41] See Trad. Freising Nos. 11, 13a, 13b, 23, 4a29, 31, 36, 37, 38, 39, 41, 42, 4851, 65, 77, 95, 97b, 100, 110, 124, 125, 139, 144, 154, 170, 171, 177, 179, 143a, 182, 198, 200a, 200c, 200d, 209, 213a, 213b, 214, 218, 226, 236, 255, 264a, 273, 278b280, 292, 293, 294, 295, 296, 300, 304, 305, 311, 313, 314, 315, 316, 320, 321, 328, 329, 330, 333b, 336, 341, 343, 346, 348, 352, 354, 371, 372, 374, 375, 376, 382, 384, 391, 394, 397a, 397b, 400a, 400c, 402, 40?, 405, 414, 421, 422, 426, 427, 434, 435a, 435b, 436, 439, 441, 442, 445, 450, 457, 459, 460, 461, 462, 470, 472, 474b, 478, 479, 486, 487, 488, 489, 492, 494, 499a, 500, 501a, 506, 508, 511, 513a, 516a, 520, 522, 528, 530, 533, 535, 536, 540a, 541, 542, 549, 550a, 574a, 588a, 588b, 594, 595, 601, 605, 607a, 608, 612, 613, 614, 621, 623, 624, 627, 630, 637, 641a, 641b, 646, 647, 653, 655a, 656b, 660, 662, 663, 665, 667a, 680a, 669, 672, 674, 675, 676, 67, 682, 683, 684, 685, 689, 690, 693, 696a, 696b, 697a, 698, 699, 701, 705, 706, 709, 714, 716, 722a, 723, 724, 725, 732, 740, 741, 743, 785, 855a, 856, 857, 859, 860, 865a, 865b, 866, 888, 899, 900, 902, 904, 910, 911, 912, 1034, 1036, 1124, 1154, 1159a, 1183, 1288, 1316; vgl. Trad. Mondsee Nr.16, 20, 31, 33, 37, 38, 42, 52b, 54, 56, 60, 61, 68, 71, 74, 76, 80, 103, 111, 113, 120, 121, 128, 130, 132, 134; Trad. Passau Nos. 8, 18, 19, 28b, 31, 32, 39, 41, 45, 51, 52, 59, 60, 63, 64, 65, 66, 69, 71,

part of the donors. Furthermore, there is evidence to indicate that the lack of conditions mentioned in the charters' texts does not necessarily mean that the respective donations were actually of unconditional nature. The sources show that in many cases an apparently unconditional donation was subsequently followed by the granting of the transferred property back to the donor, although such a condition had originally not been envisaged in the document.[42] The motives underlying such property transfers thus remain unclear and cannot be answered solely on the basis of the texts of the charters. The same applies to the *arengae* detailing possible religious contexts of the transfers. Although *arengae* can only rarely be found in private charters of early medieval Bavaria, their absence from the texts of the charters is not necessarily due to the circumstance that little importance was laid on the explanation of spiritual motives or the fixation of the conditions of the donations, which promised economic advantages for the donors. One possible explanation is that medieval Bavarian private charters have not been preserved as originals, but have only been transmitted in copied form in cartularies. After all, it cannot be ruled out that during the compilation of the cartularies and the transmission of the charters, which was often carried out long after the act of transfer, the scribes could sometimes have deliberately omitted the copying of certain components of the texts. Those components whose preservation would be of only little value long after the death of the donors (such as the mention of the exact terms of the transfer of property or the names of the witnesses involved) proved to be particularly suitable for potential abridgements of the text. Similarly, the *arengae* not necessary for the long-term preservation of the contents of the legal transaction might have been considered dispensable.

Findings concerning the shortening and rewording of charters imply that the analysis of private charters documenting donations to the church does not allow to draw sufficiently viable conclusions about the precise significance of religious and economic motives in the transfer of property. The limited informative value of these sources regarding the motives of the transfers leads to the donors themselves and if they might not provide

74, 75, 85; Trad. Regensburg/St. Emmeram Nos. 9, 12, 17, 18, 26, 27, 29, 32, 36, 46, 48, 72, 73, 86, 87, 93, 95, 112, 137, 145, 147, 151, 157, 160, 163, 164, 166, 190, 191, 195, 212a, 212b, 220, 251, 253, 257, 258, 259; e Trad. Schäftlarn No. 28a.

42 For example, the priest Wafanheri was lent back his property in Filusa, which he had transferred to Freising between 807 and 811, as a lifelong *beneficium* by Bishop Hitto of Freising on 14 June 815 (see Trad. Freising Nos. 269 and 340).

more precise information about their individual strategies in transferring property to the church. However, since most of the individuals can often only be traced once and are also only very rarely mentioned in other written sources, it is usually not possible to reveal more about them than what the only surviving charter in each case discloses about their only documented legal transaction. Only in a few individual cases several documentary testimonies of certain donors have been preserved, which, within certain limits, allow us to gain a more precise insight into the possible background of their transfers of property.

Thus, in the case of one of these donors, namely count Machelm, who was active under the Agilolfingian dukes Odilo and Tassilo, it can be ascertained on the basis of the surviving charters that he donated parts of his property to all the important ecclesiastical institutions of early medieval Bavaria.[43] At least two of these donations were made within a very short time in the summer of the year 776.[44] Hence it is quite reasonable to assume that Machelm undertook these donations in view of a very specific external occasion, perhaps his own imminent death, and that they served his own salvation. In fact, this endeavour of divine retribution and remission of sins is explicitly mentioned in some of Machelm's charters concerning donations to the church.[45] However, the fact that Machelm found it necessary to make donations to all the important Bavarian ecclesiastical institutions for this purpose cannot be attributed solely to an effort to gain as many different saints represented by these institutions as possible as advocates of his cause with God. For by favouring a large number of recipients with whom the Machelm family established and deepened connections in this way, Machelm created and strengthened a network of relationships with politically highly significant individuals and

[43] See Trad. Freising No. 74; Trad. Passau No. 9 and 10; Trad. Regensburg/St. Emmeram No. 4; Trad. Mondsee No. 1; Tiefenbach (1990, 86 no. 1).

[44] See Trad. Regensburg/St. Emmeram No. 4 on 10h of July 776 and Trad. Freising No. 74 on 8th of September 776.

[45] See Trad. Freising No. 74 ("Cogitante vel tractante me de anima mea seu de vita futura, ut in quantitate apud pio domino veniam merear accipere [...]") Trad. Mondsee No. 1 ("ego Machelm vir clarissimus cogitavi pro intuitu timoris dei vel divinam retributionem, ut in futuro seculo peccatorum meorum veniam merear consequi, dono atque transfundo [...]"); Trad. Mondsee No. 4 ("pro remedim animae meae"); Trad. Passau No. 10 ("pro redemptione anime meae vel divina retributionem"); Trad. Regensburg/ St. Emmeram No. 4 ("Ego igitur Machelm conpunctus divinae misericordiae seu aeterna retributione").

institutions (Bührer-Thierry 1999, 694). Furthermore, these donations fulfilled a political function in yet another respect: the transfers, some of which took place in the castrum Wels as well as in the ducal palatinates of Altöttingen and Ostermiething before the eyes and ears of the Bavarian nobility, also and above all served to express count Machelm's ties with the Agilolfingian ducal family, for whose salvation at least one of the donations in question explicitly was made. This donation *pro remedium et perennem salute Otilonis et Thessilonis*[46] was attributed such considerable political importance that the corresponding charter was prominently placed at the beginning of the Mondsee chartulary.[47]

While in the case of Machelm's surviving charters, both, spiritual as well as political motives were crucial for the transfers, in another exemplary case of a Bavarian count, different combinations of motives can be determined. Count Willihelm, who acted in the Traungau and who, for similar reasons like Machelm, also made donations to several different Bavarian ecclesiastical institutions for the remission of his sins and the acquisition of eternal life[48] bound the transfer of his property to a very specific condition. This condition is otherwise not detectable in other early medieval private charters of the East Frankish Empire and therefore most likely represents an individual wish of the count: According to this condition, his property transferred to the church was only to be lent to his wife if she remained loyal to him in marriage—otherwise it was to revert directly to the church.[49]

These examples demonstrate several different motives did certainly play a role in the transfers of property. Hence, on the basis of the

[46] See Trad. Mondsee No. 1.

[47] See Vienna, Haus- Hof- und Staatsarchiv, Hs. Blau 70 (Böhm Hs. 179), fol. 1r – fol. 1v.

[48] See Trad. Mondsee No. 74: "Ego Willihelmus comis cogitans de dei timore, ut mihi pius dominus de peccatis meis aliquid relaxare dignetur [...]"; Trad. Regensburg/St. Emmeram No. 26: "Quisquis in hac vita, quae cunctis mortalibus incerta est, caute semetipsum tota mentis devotione circumspicit, ad illam sine dubio perveniet feliciter vitam, ubi illi cum Christo regnant, qui hic provide gesserunt praecepta domini sui conservando."

[49] See Trad. Mondsee No. 74: "et si uxor mea tamdiu lectum meum servaverit, hoc habeat, postea in vestrum dispono [...]"; Trad. Regensburg/St. Emmeram No. 26: "et tamen coniux ipsius easdem res in ditione sua teneret, quamdiu lectum suum conservaret; si vero humano more contingeret, ut lectum suum non custodiret, mox traditio ad locum suum severteretur [...]".

surviving charters it is possible to approach the various religious and economic motives behind the donations in more detail. However, even when looking at these cases, there are insuperable limits to uncovering the individual weighting of these motives in the perspective of the donors, due to the problematic nature of tradition.

The End of Embeddedness? On the Relevance of the Increasing Number of Transactions of Exchange from the Middle of the Ninth Century Onwards

Although the problematic situation of the tradition of early medieval private charters from Bavaria does not allow for sufficiently reliable assessments of the significance of various motives for making donations to the church, it is a widespread assumption that the motives of the donors changed over the course of time. According to this idea, the acquisition of the soul's salvation as the reason for the donations was undermined in favour of an even greater emphasis on the economic interests of the donors (Borgolte 1984, 589). This supposed change was reflected accordingly in a successive decline in the nobility's willingness to undertake donations to the church (Caro 1901, 245; Rädlinger-Prömper 1987, 126–27; Störmer 1973, 374–78; Störmer 1989, 375–77). In fact, a more detailed analysis of the distribution of the contents of the Bavarian corpora of private charters shows that for the period from the middle of the ninth century onwards, only a few charters of donation can be traced in the sources from the aforementioned ecclesiastical institutions, while the numbers are higher for the eighth and early ninth centuries. Notably, charters dealing with exchanges of property form the majority of sources for the period from the middle of the ninth century onwards. Indeed, it cannot be denied that transactions of exchange lack a sacred component in some respects. However, it seems difficult to argue that the high number of exchanges is an indicator for the decrease of religious motives of the laity carrying out these transactions. Neither seems it satisfying to conclude that there was an increase of strategic and economic considerations for these transactions. In order to test this hypothesis, it is necessary to look for alternative explanations for the change observed.

Probably the most reasonable explanation for this is the possibility that the change in the legal transactions could be attributed to a natural economic logic of the development of ecclesiastical economy. According to this consideration, in the first decades after their founding, the respective ecclesiastical institutions received numerous donations, which, after a phase of consolidation, were later exchanged for other property in order to consolidate the scattered holdings that had emerged in the meantime and to round off the property as a whole (Esders 2013, 21–22). The reason for shifting character of legal transactions visible in the charters would then be an almost inevitable saturation of the land holdings of the respective recipient institution after a certain period of continuous growth. Consequently, this would lead to the rounding off of the property (Goetz 1989, 204; Kohl 2010, 107). In fact, individual strategies of the exchange partners to round off their possessions can be traced.[50]

However, further assumptions can be raised about the possible reasons behind the observed development of donations and transactions of exchange, regarding the political and legal changes of the time. The principle of the inalienability of ecclesiastical property, which had already been established in late Roman legislations and was also taken up in the Merovingian and Carolingian regulations, was probably of central importance in this context. It was precisely this principle that led Louis the Pious to initiate the annulment of transactions of exchange that could not be classified as appropriate,[51] and in this way to consolidate and expand royal control over church property (Depreux 2000, 48). According to a capitulary contained in the collection of Ansegis, transactions of exchange should only be allowed in exceptional cases where there is reasonable cause for it and the property offered to the church is equal or more valuable than the property provided by the church in return.[52] This is why the usefulness of the custom to exchange property is sometimes emphasised in the *arengae* introducing some of the charters of exchange.[53] The strict

[50] For more details, see Kohl (2013).

[51] See Capitulare missorum Wormatiense (829) (MGH Capit. 2), c. 5: "Ubicumque commutationes tam tempore nostro quamque genitoris nostri legitimae et rationabiles atque inrationabiles factae sunt, dissolvantur, et recipiat unusquisque, quod dedit. Ubi vero mortua manus ineriacet aut alia quelibet causa, quae rationabilis esse videtur, inventa fuerit, diligenter describatur et ad nostram notitiam perferatur."

[52] See Ansegisi Collectio Capitularium 553, c. 30: "Si princeps voluerit rem immobilem sanctis locis praestare et accipere ab eo aliam immobilem rem et eo modo permutationem contrahere, liceat hoc facere ei divina pragmatica sanctione ab eo promulgata."

[53] See for example Trad. Passau No. 86: "Fructuosa valde ac non solum honesta verum etiam nimium utilis consuetudo olim inter homines inoleverat commutandi videlicet

royal policy concerning exchanges was accompanied by a growing uncertainty about the validity of transactions of exchange already concluded. Therefore, royal confirmations of exchanges were increasingly requested and issued, and moreover, in the middle of the ninth century the right to barter ecclesiastical property became a privilege granted by the king. Thus, within a few years, Louis the German granted several ecclesiastical institutions the right to carry out important and useful transactions of exchange.[54] Only through these privileges dioceses and monasteries were able to carry out transactions of exchange secured by law, and without having to fear the annulment of the respective transactions. Accordingly, some of the charters documenting transactions of exchange specifically refer to a royal permission to carry out such transactions, which ultimately led to barter becoming increasingly popular.[55] As a result, the transactions of exchange themselves as well as their written fixation became so important that in the ninth century, ecclesiastical institutions created specific manuscripts intended for the collection of such charters.[56] In some of these manuscripts, the royal confirmation documents of individual exchanges as well as the respective royal privileges permitting the

quasdam res pro amborum utilitate partium"; similarly, Trad. Passau No. 87; Trad. Regensburg/St. Emmeram Nos. 33, 39, 40, 42, 50, 51, 53, 54, 55, 58, 60, 64, 69, 70, 71, 74, 75, 76, 79, 80, 82, 90, 92, 94, 95, 111, 117.

[54] In 848, Samuel, bishop of Worms and abbot of Lorsch, was granted such a privilege, followed in 851 by Gozbald, bishop of Würzburg and abbot of Niederaltaich, as well as archbishop Liupram of Salzburg. Finally, in 852, bishop Hartwig of Passau was also granted the right to conduct transactions of exchange with ecclesiastical property. See MGH DD LD Nos. 47, 59, 60 and 62.

[55] See for example Trad. Regensburg/St. Emmeram No. 40: "Fructuosa valde ac nimium utilis consuetudo olim inter homines inoleverat commutandi videlicet quasdam res pro ambarum oportunitate partium. Haec etenim modernis temporibus crebrius ac crebrius piissimorum licentia regum conficitur frequentissimeque inter nobilium substantias atque aeclesiasticarum rerum portiones contingere solet". Similarly, Trad. Regensburg/ St. Emmeram Nos. 79, 80, 95, 111.

[56] An example for this is the "Codex commutationum" from Freising (Munich, Bayerisches Hauptstaatsarchiv, HL Freising 3b).

execution of such transactions were either positioned in a prominent place within the manuscript[57] or especially emphasised in their design.[58]

The fact that, from the middle of the ninth century onwards, charters concerning donations no longer make up the main part of the tradition, but that there exist almost exclusively charters documenting transactions of exchange between the laity and ecclesiastical institutions, can hardly be attributed solely to an alleged decline in the willingness of the donors to undertake donations nor a declining importance of spiritual motives for property transfers in favour of the church. Although such an explanation cannot be ruled out, it also cannot be sufficiently proven on the basis of the tradition. It is much more likely that the growing need to round off one's own property in a useful way, rooted in the logic of economic development processes, played a significant role for the fact that transactions of exchange became more attractive in a time of consolidation of ecclesiastical land ownership. However, only with the establishment of a royal grant of respective privileges, which most Bavarian dioceses and monasteries received in the middle of the ninth century, the practice of transferring property in favour of the church in the form of transactions of exchange gradually became established. Therefore, the sparse evidence of donations can be rather attributed to these processes of socio-political change than to an increasingly lower motivation on the part of the donors to carry out transfers of property in favour of the church for religious reasons.

Conclusion

Since both religious and economic motives were behind the transfers of property in favour of the church, a more detailed analysis of precisely these acts of transfer is particularly approaching the understudied question, of

[57] Thus, the deacon Anamot has his chartulary of property transfers in favour of the dioecese of Regensburg and the monastery of St. Emmeram begin with an exchange carried out between King Louis the German and Bishop Ambricho of Regensburg (Munich, Bayerisches Hauptstaatsarchiv, KL Regensburg-St. Emmeram 5 1/3, fol. 75v, edited in Trad. Regensburg/St. Emmeram No. 44).

[58] In the "Codex antiquissismus" from Passau, the permission granted by Louis the German to bishop Hartwig of Passau to exchange property is graphically highlighted by a heading in red and a chrismon extending over almost ten lines (Munich, Bayerisches Hauptstaatsarchiv, HL Passau Lit. 1, fol. 39).

how exactly the embeddedness and complex interrelationship of religious and economic considerations were shaped in these transfers of property.

The texts of the early medieval private charters, which document these acts of donation, bestowal and exchange between the laity and ecclesiastical institutions, and of which a large number of records have survived for the Bavarian region exemplarily used here, reveal that the donation as most important form of property transfer, was not only made with the goals of receiving liturgical counter-gifts and acquiring the salvation of the soul. In many cases they served economic and strategic objectives, providing the actors involved with considerable economic advantages during their lifetime. However, a more precise examination of the question as to exactly what significance the religious and economic motives could have had in these transfers of property is limited by the available source material. Since the transmission of the charters in cartularies is likely to involve abridgements and modifications of the texts, an analysis of the texts of the charters does not allow sufficient conclusions to be drawn about the individual weighting of various motives for the donations. The widespread hypothesis that spiritual motives for the transfers of property in favour of the church played an increasingly minor role over time and are reflected in a decreasing willingness to undertake donations can therefore not be confirmed. The changing practice of transferring property to ecclesiastical institutions from the ninth century onwards, can therefore not necessarily be understood as an external expression of a decreasing importance of religious considerations in property transfers. Instead, it could rather be attributed to economic and political processes of change beginning at this time.

A more detailed analysis of private charters, which takes a closer look at the transfers of property between the laity and ecclesiastical institutions, allows us to uncover the extent to which these acts were characterised by an embeddedness of a variety of different types of motives, that can be assigned equally to the religious and the economic sphere. Accordingly, hypotheses that attribute the various forms of property transfers all too unilaterally to the supposedly dominant importance of economic considerations do not adequately consider the complex interrelationship of a variety of motives. However, a precise scaling of the weighting of these motives cannot be undertaken due to the problematic source situation. An answer to the question of how exactly the embeddedness of religion and economy in the moral economy of the early Middle Ages was structured can thus, on the basis of the study of property transfers in favour of the church, only be approached within certain limits.

References

Manuscripts

Munich, Bayerisches Hauptstaatsarchiv, HL Freising 3a.
Munich, Bayerisches Hauptstaatsarchiv, HL Freising 3b.
Munich, Bayerisches Hauptstaatsarchiv, HL Passau Lit. 1.
Munich, Bayerisches Hauptstaatsarchiv, KL Regensburg-St. Emmeram 5 1/3.
Vienna, Haus-, Hof- und Staatsarchiv, Hs. Blau 70 (Böhm Hs. 179).

Source Editions

Ansegisi Collectio Capitularium / Die Kapitulariensammlung des Ansegis. 1996. Ed. Gerhard Schmitz. MGH Leges 3a. Hanover: Hahn.

Augustine. 1862. *Sermones*. Ed. Jacques-Paul Migne. Patrologia Latina 38. Paris: Migne, cols 23-1484.

Caesarius of Arles. 1953. *Sermones*. Ed. Germain Morin. Corpus Christianorum Series Latina 104. Turnhout: Brepols.

Capitula Episcoporum. 1984–2005. Vols 1–4. MGH Capitula Episcoporum 1–4. Hanover: Hahn.

Capitularia regum Francorum. Vol. 1. 1883. Ed. Alfred Boretius. MGH Capitularia Regum Francorum 1. Hanover: Hahn.

Capitularia regum Francorum. Vol. 2. 1897. Ed. Alfred Boretius and Victor Krause. MGH Capitularia Regum Francorum 2. Hanover: Hahn.

Concilia aevi Carolini. Vol. 1. 1906. Ed. Albert Werminghof. MGH Coniclia 1,1. Hanover and Leipzig: Hahn.

Concilia aevi Carolini. Vol. 2. 1908. Ed. Albert Werminghof. MGH Concilia 2,2. Hanover: Hahn.

Das älteste Traditionsbuch des Klosters Mondsee. 1989. Ed. Gebhard Rath and Erich Reiter. Linz: Oberösterreichisches Landesarchiv.

Die Traditionen des Hochstifts Freising. 2 Volumes. 1905 and 1909. Ed. Theodor Bitterauf. Munich: Rieger.

Die Traditionen des Hochstifts Passau. 1930. Ed. Max Heuwieser. Munich: Verlag der Kommission für Bayerische Landesgeschichte.

Die Traditionen des Hochstifts Regensburg und des Klosters St. Emmeram. 1943. Ed. Josef Widemann, Munich: Beck.

Die Traditionen des Klosters Schäftlarn 760–1305. 1953. Ed. Alois Weissthanner. Munich: Beck.

Die Urkunden der deutschen Karolinger. Erster Band: Die Urkunden Ludwigs des Deutschen, Karlmanns und Ludwigs des Jüngeren. 1934. Ed. Paul Kehr. MGH Diplomata. Berlin: Weidmannsche Buchhandlung.

Formulae merowingici et karolini Aevi: Accedunt ordines iudiciorum dei. 1886. Ed. Karl Zeumer. MGH Formulae. Hanover: Hahn.

Leges Alamannorum. 1966. Ed. Karl August Eckhardt. MGH Leges nat. Germ. 5,1. Hanover: Hahn.

Leges Baiwariorum. 1926. Ed. Ernst von Schwind. MGH Leges nat. Germ. 5, 2. Hanover: Hahn.

Leo the Great. 1846. *Sermones*. Ed. Jacques-Paul Migne. Patrolocuia Latina 54. Paris: Migne, cols 138-583.

Salzburger Urkundenbuch. 3 Volumes. Ed. Willibald Hauthaler. Salzburg: Selbstverlag der Gesellschaft für Salzburger Landeskunde, 1910, 1916 and 1918.

Theodosiani libri XVI cum constitutionibus Sirmondianis et leges novellae ad Theodosianum pertinentes. Volumen 1, pars 2. 1905. Ed. Theodor Mommsen, Paul Martin Meyer and Paul Krüger. Berlin: Weidmann.

Secondary Literature

Angenendt, Arnold. 2008. Donationes pro anima. Gift and Countergift in the Early Medieval Liturgy. In *The Long Morning of Medieval Europe. New Directions in Early Medieval Studies*, ed. Jennifer R. Davis and Michael McCormick. Aldershot: Ashgate.

Arnold, Thomas Clay. 2001. Rethinking Moral Economy. *American Political Science Review* 95 (1): 85–95.

Beckert, Jens. 2002. *Beyond the Market. The Social Foundations of Economic Efficiency*. Princeton, NJ: Princeton University Press.

———. 2006. The Moral Embeddedness of Markets. In *Ethics and the Market. Insights from Social Economics*, ed. Betsy Jane Clary et al., 11–25. London and New York: Routledge.

Booth, William James. 1993a. *Households: On the Moral Architecture of the Economy*. Ithaca: Cornell University Press.

———. 1993b. A Note on the Idea of the Moral Economy. *American Political Science Review* 87 (4): 949–54.

———. 1994. On the Idea of the Moral Economy. *American Political Science Review* 88 (3): 653–67.

Borgolte, Michael. 1984. Gedenkstiftungen in St. Galler Urkunden. In *Memoria. Der geschichtliche Zeugniswert des liturgischen Gedenkens im Mittelalter*, ed. Karl Schmid and Joachim Wollasch, 578–602. Munich: Fink.

Brown, Peter. 2015. *The Ransom of the Soul. Afterlife and Wealth in Western Christianity.* Cambridge, MA: Harvard University Press.

Bührer-Thierry, Geneviève. 1999. Formes de donations aux églises et stratégies des familles en Bavière du VIIIe siècle au Xe siècle. *Mélanges de l'Ecole française de Rome* 111: 675–99.

Caro, Georg. 1901. Studien zu den älteren St. Galler Urkunden. Die Grundbesitzverteilung in der Nordostschweiz und in angrenzenden alemannischen Stammesgebieten zur Karolingerzeit, Erster Abschnitt. *Jahrbuch für schweizerische Geschichte* 26: 207–94.

———. 1902. Studien zu den älteren St. Galler Urkunden. Die Grundbesitzverteilung in der Nordostschweiz und in angrenzenden alemannischen Stammesbieten zur Karolingerzeit. Zweiter Abschnitt. *Jahrbuch für schweizerische Geschichte* 27: 187–370.

Czock, Miriam. 2021. Einführung. In *Der Wert des Heiligen. Spirituelle, materielle und ökonomische Verflechtungen*, ed. Andreas Bihrer, Miriam Czock, and Uta Kleine. Stuttgart: Franz Steiner Verlag.

Davies, Wendy. 2007. *Acts of Giving. Individual, Community, and Church in Tenth-Century Christian Spain.* Oxford: Oxford University Press.

Davis, James. 2012. *Medieval Market Morality. Life, Law and Ethics in the English Marketplace, 1200–1500.* Cambridge and New York: Cambridge University Press.

Depreux, Philippe. 2000. The Development of Charters Confirming Exchange by the Royal Administration (Eigth–Tenth Centuries). In *Charters and the Use of the Written Word in Medieval Studies*, ed. Karl Heidecker, 43–62. Turnhout: Brepols.

Devroey, Jean-Pierre. 2020. Monastic Economics in the Carolingian Age. In *The Cambridge History of Medieval Monasticism in the Latin West. Volume 1: Origins to the Eleventh Century*, ed. Alison Beach, 466–84. Cambridge: Cambridge University Press.

Esders, Stefan. 2013. Die frühmittelalterliche „Blüte" des Tauschgeschäfts: Folge ökonomischer Entwicklung oder Resultat rechtspolitischer Setzung? In *Tauschgeschäft und Tauschurkunde vom 8. bis zum 12. Jahrhundert/L'acte d'échange du VIII au XII siècle*, ed. Irmgard Fees and Philippe Depreux, 19–44. Cologne, Weimar and Vienna: Böhlau.

Esders, Stefan, and Heike Johanna Mierau. 2000. *Der althochdeutsche Klerikereid. Bischöfliche Diözesangewalt, kirchliches Benefizialwesen und volkssprachliche Rechtspraxis im frühmittelalterlichen Baiern.* Hanover: Hahn.

———. 2006. Die bairischen Eliten nach dem Sturz Tassilos III.: das Beispiel der adeligen Stiftungspraxis in der Diözese Freising. In *Les Élites au Haut Moyen Âge. Crises et Renouvellements*, ed. François Bougard, Laurent Feller, and Régine Le Jan, 283–314. Turnhout: Brepols.

Faith, Rosamond Jane. 2020. *The Moral Economy of the Countryside. Anglo-Saxon to Anglo-Norman England.* Cambridge, New York, Port Melbourne, New Delhi, and Singapore: Cambridge University Press.

Fouracre, Paul J. 2020. Lights, Power and the Moral Economy of Early Medieval Europe. *Early medieval Europe* 28: 367–87.

Fourcade, Marion, and Kieran Healy. 2007. Moral Views of Market Society. *Annual Review of Sociology* 33: 285–311.

Freudenberg, Sebastian. 2013. *Trado atque dono. Die frühmittelalterliche Grundherrschaft in Ostfranken im Spiegel der Traditionsurkunden der Klöster Lorsch und Fulda (750–900).* Stuttgart: Steiner.

Freund, Stephan. 2004. *Von den Agilolfingern zu den Karolingern. Bayerns Bischöfe zwischen Kirchenorganisation, Reichsintegration und Karolingischer Reform (700–847).* Munich: Verlag C.H. Beck.

Frevert, Ute. 2019a. Introduction. In *Moral Economies*, ed. Ute Frevert, 7–12. Göttingen: Vandenhoeck & Ruprecht.

———. 2019b. Moral Economies, Present and Past. Social Practices and Intellectual Controversies. In *Moral Economies*, ed. Ute Frevert, 13–43. Göttingen: Vandenhoeck & Ruprecht.

Goetz, Hans-Werner. 1989. Beobachtungen zur Grundherrschaftsentwicklung der Abtei St. Gallen vom 8. bis zum 10. Jahrhundert. In *Strukturen der Grundherrschaft im frühen Mittelalter*, ed. Werner Rösener, 197–246. Göttingen: Vandenhoeck und Ruprecht.

———. 1999. La circulation des biens à l'intérieur de la famille. Rapport introductif. *Mélanges de l'Ecole française de Rome* 111: 861–79.

———. 2006. Die „private" Grundherrschaft des frühen Mittelalters im Spiegel der St. Galler Traditionsurkunden. In *Tätigkeitsfelder und Erfahrungshorizonte des ländlichen Menschen in der frühmittelalterlichen Grundherrschaft (bis ca. 1000)*, ed. Brigitte Kasten. Stuttgart: Steiner.

Götz, Norbert. 2015. 'Moral Economy': Its Conceptual History and Analytical Prospects. *Journal of Global Ethics* 11 (2): 147–62.

Granovetter, Mark. 1985. Economic Action and Social Structure: The Problem of Embeddedness. *The American Journal of Sociology* 91: 481–510.

Hahn, Hans-Peter. 2014. Notizen zur Umwertung der Werte. Perspektive auf ökonomische Konzepte im interdisziplinären Diskurs. In *Kultur der Ökonomie. Zur Materialität und Performanz des Wirtschaftlichen*, ed. Inga Klein and Sonja Windmöller, 17–36. Bielefeld: transcript.

Hartung, Wolfgang. 1988. Adel, Erbrecht, Schenkung. Die strukturellen Ursachen der frühmittelalterlichen Besitzübertragungen an die Kirche. In *Gesellschaftsgeschichte. Festschrift für Karl Bosl zum 80. Geburtstag. Band 1*, ed. Ferdinand Seibt, 417–38. Munich: Oldenbourg.

Herz, Martin. 1958. *Sacrum commercium. Eine begriffsgeschichtliche Studie zur Theologie der römischen Liturgiesprache.* Munich: Zink.

Hummer, Hans J. 2005. *Politics and Power in Early Medieval Europe: Alsace and the Frankish Realm, 600–1000*. Cambridge and New York: Cambridge University Press.

Innes, Matthew. 2000. *State and Society in the Early Middle Ages: The Middle Rhine Valley, 400–1000*. Cambridge: Cambridge University Press.

Jahn, Joachim. 1988. Tradere ad sanctum. Politische und gesellschaftliche Aspekte der Traditionspraxis im agilolfingischen Bayern. In *Gesellschaftsgeschichte. Festschrift für Karl Bosl zum 80. Geburtstag*, ed. Ferdinand Seibt, vol. 1, 400–16. Munich: Oldenbourg.

———. 1991. *Ducatus Baiuvariorum. Das bairische Herzogtum der Agilolfinger.* Stuttgart: Hiersemann.

Knäble, Philip. 2017. Wucher, Seelenheil, Gemeinwohl. Der Scholastiker als Wirtschaftsexperte? In *Wissen und Wirtschaft. Expertenkulturen und Märkte vom 13. bis 18. Jahrhundert*, ed. Philip Knäble and Nina Elsemann, 115–37. Göttingen: Vandenhoeck & Ruprecht.

———. 2019. "Moralische Ökonomie?" – Zur Wirtschaftsethik der Schule von Salamanca am Beispiel von Martín de Azpilcueta und Leonardus Lessius. *Saeculum* 69: 55–77.

Kohl, Thomas. 2010. *Lokale Gesellschaften. Formen der Gemeinschaft in Bayern vom 8. bis zum 10. Jahrhundert.* Ostfildern: Thorbecke.

———. 2013. Pro ambarum utilitate und die Suche nach der melior pars – Tauschgeschäfte und Tauschstrategien in Bayern vom 8. bis zum 11. Jahrhundert. In *Tauschgeschäft und Tauschurkunde vom 8. bis zum 12. Jahrhundert/ L'acte d'échange du VIII au XII siècle*, ed. Irmgard Fees and Philippe Depreux, 201–16. Cologne, Weimar and Vienna: Böhlau.

Lutz, Martin. 2018. Religion und Wirtschaft. In *Handbuch Religionssoziologie*, ed. Detlef Pollack, Volkhard Krech, Olaf Müller, and Markus Hero, 715–40. Wiesbaden: Springer VS.

Magnani Soares-Christen, Eliana. 2003. Transforming Things and Persons. The Gift „pro anima" in the Eleventh and Twelfth Centuries. In *Negotiating the Gift. Pre-modern Figurations of Exchange*, ed. Gadi Algazi, Valentin Groebner, and Bernhard Jussen, 269–84. Göttingen: Vandenhoeck & Ruprecht.

Mauss, Marcel. 1923/1924. Essai sur le don. Forme et raison de l'échanges dans les sociétés archaïques. *L'année sociologique* 1: 30–186.

Polanyi, Karl. 1944. *The Great Transformation*. New York: Rinehart.

———. 1957. Aristotle Discovers the Economy. In *Trade and Market in the Early Empires. Economies in History and Theory*, ed. Karl Polanyi, Conrad M. Arensberg, and Harry W. Pearson, 64–96. Glencoe, IL: Free Press.

Quaas, Franziska. 2020. Formelhaftes Schreiben im Spannungsfeld zwischen Urkunden und formulae des Ostfränkischen Reiches. PhD-Thesis, University of Hamburg, Monograph forthcoming in 2023.

———. 2021a. Sakralität und Handel. Eine kulturelle Semantik des Marktbegriffs in Spätantike und Frühmittelalter. In *Der Wert des Heiligen. Spirituelle, materielle und ökonomische Verflechtungen*, ed. Andreas Bihrer, Miriam Czock, and Uta Kleine, 105–34. Stuttgart: Franz Steiner Verlag.

———. 2021b. Towards a Different Type of Market Exchange in the Early Middle Ages: The Sacrum Commercium and Its Agents. In *Markets and their Actors in the Late Middle Ages*, ed. Tanja Skambraks, Julia Bruch, and Ulla Kypta, 27–70. Berlin and Boston: De Gruyter.

Rädlinger-Prömper, Christine. 1987. *Sankt Emmeram in Regensburg. Struktur- und Funktionswandel eines bayerischen Klosters im früheren Mittelalter.* Kallmünz: Lassleben.

Rogan, Tim. 2018. *The Moral Economists: R. H. Tawney, Karl Polanyi, E.P. Thompson, and the Critique of Capitalism.* Princeton, NJ: Princeton University Press.

Rosenwein, Barbara H. 1989. *To Be the Neighbour of Saint Peter. The Social Meaning of Cluny's Property.* Ithaca: Cornell University Press.

Salzmann, Ariel. 2010. Is There a Moral Economy of State formation? Religious Minorities and Repertoires of Regime Integration in the Middle East and Western Europe, 600–1614. *Theory and Society* 39: 49–68.

Sayer, Andrew. 2006. Approaching Moral Economy. In *The Moralization of Markets*, ed. Nico Stehr, Christoph Henning, and Bernd Weiler, 77–97. London: Transaction Publishers.

Signori, Gabriela. 2003. "Family Traditions". Moral Economy and Memorial "Gift Exchange" in the Urban World of the Late Fifteenth Century. In *Negotiating the Gift. Pre-modern Figurations of Exchange*, ed. Gadi Algazi, Valentin Groebner, and Bernhard Jussen, 285–318. Göttingen: Vandenhoeck & Ruprecht.

Silber, Ilana G. 1995. Gift-Giving in the Great Traditions. The Case of Donations to Monasteries in the Medieval West. *European Journal of Sociology* 36: 209–43.

Simmel, Georg. 1900. *Philosophie des Geldes*. Munich: Duncker & Humblot.

Skambraks, Tanja. 2017. Expertise im Dienste der Caritas. Die Monti di Pietà zwischen gelehrtem Wissen und Erfahrungswissen. In *Wissen und Wirtschaft. Expertenkulturen und Märkte vom 13. bis 18. Jahrhundert*, ed. Marian Füssel, Philip Knäble, and Nina Elsemann, 169–90. Göttingen and Bristol: Vandenhoeck & Ruprecht.

———. 2018. Zwischen Kooperation und Konkurrenz. Jüdische Pfandleihe und Monti di Pietà in Italien. In *Ökonomische Glaubensfragen: Strukturen und Praktiken jüdischen und christlichen Kleinkredits im Spätmittelalter*, ed. Gerhard Fouquet and Sven Rabeler, 99–119. Stuttgart: Franz Steiner Verlag.

Sombart, Werner. 1902. *Der moderne Kapitalismus. Historisch-systematische Darstellung des gesamteuropäischen Wirtschaftslebens von seinen Anfängen bis zur Gegenwart*, 3 vols. Leipzig: Duncker & Humblot.

Staab, Franz. 1999. La circulation des biens à l'intérieur de la famille dans la région du Rhin moyen. *Mélanges de l'Ecole française de Rome* 111: 911–31.

Störmer, Wilhelm. 1973. *Früher Adel. Studien zur politischen Führungsschicht im fränkisch-deutschen Reich vom 8. bis 11. Jahrhundert*. Stuttgart: Hiersemann.

———. 1989. Frühmittelalterliche Grundherrschaft bayerischer Kirchen (8.-10. Jahrhundert. In *Strukturen der Grundherrschaft im frühen Mittelalter*, ed. Werner Rösener, 370–410. Göttingen: Vandenhoeck & Ruprecht.

———. 1994. Besitz- und Herrschaftsgefüge im Passauer Raum des 8./9. Jahrhunderts. Herzog, König, Adel und Kirche. In *Das Christentum im bairischen Raum. Von den Anfängen bis ins 11. Jahrhundert*, ed. Egon Boshof and Hartmut Wolf, 391–424. Cologne, Weimar and Vienna: Böhlau.

Thompson, Edward Palmer. 1963. *The Making of the English Working Class*. London: Gollancz.

———. 1971. The Moral Economy of the English Crowd in the Eighteenth Century. *Past & Present* 50: 76–136.

———. 1991. *Customs in Common*. London: Penguin Books.

Tiefenbach, Heinrich 1990. Die Namen des Breviarium Urolfi: Mit einer Textedition. In *Ortsname und Urkunde. Frühmittelalterliche Ortsnamenüberlieferung. Münchener Symposion, 10. bis 12. Oktober 1988*. Ed. Rudolf Schützeichel, 60–69. Heidelberg: Winter.

Todeschini, Giacomo. 1994. *Il prezzo della salvezza. Lessici medievali del pensiero economico*. Rome: Nuova Italia Scientifica.

von Schmoller, Gustav. 1893. *Die Volkswirtschaft, die Volkswirtschaftslehre und ihre Methode*. Frankfurt am Main: Vittorio Klostermann.

Weber, Max. 1920. *Die protestantische Ethik und der Geist des Kapitalismus. Die protestantischen Sekten und der Geist des Kapitalismus sowie Die Wirtschaftsethik der Weltreligionen – Konfuzianismus und Taoismus*. Tübingen: Mohr.

Wood, Ian. 2018. *The transformation of the Roman West*. Leeds: ARC Humanities Press.

———. 2019. The Early Medieval West as a Temple Society. *Rivista storica dell'antichità* 49: 117–46.

Wrightson, Keith. 2000. *Earthly Necessities. Economic Lives in Early modern Britain*. New Haven, CT: Yale University Press.

CHAPTER 4

Between *Pietas* and Usury: Dynamics of a Moral Economy in the Middle Ages

Tanja Skambraks

Introduction

In the Middle Ages, religion and the Catholic Church—as an institution based on as well as creating moral values—exerted a strong influence on economic thought and economic practices. Especially the commercial revolution between the eleventh and the fourteenth century fostered the development of new economic practices and instruments, such as new trade contracts or forms of credit. Technical innovation and favourable climate resulted in population growth and raised economic productivity in the high Middle Ages. The commercial revolution describes the subsequent process of economic expansion, effecting the scale of local and foreign trade, urbanisation, banking and finance as well as legal institutions. This transformation of the medieval agrarian society into a monetarised consumer society is also regarded as the beginning of proto-capitalism (Lopez 1976).

T. Skambraks (✉)
Karl-Franzens-Universität, Graz, Austria
e-mail: tanja.skambraks@uni-graz.at

T. Skambraks and M. Lutz (eds.), *Reassessing the Moral Economy*, Palgrave Studies in Economic History,
https://doi.org/10.1007/978-3-031-29834-9_4

The abovementioned intensified use of money and credit fueled debates on legitimate profits, interest and usury especially from the thirteenth century on. Using scholastic treatises, preachers and confessors worked hard to integrate the economic effects of the newly developed consumer society in late medieval cities and the question of the personal conscience of merchants, moneylenders and pawnbrokers (Gilomen 1990, 2010; Todeschini 2002, 2009; Skambraks 2023).

The foundation of Christian pawnbroking houses (Monti di Pietà) implementing new forms of credit and investment in Italian cities in the fifteenth century was one such crucial catalyst of this discourse in the later Middle Ages. This institution tried to unite the spheres of credit and charity, thus pointing to a medieval moral economy where the Church, represented by the Order of St. Francis, took over a leading role in the foundation and propagation of a credit and banking institute that also took interest from its clients. The small loans provided by the Monti worked quite similar as today's micro-loans, such as the Grameen Bank of Nobel Prize winner Muhammad Yunus (Yunus 2007). The source material connected to the Monti di Pietà offers an exceptional opportunity to examine the levels of mutual influence between economic practice, canon law and Christian economic ethics at the end of the Middle Ages (Skambraks 2023).

Dealing with premodern credit and banking, I regard the concept of moral economy (Thompson 1963, 1971) as a most useful heuristic tool for the analysis of religious values shaping the connected practices and economic ethics. Although there has been a number of influential articles and books reflecting on the usefulness and adaptability of Thompson's concept to other spheres of historical research (Fontaine 2008; Frevert 2019; Rogan 2017), one central desideratum remains the aforementioned operationalisation of this concept for premodern times.

The aim of this chapter is thus twofold: Broadly, it will focus on the relationship between religion and economy[1] in the Middle Ages, which can be described as a moral economy. More concretely, it will suggest three terms for operationalising the dynamics between both intertwined

[1] I understand economy here as a complex of human actions and social structures that was directed towards securing the material basis of life. Economy encompasses the expenses and returns of both subsistence-securing and profit-oriented activities. This includes the large areas of production, marketing and financing, but also the discourse on economic practices.

spheres: (1) embeddedness, (2) innovations and (3) feedback. These concepts are employed as tools for the description and analysis along three concrete thematic fields: medieval canon law, economic ethics and, of course, economic practices and institutions. The case studies presented here focus on the medieval theory of credit and interest (reflected in the canon law and sermons, treatises and regulations) as well as on the propagation and realisation of innovative economic thoughts linked to Christian pawnbroking houses in late medieval Italy.

Based on latest research results on business ethics and credit in the Middle Ages, this chapter aims at demonstrating the connectivity of this topic for an epoch-spanning and interdisciplinary research perspective that can enrich the study of dynamics between religion and economic practices.

Among the main themes of medieval economic thought were the topics of profit and wealth as well as solutions to the omnipresent problem of resource distribution in a world of economic precarity. These topics were continuously evaluated and negotiated in the Middle Ages against the backdrop of a Christian worldview. The media of this discourse were mostly tracts, sermons and reports by theologians and legal scholars. The ideals of Christian charity (*caritas*), mercy and piety (*pietas*) played just as important a role in the formulation of economic ethics as the omnipresent problem of mortal sins, such as greed (*avaritia*), gluttony (*gula*) and luxury (*luxuria*). Another central thematic area in which the basic values of economic action were negotiated was the discourse on usury and interest, which dealt with the unlawful or lawful profit from lending. Linked to the research on medieval canon law and economic ethics even in current scholarly literature is the grand narrative of the general hostility of the medieval church towards economy and the all-encompassing question of the emergence of capitalism. This discussion is depicted in works by various social and economic historians like Werner Sombart (Sombart 1902), John Noonan, John Munroe (Noonan 1957; Munroe 2002) and Hans-Jörg Gilomen (Gilomen 1990, 2010) and Giacomo Todeschini (2002, 2009, 2016). On the one hand, Sombart in his "History of Capitalism" proclaimed the seemingly overall mightiness of Christian religion as a hindering force to economic development. In the footsteps of Sombart, authors like Raymond de Roover interpreted the role of the church as a restrictive one; as circumvention strategies such as hidden interest and too high costs of credit would have inhibited the economy (de Roover 1958). Notably, both perspectives are based on a growth-oriented model of progress, not on a subsistence model that is perhaps more prevalent in the Middle Ages.

On the other hand, Munroe and lately Gilomen have emphasised the productive role of religious restrictions as driving force for economic development, for instance concerning the use of money, credit and rents as part of the financial revolution. Gilomen also made clear that despite the Church's ban on usury, there was a high number of 'circumvention strategies' including the widespread use of interest and usury in disguise. Similarly, Laurence Fontaine states in her book Économie Morale that 'ecclesiastical and lay prohibitions resulted in increasingly sophisticated drafting of loan contracts in order to preclude the possibility of prosecution' (Fontaine 2008, 191). John Noonan employed the same interpretative path decades earlier in 1957, pointing out that economic innovation in the Middle Ages was achieved through prohibitions and circumvention strategies (Noonan 1957). These were a productive force because they led to the emergence of financial investments (shared investments with high returns and freeing up capital on the market), which in turn contributed to economic growth. The development of innovations regarding loan and business contracts is closely linked to the so-called commercial revolution. It brought about various new ways of credit and money use, which, although obviously contrary to the canon law—were widely accepted practices and eventually led to the questioning and transformation of the legal and moral system. Recent research, such as Todeschini's as well as my own (Skambraks 2017, 2023) shows that the Christian theologians' confrontation with the manifestations of an expanding economic system by no means led to a pure rejection of profit, interest and prosperity. On the contrary, it rather incited a process of integration and adaptation of theory to economic reality.

In this chapter I will first propose a conceptual framework regarding the general relationship between religion and economy, then briefly discuss the problem of usury and interest taking in the Middle Ages and thirdly, apply the conceptual framework to the emergence of a Christian small-scale credit institution.

Operationalising Moral Economy

Moral economy can be used as an essential heuristic concept for the analysis of the relationship between premodern economy and religion, but has hitherto not been conceptualised for the premodern epoch. In his definition of the term Thompson emphasised the role of the traditional moral concepts of the English working-class during the Food Riots of the eighteenth century, regarding for instance the just price and fair wages. In contrast to the rational choice approach, which focuses on the motive of profit, moral economy thus implies a set of basic assumptions about how economic behaviour is guided by certain values and beliefs, consequently linking the fields of economics, perception and behaviour. The New Cultural History—represented, for example, by Laurence Fontaine and Ute Frevert—has recently tackled the topic of moral economy from an early modern and contemporary historical perspective, leaving the Middle Ages largely unconsidered. This gap in the moral economy of the medieval period is another starting point for this paper, which aims at examining the role and change of attitudes, values and maxims of action for economic action in the Middle Ages.

As mentioned above, one crucial question is how the concept of moral economy can be operationalised. I would like to propose the following model showing three fields of investigation: economic practice, economic ethics and canon law. My hypothesis is that there was an interaction, i.e. an ongoing dynamic, between these three areas. I characterise this dynamic with the terms: embeddedness, innovation and feedback (Fig. 4.1).

The term embeddedness, used by representatives of economic sociology, such as Karl Polanyi (Polanyi 1968) and Mark Granovetter (Granovetter 1985, 2017), refers to the close interconnection of religious values, economic ethics and economic activity. Following Polanyi, embeddedness is considered an indicator for the influence and control of economic activities by "non-economic" institutions, such as religion. The emergence of charitable urban institutions, medieval poor-relief and Christian microcredit are fields of premodern social and economic history that show interesting evidence for the embeddedness thesis. This will be illustrated by two case studies dealing with charitably motivated small loans, pointing out the integration of money-handling and Christian ethics or Christian rituals. The second level of the dynamics of the moral economy are innovations in economic ethics. Regarding the topics of usury and interest, scholastic literature from the thirteenth century provides us with a series of conceptual innovations, emerging in the course of new trade practices, i.e. the aforementioned commercial revolution from the eleventh to the fourteenth century (Lopez 1976).

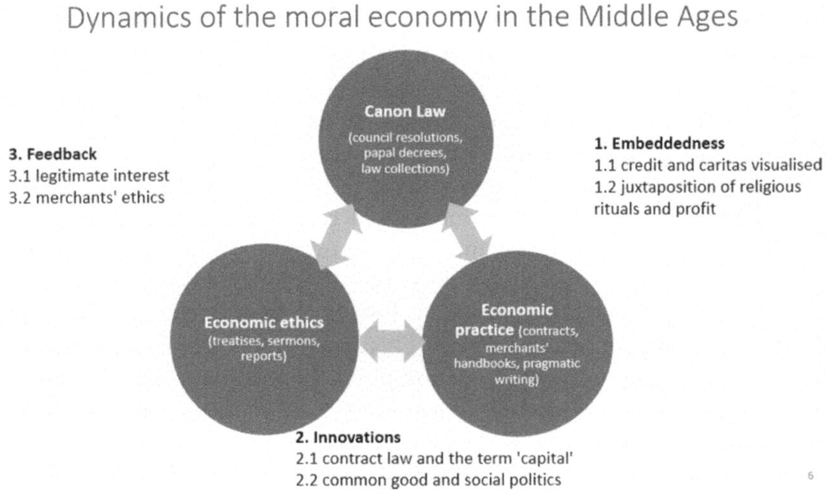

Fig. 4.1 Dynamics of the moral economy in the Middle Ages

This transformation not only shaped the discourse on right economic activity, but also had concrete socio-political and institutional consequences. New ideas included, for example, the definition of *capital* or new socio-political concepts for fighting poverty in the fifteenth century, which will be pointed out in this chapter later on. Thirdly, as the model shows, I will examine the feedback processes between economic practice and religious theory. Using the example of small loans provided by Christian welfare institutions, which helped to legitimise certain forms of interest, it is possible to show the feedback of economic practice on economic ethics and the associated religious norms.

Connected to the existence and use of credit were the key problems of usury and interest. Throughout the high and late Middle Ages, scholastics like Thomas Aquinus, Johannes Duns Scotus, Petrus Iohannis Olivi or Antonin of Florence intensively discussed these problems which were important topics of the canon law, most importantly the Decretum Gratiani and the decrees of Church councils. The discussion on usury and interest both limited and expanded the scope of action of medieval merchants, money lenders and bankers. According to traditional canon law the profit made through the lending of money or fruit-bearing goods was strictly forbidden and regarded as unfair until the high Middle Ages.

This attitude was based on three reasons: firstly, money was considered a sterile medium of exchange in the Aristotelian interpretation. Secondly, the usurer lent something that belonged to God only, namely time. Thirdly, the very *intention of profit*, thus usury, was regarded as a variety of *avaritia* and thus a mortal sin.

Looking at the guidelines in the Old and New Testament (for instance Lev. 25,36; Luke 6,35), council resolutions (e.g. Nicäa 325, 4th Lateran Council 1215, Council of Vienne 1311) and the most important canonical collection of law, the Decretum Gratiani, the comprehensive rejection of any enrichment through interest becomes absolutely clear: "Everything that surpasses the basic loan sum is regarded as usury" (*Quiquid ultra sortem exigitur usura est*). In this strict sense, every claimed sum above the original loan was considered usurious. The core of this argumentation against usury was the protection of the soul of the faithful on the one hand and the violation of the principle of Christian *caritas* on the other hand. Biblical tradition and canon law considered both violations as the basis of enrichment at the expense of others as well as the exploitation of a person's weakness.

Despite these clearly formulated rules, there was a considerable gap between the codes of canon law and economic reality, especially since the eleventh century. There are various examples illustrating this discrepancy. The granting of loans and credits, for instance, was a common practice in the Middle Ages, fostering numerous circumvention strategies. The hiding of interest took place when interest was included in the loan sum or the masking of a loan contract as contract of sale. One result was the emergence of acceptable forms of interest, for instance in case of deferred payments (*damnum emergens*). Furthermore, new forms of contracts connected to maritime trade credit emerged, putting the problem of risk (*periculum sortis*) and profit-loss (*lucrum cessans*) onto the scholastics' agenda.

The Emergence of Christian Small-Scale Credit

Among these developments, the history of Christian small-scale credit institutions stands out as an impressive example of ethical innovation linking credit to *caritas*. The foundation of institutions, such as the Monti di Pietà set in motion another wave of innovation regarding the regulation and definition of interest and the handling of money. The so-called *Mountains of Piety* were urban pawnbroking institutions, founded in Italy in the second half of the fifteenth century. Their story was highly successful. Over 200 such Monti were founded between 1462 and 1550. They granted small loans against a pledge for a short term between three and twelve months. Their clientele consisted of people who possessed enough objects they could use as pledges, thus, members of the so-called working poor, craftsmen, day labourers, widows and sometimes also other charitable institutions. The loans were provided at a low interest rate (of between 4 and 10%), a fact that caused a long and controversial debate between the Monti's supporters and their critics (Skambraks 2017).

The successive legal development in favour of certain forms of interest since the thirteenth century was thus linked to the emergence of new contract forms regarding trade as well as new credit instruments. The underlying process of change and interaction between law, theology and economics is still an unexplored part of medieval research. However, this complex interrelation is a formidable starting point for the analysis of the moral economy focusing on the connection between religion and economy.

Embeddedness of Piety and Economy

Programmatic Images

After this short introduction into some basic problems of medieval economic ethics, let us now look at the three aforementioned levels of operationalisation. There is a very rich source tradition of the above-mentioned Monti di Pietà consisting of legal treatises, sermons, pictures, statutes and a plethora of different types of account books. The close interweaving/embedding of economy and religion becomes particularly clear in the visual programme accompanying the establishment of the pawnshops. This programme was consciously established and used by the Franciscans (Helas 2004; Puglisi and Barcham 2008). The images in question appeared not only on the walls of the buildings housing the pawnshops, but also in printed form in theological and juridical treatises since the late fifteenth century. Thus, the pictures (per)formed a kind of visual synthesis of the ideas conveyed in these often very extensive tracts (Fig. 4.2).

The engraving by Francesco Roselli from 1485, for example, attached to a treatise in favour of the Monti provides an intriguing example. The

Fig. 4.2 Marco da Montegallo: Tabula della Salute, 1486, Copperplate Engraving c. 1485 (Firenze, Uffizi)

text containing the picture is the *Tabula della Salute* written by the Franciscan Marco da Montegallo in the year 1486 (Marco del Monte S. Maria printed in 1494). In the picture's foreground on the left, we see the preacher Montegallo on the pulpit in front of an audience consisting of children, women and some men. On the left, behind the preaching scene, the view opens into a hospital, leading the viewers to glance at sick people in beds. Opposite on the right side of the picture is an important main motive of the Monti iconography: Jesus as the Man of Sorrows, the *imago pietatis* (an emblem of suffering which should induce compassion), in front of which believers have gathered in prayer. Further back we see a depiction of the biblical motive of the five works of mercy (based on Matthew 25,34–46: clothing the naked, feeding and watering the hungry and thirsty, visiting the imprisoned and sick and sheltering the homeless). In the image's centre we see a mountain of coins, literally depicting the Monte. It is surrounded by a number of people from different social backgrounds of the city, among them a rich, well-dressed man giving alms to an old beggar as well as two poor people (a woman with a baby and another vagabond or pilgrim). Needy people are taking some pieces from the pile of coins, while some richer people are adding money to it. The picture thus conveys the idealistic impression of a consistent sequence of charitable deeds provided by a well-functioning network of city institutions, taking care of those in need. The mountain formed of money in the picture's centre also occupied a central place in the Franciscans' socio-political programme. Here, the Christian virtue of *pietas* merged with the concrete image of capital forming a particular synthesis of three motives: poor-relief, money and Franciscan preaching. The Franciscan observants deliberately made use of such an elaborate complex of motives to represent and promote their own activities connected to the significance of the Monti di Pietà for salvation, based on the biblical tradition.

Ritual and Performance

A second impressive example of the discursive and performative embeddedness of capital and piety is offered by the statutes of the Monte di Pietà of Verona, written by the Franciscan friar Michele d'Acqui in 1490 (Delcorno 2015). The Monte of Verona was—like other Monti—organised as a brotherhood raising part of its basic capital from its members' annual payments and donations, for which they obtained indulgences as a form of spiritual capital.

The statutes describe in detail how donations were collected during the annual procession on 29 August. Singing children led the procession, followed by Franciscans carrying five statues of martyrs. Next came the members of the Monte's board and the brotherhood, as well as the city's people. A sculpture of the Monte symbolising the heavenly hierarchy with an allegory of the Trinity was carried around. The purpose of the procession accompanied by singing, ornaments and the statutes of the martyrs was to attract people, to involve them in the procession as spectators and to encourage them to make donations to the Monte. In addition to describing the procession itself, the author Michele d' Acqui mentions the sum that should be raised: 2000 ducats from 40,000 donors. The text suggests that the religious and ceremonial form was purposefully used to achieve a monetary goal. The donors thus supported urban welfare and contributed to the salvation of their souls. The following quotation shown in the illustration invalidates the accusation of usury by emphasising the charitable character of the pietas of the Monte:

> Thus it is advised and resolved that this Holy Mount of Mercy be established in honour of our Lord Jesus Christ, and that it may and shall support the poor Christians out of the money of the Most Pious Mount of Holy Mercy without usury. (Delcorno 2015, 151, translation of the author)

Hence, the brotherhood under Franciscan guidance used religious rituals and familiar institutional forms to gain the attention and support of the city community for a socio-political goal, namely microcredit. The leitmotivs *caritas* and *pietas,* staged through image and performance, were quite naturally linked with the representation of money, specifically the capital of the credit institution.

Innovations

Petrus Iohannis Olivi's Treatise De Contractibus

As already mentioned, new economic developments, like private loans and risky maritime trade led to the extensive discussion of legitimate profits from credit transactions as early as the thirteenth century. The Franciscan observant friar Petrus Iohannis Olivi developed decisive new ideas in his work on the theory of commercial contracts *De contractibus* from 1294/95. Olivi is perhaps the most influential thinker on economic theory in the Middle Ages (Todeschini 1977; Wolf 1994; Piron 2020). His ideas were taken up and further disseminated by numerous Franciscan preachers (such as Bernardino da Siena). Perhaps Olivi's most important innovation concerns the concept of capital. He formulated in terms of the profit from a maritime trade contract:

> That which, according to the firm determination of the owner, is destined to a probable profit, has not only the force of mere money or of a mere commodity, but, in addition, a certain potentiality (or essence) of profit, which we commonly call capital. Therefore, not only should the actual value be returned, but also a surplus value. (Olivi, ed. Franco 2021, No. 63, 232)

Contrary to the thesis of the sterility of money, as claimed by Aristotle and Thomas Aquinas, money thus carries a productive value that is created by feeding it into the economic cycle. The productive value of money thus arises from the dynamic transfer of human activity to an infertile medium. The transfer of the right to use this potential beyond its actual value legitimises a compensation in the form of interest. Olivi broadened the meaning of the term money adding the dimension of capital and thus removing profit from its classical definition as a labour wage. At the same time he reinterpreted it as the inherent productive force of a good, as a productive force (*ratio seminalis*) inherent in money like the "merchant's tool of the trade" (Wolf 1994, 418). This tool can and should be used productively by the merchant, i.e. for the common good. The conclusion of contracts is one form of such productive usage.

From the potential of money, the *ratio seminalis,* Olivi derived certain legitimate forms of interest in the same treatise, such as compensation for risk (*periculum sortis*) and for lost profit (*lucrum cessans*). Both exceptions signify important innovations concerning the flexibilisation of the concept of usury.

The legitimate profit discussed by Olivi was based on another crucial aspect of medieval economic debate, namely the just price, which he also analysed in detail in his treatise. Based on the basic principle of the common good, a fair price, according to Olivi, should always be aimed for and should be based on justice or balance between buyer and seller. Neither of them—according to the law of charity—should be taken advantage of. Seven *quaestiones* connect the topic of price formation with the sales practice of negotiating and bargaining. They deal with the sale of goods that are too expensive or too cheap (1), the relationship between the price and the use value of a good (2), the question of whether a price increase can be derived from need/increased demand (3), whether defects in the traded good must be disclosed (4) and whether the buyer is entitled to compensation for excessively high prices (5). The sixth *quaestio* examines whether the resale of a thing at a higher price is a mortal sin (6) and finally Olivi discusses the question of the legitimacy of manipulating a commercial good, for example through additions (7).

Here I will only deal with the first *quaestio* on price formation, which contains essential aspects of the roles of buyer and seller and thus allows us to better understand the basics of the relations between the contracting parties. Olivi first affirms the question of whether goods may be sold above or below their actual value in case of doubt. After all, almost everyone wanted to sell expensively and buy cheaply. Moreover, the act of buying is voluntary, i.e. free will moves the seller to set the price and the buyer to acquire a good. The principle equality of both partners is emphasised here. "A thing is worth as much as it can be sold for", he concludes (Olivi, ed. Franco 2021, 3). The agreed price is the result of a consensus between both parties. In the following scholastic counter-arguments, Olivi first emphasises the aspect of charity and justice of the exchange and thus refers to the social and ethical dimension of the act of purchase. It is against divine law to deliberately harm someone through overpricing (Olivi, ed. Franco 2021, 5).

In the following distinctions, he names the three objective factors in price formation. First, there is the usefulness (*utilitas*) of a thing (a strong and healthy horse is worth more than an old horse), secondly its rarity (*raritas*), thirdly the pleasure (*beneplacitum*) that people find in a thing (e.g. a piece of jewellery). Finally, in the *responsio*, Olivi speaks out in principle against an overpriced sale, whereby—interestingly—the intention of the agents serves as a measure of the judgement of the actions. Olivi writes:

> However, in the transgression of these limits there need not always be a mortal sin, unless this is so great and so monstrous that already in the contract itself inequality and injustice prevail over equality and justice. Therefore, it is ensured in the civil law that if the buyer or the seller is defrauded of more than half of the just price, that contract is void and must be declared void by the judges. (Olivi, ed. Franco 2021, 11)

Notably, the guarantor of contractual righteousness here is civil legislation, not canon law. This seems only logical, since the growing importance of towns as economic centres led to the development of communal institutions like the city council or city courts providing jurisdiction and governmental rules based on the reality and needs of the city community. Consequently, secular courts—according to Olivi—were the ones who supervise the observance of the law. The rule of law and justice is decisive for the act and contract of selling (Olivi, ed. Franco, 2021, 13), therefore it is not permissible to set a more unjust price. In addition to the principle of equality, reason (*ratio*) is regarded as the guiding principle of the trader in setting prices. In barter transactions, the equality of value results from the consideration of the use and utility of a commodity. Since these two quantities can in turn vary, Olivi allows for a certain flexibility of prices at this point. These few examples from Olivi's fascinating work show the potential for innovation of the discourse on economic ethics as a reflection of the expanding economy at the end of the thirteenth century. Olivi's work laid the foundation for long-lasting process of development of central economic terms such as profit, capital and pricing. These newly defined terms were received and implemented in treatises and sermons by later authorities on economic ethics like Bernardino da Siena, one of the most famous late medieval preachers on economic topics.

The Monte as Depositum Apostolicum in Annio da Viterbo's Questiones

A second example of innovative thinking about economic ethics, which has hitherto been completely unknown in the scholarly literature, concerns the solution of the problem of poverty and stems from the Dominican author Annio da Viterbo. As mentioned before, the Franciscans founded the Monti di Pietà in the middle of the fifteenth century with the aim of granting small loans to those in need. The Monte's interest rate of 4 to 10% became the cause of a far-reaching dispute between Franciscan and Dominican legal scholars as well as Augustinian eremites in the 1480s and 1490s, producing numerous expert reports and treatises marking another important step in the development of the concepts of usury and interest. However, only few of the non-Franciscan authors argued in favour of the Monti's aims and business, and very few even developed new ideas regarding their ethical foundations.

One such treatise was written by one of the most innovative thinkers on the subject, the Dominican Annio da Viterbo. In his *Quaestiones due disputate super mutuo iudaico et civili et divino* published in 1492, he draws the picture of an apostolic community of the poor who—empowered by the Monti's loans—not only could achieve a dignified livelihood in a cycle of self-help, but could also improve the whole society. In contrast to the Franciscan treatises, which argued primarily on the basis of contract law, Annio shows himself as an independent thinker in a different, one could say much more socio-politically arguing tradition. He describes the Monte as one part of a social contract and thus as a building block of a cities' socio-political scheme.

> This, therefore, is the aim of civil society. The provision obliges bishops, rectors and magistrates to provide beggars with at least a permanent hospitality allowance and poor citizens with an always available permanent loan: as is precisely the case in this Apostolic Deposit. (Annio da Viterbo, Quaestiones 1492, cit. in: Amadori 2007, 258)

From Aristotle's Politics and the 15th chapter of Deuteronomy, he derives the duty of care of politicians for the welfare of their citizens. The commandment obliges bishops, rectors and city magistrates to provide at least a permanent lodging allowance for beggars and a perpetual loan for poor citizens to meet their needs, as is the case in this apostolic deposit.

On the one hand, poor-relief activities should take the form of the statutes of the city fathers, ensuring welfare and the *bonum commune*. On the other hand, the debtors ultimately made a profit for themselves through the interest paid. Hence, the poor themselves *and* the Monte become benefactors, linking the profit to the desirable growth of the charitable institution. Notably, profit for the sake of the *bonum commune* had a positive connotation. The Monti's general non-profit character (all profits should be redistributed among the poor) is also Annio's main argument against the accusation of usury claimed by critics. In this system, the poor formed a legal community supporting each other through loans on the basis of several legitimate contracts. (Annio da Viterbo, Quaestiones 1492, cit. in: Amadori 2007, p. 262).

These contracts were formed on various levels and with various social goals, depicted in this overview (Table 4.1).

Through this charitable institution, not only poverty is fought, but the entire community is improved. The communal *depositum* of the poor also transformed them into better people. This would create an urban society modelled on the apostolic community who shared everything:

> The deposit of the community of the poor, called apostolic, also ensures that the city is well managed. In fact, life in a city where all things are common and no one is destitute, with no one pursuing his own interests, resembles that of the city of the apostles. In this way, natural law is upheld and civil society is optimally organised. (Annio da Viterbo, cit. in: Amadori 2007, 266)

Table 4.1 Types of contracts established by the Monte di Pietà's small-scale credits according to Annio da Viterbo

Type of contract	*Goal of the contract*	*Contract partners*
1. Contract of help	Care of the very poor	Monte an donors from the city
2. Loan contract	Care for the working poor	Monte and citizens, donating money to it
3. Contract about work/ services	Wages	Working Poor and officers of the monte
4. Loan contract (small-scale credit)	Welfare	Working poor and rich people
5. Contract about the divine mandate	Welfare and provision, enhancement of the common good	Monte and city government
6. Contract of positive growth	Growth of capital	Working Poor and the Monte

Annio da Viterbo sketches a highly interesting utopia of a moral economy based on common property; an idea that has not been associated with the Monti in this clarity before, and which is still reviving today in various political and economic alternatives to capitalism. The ethical basis of this welfare is Christian *caritas* and *pietas*. However, this only regards a certain group: namely Christians.

The innovations of the discourse on economic ethics circling around interest and usury were entirely directed towards the Christian community. Their flipside was the antisemintic marginalisation of Jewish moneylenders, which repeatedly stands out in the expert's reports and treatises—Annio da Viterbo's *Quaestiones* are no exception here. In spite of this discrimination, the foundation of the Monti di Pietà did in many cases not lead to the abolishment of Jewish moneylending. Many Jewish moneylenders often moved to the outskirts of towns and continued their business. In many cases, the basic capital for the institutions' installation often came from "credits" provided by the Jewish community. Furthermore, city authorities, like in Siena, asked the pope for the reinstallation of Jewish moneylenders, because the Monti were not able to provide enough credit for its inhabitants. In Rome, the pope granted exceptional rights to Jewish banking houses long after the foundation of the Monti. This dimension points to the exclusion and inclusion mechanisms of the medieval moral economy against the background of religious and social diversity. The issue of inclusion and exclusion of other religions as one element of the discourse on business ethics and economic practices offers another intriguing aspect of this field of research, which has been dealt with elsewhere (Skambraks 2023; Pullan 2001; Todeschini 2008, 2004, 2016; Toaff 2004).

Feedback Effects

In the third part of this chapter, I will look at feedback effects between business practice, business ethics and canon law. As already indicated previously when dealing with Petrus Iohannis Olivi's treatise on contract law, there remains the crucial question of the extent to which innovations in business ethics affected contemporary norms, urban laws and, of course, canon law. There is proof from different thematic areas for an influence or feedback effect between those spheres. In the following, I will present two examples.

The first case regards the starting point of this paper, the prohibition of usury by canon law. The foundation of the Monti di Pietà led to a heated debate about the taking of interest and finally resulted in the decision of the 5th Lateran Council in 1515, stipulating the legitimate payment of interest, to be used for the maintenance of the Christian institution of the Monti. This form of interest was defined as *stipendium laboris*, as an allowance for expenses by the pawnshop's employees. Pope Leo X. formulated in his decree *Inter multiplices* of 1515:

> For the indemnity of the montes, i.e. for the expenses of their servants and all other things extending to the necessary maintenance, it shall be lawful, if the pawnshops make no profit, to demand and receive a moderate and necessary sum over and above the capital lent, from those who are to be paid out of such a loan (...) Such a loan business deserves praise and approval, and shall in no way be held to be usury (...). (Wohlmuth 2000, 625)

This decision was an important step towards making the law on interest and usury more flexible on the basis of a religious justification, based on *caritas* and *pietas* as moral values.

Usury was not only a problem of the credit economy, trade also was presumably endangered by it. The dangerous character of trade and commerce was discussed in detail in various sermons, most famously by

Bernardino da Siena. Traces of the aforementioned feedback effects of those sermons (as a form of popular didactics) can be found in handbooks written by late medieval merchants. In addition to information on measurements, exchange rates and commodity prices, these books often contain moral advice on how a good merchant should behave. These entries show that even merchants who were repeatedly accused of being driven by search for profit only were guided by moral values such as diligence, care and moderation, which illustrate the influence of Christian business ethics.

One example comes from the famous *Pratica della Mercatura* by Francesco Pegolotti. The Prologue of the book contains a poem praising the virtues of the good merchant:

> He must always act with integrity, farsightedness will be useful to him. He should always keep his promises. If possible, his appearance should be plain and his behaviour amiable and in harmony with reason: let him be careful in buying and generous in selling. Let him avoid quarrels and keep a friendly disposition. He should attend church and give out of love for God. He should increase his reputation and not haggle, avoid usury and gambling and renounce them altogether. Finally, he should manage his accounts sensibly and commit no mistakes. Amen (Pegolotti, ed. Evans, 1936, xxiv)

Clearly, the inclusion of such a text into a handbook for merchants written by a merchant emphasises not only a literary convention, but the need and wish for moral orientation. Values like honesty, efficiency and reason are mentioned as are the love for God as a source of motivation for charitable acts.

Looking at a different example from the famous German Fugger company from the year 1520, we see a very similar approach. In his treatise on bookkeeping, the Fuggers' chief accountant, Matthäus Schwarz, repeatedly inserted ethical notes, as we see in this example on dealing with creditors.

> Now many a merchant thinks he is rich if he has a large capital and does not pay attention to his creditors whom he has to pay off, whether he expects more or less from his debtors. Such people lose in a dissolute manner and go bankrupt and do not know how, when or where it happened to them. Recklessness, when it takes possession of a merchant, brings arrogance with ambition and profiteering; sells his goods at a loss, and brings in

> his debts that he may buy dominions; forgets his creditors. [...] Then one goes bankrupt, compares himself with his creditors, gives them barely a third. He has stolen the rest from them. But if you want to succeed, look to your own affairs with reason. (Matthäus Schwarz, Musterbuchhaltung, Weitnauer 1931, 270)

In the texts of Pegolotti and Schwartz, the role of the merchants is not portrayed exclusively positive. They might be driven by wrong motives on an individual level, but in society they are considered productive and dignified because they feed money into the economic cycle and are thus useful to the *bonum commune*. If they are ready to behave according to a moral code, avoid gambling and do not strive for excessive gain, their performance becomes compatible with the moral economy. This finding reflects the prevailing perception of the late Middle Ages that it was the individual who erred, as trade became more and more accepted.

Conclusion

Piety and usury, Christian religion and economic activity were inextricably linked in the Middle Ages, they influenced each other and contributed to the development of economic ethical innovations. In the Middle Ages, the Christian religion provided the impetus for economic ethics and was in turn subject to influences from economic practice, which contributed to the dynamisation of these basic values. The embeddedness and entanglement of religious values and economic practices and ideas became obvious in the visual and ritual programme of the Monti di Pietà, clearly depicting the handling of money with charitable works for the *bonum commune*. This chapter highlighted innovations and feedback effects using the example of the discourse on interest and usury. The commercial revolution induced a number of innovations visible in the changing discourse on the terms like capital or profit. These new ideas evolved in the thirteenth century with Petrus Iohannis Olivi's works and were finally integrated in the canon law two hundred years later at the 5th Lateran Council in 1515. The third level of the dynamics of religion and economy, namely feedbacks, proved a useful operator for the analysis. Not only were new ideas on economic ethics integrated into canon law, but they are also visible in the handbooks and guidebooks for merchants.

Consequently, the hypothesis of the general anti-business theology within the medieval church can be refuted. Furthermore, embeddedness, innovation and feedback could be useful operators for analysing the dynamics between Christian religion and economy, hence the Moral economy of the Middle Ages.

References

Amadori, Severio. 2007. *Nelle bisacce di Bernardino da Feltre: Gli scritti giuridici in difesa dei monti di pietà*. Bologna: Compositori.

Annio da Viterbo. 1492. *Questiones due disputate super mutuo iudaico et civili et divino,* edite in Mons Pietis. Pro Monte Pietatis consilia. Venedig: Giovanni Tacuino.

Delcorno, Pietro. 2015. Micquel de Acqui and the foundation of the Monte di Pietà in Verona. An unpublished incunabula. *Varia Historia* 31 (55): 127–60.

de Roover, Raymond. 1958. The Concept of the Just Price: Theory and Economic Policy. *Journal of Economic History* 18 (4): 418–434.

Evans, Allan, ed. 1936. Francesco Pegolotti, Pratica della Mercatura: Book of Descriptions of Countries and of Merchandise. Cambridge, MA: Medieval Academy of America.

Fontaine, Laurence. 2008. *L'économie morale: pauvreté, crédit et confiance dans l' Europe preindustrielle*. Paris: Gallimard.

Frevert, Ute, ed. 2019. *Moral Economies*. Göttingen: Vandenhoeck & Ruprecht.

Gilomen, Hans-Jörg. 1990. Wucher und Wirtschaft im Mittelalter. *Historische Zeitschrift* 250: 265–301.

———. 2010. Kredit und Innovation im Spätmittelalter. In *Aufbruch im Mittelalter. Innovationen in Gesellschaften der Vormoderne*, ed. Christian Hesse and Klaus Oschema, 35–68. Ostfildern: Jan Thorbecke Verlag.

Granovetter, Mark. 2017. *Society and Economy. Framework and Principles*. Cambridge, MA and London: The Belknap Press of Harvard University Press.

———. 1985. Economic Action and Social Structure: The Problem of Embeddedness. *American Journal of Sociology* 91 (3): 481–510.

Helas, Philine. 2004. Die Predigt in der Weltenlandschaft: zur Agitation von Fra Marco da Montegallo für den Monte di Pietà in einem Stich von Francesco Rosselli (c.1485). *Marburger Jahrbuch für Kunstwissenschaft* 31: 105–44.

Lopez, Robert S. 1976. *The Commercial Revolution of the Middle Ages, 950–1350*. Cambridge: Cambridge University Press.

Marco del Monte S. Maria. 1494. *La tabula della salute*. Firenze: Antonio Miscomini. https://gutenberg.beic.it/view/action/nmets.do?DOCCHOICE=9925126.xml&dvs=1642503282339~426&locale=de_DE&search_terms=Marco+da+Montegallo&show_metadata=true&adjacency=&VIEWER_URL=/view/action/nmets.do?&DELIVERY_RULE_ID=7&divType=&usePid1=true&usePid2=true.

Munroe, John H. 2002. The Medieval Origins of the Financial Revolution: Usury, *Rentes* and Negotiability. *The International History Review* 25 (3): 505–62.

Noonan, John Thomas. 1957. *The Scholastic Analysis of Usury*. Cambridge, MA: Harvard University Press.

Olivi, Petrus Iohannis. 2021. *Traktat über Verträge*, ed. G. Franco. Hamburg: Meiner.

Piron, Sylvain. 2020. *Généalogie de la morale économique*. Bruxelles: ZONES SENSIBLES.

Polanyi, Karl. 1968. The Economy as Instituted Process. In *Economic Anthropology. Readings in Theory and Analysis*, ed. Edward LeClair and Harold K. Schneider, 122–42. New York: Holt, Rinehart and Winston.

Puglisi, Catherine, and William Barcham. 2008. Bernardino da Feltre, the Monte di Pietà and the Man of Sorrows: Activist, Microcredit and Logo. *Artibus et Historiae* 58: 35–63.

Pullan, Brian. 2001. Jewish Banks and Monti di Pietà. In *The Jews of Early Modern Venice*, ed. Robert. C. Davis and Benjamin Ravid, 53–72. Baltimore/London: Johns Hopkins University Press.

Rogan, Tim. 2017. *The Moral Economists*. Princeton and Oxford: OUP.

Skambraks, Tanja, 2017. Expertise im Dienste der Caritas. Die Monti di Pietà zwischen gelehrtem Wissen und Erfahrungswissen. In *Wirtschaft und Wissen. Expertenkulturen und Märkte vom 13. bis 18. Jahrhundert*, ed. Philip Knäble, Marian Füssel, and Nina Elsemann, 169–90. Göttingen: Vandenhoeck & Ruprecht.

Skambraks, Tanja. 2023. *Karitativer Kredit. Monti di Pietà, franziskanische Wirtschaftsethik und städtische Sozialpolitik in Italien (15. und 16. Jahrhundert)*. Stuttgart: Steiner.

Sombart, Werner. 1902. *Der Moderne Kapitalismus. Vol. 1: Die Genesis des Kapitalismus*. Leipzig: Duncker & Humblot.

Thompson, E.P. 1963. *The Making of the English Working Class*. London: Victor Gollancz.

———. 1971. The Moral Economy of the English Crowd in the Eighteenth Century. *Past and Present* 50: 76–136.

Toaff, Ariel. 2004. Jews, Christians and the First Monti di Pietà in Italy (1462–1500). In *Friars and Jews in the Middle Ages and Renaissance*, ed. Steven J. McMichael, 239–253. Leiden: Brill.

Todeschini, Giacomo. 1977. Oeconomia Franciscana II: Pietro di Giovanni Olivi come fonte per la storia dell'etica-economica medievale. *Rivista di storia e letteratura religiosa* 13: 461–494.

———. 2002. *I mercanti e il Tempio. La società cristiana e il circolo virtuoso della ricchezza fra Medioevo ed età moderna*. Bologna: Il Mulino.

———. 2004. Franciscan Economics and Jews in the Middle Ages: From a Theological to an Economic Lexicon. In *Friars and Jews in the Middle Ages and Renaissance*, ed. Steven J. McMichael, 99–117. Leiden: Brill.

———. 2008. Christian Perceptions of Jewish Economic Activity in the Middle Ages. In *Wirtschaftsgeschichte der mittelalterlichen Juden: Fragen und Einschätzungen*, ed. Michael Toch, 1–16. Oldenbourg: De Gruyter.

———. 2016. *La banca e il ghetto. Una storia italiana (secoli XIV–XVI)*. Rom/ Bari: Editori Laterza.

———. 2009. *Franciscan Wealth: From Voluntary Poverty to Market Society*. New York: Franciscan Institute Publications.

Weitnauer, Alfred. 1931. *Venezianischer Handel der Fugger: nach der Musterbuchhaltung des Matthaeus Schwarz*. Berlin: Duncker & Humblot.

Wohlmuth, Joseph. 2000. *Dekrete der ökumenischen Konzilien, Bd. 2: Konzilien des Mittelalters*. Paderborn: Schöningh.

Wolf, Michael. 1994. Mehrwert und Impetus bei Petrus Iohannis Olivi. Wissenschaftlicher Paradigmenwechsel im Kontext gesellschaftlicher Veränderungen im späten Mittelalter. In *Sozialer Wandel im Mittelalter. Wahrnehmungsformen, Erklärungsmuster, Regelungsmechanismen*, ed. Jürgen Miethke and Klaus Schreiner, 413–423. Sigmaringen: Thorbecke.

Yunus, Muhammad. 2007. *Banker of the Poor. Micro-Lending and the Battle Against World Poverty*. New York: Public Affairs.ss

CHAPTER 5

Past the Limits of Usury: Jews and the Moral Economy of Moneylending in the Late Medieval German Territories

Aviya Doron

Introduction

> If thou wilt lend this money, lend it not as to thy friends, for when did friendship take a breed for barren metal of his friend?
>
> Shakespeare, The Merchant of Venice, Act I Scene 2

The Merchant of Venice and its protagonist Shylock are frequently evoked in the context of medieval Jews' economic activities and the moral pitfalls of credit exchange, or, in its nefarious and predatory form, usury. In the above quote, Shakespeare expresses a moral stance toward moneylending—that taking interest is not compatible with friendship.

A. Doron (✉)
Department of Jewish History,
Hebrew University of Jerusalem, Jerusalem, Israel
e-mail: aviyadoron@gmail.com

T. Skambraks and M. Lutz (eds.), *Reassessing the Moral Economy*, Palgrave Studies in Economic History,
https://doi.org/10.1007/978-3-031-29834-9_5

The idea that charging interest is contrary to friendship or a general state of kinship, is rooted in the biblical prohibition on usury: "Thou shalt not lend upon interest to thy brother" (Deuteronomy 23:19). Though the biblical prohibition was shared by both Jews and Christians, the two religions varied on its basic interpretation (Soloveitchik 2013; Kirschenbaum 1985; Todeschini 2020). Setting the boundary between the brother, one's self, and the other lay at the heart of the majority of medieval polemics regarding the biblical ban, with Jewish scholars interpreting the prohibition to apply only within the boundaries of the Jewish faith, and Christian theologists viewing any transaction in which one received more than was given as unjust (Kirschenbaum 1985). However, the moral ideal expressed in both the biblical prohibition, and in The Merchant of Venice, warrants the obverse question: are credit relations always rooted in enmity, and is enmity their inevitable outcome?

The constant intersection of Jews and Christians in urban credit markets in the German-speaking Territories of the Holy Roman Empire, which expanded as of the late twelfth century (Howell 2010; Fouquet 2010; Elbl et al. 2007), forged a broad range of relationships between Jews and Christians, from incidental pawnbroking to long-term business connections. These complex relationships in turn provoked many ethical and moral questions, beyond the fundamental debate over usury. While the moral outlooks connected to the usury prohibition have dominated scholarship on Jews and the moral foundation of their economic dealings with Christians, Jewish-Christian economic exchange cannot be collapsed solely into the usury debate, as moneylending itself raised other moral concerns. In this paper, I aim to broaden previous discussions on Jews' moral perceptions of their economic activities by shifting attention from the question of usury to other ethical concerns arising from the practice of extending credit. Based on the complex and overlapping interpersonal relationships that credit transactions created between Jews and Christians, this paper will illuminate the more mundane moral hazards that occupied Jews' conceptions of their credit exchange with Christians, mainly regarding limits of competition.

To gather evidence on Jews' moral outlooks, this paper relies on responsa literature, documenting queries Jewish communities or individuals sent to esteemed rabbis over debates concerning the application of Jewish law, often involving economic disputes (Soloveitchik 2013). Although responsa literature intrinsically addresses conflicts between Jews, many such disputes arose from previous exchanges with Christians, emphasizing the interconnectedness of Jews and Christians in the urban credit market. Thus, closely investigating these sources provides insight into how moral norms and legal practices, at times formulated by Christian theologians, penetrated into the mentalities and daily activities of individual Jews, and how market forces shaped the religious and moral perceptions of Jewish scholars.

In order to examine Jews' formulation of a certain moral economy of moneylending, this article will be divided into three sections: the first providing a brief summary of current literature related to the prohibition on usury and how it relates to Jews' economic activities at the time, the second detailing Jews' moral attitudes toward economic exchange and coexistence with Christians, and the third examining moral concerns in inter-Jewish economic exchange, focusing on regulations of economic competition. Although Jews' moral attitudes toward exchange with both Christians and Jews were shaped by their constant daily interactions with Christians, Jews saw themselves as a distinct group, and Jewish law likewise treated matters between Jews according to different legal and moral standards than that applied to interactions between Jews and non-Jews. Thus, to trace Jews' formulation and negotiation of the ethical framework shaping their economic activities, this paper will examine Jews' moral ideas both within their own community and toward the Christian environment in which they lived, providing a complex view of the intricacies of Jews' conceptualization of a moral economy.

Usury, Moneylending, and Jews' Involvement in the Medieval Economy

The pervasive need for credit and its ubiquity in the medieval economy has long been recognized (de Roover 1974; Smail 2016; Gilomen 1990; Howell 2010; Spufford 2003). The expansion of trade and commerce as of the twelfth century, together with coin shortages (Lopez 1976; Fouquet 2010), rendered credit vital for engaging in and maintaining commercial activity. In this market environment, scholars have stressed the enduring dissonance between the use of credit and the accompanying theological debate on the moral implications and dangers of usury (Langholm 1998; Little 1978; Gilomen 1990; de Roover 1967). In addition to the biblical prohibition against usury, Medieval Christian theologians engaged with several argumentations on the immorality of moneylending, ranging from the sterility of money, through imbalances between two sides of the exchange leading to injustices, to the idea that in credit one sells time, which is created by God and not for man to sell (Le Goff 1970; Langholm 1998; Wood 2002; Todeschini 2012; Dorin 2023; Kaye 2014). At the same time, as Giacomo Todeschini indicated, the idea that a complete dichotomy existed between moral norms condemning usury, and the ever-presence of credit in actual practices is problematic (Todeschini 2012). He demonstrated that medieval theologians often employed anti-usury rhetoric as economic metaphors used to demarcate social and political boundaries, whereas the provision of credit was in essence acceptable through different qualifications (Todeschini 2012).

Scholarly concentration on the disparity between the need for credit and its moral condemnation also cultivated one of the most contentious topics in the historiography of medieval Jews: the categorical association between Jews and moneylending (Dorin 2023; Todeschini 2008; Mell 2017; Toch 2000). Indeed, medieval Christian moral perceptions of Jews and their economic activity identified Jews almost entirely with usury, viewing this as a manifestation of greed (Todeschini 2008; Toch 2000). The theological and moral debates that the prohibition on usury spurred, especially in Jewish-Christian contexts, have likewise occupied much of the scholarship on medieval Jews' moral views of the economy, and Jewish economic thought more broadly (Gemorah 2008; Soloveitchik 2013). In this context, the expansive studies of Haym Soloveitchik on the development of Jews' attitude toward usury and lending on interest stressed that contrary to Christian theological perceptions of usury as a moral sin, Jews never assigned any moral vice to the biblical prohibition (Soloveitchik 2013: 51). As a result, especially with the expansion of commerce as of the twelfth century, Jewish sages increasingly viewed the prohibition on lending on interest as a legal proscription, devoid of any moral implications. Thus, it could be circumvented using legal technicalities, such as a Christian strawman serving as middleman in a loan between two Jews, consequently bypassing a forbidden loan (Soloveitchik 2013: 53).

Beyond scholarly debates surrounding the divergence between Jews' and Christians' conceptualization of usury, previous generations of scholars also stressed the special role Jews played in the development of the European economy, as sole providers of credit (Mell 2017; Toch 2000; Todeschini 2020). However, scholarship over the past two decades has demonstrated that credit was prevalent throughout and across medieval society, with practically all segments of society extending and relying on credit in their economic activities (Howell 2010; Signori 2015;

Smail 2016). The ubiquity of credit meant that Jews were not the sole providers of credit in the medieval economy, and that the usury prohibition did not prevent Christians from engaging in credit. Accordingly, many Jewish-Christian economic interactions in the German-speaking territories of the Holy Roman Empire and well beyond, revolved around moneylending and credit (Toch 2008; Wiedl 2009; Shatzmiller 2017), producing numerous moral concerns other than the permissibility of moneylending.

Living as a distinct minority group, Jews were granted settlement rights in towns of the German territories entitling them to both legal and religious freedoms, recognizing Jewish law as a binding legal system for Jews (Cluse 2009; Haverkamp 2015). Jews' legal and religious precepts were rooted in and governed by the *halakhah*, the body of Jewish law derived from written and oral traditions. The *halakhah* was thus an encapsulation of both Jewish law and religion, and rabbinic scholars provided Jewish communities with guidance on how to conduct their lives according to the *halakhah*. At the same time, Jews lived in close proximity to their Christian neighbors and shared their daily routines and concerns, maintaining constant contact with Christians. The inevitable tension between the realities of daily life and their resulting cultural transfers and the traditions of Jewish law have occupied many scholars, who stressed the different ways in which Jews adapted and appropriated Christian cultural norms and ideas, demonstrating Jews' deep embeddedness in Christian society (Baumgarten 2014, 2018; Marcus 2014; Yuval 2008). Thus, Jews' ideas of the accepted norms of conduct toward their Christian counterparts were in constant negotiation between the prevalent norms of the Christian environment in which they were embedded, Judaism's religious dictates, and their often-precarious position in Christian society as a religious group subject to great hostilities and even violence.

Between Jews and Christians

Among the different forces shaping Jews' conceptualizations of a moral economy of moneylending, it is often easiest to detect the impact of religious concerns, although these were not necessarily predominant factors for many Jews. As a result, much attention has been paid to corresponding discussions of Jewish sages and Christian theologians regarding the pawning with Jews of ecclesiastic objects, such as chalices, priestly garments, and other objects of the church (Shatzmiller 2008, 2017;

Müller 2012; Wiedl 2016). Despite religious concerns, such transactions still occurred, presumably without much moral quandaries. Furthermore, such high-profile ecclesiastic objects represent a small fraction of Jewish-Christian credit transactions. With most interreligious credit transactions secured by unexceptional objects, the moral attitude of most Jews toward their exchange with Christians was occupied by far more mundane issues.

Indeed, responsa literature reveals the close contacts Jews maintained with Christian clients and their resulting ethical obligations. A responsum sent to Rabbi Meir of Rothenburg (~1220–1293), the most revered religious authority among the Jewish communities in thirteenth-century Germany (Emanuel 2004), provides an example. As with most responsa, an account of the events is presented through the sides to the dispute using generic aliases, the most common for men being Reuven and Shimon, and for women Rachel and Lea. The responsum begins with a dispute between a father and son-in-law: the son-in-law, given the alias Reuven, blamed his father-in-law, Shimon, for informing his Christian creditors that he was planning to flee the city, causing him to lose two marks. The father-in-law strongly denied this had occurred.[1]

While the initial query does not reveal much more than a family dispute, Rabbi Meir's reply provides insight into moral assumptions regarding credit exchange with Christians. First, Rabbi Meir asked Reuven to explain what he meant by this loss. If it was his original debt to the Christian debtors, which he was now made to pay, Rabbi Meir explains that the father-in-law "did not cause any losses, for clearly Reuven who borrowed from the Christians must pay them. And even if the Christians die, he must pay their heirs." Thus, Rabbi Meir expressed a clear stance that Jews must uphold their credit obligations to Christians. Although this might seem like a trivial statement, there is overwhelming contemporaneous evidence of Christian debtors reneging on their loans to Jewish creditors, and of a general non-compliance with loan obligations (Doron 2021). Contrary to prevalent norms of conduct, Rabbi Meir established that paying one's credit obligation cannot be considered a loss and is the required and expected norm. Subsequently, Rabbi Meir explored another option of what the said loss could have been: perhaps, upon learning of Reuven's plans to flee, the Christians accused him of greater crimes, extracting payments beyond the debt. If this were the case, then the

[1] R. Meir b. Baruch of Rothenburg, Cremona Edition (Budapest: Buchhandlung Sternberg & Co., 1895), 20b–21a §35.

father-in-law must swear an oath in the synagogue confirming that he did not inform the Christians. However, if the Christians testify that the father-in-law did inform them, then he must swear an oath in front of the Christians confirming that he did not inform them. The opinions and accounts of the Christians were given considerable weight in the outcome of the dispute and applied to solve the conflicting reports of the in-laws. Thus, Rabbi Meir's ruling officially acknowledged Jews' and Christians' co-dependence in the urban credit market.

Moving from the intricate details of Jewish-Christian interpersonal relationships, a later responsum following the Black Death presents a more general moral position toward Jews' economic coexistence with Christians. The query was sent to Rabbi Yaakob Levi Moelin (~1365–1427), the leading Jewish legal authority in northern Europe in the second half of the fourteenth century, called by his acronym, Maharil. Following the general upheaval brought on by the Black Death, the nature of Jewish settlement changed, especially due to the pogroms and expulsions directed against them throughout the German lands (Gilomen 2011; Barzilay 2022; Toch 1992). The devastation of large and established Jewish communities led many Jews to live in smaller settlements, leading to obstacles in the fulfillment of ritual obligations requiring at least ten Jewish men present (Kaplan 2011). In this context, Maharil received a query over a conflict between Jews local to these small settlements and non-local Jews, living in their environs, over the division of the expenses of hiring additional Jews for the High Holidays' prayers. In response to the argument of the Jews from the environs that their arrival to the small towns causes no harm to the local Jews, the local Jews replied:

> No, for you cause us malice, as the Christians will say that the town is full of Jews which they are not used to. And also, you grab and buy what they [the Christians] are not accustomed to during the rest of the year, and we are uncomfortable with that.[2]

The Jews living in these small communities express an understanding of the function of their local market as well as their concern that lodging additional Jews would cause market shortages, depriving their Christian neighbors of necessities. While it is difficult to judge whether this concern

[2] Yitchak Satz, ed., *Shut Maharil Hahadashot* (New Responsa of Rabbi Yaacov Molin-Maharil) (Jerusalem: Jerusalem Institute, 1997), §59.

was a result of their precarious position in the post-Black Death period, it nonetheless demonstrates Jews' awareness of their part in the whole of the community, and a sense of ethical obligation to prevent changes to their portion of the market that could harm the Christians with whom they share their living environment and market. Moreover, these Jews on some level displayed a greater obligation toward their Christian neighbors than their non-local coreligionists, reenforcing the perception that these Jews felt themselves responsible and accountable for the function of the local market.

Although not directly mentioned, this stance reflects two existing Jewish legal concepts: the Right of Settlement (*Heskat HaYeshuv*), and the Ban on Settlement (*Herem HaYeshuv*). These two closely linked concepts, created by medieval Jewish communities in the German Empire (Schwarzfuchs 1993), allowed Jews who resided in a certain place to prevent other Jews from settling there (by the Right of Settlement), using the threat of ban as a punishment for those who did not respect the boundaries of settlement (through the Ban on Settlement) (Gladstein-Kestenberg 1978). The right to settle in a place was completely linked with the right to conduct business in that location. While these concepts were used to restrict new Jews from residing in a settlement, consequently entering into competition with the Jews already living there, in this case brought to Maharil, the same moral principle was applied, but in order to prevent Jews from entering into competition with Christians.

In his reply, Maharil addressed the problem of Jews from the environs buying out market supplies, suggesting a solution:

> ...the local Jews should establish an ordinance that the non-local [Jews] shall not [grab everything from the market] and shall not buy more than is necessary for their sustenance, and not from merchandise that a Christian wants to buy...[3]

Addressing the small-town Jews' objection to non-local Jews abusing their market, Maharil confirms their concerns and suggests a communal legal mechanism that could prevent such behavior. He thereby instructed the local Jews to instate an ordinance, a Jewish communal regulation,

[3] Yitchak Satz, ed., *Shut Maharil Hahadashot* (New Responsa of Rabbi Yaacov Molin-Maharil) (Jerusalem: Jerusalem Institute, 1997), §59.

to prevent the non-local Jews from abusing their local market. In addition, not only should these Jews be restricted to buying only the most necessary items for their sustenance, but they should also refrain from buying merchandise that Christians intend on buying. In this way, Maharil attempted to prevent the non-local Jews from disrupting Christians' routines in the local market, essentially prohibiting the non-local Jews from functioning as a competing economic force. Finally, in order to ensure compliance with this ordinance, Maharil suggested a punishment for violating the ordinance: those offenders would be prohibited from participating in the High Holidays' prayers. As participating in these prayers was the fundamental reason the non-local Jews arrived at these small towns, and is also an essential precept in the Jewish faith, prohibiting participation in the prayers was a considerable threat. Setting the stakes so high stresses the commitment to the integrity of the local market and its norms, and a willingness to use religious levers to ensure this integrity.

While the discussion in the responsum focuses on the possibility of shortages of supplies, it might also echo contemporaneous concerns in Christian society over forestalling—the act of buying out a certain basic commodity to create scarcity and drive-up prices (Britnell 1987; Wood 2002, 139). Such activities were seen as interference with the natural, just, or common prices in the market, associated with the vice of monopolies (Wood 2002; Kaye 2014; Langholm 2006). As the reply of Maharil repeatedly states that the non-local Jews should cease from purchasing more goods than are necessary for their sustenance, this implies some form of wholesale purchasing, perhaps with the intention of reselling it in their places of origin. Maharil's suggestion to restrict the non-local Jews from engaging in commercial exchange is consistent with regulations across the empire attempting to restrict forestalling practices. Thus, not only does the reply reveal a moral obligation to maintain the integrity of a local market, but it also suggests the permeation of the prevailing moral ideas on prices and their manipulation into Jewish norms.

The question sent to Maharil, although not relating to the practice of moneylending, exhibits Jews' moral obligation to the marketplaces in which they were active and their appropriation of similar norms of behavior as accepted in Christian society, specifically a similar unease about forestalling. Whereas the moral obligation was toward Christians, ensuring their access to supplies in the market, the group upon which restrictions were placed to meet this obligation was non-local Jews, using Jewish legal mechanisms: a communal ordinance and a threat to prohibit participation in prayer. In this particular case, the questions of competition and distribution of resources were expressed in the context of potential competition with local Christians. As the following section demonstrates, similar concerns over competition and distribution of resources were a central and significant moral concern in the management of economic activities among Jews.

Within the Jewish Community

The regulation of competition was crucial to Jewish communities in the German Empire, whose members often relied on similar occupations for their livelihood. Several communal legal concepts, including the right to prohibit new Jews from residing in a certain location and the demarcation of certain Christians as off-limits, express a strong moral position taken toward the management of competitive forces. Indeed, regulation of competition was a common feature of the medieval economy, and the Right and Ban on Settlement have previously been compared to the function of guilds in medieval society (Gladstein-Kestenberg 1978). While merchant and trade guilds established monopolistic practices, the moral issues related to restriction of competition were also addressed by medieval Christian moralists. Around the second half of the thirteenth century, moralists largely condemned monopolies as destructive forces interfering with the just, competitive price of the market, causing harm to the community (Langholm 2006). Monopolies and competitive practices were not only addressed in relation to price control, as Joel Kaye demonstrated, between 1280 and 1360 the idea of balance within the community or the well-functioning political system was seen to be achieved when "the very massing of competing private desires and functions within the aggregate whole creates a "tempered" product, the Common Good, when aided by the equalizing instrument of law and custom" (Kaye 2014, 333). Thus, competition was part and parcel of medieval moralists' conception of the healthy functioning of a moral community and economy.

Although not expressing a moral stance toward prices and value control, Jews too engaged in discussions on competitive practices and their management for maintaining a common good among Jews. Through their own legal concepts and norms, Jews negotiated how to strike a balance between the competing interests of varying community members and the growing and ever more complex credit market. An example is the legal concept of *ma'arufia*, deriving from Arabic from the semantic field of acquaintance or familiarity, evidenced in the writings of Jewish sages as of the eleventh century (Steiner 2011). The concept provided certain Jewish moneylenders exclusivity over a particular Christian client (Agus 1996; Eidelberg 1999; Shoham-Steiner 2020). Once this exclusivity was established between a Jewish moneylender and a Christian client, often wealthy or politically important, no other Jew was supposed to offer services to that Christian. While the concept of *ma'arufia* was most likely no longer strictly practiced by the thirteenth century (Baumgarten 2021), there is evidence of similar questions of competition between Jews for the same Christian clients debated through the legal concept of *ma'arufia* and its moral implications.

A mid-thirteenth-century example is found in a question sent to Rabbi Yekutiel bar Avraham, who corresponded with Rabbi Meir of Rothenburg, and was likely a generation his senior. In a query sent to him, the term *ma'arufia* is explicitly mentioned to describe a relationship between a Jew and his Christian client that was threatened by another Jew.

> Reuven pleaded with Shimon: "do not lend [money] to that knight, my *ma'arufia*, which my life depends on." And Shimon replies: "I intend to lend him [money] for less..." and again Shimon said: "I did not lend him [money] and if I did, what do I owe you."[4]

The conflict between the two parties shows a clash between the perhaps dated laws of *ma'arufia*, actually using the term to define his relationship with the knight, and a different approach, which considers an intrusion into a long-established credit relationship as morally acceptable. The conflict between these approaches is stressed by Reuven's claim that his life depends on that knight, calling into question whether his livelihood was dependent on him, or that he required his protection in non-financial form. In opposition to Reuven's strong claims, Shimon not only blatantly declared that he intends to offer the knight a loan on better terms, but also later denied any connection to the knight, while stating that if he hypothetically had any business with him, it was of no concern to Reuven.

The stark difference between these moral approaches to competition among Jews was not only an issue of high-stakes loans to knights or

[4] Simcha Emanuel, ed., *Responsa of Rabbi Meir of Rothenburg and His Colleagues* (Jerusalem: World Union of Jewish Studies, 2012), 894–95 §460.

wealthy individuals. Although it has been argued that the *ma'arufia* was economically viable only with elite or extremely wealthy clients (Toch 2008), the same moral concerns and presumptions underlying the concept of *ma'arufia* found expression in different forms of exchange. The need to mark competitive boundaries among community members of different social standing is illustrated in an additional thirteenth-century responsum, sent to Rabbi Moshe Azriel of Erfurt. The query begins with a detailed depiction of an unsuccessful Jew who interfered with the business of other Jews in town:

> Aaron sits in a community in a city… and he was never able to earn anything through bargaining and lending, and in time the heavens had mercy on him, as he earned a small amount, bringing bargaining within his reach. And he had no acquaintances, and the rest of the community had many, and at times he speaks to the Christians walking through the street and he knows not where they intend on going, and sometimes they carry pawns with them and sometimes they carry nothing. And Aaron talks to the gentiles, inquiring to their interests and speaking to their hearts, and says to them "if you need anything come and I shall meet your hearts' desire…"[5]

The responsum vividly portrays the realities of moneylending in town, with Christians coming and going through the street where Jews live, at times with objects in their hands to offer as pawns. Amidst this reality, one unfortunate Jew, Aaron, was unsuccessful in business and had no acquaintances as had the other Jews. He attempted to improve his economic situation by approaching Christians on the streets and offering his services. The depiction, although detailed, does not tell us much about the relationship between Aaron and the rest of the Jews in the town, nor about the relationships other, more successful, Jews had with the Christians, and whether he inserted himself in direct competition with certain individuals. Nonetheless, it is clear that on the one hand, Aaron could not have been much of a threat to other Jews, but on the other hand, his actions were seen as a nuisance that contravened the moral codes of practice among Jews, leading to a request for redress from the rabbi.

[5] Simcha Emanuel, ed., *Responsa of Rabbi Meir of Rothenburg and His Colleagues* (Jerusalem: World Union of Jewish Studies, 2012), 896–900 §461.

The boundaries of economic competition between Jews were also addressed when Christians were those attempting to play Jews off each other in order to benefit from the competition. This is discussed in a responsum of Rabbi Meir of Rothenburg, stating:

> You inquired regarding Reuven who lent money to a Christian on interest, and that same Christian came to Shimon and said to him: "[lend me] at the rate of your fellow Jew, [or] if you would like to lend me at a cheaper [rate] I will redeem [my loan] from him and take [out a loan] from you."[6]

The redress to Jewish legal authority was triggered by an attempt of a Christian to harness the competition between Jewish moneylenders to his advantage. As with the previous responsum, there is no reason to believe that the Christian maintained an exclusive relationship with Reuven, or even a longstanding one. Although neither Jew solicited the Christian's business, it is clear that the possibility of overstepping the boundaries of competition was a serious moral concern for Jewish authorities, as well as for members of the community who needed to maintain peace among themselves.

In his reply, Rabbi Meir explores two different scenarios that could have taken place once the Christian had borrowed the initial loan from Reuven: either the loan from Shimon was used to provide liquidity so that the Christian could repay Reuven, or the new loan was intended to replace the Christian's commitment to Reuven. In the first scenario of a loan supplying liquidity to an almost defaulting debtor, Rabbi Meir permitted the cross loan. In the second scenario of reissuing a new loan on better terms, he forbade it, stating that one should stay away from such wickedness or anything that resembles it. To stress the severity of the wicked behavior, he provided an example of a community that enacted an ordinance with the threat of a ban regarding such cross loans. According to his account, this ordinance decreed the following:

> If a Christian would come to a Jew asking to borrow money, even if that Jew knows that the Christian owes money to another Jew... he need not ask him if he wants to pay [the other Jew's loan], but rather assume that he needs [the loan] for other purposes. But if the Christian would ask to

[6] Simcha Emanuel, ed., *Responsa of Rabbi Meir of Rothenburg and His Colleagues* (Jerusalem: World Union of Jewish Studies, 2012), 930–31 §477.

> borrow money and say: "I need the money in order to redeem [a loan] to so and so, a Jew," one should reply: "I have no money," once gaining knowledge that he wants to redeem [the loan] of another Jew, so as not to harm his fellow...

In the quoted ordinance, we learn of the ramifications of the growing credit economy for the management of competition between Jews. Whereas the legal construct of *ma'arufia* may have sufficed to manage competition between Jews in a market where credit was consumed mostly by the elite, as credit seeped into all segments of society, creating overlapping networks of credit, new mechanisms were necessary. The solution found in this ordinance was to demarcate the boundary of permissible competition through the intention of the Christian requesting the loan. If the Christian did not specify the purpose of the loan, despite having knowledge of his indebtedness to other Jews, the Jewish moneylender should assume that the loan was for another purpose. This corresponds with contemporaneous evidence of loans and their litigation, demonstrating that many people in the urban economy were involved in multiple non-related credit transactions with several Jews at the same time (Schnur 2014; Doron 2021).

On the other hand, if the Christian, upon approaching a Jewish moneylender mentions that the loan is for the purpose of redeeming a loan with another Jew, then he should simply be refused the loan, in order to avoid the ethical question addressed earlier in the reply. Rabbi Meir found this ordinance so vital in maintaining the boundaries of competition, that he continued to state:

> And it is right for all god fearing [Jews] to do so, even where there is no ordinance. But if he [a Jew] came to a Christian and said: "I will lend you [money] so that you redeem your deposit from another Jew and give it to me... he shall be called a wicked man... and it is permitted to call him a wicked man.[7]

Thus, according to Meir of Rothenburg, all God-fearing Jews should abide by the aforementioned ordinance, even if not formally instated in their place of residence. Such broad applicability demonstrates how well

[7] Simcha Emanuel, ed., *Responsa of Rabbi Meir of Rothenburg and His Colleagues* (Jerusalem: World Union of Jewish Studies, 2012), 930–31 §477.

it balanced the realities and needs of the credit market with the moral caution and responsibility necessary toward fellow Jews. Rabbi Meir then concluded his reply with the reverse scenario: a Jew approaching a Christian in the attempt to win over his business from another Jew. In this case, not only is it forbidden, but Rabbi Meir also states that he who behaves in such a way shall be called wicked, which is not only a moral accusation according to the *halakhah*, but also carries with it practical legal ramifications: the wicked man's right to swear an oath is revoked, a practice which was critical for economic and legal conduct in the medieval world (Ziegler 1992; Linder 2014). The grave consequences of being called a wicked man required that an ungrounded allegation of a person as a wicked man was likewise punishable. However, Rabbi Meir made it clear that approaching a Christian client of another Jew to solicit their business is such a vice that he endorsed the public designation of the transgressor as wicked. Although the strong language may in fact point to the Rabbi's powerlessness in the face of a changing reality, through his ruling, he cemented his moral stance against the interference of one Jew in another Jew's business, instating a harsh punishment for those who attempt to transgress these boundaries.

Conclusion

The moral obligation to maintain economic boundaries between Jews by curbing competition was solidified in the legal concepts of the Right and Ban on Settlement and *ma'arufia*, legal concepts which were constructed in the early stages of Jewish settlement north of the Alps, reflecting a distant economic reality from that of the thirteenth century. By the thirteenth century, individual Jews no longer held monopolies over specific Christian clients, nor was it considered the moral norm. Still Jewish legal and moral authorities—rabbinic scholars—wrestled with the same questions of competition as their economic reality transformed. In these, the guiding moral principle of refraining from interfering with other Jews' business to their harm still prevailed, revealing a discerning sensitivity to the realities and complexities of the urban credit market. Yet not only Jews grappled with managing competitive forces in the urban economy: often Jews' application and adaptation of their legal concepts are far more emblematic of dynamics occurring in Christian urban society.

Returning to the Merchant of Venice and the question of usury, the assumptions and concerns Jews expressed in responsa literature present the intimate connections between creditors and debtors in the urban market. With Jews maintaining long-term credit ties with specific Christians, and Christians obtaining credit from several different Jews, the overlapping relationships credit transactions created were often far from adversarial. Shifting the gaze away from the polemics surrounding usury toward the moral concerns framing Jews' actual moneylending practices provides an opportunity to examine Jewish-Christian credit relations as social exchange, as well as an exchange of values, as Laurence Fontaine indicated (Fontaine 2014). As such, credit transactions between Jews and Christians in the German Territories were embedded in complex webs of social interactions, between Jews and Christians and among Jews, in which Jews constantly reformulated their moral economy according to the changing environment of the medieval marketplace and its moral norms.

References

Agus, Irving. 1996. *The Heroic Age of Franco-German Jewry*. New York: Yeshiva University Press.

Barzilay, Tzafrir. 2022. *Poisoned Wells: Accusations, Persecution, and Minorities in Medieval Europe, 1321–1422*. Philadelphia: University of Pennsylvania Press.

Baumgarten, Elisheva. 2014. *Practicing Piety in Medieval Ashkenaz: Men, Women, and Everyday Religious Observance*. Philadelphia: University of Pennsylvania Press.

———. 2018. Appropriation and Differentiation: Jewish Identity in Medieval Ashkenaz. *AJS Review* 42 (01): 39–63.

———. 2021. Money Matters: Individuals, Communities and Everyday Economic Interactions Between Jews and Christians in Medieval Europe. *Medieval Encounters* 27 (4–5): 293–307.

Britnell, Richard. 1987. Forstall, Forestalling and the Statute of Forestallers. *The English Historical Review* 102 (402): 89–102.

Cluse, Cristoph. 2009. Jewish Community and Civic Commune in the High Middle Ages. In *Strangers and Poor People: Changing Patterns of Inclusion and Exclusion in Europe and the Mediterranean World from Classical Antiquity to the Present Day*, ed. Andreas Gestrich, Raphael Lutz and Herbert Uerlings, 165–91. Frankfurt a.M.: Peter Lang.

de Roover, Raymond Adrien. 1967. The Scholastics, Usury, and Foreign Exchange. *Business History Review* 41 (3): 257–71.

———. 1974. *Business, Banking, and Economic Thought in Late Medieval and Early Modern Europe: Selected Studies of Raymond de Roover*. Chicago: University of Chicago Press.

Doron, Aviya. 2021. Pawned Horses: Risk and Liability in Fourteenth Century German Small-Credit Market. *Medieval Encounters* 27 (4–5): 387–409.

Dorin, Rowan. 2023. *No Return: Jews, Christian Usurers, and the Spread of Mass Expulsion in Medieval Europe*. Princeton: Princeton University Press.

Eidelberg, Shlomo. 1999. 'Maarufia' in Rabbenu Gershom's Responsa. In *Medieval Ashkenazic History: Studies on German Jewry in the Middle Ages*, ed. Shlomo Eidelberg, 11–20. New York: Sepher-Hermon Press.

Elbl, Martin, Ivana Elbl, and Lawrin D. Armstrong, eds. 2007. *Money, Markets and Trade in Late Medieval Europe: Essays in Honour of John H.A. Munro*. Leiden and Boston: Brill.

Emanuel, Simcha. 2004. Unpublished Responsa of R. Meir of Rothenburg as a Source for Jewish History. In *The Jews of Europe in the Middle Ages (Tenth to Fifteenth Centuries)*, ed. Christoph Cluse, 283–93. Turnhout: Brepols.

Fontaine, Laurence. 2014. *The Moral Economy: Poverty, Credit, and Trust in Early Modern Europe*. New York: Cambridge University Press.

Fouquet, Gerhard. 2010. Netzwerke im Internationalen Handel des Mittelalters - Eine Einleitung. In *Netzwerke im Europäischen Handel des Mittelalters*, ed. Gerhard Fouquet and Hans-Jörg. Gilomen, 9–20. Ostfildern: Jan Thorbecke Verlag.

Gemorah, Hillel. 2008. *Jewish Law in Transition: How Economic Forces Overcame the Prohibition Against Lending on Interest*. Detroit: Wayne State University Press.

Gilomen, Hans-Jörg. 1990. Wucher und Wirtschaft im Mitteralter. *Historische Zeitschrift* 250: 265–301.

———. 2011. Jüdische Migration in die Städte im Spätmittelalter – „Ganz Israel ist füreinander verantwortlich beim Tragen der Last des Exils“. In *Migration als soziale Herausforderung. Historische Formen solidarischen Handelns von der Antike bis zum 20. Jahrhundert*, ed. Joachim Bahlcke, Rainer Leng, and Peter Scholz, 123–48. Stuttgart: Steiner Verlag.

Gladstein-Kestenberg, Ruth. 1978. The 'Right of Settlement', the 'Ban on Settlement', and Medieval Reality. *Tarbiz* 47 (3/4): 216–29.

Haverkamp, Alfred. 2015. Jews in the Medieval German Kingdom. In *Corpus der Quellen zur Geschichte der Juden im spätmittelalterlichen Reich*. Arye Maimon Institut für Geschichte der Juden, Universitätsbibliothek Trier.

Howell, Martha. 2010. *Commerce Before Capitalism in Europe, 1300–1600*. Cambridge: Cambridge University Press.

Kaplan, Debra. 2011. *Beyond Expulsion: Jews, Christians, and Reformation Strasbourg*. Stanford: Stanford University Press.

Kaye, Joel. *A History of Balance, 1250–1375: The Emergence of a New Model of Equilibrium and Its Impact on Thought*. New York: Cambridge University Press.

Kirschenbaum, Aaron. 1985. Jewish and Christian Theories of Usury in the Middle Ages. *The Jewish Quarterly Review* 75 (3): 270–89.

Langholm, Odd. 1998. *Legacy of Scholasticism in Economic Thought*. Cambridge: Cambridge University Press.

———. 2006. Monopoly and Market Irregularities in Medieval Economic Thought: Traditions and Texts to A.D. 1500. *Journal of the History of Economic Thought* 28 (4): 400–1.

Le Goff, Jacques. 1970. Church Time and Merchant Time in the Middle Ages. *Social Science Information* 9 (4): 151–67.

Linder, Amnon. 2014. The Jewry-Oath in Christian Europe. In *Jews in Early Christian Law (Byzantium and the Latin West, 6th–11th centuries)*, ed. John Tolan, Nicholas de Lange, Laurence Foschia, and Capucine Nemo-Pekelman, 311–58. Turnhout: Brepols.

Little, Lester. 1978. *Religious Poverty and the Profit Economy in Medieval Europe*. Ithaca: Cornell University Press.

Lopez, Robert. 1976. *The Commercial Revolution of the Middle Ages: 950–1350*. Cambridge: Cambridge University Press.

Marcus, Ivan. 2014. A Jewish-Christian Symbiosis: The Culture of Early Ashkenaz. In *Jewish Culture and Society in Medieval France and Germany*, 147–214. Farnham, Surrey: Ashgate.

Mell, Julie. 2017. *The Myth of the Medieval Jewish Moneylender*, vol. 1. New York: Palgrave Macmillan.

Müller, Jörg R. 2012. Zur Verpfändung sakraler Kultgegenstände an Juden im mittelalterlichen Reich: Norm und Praxis. In *Pro multis beneficiis. Festschrift für Friedhelm Burgard: Forschungen zur Geschichte der Juden und des Trierer Raums*, ed. Sigrid Hirobodan and Friedhelm Burgard, 179–204. Trier: Trierer historische Forschungen.

Schnur, David. 2014. Juden und Gerichtsbücher am Beispiel der Reichsstadt Frankfurt am Main (1330–1400). In *Verschriftlichung und Quellenüberlieferung: Beiträge zur Geschichte der Juden und jüdisch-christlichen Beziehungen im spätmittelalterlichen Reich (13./14. Jahrhundert)*, ed. Alfred Haverkamp and Jörg Müller, 217–74. Peine: Hahnsche Buchhandlung.

Schwarzfuchs, Simon. 1993. Hishtalsheluto shel Herem Hayeshuv- Reiya mezavit aheret. In *Shlomo Simonsohn Jubilee Volume, Studies on the History of the Jews in the Middle Ages and Renaissance Period*, 105–17. Tel Aviv: Tel Aviv University School of Jewish Studies.

Shatzmiller, Joseph. 2008. Church Articles: Pawns in the Hands of Jewish Moneylenders. In *Wirtschaftsgeschichte der mittelalterlichen Juden: Fragen und Einschätzungen*, ed. Michael Toch, 93–102. München: Oldenbourg.

———. 2017. *Cultural Exchange Jews, Christians, and Art in the Medieval Marketplace*. Princeton: Princeton University Press.

Shoham-Steiner, Ephraim. 2020. *Jewish Medieval Underworld: Jews and Crime in Medieval Europe*. Detroit: Wayne State University Press.

Signori, Gabriela. 2015. *Schuldenwirtschaft: Konsumenten- und Hypothekarkredite im spätmittelalterlichen Basel*. Konstanz: UVK Verlagsgesellschaft.

Smail, Daniel Lord. 2016. *Legal Plunder: Households and Debt Collection in Late Medieval Europe*. Cambridge, MA: Harvard University Press.

Soloveitchik, Haym. 2013. *Collected Essays*, vol. 1. Portland: Littman Library of Jewish Civilization.

Spufford, Peter. 2003. *Power and Profit: The Merchant in Medieval Europe*. New York: Thames & Hudson.

Steiner, Richard. C. 2011. Linguistic Traces of Jewish Traders from Islamic Lands in the Frankish Kingdom. *Lĕšonénu: A Journal for the Study of the Hebrew Language and Cognate Subjects* 73 (3/4): 347–70.

Toch, Michael. 1992. Siedlungsstruktur der Juden Mitteleuropas im Wandel vom Mittelalter zur Neuzeit. In *Juden in der christlichen Umwelt während des späten Mittelalters*, ed. Alfred Haverkamp and Franz Josef Ziwes, 29–39. Berlin: Duncker & Humblot.

———. 2000. Jews and Commerce: Modern Fancies and Medieval Realities. In *Il Ruolo Economico Delle Minoranze in Europa, Secc. XIII–XVIII*, ed. Simonetta Cavacchio, 43–58. Firenze: Le Monnier.

———. 2008. Economic Activities of German Jews in the Middle Ages. In *Wirtschaftsgeschichte Der Mittelalterlichen Juden*, ed. Michael Toch, 181–210. Berlin and Boston: De Gruyter Oldenbourg.

Todeschini, Giacomo. 2008. Christian Perceptions of Jewish Economic Activity in the Middle Ages. In *Wirtschaftsgeschichte der Mittelalterlichen Juden*, ed. Michael Toch, 1–16. Berlin and Boston: De Gruyter Oldenbourg.

———. 2012. Usury in Christian Middle Ages. A Reconsideration of the Historiographical Tradition (1949–2010). In *Religion and Religious Institutions in the European Economy. 1000–1800*, ed. Francesco Ammannati, 119–30. Firenze: Firenze University Press.

———. 2020. Jewish Usurers, Blood Libel, and the Second-Hand Economy: The Medieval Origins of a Stereotype (from the Thirteenth to the Fifteenth Century). In *The Medieval Roots of Antisemitism Continuities and Discontinuities from the Middle Ages to the Present Day*, ed. Jonathan Adams and Cordelia Heß, 341–51. New York: Routledge.

Wiedl, Birgit. 2009. Jews and the City: Parameters of Jewish Urban Life in Late Medieval Austria. In *Urban Space in the Middle Ages and the Early Modern Age*, ed. Albrecht Classen, 273–308. Berlin: De Gruyter.

———. 2016. Sacred Objects in Jewish Hands. Two Case Studies. In *Jews and Christians in Medieval Europe: The Historiographical Legacy of Bernhard Blumenkranz*, ed. Philippe Buc, Martha Keil, and John Victor Tolan, 57–78. Turnhout: Brepols.

Wood, Diana. 2002. *Medieval Economic Thought*. Cambridge: Cambridge University Press.

Yuval, Israel Jacob. 2008. *Two Nations in Your Womb: Perceptions of Jews and Christians in Late Antiquity and the Middle Ages*. Berkeley: University of California Press.

Ziegler, Joseph. 1992. Reflections on the Jewry Oath in the Middle Ages. *Studies in Church History* 29: 209–20.

CHAPTER 6

Fiscality, Debt, and Moral Economy: The View from Florentine Civic Chronicles

Giorgio Lizzul

Introduction

The fourteenth-century Florentine chronicler Matteo Villani (d. 1363) worried that high yields on government credits might be harmful to the spiritual health of his fellow citizens, many of whom were creditors to the Republic. Of great concern were widowed women who had chosen to invest in the market for government debt. Were they potentially involved in usurious contracts and therefore risking their souls? When the Venetian diarist Girolamo Priuli (1476–1547) lamented the impact of the crash in prices of government obligations following the defeat at the battle of Agnadello in 1509, he judged that this was a particularly grave matter because it was not simply a matter of monetary loss to high financiers but rather a threat to the well-being of the whole community. He reflected on

G. Lizzul (✉)
University of Warwick, Coventry, UK
e-mail: Giorgio.Lizzul@warwick.ac.uk

Fondazione 1563, Turin, Italy

T. Skambraks and M. Lutz (eds.), *Reassessing the Moral Economy*, Palgrave Studies in Economic History,
https://doi.org/10.1007/978-3-031-29834-9_7

how investment in government debt had been a mechanism to provide for the poor and vulnerable: it was through government credits that charitable provision to orphans and the needy were made. These securities were also key for funding brides' dowries. The right to be a creditor to the state was deeply embedded in republican ideologies: these credit instruments were seen to foster the well-being and reproduction of the political community. The market for government debt, legitimated as a mechanism for providing for the common good, was also considered by many as a site for potentially avaricious accumulation. Fluctuations in the prices of government obligations attracted the attention of a range of chroniclers across late medieval and early modern Italy. How civic chroniclers and historians understood the moral logic and potential salvific challenges posed by these interest-bearing securities, which characterised the tax systems of the largest Italian city-republics, offers an interesting case study to consider the conceptualisation of fiscality and pre-modern moral economy from a more secular viewpoint. Moral economy offers a prism through which to understand how late medieval and early modern historians framed ethical concerns on the social impact of public credit, connecting taxation and markets to religion and moral philosophy. Historical representation of consensus and contestation on the use of loans and credit markets was articulated through ideas of the common good rooted in both religious beliefs and norms, as well as civic ideologies, that could compliment the teaching of the Chruch or have their own autonomous moral logic.

From the thirteenth century on communes in north and central Italy began to institutionalise funded debts as key elements in their fiscal architecture. The maritime republics of Genoa and Venice were the first. Florence followed with the creation of the Monte Comune, its consolidated debt of the mid-fourteenth century, which remained a core part of the city's fiscal system until the sixteenth century. These debts were based on borrowing from citizens through forced or voluntary loans. Capital repayment of creditors' loans was eventually replaced by titles with rights to perpetual interest payments. These bond-like financial instruments would in all three republics become tradeable assets by the fourteenth century, attracting investment and speculation according to their price and yield. Both the interest-carrying nature of these loans and the emergence of a market, with variable and potentially very high yields, attracted the scrutiny of theologians and lawyers, many of whom were invited to judge on their potentially usurious nature. The very real concerns of governments, investors, and intellectuals have been shown to be a rich area for investigation into pre-modern economic ideas and values (see the studies of Kirshner 1982, 1983, 1984 amongst many others, and Armstrong 2003, 2004).

In a neat and pithy formulation, Diana Wood has argued that in approaching the economic thought of the Middle Ages, we need to consider that "the medieval world was not of econometrics and global markets, but one of 'theological economy'" (Wood 2002, 1). Lawrin Armstrong has recently suggested that scholastic economics should be considered part of the moral economy of pre-modern Europe (Armstrong 2016, 26). E. P. Thompson's formulation of moral economy in his study of eighteenth-century food riots was as a system of popular beliefs and deeply embedded social values that curbed and confronted laissez-faire market ideology (Thompson 1971). The moral economy of the eighteenth century drew upon laws and norms from the medieval past that had curbed unhampered market prices. These traditional and embedded crowd rights that would come into conflict with the new political economy, were understood as something akin to a *mentalitié* or popular political culture. Recent studies such as those of Davis (2011) and Armstrong (2016)—arguably drawing on a longer tradition stretching back to R. H. Tawney (1926)—have shown that medieval values about markets and credit were closely related to scholastic social thought. It was these Christian ideas that ultimately formed the basis for many early modern popular traditional expectations over economic activity.

Tracing the degree to which learned discourses were absorbed into more popular beliefs and actions, as well how popular consciousness fed into economic doctrines is of course difficult. In this chapter I will examine late medieval and Renaissance thought about fiscality not from scholastic writing but from historiographical literature. In Italy from the late thirteenth century, chronicles, diaries, and histories offer rich sources for studying economic attitudes from outside the university, which on occasion offer alternative perspectives and ways of thinking about the economy. These chronicles often give a lay viewpoint—frequently written by notaries (Zabbia 1999)—or at the least a deeply civic conception of political morality and shed light on the public reception of theological controversies over markets, whilst also giving witness to different discourses that shaped fiscal policy and citizen behaviour. To explore how chroniclers and historians wrote about the institutionalisation and investment in urban debts, I will focus on Florentine historiography from the fourteenth to the mid-sixteenth century. I survey authors that wrote about the city's funded debt and attendant market, its legitimation, operations, and discontents. I will concentrate on three themes that show shared concerns and chart historiographical developments from the late Middle Ages to the sixteenth century. First, the discussion of the initial consolidation. Here, I concentrate on the chronicle of Matteo Villani, which placed institutional formation in context with a public understanding of the theological debate over usury. His account provided a model for subsequent Florentine writers. Second, I analyse the representation of the relationship between fiscal reform and the explanation of citizen-investor behaviour in debt markets. I draw on examples from Villani, Baldassare Bonaiuti, Leonardo Bruni, and Benedetto Varchi. Last, I show how popular discontent and social participation in the debts were represented by writers that emphasise not only the regressive facets of funded debt but also their role in charitable provision. Here, I draw a comparison between Florentine writers and the Venetian Girolamo Priuli.

Italian civic chronicles' rich depictions of the social landscape lend themselves for research into the classic themes of moral economy. Reports of grain prices and the motivations behind social revolts offer insights into the world of popular beliefs and values, as well as the intellectual world of the chronicler (see for example Cohn 2006; idem 2021). Take, for example, the Franciscan Salimbene de Adam of Parma (1221–1288) who in his account of the year 1286 dedicated space to narrating the grisly death of a holy pauper. Reportedly the holy man had continuously set aside small rations of food for fear of future famine yet, Salimbene notes, this was during a time of abundance. When his emaciated body was discovered alongside a rotting pile of bread and grain, his corpse was humiliated and abused by local children, whose behaviour was incited by his miserliness (Salimbene de Adam 1966, 905–906; Jordan 1996, 3). Such an episode not only tells us about the social reality of the fear of famine and popular responses to hoarding, but its inclusion shows how history writing could weave a moral tale about the dangers of hoarding in times of abundance into a narrative of the past. Domenico Lenzi (fl. 14th c.), Florentine grain merchant and chronicler of the grain market, represented concerns over just price in the market for grain and popular voices on customary rights to affordable grain. He reported Florentine's popular grievances on the role of merchants in causing high prices "that sought to starve them," and reported popular solutions to correct inflated prices: "you would like to kill all of them and steal from them" (Nanni in Bauch and Schenk 2019, 183–186).

Chroniclers' portrayal of the ethics of taxation has been much less studied (see, however, Kirshner 1984; Kaye 1998; Armstrong 2003, 53, 72–73). Should medieval and early modern thinking about fiscality be placed alongside writing on the marketing of commodities and foodstuffs under the conceptual frame of moral economy? Considering moral economy more broadly, not necessarily as popular but as shared economic values that are part of larger moral frameworks within which ethical norms penetrate economic decision-making, and also along the lines of invoking non-monetary rights which third parties will act to support, where, as Charles Tilly put it, "for example, community membership supersedes price as a basis of entitlement" (cited in Thompson 1993, 338), can offer a useful frame for interpreting the ideology of pre-modern taxation. Citizen rights to lend rather than pay all exactions as direct or non-redeemable taxes can be understood as a customary privilege enjoyed by virtue of citizenship in a political community. This was a traditional right in many Italian city-republics that saw a variety of social groups from wealthy urban elites to much lower social strata, such as artisans and workers, become creditors to the state. An understanding of the extension of credit and participation in debt markets in the Italian republics cannot simply rely on an interpretative framework that reduces governments' raising of capital and agents' investment to profit-seeking market activity. It is essential to recognise how practices of credit were deeply embedded in republican political ideologies, and in particular, values constellated between ideas of justice, private property, and active citizen obligations. The moral-political ideas that legitimated these fiscal systems, however, were by no means uncontested nor insulated from accusations of individual greed at the expense of the common good.

Fiscality and Usury

In the continuation of his brother Giovanni Villani's (d. 1348) *Nuova cronica*, Matteo provided a contemporary narrative of the creation of Florence's Monte Comune (1343–1345). He fleshed out Giovanni's brief description and offered a lay perspective on the theological controversy that ensued. The Villani's fortunes were closely tied to the Monte—they had invested heavily in the city's debt and Matteo was himself a scribe of the new institution (Zabbia 2020). Matteo described the establishment of the public debt through a fiscal-moral language that rationalised the Commune's continued reliance on credit and the decision to compensate its citizens. Consolidation was not so much a choice, rather it had been obliged by necessity as the city was "overcome by many grave fortunes and immeasurable needs" (Matteo Villani 1995, *Cronica* 1.460).[1] A crisis created by military indebtedness necessitated debt consolidation for the city to repay citizen creditors:

> Because of the war with the Pisans over the matter of Lucca, our commune found itself having borrowed 600,000 gold florins from its citizens. Not having any source to restitute the loans, it purged the debt and reduced it to 504,000 gold florins and some hundreds more and made a Monte. It created four books, one for each quarter, and recorded in alphabetic order every creditor. (Villani 1995, *Cronica* 1.459–60)

Importantly Matteo listed the measures the Commune took to secure creditors' trust in the fund to "fortify who had money in the Monte" (Villani 1995, *Cronica* 1.460).[2]

Although Matteo dates the moral controversy that accompanied the formalisation of the public debt to 1353–1354, almost a decade after the initial consolidation, his account is placed in the narrative of the moment of consolidation. He was not particularly concerned by the five per cent interest paid to the original creditors being usurious, notwithstanding that this was a source of controversy and his vocabulary implicitly legitimised creditors' right to receive interest and for the city to use credit mechanisms. He described the payments on the Monte credits as both gift, *dono*, and *interesse* (the jurist Azo's (c. 1150–1230) term for compensation for damages to the creditor, see Armstrong 2003, 62). This compensation replaced the repayment of the principal of the loan. Giovanni had earlier

[1] All translations are my own unless stated.

[2] See Matteo Villani, *Cronaca*, 1.460: "[The Comune] decreed certain penal laws obliged to the papal the privilege and immunity of the Monte monies (*munità ch'avessono I danari del Monte*). It decreed that for every month in perpetuity every creditor should have, and will have, as a gift per year and monetary interest one denaio per lira, and that nobody's money in the Monte could be taken away for any reason, wrongdoing, banishment, or any condemnation that one might receive. The said monies could not be taken as security for any debt, nor for dowry, nor could any exaction be made on them. It was licit for anyone to be able to sell and transfer them, and these privileges, security and gift [i.e. interest] the recipient would have like the first owner."

described the interest as a reward, *guiderdone*, derived from income from excise duties, *gabelle* (Giovanni Villani 1990, *Nuova cronica* 3.384). If creditors had lent to the commune without the expectation of receiving interest payments, returns on their loans could be described as gifts. This was not, however, an uncontroversial position as certain theologians, such as John Klenkock (d. 1374) and Guido de Belloreguardo (d. 1377), denied any right to payments of increments, even on compulsory loans, as this was usurious and encouraged greed (see Kirshner 1970, 121–122; Armstrong 2003, 6). Matteo's real concern over the legitimacy of the Commune's fiscal actions and for his fellow citizen creditors' consciences was in the area we might call in contemporary financial terminology the secondary market. After the initial restructuring of the debt, Florence had decided against repaying capital and made the unpaid citizen loans permeant interest-carrying credits to the Commune which could be bought and sold on the market. This led to the flaring up of a theological dispute, which Matteo shows was a concern to himself, his fellow citizens, and leading mendicant authorities in the city:

> About these contracts of buyers [of public debt shares] many questions were posed in Florence between 1353–4: was the purchase licit without required restitution or not? Again, was it licit that the purchaser makes [the purchase] with a view to receiving the profit [*utile*] that the Comune ordered to the creditors. [Was it licit] if the 100 florins lent to the Comune were purchased for 25 gold florins, or more or less as was their course [i.e. market price]? The opinion of the theologians and legists in many disputations were varied. One held that it was illicit and required restitution, the other not. And the friars preached on it differently, those of the order of St. Domenic said that it could not be done licitly, the Augustinians argued the same as them. The friars minor preached that it could be done. And for this reason the people were left in profound obscurity. (Matteo Villani 1995, *Cronica* 1.460–2)

Villani's account is interesting as it evidences a lay reception of what the key issues were in the theological debate (for their accuracy and a more detailed account of the terms of the dispute see Kirshner 1984; Armstrong 2003, 70–78). It likewise articulates his own and his fellow citizens' personal stakes in the contention. Villani portrayed the dispute as centring around the Dominican Piero Strozzi (d. 1362) and the Franciscan Francesco da Empoli (d. 1370). Villani's verdict was that Piero, who argued the contracts were illicit, had failed to demonstrate this "clearly." In contrast, Francesco is portrayed as having greater experience in disputation with masters of divinity on the matter and with "diligence" and "clarity" he preached and wrote that these contracts were licit; therefore, the contract did not require restitution from those who made these purchases, "who could do so without opposition to his conscience" (Villani 1995, *Cronica* 1.462). The surviving accounts of their opinions show that central to the dispute was that Francesco defended the right of creditors to receive *interesse* whereas Strozzi accepted the right of citizens to receive a *dono* for their services, with the right to a gift being non-transferrable and therefore excluding the legitimacy of purchasers to receive compensation (Armstrong 2003, 75). Although Villani was more favourable to Francesco's judgement, he represents the compensation to creditors as both gift and *interesse*.

Matteo states Francesco disseminated his judgement to all the orders and preached what he wrote. However, Villani recounts, many preachers and their masters refused to alter their position that purchases of credits on the market required restitution. Because of this "many remained in doubt over these contracts" (Villani 1995, *Cronica* 1.462). Despite this, Villani claims, because many Florentines were in clear agreement with Francesco they bought and sold titles in the debt without reprehension from their conscience, "trading like any other trader" (Villani 1995, *Cronica* 1.462). Villani states if the contract was usurious, it was the duty of preachers to disprove those who maintained the opposite and their responsibility to draw people from error:

> If it was licit, considering men are desirous to make money (*guadagnare*) it is evil to cast them in suspicion and contaminate their conscience of that which is licit through unreasonable sermons. (Villani 1995, *Cronica* 1.462)

Theological censure of market activity if not rationally explicable to the laity, Matteo argued, is immoral as there exists a shared set of commercial profit-seeking instincts amongst Florentine citizens (for the general medieval roots of this idea, see Nederman 2003).

Prices, Investment Behaviour, and Ethics

That government obligations could be purchased at prices below par on the market by investors seeking a profit through exploiting much higher yields than the original five per cent interest was a particular concern for theologians and jurists. Florentine chronicles described how citizen investors responded to depressed prices to maximise their return on investment. They also show how the communal authorities reasoned and made assumptions about citizen-investor behaviour in order to raise capital. Returning to Matteo Villani's chronicle, he presented an account of the establishment of the Monte Uno Tre (1358). This Monte was created by the Commune, according to Matteo, to "preserve *suo stato*" and finance defence from the mercenary companies at a time when customs revenue was low. This new Monte sought to avoid recourse to forced loans by raising voluntary credit. In order to attract investments a 100 florin loan was recorded as a 300 florin loan. The creditor would therefore receive a much higher return on his investment (the right to three times the nominal interest). As Matteo shows, this made the government debt a very attractive site for investment. Unlike in his earlier discussion of Monte credits, where he felt it was wrong to challenge the legitimacy of profit-seeking in the debt market, he was critical of the social and spiritual consequences of raising capital with such high-interest rates. He complained that lending to the city was now motivated by extreme greed rather than civic charity or affection for the republic; this shifted the city's ancient customs from commerce to usury (Matteo Villani 1995, *Cronica* 2.218–19).

Baldassare Bonaiuti (1336–1385) also described how the Florentine government could manage the debt through knowledge of how citizens would respond to the possibility of profiting from exploiting the difference between the face value of credits and their actual market price. He gave both an account of how discounting the price of government securities was used to attract capital in the Monte Uno Tre as well as the Monte Uno Due (1362). With regard to 1362 Florence needed to raise money for the Pisan war. Bonaiuti states the Commune recognised there was a general sense amongst citizens that being forced to lend at five per cent was considered an injustice, however, the ability to vary the interest rate was limited by laws that had sought to secure the trust of creditors by restricting adjustments to the terms on which capital was held in the Monte. To navigate this it was decided to issue new credits at a discounted price, such that a 100 Florin loan with five per cent interest would be sold at the discounted price of 50 Florins but, this loan would retain the face value five per cent coupon payment, which represented a current yield of 10%. When discussing the problems that stemmed from the Uno Tre and Uno Due, Bonaiuti observed how high yields were successful in raising capital, as voluntary investors were attracted by the rate of return. Although in effect, this moved capital away from commercial investment to the government debt market and entailed very high carrying charges for the Commune (Bonaiuti 1903–1955, *Cronaca fiorentina* 384–385). Bonaiuti also recorded how the government introduced a tax on exchanging Monte credits to reduce speculative trading on future returns (Kirshner 1970, 21; Armstrong 2003, 40).

The impact of humanism on Florentine historiography erased the moral and theological controversy from new descriptions of the monti. Leonardo Bruni (1370–1444) in his *History of the Florentine People*, despite his heavy use of the Villani brothers' chronicles, omitted Matteo's record of the controversy and personal complaints about usurious yields. He replaced it with a Ciceronian legitimation of the centrality of the Monte Comune to the Republic—it was one of the "foundations of the Republic" (Bruni 2001–2007, *History* 2.302)—and a more mechanical explanation of how it operated. Bruni stated that trade in Monte credits was like that for any other merchandise, with the price of the titles being determined by "time, investor confidence and yield" (Bruni 2001–2007, *History* 2.302)[3] Bruni's secularised treatment can be observed to be tacitly criticised by the Dominican Archbishop of Florence Antonino Pierozzi (1389–1459), when in his *Chronicon* of 1456 he copied Bruni's description of the Monte but restored Matteo Villani's choice to report the controversy—no doubt because he himself had dealt with the matter in his *Summa theologica*. He described how the price of credits changed in correspondence with war and peace. Antonino stated that with regard to the market and the right to acquire the credits' interest payments "there were many doubts" (Antoninus 1484, *Chronicon* fol. 107r). The *Chronicon* acknowledged how it was contentions whether one could sell the right to the interest of forced loans.

In the sixteenth century, Benedetto Varchi (1504–1563) in his *Storia Fiorentina* (1546) returned to the monti, following their general absence

[3] Trans. Hankins.

from the later fifteenth-century humanist histories of Poggio Bracciolini (1380–1459) and Bartolomeo Scala (1430–1497), and in distinction from his contemporaries Niccolò Machiavelli (1469–1527) and Donato Giannotti (1492–1573) who cast their more detailed scrutiny instead on the debts of Genoa and Venice, respectively. Like Bruni, Varchi omitted a description of the theological contentions surrounding the debt market. This would only reappear in Scipione Ammirato's (1531–1601) *Istorie fiorentine*, where he wryly remarked the controversy had only flared up in a moment of idleness following war, which led people to pay attention to a religious dispute (Ammirato 1848, *Istorie fiorentine* part 1 vol. 4 186). Varchi instead used the fiscal reforms of the Decima and Monte in 1532, which he framed as responses to war and plague that had led to a dearth of workers, high labour costs, and suppressed commerce, to present a history of the origins of Florentine monti and description of investor rationality (Varchi 1858, *Storia fiorentina* 3.20–31). In his account he explains what forms the price of Monte credits and how investors operate in the market. Varchi cautions that in order to analyse the return from these funds, the *paghe*, one has to look beyond their instituted rates reflected in their names, i.e., the "Monte of 3%." The size of *paghe* (understood as yield rather than nominal coupon), whether they were high or low, he states, depends on their public reputation. This was based on their expected return that depended on Monte legislation or the scarcity of specie. During peace, when commerce is not impeded and there is an abundance of money, the Monte earns reputation ("acquista riputazione") amongst citizens and they are worth their face value, this means the *paghe* are small. In contrast, when there is a scarcity of money ("carestia di danari"), which happens during war and sedition when citizens hold on tight to their money, commerce decreases and the reputation of the Monte falls (presumably because little money is spent on goods, reducing the *gabelle* which serviced the debt) and the credits are worth little. This is when the *paghe* are large as the capital does not cost the investor much. It is this movement, he states, which explains the trade in Monte credits (Varchi 1858, *Storia fiorentina* 3.28).

A Regressive or Charitable Institution?

Although Matteo Villani described Florentines as enthusiastic investors in the debt due to their natural propensity to seek money, fellow chroniclers represented the socially contested nature of the monti. In narratives of the Ciompi revolt of 1378 we see how regressive facets of the monti made the institution a target. Indirect consumption taxes paid at a flat rate by citizens and non-citizens serviced the interest of creditors. An anonymous chronicler of the Ciompi revolt recorded how the revolt on 25 July attacked the fiscal institutions of the Republic, such as the gabelles and Monte, by seeking to reduce the duties on grain and flour and suspend interest payments on the Monte (*Cronaca terza d'Anonimo* in Scaramella 1934, 130).[4] Alamanno Acciaioli (fl. 1378) reports how it was decided to replace interest with capital repayment so that creditors no longer held capital in the debt (Acciaioli *Cronaca* in Scaramella 1934, 28). Another chronicler states the Ciompi planned to replace citizen loans with a proportional direct property tax, the *estimo* (*Cronaca Seconda d'Anonimo* in Scaramella 1934, 111). One sympathetic chronicler to the Ciompi records how it would have been a death penalty to discuss forced loans (*prestanze*) without an *estimo* in Florence (*Cronaca Prima d'Anonimo* in Scaramella 1934, 87).[5] Machiavelli's *Istorie fiorentine* noted how the representatives of the plebian revolt in their designs to seize the Republic demanded the Signoria legislate "that the Monte will end its interest payments, returning only capital" to the benefit of their specific supporters (Machiavelli 1988, *Istorie*, 126).[6]

Despite the system of monti being clearly favourable to the interests of elements of the elite rich in liquid wealth, investment in the debt was not an exclusive preserve of the wealthiest citizens. Several diaries and chronicles celebrate the social function played by the market in government credit. Bonaiuti argued the stakes were so high in overturning the Ciompi's monti reforms because it concerned "a large sum of money and the number of men and women [investors] was so big" (Bonaiuti 1903–1955, *Cronaca* 329). In Matteo Villani's complaint that widows who invested in the high returns of the Monte Uno Tre were "taking little care of their

[4] See in idem, *Lettera d'anonimo sul tumulto dei Ciompi*, on the third demand of the popolo minuto in their petition of 22 July, 146: "If someone is owed by the Comune, they will be restituited in 12 years, every year a penny per shilling."

[5] On the deliberations to return to the use of the estimo 21 October, see idem, 87: "Ancora sì si fece un consiglio di popolo e di comune: che si dovesse fare l'estimo nella città di Firenze, sì com'egli si fa nel contado; a pena la testa chi ragionasse di fare prestanza niuna se non per estimo. Così si vinse per lo consiglio del popolo e del comune, e ch'el monte non rendesse, se non fatto l'estimo com'è detto."

[6] Trans. Banfield and Mansfield.

souls, so long as the Monte attended to their own assets," he drew attention to the significant presence of women investors in the funded debt (Matteo Villani 1995, *Cronica* 2.219). Securities in the republican debts were often used as financial instruments to provide a stable income to the investor and were bought by those interested in smoothing income over the life-cycle (see Shaw 2018) or making endowments as they were seen as stable and reliable forms of investment. Recipients of government obligations, tied into political circuits of credit, included brides (as part of their dowry), widows, orphans, and religious foundations such as monasteries and hospitals. The impact of price movements in the market for government debt, in particular collapses in value, were described through the presentation of the civic bonds that connected these instruments to charitable institutions and the vulnerable who were dependent on them for alms. Descriptions moved the moral justification of these instruments away from the pursuit of the common good in matters of military expediency and the preservation of the economic interests of creditors to a conception of the common good concerned for the provision of the poor or vulnerable.

Giovanni Rucellai's (1403–1481) description of the creation of the Monte delle Doti (1425) emphasised the importance of government credits for Florentine families and women. This was an institution that allowed fathers at the birth of a daughter to invest in a communal fund to provide for their future marriage. The investment was released as principal and compound interest for the dowry once the daughters consummated their marriage (Molho 1994, 27–79). The credits were used to pay off the capital of the Monte Comune and facilitate the raising of a dowry in a period where dowry inflation was harming the ability of families to marry their daughters (Kirshner and Molho 1978). Rucellai described the fund as "a great adaption for citizens and subjects, and a profit to the commune. Through it huge dowries are given, more than in any other age" (Rucellai 2013, *Zibaldone* 181). Benedetto Dei lauded the Monte delle Doti "a beautiful discovery of great profit and advantage to the Florentine nation" (Dei 1984, *Cronica* 78); it was an institution that elicited civic pride as he claimed it was unique amongst the Italian republics. The fund welded the exigencies of public finance and Florence's war machine to families' private financial needs for planning and effecting marriage alliances.

We can see parallel concerns in linking government obligations to dowries and charitable provision if we look at Venice for comparison.

Girolamo Priuli lamented how the battle of Agnadello lead to "the ruin of the Venetian state," ushering a collapse in the market for Monte Nuovo credits, which had plummeted to prices sixty per cent below par (Priuli 1912–1941, *Diarii* 4.16). Priuli argued it was impossible to judge the full impact of the closure of the Camera of the Monte Nuovo on the city as so many classes and sections of Venetian society had invested and placed their hopes in the debt: "how many commissaries for the poor, widows, wards, monasteries, hospitals, alms, craftsmen, rich, mediocre, poor, nobles, citizens, and *popolari* all of whom had placed their meagre capital in this Camera for the preservation of their own life, that of their children and family in accordance with their status" (Priuli 1912–1941, *Diarii* 4.16). The collapse had, therefore, not only devastated commercial profit and livelihoods based on the investment of capital in the Venetian state, but also the charitable and religious establishments of Venice, as well as disrupt Venetian marriage strategies: "how many poor maidens and virgins who hoped to get married had to agree to another match" (Priuli 1912–1941, *Diarii* 4.16).

Conclusion

Florentine civic chroniclers and historians from the fourteenth to the sixteenth century provide a window into how problems of public finance were conceptualised within broader and complex frameworks of moral and religious ideas. Certain authors, however, were unconcerned with relating activity in the market for government obligations to moral-theological concerns. At times they described creditor motivations as distinct and autonomous from religious norms. As Matteo Villani's description of the Monte and the usury controversy makes clear, moral economy in this context cannot be understood as a unitary system of shared beliefs by all members of a society relating to market activities, nor as a language of economics that can be entirely subsumed to the vocabulary of scholastic theologians and legists. In his account, Florentines were profit-seeking but this was not a vision positing that citizens were or ought to be profit maximisers. Gains ought to be moderate and profitable lending should be accompanied by charitable intentions towards the well-being of the political community. Nor should financial investment be at the expense of the commercial exchange of merchandise. Although Villani presented citizen economic activity somewhat in parallel to the settlement of questions of conscience, with adherence to theological positions following existing behaviour and values, his description was full of normative prejudices regarding economic behaviour. Even if his outlook was unashamedly commercial, he had absorbed a concern with usury and avarice framed around intention and excessive profit in relationship to the common good. Some chroniclers and historians consciously choose to excise reports of the theological controversy surrounding interest-carrying public loans and their exchange that had been central in their source material and remained a lively and contentious issue. Villani's contemporary Baldassare Bonaiuti offers an interesting point of comparison, where concerns over the debt market were not tied to the usury controversy but were framed with reference to concerns over the burden of debt and the social impact of speculation. Fiscal-political description and analysis were bound with the question of the preservation of the republic, a concern that had its own moral emphases and logic.

Aspects of the humanist cultural milieux of figures such as Leonardo Bruni and Benedetto Varchi, as well as their lay notarial formation, may in part explain a secularisation of their economic narratives—as too might their literary ambitions of providing official historiography that excised overly contentious economic questions. Their descriptions of the prices and trade in Monte credits omitted reference to theological doctrine and contention over just price and usury. In Bruni's ideological history of the Florentine *popolo* we see in his description of the Monte market something coming close, albeit on a small and singular case, to Thompson's characterisation of Adam Smith's political economy as "disinfested of intrusive moral imperatives" (Thompson 1993, 268), which is of course not to say either were disinterested with morality, but that economics could be described "mechanically." Yet the absence of economic theology in Bruni and Varchi was not an absence of moral economy. These historians articulated complex systems of values, rights, and privileges that were at the core of what it meant to be a citizen in a republic. Their descriptions of capital markets and participants' behaviour were not external to a broader sphere of ethico-political action.

All the above history writers by no means offer objective reports on the economic values of their fellow citizens. Their accounts are an important reminder that we approach late medieval and early modern moral economy through the eyes of an author who has his own ambitions and class prejudices when describing social reality. Medieval chronicles do, however, occasion a study of moral economy beyond the opinions of an intellectual elite of theologians, canonists, and romanists. Their portrayals of fiscal systems were embedded in discourses that were inherently normative, shaped by their authors' social-cultural formation and proximity to ruling groups. Many chroniclers, however, were not in any simple sense ideologues for the governing class and we find in them evidence of the contested nature of the republic's fiscal institutions that offer traces of counter-hegemonic beliefs. In all these cases, even where the representation of citizen behaviour seems distant from scholastic moral teaching, and may even seem to share some characteristics with *homo economicus*, these chroniclers' and historians' beliefs and analyses were part of larger ethical and religious structures of belief, where profit making actions were seldom legitimised outside of a framework of virtuous action, where the private accumulation of wealth was legitimate when understood for its potential to render benefits to the community and an individual's soul through good deeds.

References

Ammirato, Scipione. 1848. *Istorie fiorentine*. Ed. F. Ranalli. Florence: V. Batelli e Compagni.

Antoninus, Florentinus. 1484. *Chronicon*. Nuremberg: Koberger.

Armstrong, Lawrin. 2003. *Usury and Public Debt in Early Renaissance Florence: Lorenzo Ridolfi on the Monte Comune*. Toronto: Pontifical Institute of Medieval Studies.

Armstrong, Lawrin. 2004. Usury, Conscience and Public Debt: Angelo Corbinelli's Testament of 1419. In *A Renaissance of Conflicts*, ed. John A. Marino and Thomas Kuehn, 173–240. Toronto: Centre for Reformation and Renaissance Studies.

Armstrong, Lawrin. 2016. *The Idea of a Moral Economy: Gerard of Siena on Usury, Restitution and Prescription*. Toronto: University of Toronto Press.

Bauch, Martin, and Gerrit Jasper Schenk, eds. 2019. *The Crisis of the 14th Century, Teleconnections Between Environmental and Societal Change?* Berlin: De Gruyter.

Bonaiuti, Baldassarre. 1903–1955. Cronaca fiorentina di Marchionne di Coppo Stefani. Ed. Niccolò Rodolico, *Rerum italicarum scriptores 2 serie*, 30.1. Città di Castello: Coi Tipi dell'editore S di Lapi – Bologna: Zanichelli.

Bruni, Leonardo. 2001–2007. *History of the Florentine People*. Ed. and trans. James Hankins, 3 vols. Cambridge, MA: Harvard University Press.

Cohn, Samuel K. 2006. *Lust for Liberty: The Politics of Social Revolt in Medieval Europe, 1200–1400: Italy, France, and Flanders*. Cambridge, MA: Harvard University Press.

Cohn, Samuel K. 2021. *Popular Protest and Ideals of Democracy in Late Renaissance Italy*. Oxford: Oxford University Press.

Davis, James. 2011. *Medieval Market Morality*. Cambridge: Cambridge University Press.

Dei, Benedetto. 1984. *La cronica*. Ed. Roberto Barducci. Florence, 1984.

Jordan, William Chester. 1996. *The Great Famine: Northern Europe in the Early Fourteenth Century*. Princeton NJ: Princeton University Press.

Kaye, Joel. 1998. Monetary and Market Consciousness in Thirteenth and Fourteenth Century Europe. In *Ancient and Medieval Economic Ideas and Concepts of Social Justice*, ed. S. Todd Lowry and Barry Gordon, 371–404. Leiden: Brill.

Kirshner, Julius. 1970. From Usury to Public Finance: The Ecclesiastical Controversy Over the Public Debts of Florence, Genoa and Venice (1300–1500). PhD diss. Colombia University.

Kirshner, Julius. 1982. Reading Bernardino's Sermon on the Public Debt. In *Atti del simposio internazionale caterinianobernardiniano, Siena 17–20 aprile 1980*, ed. Domenico Maffei and Paolo Nardi, 547–622. Siena: Accademia senese degli Intronati.

Kirshner, Julius. 1983. Storm Over the Monte Comune: Genesis of the Moral Controversy Over the Public Debt of Florence. *Archivum Fratrum Praedicatorum* 53: 219–276.

Kirshner, Julius. 1984. "Ubi est ille?" Franco Sacchetti on the Monte Comune of Florence. *Speculum* 59 (3): 556–584.

Kirshner, Julius, and Anthony Molho. 1978. The Dowry Fund and the Marriage Market in Early Quattrocento Florence. *The Journal of Modern History* 50 (3): 403–438.

Machiavelli, Niccolò. 1988. *Florentine Histories*. Trans. Laura F. Banfield and Harvey C. Mansfield. Princeton, NJ: Princeton University Press.

Molho, Anthony. 1994. *Marriage Alliance in Late Medieval Florence*. Cambridge, MA: Harvard University Press.

Nanni, Paolo. 2019. Facing Crisis in Medieval Florence. In *The Crisis of the 14th Century: Teleconnections Between Environmental and Societal Change?* ed. Martin Bauch and Gerrit Jasper Schenk. Berlin: De Gruyter.

Nederman, Cary J. 2003. Commercial Society and Republican Government in the Latin Middle Ages: The Economic Dimensions of Brunetto Latini's Republicanism. *Political Theory* 31 (5): 644–663.

Priuli, Girolamo. 1912–1941. *I diarii di Girolamo Priuli*. 4 vols, ed. Arturo Segre and Roberto Cessi, *Rerum italicarum scriptores 2 serie*, 24.3.

Rucellai, Giovanni di Pagolo. 2013. *Zibaldone*. Ed. Gabriella Battista. Florence: SISMEL/Edizioni del Galluzzo.

Salimbene de Adam. 1966. *Cronica*, 2 vols, ed. Giuseppe Scalia. Bari: Laterza.

Scaramella, Gino, (ed.). 1934. *Il tumulto dei Ciompi: Cronache e memoria* in *Rerum italicarum scriptores 2 serie*. 18.3: Bologna: Zanichelli.
Shaw, J. E. 2018. Women, Credit and Dowry in Early Modern Italy. In *Women and Credit in Pre-Industrial Europe. Early European Research*, ed. E. Dermineur, 173–202. Turnhout: Brepols.
Tawney, R.H. 1926 [2015]. *Religion and the Rise of Capitalism*. London: Verso.
Thompson, E.P. 1971. The Moral Economy of the English Crowd in the Eighteenth Century. *Past and Present* 50: 76–136.
Thompson, E.P. 1993. *Customs in Common*. London: Penguin Books.
Varchi, Benedetto. 1858. *Storia fiorentina*. Ed. Gaetano Milanesi, 3 vols. Florence: Le Monnier.
Villani, Giovanni. 1990. *Nuova cronica*. Ed. Giuseppe Porta, 3 vols. Parma: Fondazione Pietro Bembo.
Villani, Matteo. 1995. *Cronica*. Ed. Giuseppe Porta, 2 vols. Parma: Fondazione Pietro Bembo.
Wood, Diana. 2012. *Medieval Economic Thought*. Cambridge: Cambridge University Press.
Zabbia, Marino. 1999. *I notai e la cronachistica cittadina italiana nel trecento*. Bologna: Istituto storico italiano per il Medioevo.
Zabbia, Marino. 2020. Matteo Villani. *Dizionario Biografico degli italiani*, vol. 99. Rome, Istituto della Enciclopedia italiana, 338–341.

PART II

Early Modern Period

CHAPTER 7

The Moral Economy of Epidemics: Emergency, Charitable Institutions and Poor Relief in Early Modern Italian Plague Regulations

Lorenzo Coccoli

Introduction

Commenting in *The New Yorker* on the introduction of mandatory self-confinement during the 2003 SARS epidemic in Singapore, Ali Khan—the then member of the committee of experts sent by the WHO to cooperate in the elaboration of an effective national health crisis management plan—thus recalled the logistical difficulties involved in the adoption of mandatory quarantine measures: "'The moment you hold'em, you

An earlier version of this article has already appeared in Italian in *Politics. Rivista di studi politici* 15 (1) (2021): 75–91.

L. Coccoli (✉)
Università degli Studi dell'Insubria, Varese, Italy
e-mail: coccoli@hotmail.com

T. Skambraks and M. Lutz (eds.), *Reassessing the Moral Economy*, Palgrave Studies in Economic History,
https://doi.org/10.1007/978-3-031-29834-9_6

own'em', is what we say. You've got to feed these people, see to their health care, make sure they are housed and clothed. Who takes care of them? Who pays for them? If you're the government ministry enforcing self-quarantine, you do" (Quammen 2020).

This could seem an obvious, even trivial answer. But its apparent insignificance risks diverting attention from the seriousness of the two questions that precede it. In fact, on closer inspection, there does not seem to be any logical or natural necessity linking a governmental decision to segregate a part of the population in order to prevent the spread of contagious diseases with the related obligation to care for the people thus segregated. One can easily conjure up a futuristic dystopia in which a cruel totalitarian regime forces its citizens to lock themselves in their homes without providing them with any kind of material support, and leaves them to starve—something similar, say, to the situation in which the protagonists of José Saramago's *Blindness* find themselves, forcibly confined in a former asylum and soon abandoned to their fate by the authorities. But then, is there really any need for that level of imagination? Between 1940 and 1943, almost half a million Polish Jews were "quarantined" in the Warsaw ghetto, the establishment of which had been justified, among other reasons, by the need to avert an alleged epidemic threat. What followed is, unfortunately, well known: not only did the German General Government do nothing to provide for the internees, but it also actively impeded any significant supply of food and medicine, condemning thousands to death from disease and starvation (Roland 1992). Other, less tragic examples could be adduced, but the main point should already be clear: that an obligation exists for rulers to support the people affected by their health policies, is by no means axiomatic. *Why*, after all, should they take care of them? *Why* should they pay for them?

This is not to suggest that there are no plausible answers to these questions, but only that these answers are far from self-evident. Although we usually take it for granted, there is in fact no direct and necessary causal relationship between the socio-economic implications of a given epidemic episode (or any other natural disaster) and the measures that governments may or may not take to alleviate their impact. In order to connect the former to the latter and build a stronger explanatory chain, some additional links are needed. In this contribution, I intend to draw attention to *one* of these missing links, thus rescuing it from its relative invisibility. This is where E. P. Thompson's well-known formula comes into play: I propose to label this additional *explanans* the "moral economy of epidemics", using the term to refer to a set of religious, legal, moral and political practices and values, that are at least partially shared by rulers and ruled, and that compel the former—even if within certain limits—to provide relief to the latter in time of health emergencies. Although this study is limited to the experience of early modern Italian cities, I am confident that the same explanatory model may also prove useful when applied to the analysis of similar situations in different contexts.

I start with a brief methodological excursus on the use of Thompson's categories, and the adjustments they needed in order to be employed here. I then show how the institutional response given by some of the most relevant political realities of early modern Italy to recurrent plague-induced crises, almost invariably included an attempt to organise some form of aid to the hardest-hit sections of the population. Finally, I proceed to disentangle—without any claim to completeness—the different and sometimes conflicting values that explicitly or implicitly underlay these emergency relief schemes, while at the same time allowing their recipients some room for manoeuvre. It is here that the major role played by religious principles in shaping this peculiar version of the moral economy becomes apparent.

What Kind of Moral Economy?

After an earlier appearance in the pages of *The Making of the English Working Class* (1963), the notion of moral economy was first extensively discussed by E. P. Thompson in his much-celebrated article of 1971, *The Moral Economy of the English Crowd in the Eighteenth Century*, and subsequently added from there—although not without further discussion and different modifications—to the methodological toolbox of the humanities (Götz 2015). Thompson's aim was twofold: first, he wished to restore rationality to the food riots that had swept England in the second half of the eighteenth century, by rediscovering their inherent logic. Second, he wanted to break away from the then-current economic and biological determinism that understood them as mere physiological reactions to misery and starvation. According to Thompson, the crowd attacked bakeries and mills not because it was driven by blind desperation and empty stomachs, but because it was endowed with its own moral code that gave method, legitimacy and meaning to its actions. There were no "rebellions of the belly", but rather a "more complex, culturally-mediated function", irreducible to "the primary stimulus of 'distress'"

(Thompson 1971, 77–78). Behind those "risings of the poor" lay in fact a sense of violated justice, and the urgency of a wrong to be righted.

Thompson later cautioned against turning the moral economy into a *passepartout* for all occasions and recalled how its original context of application was limited to a given practice in a given period: i.e., popular conflicts over market access to essential goods at a time when liberal deregulation and incipient capitalism were disrupting age-old arrangements supposedly sanctioned by secular customs. However, he did not exclude the possibility of an extensive use of the notion, knowing that, as with all inventions, even conceptual ones invariably end up exceeding the range of uses foreseen by their inventor. He just warned that if the term was to be expanded beyond its initial meaning, a redefinition of it would then become necessary to avoid the risk of "some loss of focus" (Thompson 1993, 338). This is what I intend to do here. I will keep some elements of the original proposal, while revising others and adding new ones, in order to fine-tune it to the specific topic of these pages.

Thompson's lesson has at least one core content that is important to retain. His moral economy consists in fact of an essential attempt at denaturalisation: it breaks the stimulus–response causal relation by inserting in the middle of it a symbolic transmission belt made up of beliefs, customs and cultural traditions, but also "deep emotions", "claims" and a sense of "outrage" (ibid.). In the mutual confrontation between rulers and ruled—of which riots represent only one of many possible declinations—there is nothing immediate. Instead, there is a whole host of beliefs and practices, strategies and tactics, values and representations that are more or less shared on both sides of that relationship. It constitutes an intermediate space that provides those involved with leeway for agency and the ability to choose, freeing them from the force of gravity that would have them nailed to a single deterministic course of action and handing them back to the contingency of political deliberation.

However, with respect to the Thompsonian formulation, some modifications are required here. First, a shift in emphasis is needed. In his 1971 article, the moral economy was mostly the business of the dominated. In line with the methodological programme of history from below, Thompson's angle coincided almost entirely with that of the "English crowd": it was its moral logic that he was trying to uncover, just as it was its revolts that he was trying to explain. And yet, this "consistent theoretical model" was presented as "a selective reconstruction of the paternalist one" of the elites (Thompson 1971, 98). The effectiveness of popular "direct action" and its claim to legitimacy depended, in other words, on the fact that the expectations and ethical concerns of the "plebs" were at least in part the same as those of the "patricians" in charge of managing markets and preserving order. A common normative ground ensured that the demands coming from "below"—even when expressed in the language of tumults—could be accepted by those "above" as partially justified, and sometimes translated into special regulatory provisions for the benefit of the governed. The circulation of a somewhat shared religious and political culture provided the crowd with the fulcrum on which to rest the lever of its claims, an instrument of pressure echoed on the other side of the social spectrum by the *noblesse oblige*. I am not interested here in establishing whether the (logical or chronological) primacy in the construction of this collective cultural *milieu* belongs to one party or the other, a question that risks slipping into "one of a political chicken and egg" (Bohstedt 1992, 273). It suffices to gesture towards the existence of this space of communication and bargaining among different ends of social power relations, a middle ground that was also the "theatre" in which "some reciprocity in the relations between rich and poor" could be staged (Thompson 1974, 395). In this sense, a good definition of moral economy will have to include, in Didier Fassin's words, "the production, distribution, circulation and use of moral sentiments, emotions and values, norms and obligations in the social space", thus extending its scope beyond just the "dominated groups" (Fassin 2009, 1257).

But we need to stretch the notion in other directions too. Thompson basically limited his formula to the food market. However, as we shall see, this was not the only field in which economic relations could be "regulated according to non-monetary norms" (Thompson 1993, 340). Under more or less exceptional circumstances, the "moral" factor could also intervene in facilitating access to very different kinds of goods and services (health, housing, justice) by loosening the criteria presiding over the allocation of community resources, which normally followed the stricter logic—though always tempered by political and status considerations—of supply and demand. Moreover, this alternative regulatory standard does not appear to have been evoked only at the time of the transition from *ancien régime* paternalism to eighteenth-century liberalism. Although Thompson believed that moral economy had been "summoned into being in resistance to the economy of the 'free market'" (ibid.), it seems more convenient to detach it from any exact chronological placement. Not only does moral economy predate by centuries of the advent of political economy, but it also survives it. Better still, moral economy and political economy do not stand to each other in a relation of historical succession, but in a constant dialectic of mutual articulation and "simultaneous reconfiguration" (Fassin 2009, 1259). It is only once the notion of moral economy is liberated from the exclusive reference to a precise historical moment, that it can become a valuable analytical tool for historians of all periods to work with.

Discipline, but Not Just Punish

In the already vast and ever-growing social history scholarship on medieval and early modern epidemics, a tendency exists to observe the relationship between "the plague and the poor" (Carmichael 1986) mostly through the lens of criminal justice and the repressive power deployed by the authorities to keep marginal sectors of society in check (Pastore 1991). Emphasis is thus placed on the repeated attempts by rulers and legislators to expel or confine beggars, vagrants, prostitutes and other "undeserving poor", accusing them of contaminating—both literally and metaphorically—the social body. In what was probably the first legal treatise entirely devoted to the issues raised by epidemic occurrences (Ascheri 2020), the Pavese jurist Gianfrancesco Ripa di San Nazzaro repeated an admonition that was already more than a century old: "Whenever the threat of mephitic disease is imminent, those in charge of public affairs must banish from the city not only the pimps and harlots, but also all able-bodied beggars. They are indeed the ones who bring in the disease, and once they have introduced it, they feed it by wandering about, haunting every corner of the city, gorging themselves and leading a shameful life" (Ripa di San Nazzaro 1598, 147). In fact, health regulations issued by city authorities to deal with the emergency were often replete with harsh measures against these and other categories of undesirables. As Paul Slack puts it, "[t]here is no doubt that plague regulations were designed as more than instrumental measures against contagion. They were methods of social control" (Slack 1988, 447).

However, the dominant and still persisting (Boiteux 2007; Beauvieux 2014; Henderson 2019) interest in the disciplining, regimentation and "meticulous tactical partitioning" of society in time of plague—behind which one can perhaps recognise the influence of Michel Foucault's pages on "the plague-stricken town" in *Discipline and Punish* (1995, 195–200)—has forced another and equally relevant aspect into the background. As a matter of fact, not everything public authorities devised to manage their communities in general and the poor in particular can be reduced to punishment, confinement, exile or surveillance. Indeed, the penal facet was always a prominent feature of early modern political responses to epidemic crises, but it was never the only one. Contemporary authors were well aware of that. This is testified, for example, by Giovanni Filippo Ingrassia's much-quoted treatise on the 1575–1576 plague outbreak in Palermo. Three figures stood out on its frontispiece: a pair of bags full of money, some bonfires, and a landscape grimly dominated by the well-recognisable shapes of two or three gallows. A distich by a certain Maurizio Martelli helped make the message clearer: "*Lana, aura, et Linum captant contagia pestis / Ignis, furca, aurum sunt medicina mali*". According to Ingrassia, fire, the gallows and money were in fact the three main weapons to be used against the contagion: the first represented the need to burn and destroy all infected or infectible objects, the second embodied the punitive threat necessary to keep potential transgressors in line, while the third symbolised the large amount of resources needed to finance the city's costly health policies.

But what was all that money for? Breaking down expenditures into disaggregated items, Ingrassia listed the salaries of "guards, carters and gravediggers"; the fodder for horses and oxen used to pull carts and caskets; and the single biggest item of all, "alms (*limosine*) for the support of so many poor people" (Ingrassia 1576, 158). Starting at least from the sixteenth century, this was another fixture of almost every package of measures adopted by Italian cities in order to fight the plague and its social consequences. To those who were forced to isolate themselves in their homes because of their actual or suspected illness, the city usually delivered food and other essential goods, in case they were unable to procure them for themselves. When a general quarantine with the ensuing closure of all non-necessary economic activities was declared—a measure of last resort, but one that was employed with increasing frequency from the second half of the sixteenth century onwards—the ruling elites felt compelled to take care of all the poor in the city and the *contado* through public funds and private charitable initiatives, sometimes offering aid also in the form of cash grants.

To be sure, welfare arrangements were not always able to keep up with the emergency. This is what, for example, the apostolic nuncio lamented when he wrote to the Viceroy of Naples at the height of the 1656 plague, to denounce the misconduct of his ministers: "when some poor man's home was locked up, no thought had been given to how to feed him, so that, with greater scandal, many died of mere necessity" (cited in Calvi 1981, 442). But in most cases, the figures detailing the economic efforts put in for relief purposes were remarkable, and represented a source of civic pride for chroniclers recording them (Cohn 2010, 278–80). Thus, the Milanese Paolo Bisciola estimated at 571,032 *lire*, 14 *soldi* and 5 *denari* the costs incurred by the Treasury just to feed "the poor of the city" during the general confinement imposed from the end of October 1576 to the beginning of March 1577, and that was without counting the almost equally considerable outlay required for those of the nearby *Borgo degli Ortolani*, for "the poor clergy", and for local beggars hosted in special hospices (Bisciola 1577, n.p.). Ingrassia reported that more than 60,000 *scudi* were spent by the city of Palermo in only five months between 1575 and 1576, a significant part of which was allocated to alms for the poor (Ingrassia 1576, 235). Giovanni Francesco Fiochetto, first physician of the Duke of Savoy, recalled that between 1630 and 1631, 14,000 *scudi* were spent every month in Turin to support "with great charity" the poor in the lazaretto, the city and the countryside, granting them "wood, bread, wine, meat, cheese, oil, butter" (Fiochetto 1631, 142–43).

Likely exaggerations aside, such impressive figures can be explained by the large number of people to be assisted. According to Giacomo Filippo Besta's account of the 1576–1577 plague in Milan, at the beginning of the quarantine the city deputies counted 42,710 paupers to be fed at home, not including the 5,000 people in hospitals and temporary huts built outside the city walls to house for the sick, and the 1,000 religious in convents and monasteries (Besta 1578, 24*v*). During the Florentine epidemic of 1630–1631, an official document reported the existence of 30,452 individuals in need of assistance, out of a resident population of 61,408 (Henderson 2019, 136). These somehow striking figures may perhaps require some terminological clarification. In the *ancien régime* vocabulary, "the poor" were not just the absolutely destitute and needy. Rather, the term referred to all those propertyless people who were wholly or largely dependent on their labour for their daily survival, and were thus vulnerable to wage reductions, unemployment, illness, and other more or less predictable circumstances (Coccoli, forthcoming). It is evidently in this sense that the expression is used in the narratives we are dealing with. Thus, Bisciola could say that "the city's poor have been assisted up to these days; those, I say, who could not support themselves without working, and those who could not gain their living without their trade" (Bisciola 1577, n.p.). Reporting the concerns of the Milanese Health Board about the lot of the poorer sort in the 1630–1631 outbreak, Alessandro Tadino wrote that "since the manufacturing of silk, tissues, gold and other kinds of good was ceasing because of the disease, the poor were running the risk of dying of starvation" (Tadino 1648, 79). Here, the close relationship between poverty and labour is absolutely apparent. But the widespread currency of this association went beyond the Italian context. Musing over the disastrous social consequences of the Great Plague of London in 1665, the anonymous protagonist of Defoe's *A Journal of the Plague Year* (1722) recalled how "all Trades being stopt, Employment ceased; the Labour, and by that, the Bread of the Poor were cut off; and at first indeed, the Cries of the poor were most lamentable to hear; tho' by the Distribution of Charity, their Misery that way was greatly abated" (Defoe 2003, 93).

The supply of food and heating material was not the only form of public relief for "the poor". Sometimes the aids preceded the outbreak and were conceived in terms of prophylactic measures. In an effort to prevent the corruption of the air, which is a long-standing medical tradition considered to be one of the main causes of the spread of the disease (Snowden 2019, 14–26), the *Sanità* of Florence embarked in 1630 on a vast campaign to repair leaking cesspits and replace rotten mattresses in the poorer parishes of the city. At the beginning of September, the magistrates recorded that a total of 2,347 straw mattresses had been distributed at public expense, corresponding to approximately 3% of the resident population (Henderson 2019, 60–70).

Goods were not, however, the only object of this public liberality, which could just as often take the form of the provision of services. They were, first and foremost, services aimed at the health of the body and the soul. Physicians and surgeons were specially hired by the cities to treat the poor for free, hospitals were opened or strengthened to accommodate the sick who could not afford private care, and priests were charged with administering the last sacraments in the lazarettos (Fiochetto 1631, 170; Carmichael 1983, 519; Cipolla 2007, 63–64). But public authorities could exceptionally intervene also in the sphere of civil law, to ease the distress of those who had not been able to work during the epidemic and had thus been forced into debt or to fall behind with their rent. Thus, for example, the Senate of Milan ordered in 1576 the release of all prisoners for debt, and in 1577 it declared a six months moratorium on evictions (Centorio degli Ortensi 1579, 114 and 344–45). Similar measures were repeated half a century later, during the plague of 1630–1631 (Tadino 1648, 125–26 and 137).

Moral Bending

One thing clearly emerges from the picture sketched above: in time of health emergencies, the logic that normally governed the social distribution of goods, services and rights could be bent by direct intervention of public authorities to the benefit of the usually disadvantaged. However, the causes of this extraordinary alteration capable of temporarily reconfiguring the economic and legal field remain to be clarified.

When existing scholarship considers, albeit cursorily, this more benign aspect of plague regulations, explanations seem to oscillate between an appreciation of the special "commitment [...] to the cause of the poor" (Henderson 2019, 82) shown by private organisations or individual figures—as, for instance, those of Carlo and Federico Borromeo in sixteenth and seventeenth-century Milan, or the Grand Duke Ferdinand II in 1630 Florence—and a more functionalist approach pointing to the necessity of preventing disorders and revolts. Both solutions are not fully satisfactory, though. The first one results in an excess of personalisation, making such complex and relatively well-coordinated strategies depend on the benevolence and goodwill of isolated individuals. The second one fails to explain *why* the poor could feel entitled to revolt, and why on the other hand the response from above did not consist of mere repression. The hypothesis of a moral economy of epidemics, as previously (re)defined, helps solve these problems. The idea is that, in time of plague outbreaks, the existence of a certain set of partially shared norms, constraints and values obliged the rulers—no matter if through social pressure or intimate personal conviction—to take care of the ruled, legitimising the latter to rise up if they believed that this implicit social pact had been violated.

What elements did this set consist of? There is obviously no simple answer to that question. First, values and norms are not inert entities with well-defined boundaries: they are cultural and historical artefacts, entangled with one another and characterised by ever-shifting contours, that can therefore be disentangled only on an analytical level. Second, being the product of historically and geographically variable practices, traditions and institutions, they are also highly context-dependent: what is true for a certain region at a certain time may not be true for another region, or for the same region at a different time. Finally, moral economies are, more often than not, implicit infrastructures: they are usually taken for granted, and only rarely do social actors feel the need to make them explicit. That said, epidemic crises—as well as other situations of comparable intensity—represent one of the best opportunities to cast a glance at these otherwise invisible symbolic structures: it is when the normative subtext that tacitly regulates ordinary social exchanges comes under increasing pressure from extraordinary circumstances that it begins to emerge under the pen of the authors interested in its defence.

It is then possible to unravel the various threads that make up the fabric of the moral economy of epidemics in early modern Italian cities, following the scattered traces that appear in the sources. The religious ideal of charity was undoubtedly a prominent factor, and the traditional catalogue of the seven works of mercy definitely played a role. It is no coincidence that, as we seen above, "alms" (*limosina*) was usually the term of choice for public aid granted to individuals in need. As Colin Jones has shown with regard to pre-revolutionary France, even in normal times the "charitable imperative" to give to the poor, and the social expectations that went with it, were so powerful in Catholic countries that the line between voluntariness and obligation was actually blurred (Jones 1989). Reaffirming this imperative became all the more urgent in the exceptional time of epidemic outbreaks, when the raging disease threatened to break social ties and "destroy the illusion of paternalistic care on the part of the rich for the poor" (Pullan 1992, 117). Indeed, as Lodovico Antonio Muratori still recalled at the beginning of the eighteenth century, it was absolutely legitimate for those who had the means to try to save themselves by fleeing the plague-ridden city. They should not, however, make the mistake of believing themselves

> exempted also from certain laws of Christian charity. Since beggars, craftsmen, and so many others who are used to earning their bread day by day remain in the cities, because they lack the opportunity to go elsewhere; and since, conversely, only the better off are able to seek asylum in the countryside, everyone sees how the poor people of the city are going to be left with no one to give them alms and provide them with work [...]. Thus, it is not only a counsel, but also a clear precept of Christian charity, that even when the citizens are outside the city, they have to help

> and succour those left behind in such extreme necessity [...]. (Muratori 1714, 33–34)

Moreover, in its Catholic understanding, charity was not just a binary relationship. The act of giving and receiving was always mediated by the divine presence, since it was before God that men earned credit for their good works. Feeding the hungry at public expense could thus be seen as the best way to appease "the righteous wrath of God against our sins" (Tadino 1648, 10). When one considers that God's wrath had long figured as the main cause of the plague (Snowden 2019, 10–13), while still playing a central role in seventeenth- and even eighteenth-century treatises, it becomes easy to understand why the relief of the poor was deemed to be so important not only for their survival, but for the survival of the city as a whole.

Legal and political representations also had their say. Arguing in favour of the imposition of a general *collecta* to finance public assistance when public funds were not sufficient, Ripa explained that "it is indeed in the interest of the state that the poor do not die, because without the poor the city is not complete (*perfecta*)" (Ripa di San Nazzaro 1598, 149). He referred the reader to a passage in the *Digest* (50.11.2) in which Callistratus, quoting from Plato's *Republic*, asserted that in order for a city "to be prosperous, and its people to be happy", it needed a large number of peasants, labourers and merchants to cater for its material needs. It is quite clear, then, that a very specific socio-economic reality hid behind Ripa's organicist image of the "*communitas perfecta*", one that once again confirms the modern identification of work and poverty. The poor were needed to perform those basic tasks that literally made associate life possible. This is why, as Muratori wrote, supporting them by public money "in time of contagion" was not only "an act of supreme Charity", but also "something of the highest interest, since once the craftsmen, peasants, tradesmen, and other such workers are lost, one cannot say what harm will come to those who remain alive. The head is miserable, when the members do not serve it, or it lacks them" (Muratori 1714, 136–37).

Civic pride was another relevant piece of the mosaic. The humanist ideal of honour could function as a further stimulus for rulers to keep the paternalistic machine up and running. In Centorio's words:

> Since we put every effort into enhancing and preserving in the minds of men the memory of excellent actions (as if it can last for eternity) in order

> to incite them to glorious deeds [...]. How much we must therefore, with every reason, exalt that of those who, as true lovers of their country, never abandoned it, nor failed in all its afflictions and calamities to give it all the help and assistance they were capable of. (Centorio degli Ortensi 1579, 350)

Writing in June 1630 to the College of Physicians to urge them to take better care of the poor in hospitals and lazarettos, the Milanese magistrates reminded them that, by doing so, "not only they will acquire copious merit in the eyes of God, but the city will also preserve the immortal memory of their actions and will be forever indebted to them" (Tadino 1648, 104).

Starting from the second half of the sixteenth century, prescriptions derived from medical knowledge were also increasingly relevant in determining the attention paid by local authorities to the living conditions of the poor. Helping them was no longer just a matter of charitable obligation or economic interest, but also a public health concern. Thus, for example, the *Istruzione* drafted in September 1576 by the Milanese *Sanità* and addressed to the deputies in charge of enforcing sanitary regulations in the various districts of the city, exhorted them as follows: "It will be reasonable above all to ensure that the poor do not suffer, either from lack of food or medications, so that they do not die for this reason, which otherwise might cause the air to be infected" (Centorio degli Ortensi 1579, 109). At the same time, physicians and surgeons insisted in their works on the need to guarantee "a rich and appropriate diet" for the lower sorts, not only as an act of mercy but also as a reliable method of disease management (Conforti 2006, 145).

However, it would be a mistake to look at the moral economy of epidemics as something entirely pacified, in which the poor only appear as passive objects of public benevolence. Quite on the contrary, their agency is always clearly legible even between the lines of the official discourse, where the role the threat of popular "direct action" played in political choices is undeniable. Opportunities for appropriation and conflict were everywhere. At a most basic level, an expression of this antagonistic relation can be recognised in the numerous attempts to further twist public relief to private advantage, integrating it into autonomous survival strategies. Evidence of this can be found in the repeated complaints by jurists, magistrates, and chroniclers who warned against those many who simulated symptoms of the plague in order to be fed in hospitals

(Ascheri 2020, 117–18), or who stayed "confined in their homes so as to get the daily allowance even after the quarantine period had expired" (Cipolla 1973, 77).

There were also more collective and noisier forms of negotiation and protest. According to Galeazzo Capella's account, "a very large number" of people who had been expelled from Milan in 1524 because suspected of having plague, finding nothing to eat outside, caused a "sedition" and entered the city in arms; so that the Duke, "having consideration for the poor" (as Capella euphemistically put it), ordered to feed them at public expense (Capella 1538, 82). Centorio reported that, for example, the decision of the Milanese Senate to suspend evictions for six months was taken in response to a "very big upheaval" born "among the inhabitants of the houses" who, finding themselves impoverished by the interruption of their trades, were clamouring for a reduction of rents, and for this reason "went around Milan fuelling many bad feelings and disturbances" (Centorio degli Ortensi 1579, 344–45). When, in June 1656, a palisade was erected by Roman authorities to isolate the *Trastevere* district and prevent a plague outbreak from spreading to the whole city, the people there rose up against the closure and rioted to demand adequate support (Boiteux 2007, 176 and 190).

The passage to action was not always necessary. The mere possibility of a popular uprising was often sufficient for the "moral" infrastructure to be translated into a concrete "economy"—i.e., into a redistribution of collective resources consistent with the principle of "paternalistic care on the part of the rich for the poor". Fear of riots was almost invariably one of the elements considered by rulers when deciding on a given course of action, and gave ammunition to those opposed to strict confinement and quarantine measures. Once economic activity had ceased and the poor had been forced to stay at home without any concomitant subsidy, the danger "that the plebs would riot, having nothing to live on" was just around the corner (Besta 1578, 25*r*; see also Roscio 1665, 31–32). The *provisioni* (supplies) that were to accompany generalised lockdowns were therefore essential to defuse the risk of "popular tumult" (Besta 1578, 25*v*). Or, to put it the other way around, it was the prospect of tumult that actually led to the adoption of the *provisioni*.

Conclusion

In early modern Italy, the moral economy of epidemics took shape at the intersection of two different axes. First, a network of norms, obligations and values, constantly reproduced through formal and informal channels, and circulating—despite multiple differences and variations—from one end of the social ladder to the other. Here, religion took centre stage, as the notions of charity and almsgiving stood at the heart of this normative background, but other legal, economic and medical considerations were also important. Second, the ability—or, better, the threat—of direct action by the ruled. This last aspect in particular is still largely to be explored, and it does not seem unreasonable to hope that even in this case, as has already happened with other areas of social history, further archival research can restore a meaningful voice to a supposedly inarticulate "plebs" in turmoil. What is certain is that, contrary to what was believed in a different historiographical season, the coming of the plague did not at all coincide with an alleged "muteness of the poor" (Baehrel 1952, 352).

These two facets were in a dialectical relationship with each other. The "conflicting" level interacted with the "moral" one either by modifying its internal structure and overall configuration, or by provoking its actualisation into a particular welfare policy—i.e., into a particular *economy*. Conversely, the existence of a paternalistic horizon of values made it possible to recognise as legitimate, at least in part, the poor's claim to be helped in time of need, thereby allowing them some sense of entitlement and room for protest. This was true, of course, only within certain limits: episodes of exemplary punishments inflicted upon suspected instigators of riots were not uncommon (Calvi 1981, 429; Boiteux 2007, 190). Yet, it is undeniable that this peculiar belief system helped keep the bar of tolerance relatively high, providing leeway for even vigorous expressions of discontent. Just as it is undeniable that, without those expressions of discontent, the moral economy of epidemics would probably have been bound to remain on paper.

More research is also needed to extend the scope of the analysis beyond early modern Italy. However, some general points can already be made. Firstly, it is important to notice the political relevance of public welfare measures implemented during plague outbreaks, often in conjunction with those disciplinary and repressive solutions on which scholars have traditionally focused their attention. Secondly, it must be stressed how these "charitable" policies cannot be taken for granted as requiring no explanation, nor can they be interpreted solely in terms either of the subjective generosity of their proponents or the elites' willingness to buy the silence of the poor (Baehrel 1952, 352). Instead, a set of partially shared norms must be supposed, the existence of which can account for both the obligation of the rulers to take care of their subjects and the possibilities for self-legitimation of the direct action of the ruled. Finally, as the moral economy of epidemics is highly dependent on its context, it might vary according to time, place, confessional affiliation, institutional fabric and power relations. This is to say: moral economies are entirely *historical* constructs.

This is perhaps one of the main lessons to be drawn from the Thompsonian notion, even beyond Thompson himself. Once one recognises that there is nothing "natural" in the choice of granting public aid to those who bear the brunt of epidemic outbreaks, it becomes possible both to appreciate the "cultural" and strategic factors lying behind it and to compare across time and space the changing relative weight carried by religious, economic, legal and political dimensions in determining it. "The moment you hold'em, you own'em": the same motto can mean two quite different things in, say, sixteenth-century Milan and twenty-first-century Singapore.

References

Ascheri, Mario. 2020. *Rimedi contro le epidemie. I consigli di diritto europeo dei giuristi (secoli XIV–XVI).* Canterano: Aracne.

Baehrel, René. 1952. La haine de classe en temps d'épidémie. *Annales. Economies, sociétés, civilisations* 7 (3): 351–60.

Beauvieux, Fleur. 2014. Justice et répression de la criminalité en temps de peste. L'exemple de l'épidémie marseillaise de 1720–1722. *Criminocorpus.* https://doi.org/10.4000/criminocorpus.2857.

Besta, Giacomo Filippo. 1578. *Vera narratione del successo della peste, che afflisse l'inclita città di Milano, l'anno 1576. & di tutte le provisioni fatte a salute di essa città.* Milan: per Paolo Gottardo e Pacifico Pontij, fratelli.

Bisciola, Paolo. 1577. *Relatione verissima del progresso della peste di Milano. Qual principiò nel mese d'Agosto 1576 e seguì fino al mese di Maggio 1577.* Bologna: per Alessandro Benacci.

Bohstedt, John. 1992. The Moral Economy and the Discipline of Historical Context. *Journal of Social History* 26 (2): 265–84.

Boiteux, Martine. 2007. Le bouclage. Rome en temps de peste (1656–1657). *Roma moderna e contemporanea* 14 (1–3): 175–201.

Calvi, Giulia. 1981. L'oro, il fuoco, le forche: la peste napoletana del 1656. *Archivio Storico Italiano* 139 (3): 405–58.

Capella, Galeazzo F. 1538. *Commentarii Galeacii Capellae de rebus gestis pro restitutione Francisci Sfortiae II. Mediolani Ducis*. Strasbourg: apud Cratonem Mylium.

Carmichael, Ann G. 1983. Plague Legislation in the Italian Renaissance. *Bulletin of the History of Medicine* 57 (4): 508–25.

———. 1986. *Plague and the Poor in Renaissance Florence*. Cambridge: Cambridge University Press.

Centorio degli Ortensi, Ascanio. 1579. *I cinque libri degl'avvertimenti, ordini, gride et editti: fatti, et osservati in Milano, ne' tempi sospettosi della peste; ne gli anni MDLXXVI et LXXVII*. Venice: appresso Giovanni e Gio. Paolo Gioliti De' Ferrari.

Cipolla, Carlo M. 1973. *Cristofano and the Plague: A Study in the History of Public Health in the Age of Galileo*. Berkeley: University of California Press.

———. 2007. *Contro un nemico invisibile. Epidemie e strutture sanitarie nell'Italia del Rinascimento*. Bologna: il Mulino.

Coccoli, Lorenzo. Forthcoming. Defining Poverty. In *A Cultural History of Poverty*. 4: *A Cultural History of Poverty in the Age of the Emerging Atlantic World (1650–1800)*, ed. Laurinda Abreu. London: Bloomsbury Academy.

Cohn, Samuel K., Jr. 2010. *Cultures of Plague: Medical Thinking at the End of the Renaissance*. New York and Oxford: Oxford University Press.

Conforti, Maria. 2006. Peste a stampa: TRattati, relazioni e cronache a Roma nel 1656. *Roma moderna e contemporanea* 14 (1–3): 135–58.

Defoe, Daniel. 2003. *A Journal of the Plague Year*, ed. C. Wall. London: Penguin.

Fassin, Didier. 2009. Les économies morales revisitées. *Annales. Histoire, Sciences Sociales* 64 (6): 1237–66.

Fiochetto, Giovanni Francesco. 1631. *Trattato della peste, et pestifero contagio di Torino*. Turin: appresso Gio. Guglielmo Tisma.

Foucault, Michel. 1995. *Discipline and Punish. The Birth of the Prison*, trans. A. Sheridan. New York: Vintage Books.

Götz, Norbert. 2015. 'Moral Economy': Its Conceptual History and Analytical Prospects. *Journal of Global Ethics* 11 (2): 147–62.

Henderson, John. 2019. *Florence Under Siege. Surviving Plague in an Early Modern City*. New Haven and London: Yale University Press.

Ingrassia, Giovanni Filippo. 1576. *Informatione del pestifero, et contagioso morbo: il quale affligge et haue afflitto questa Città di Palermo, & molte altre Città, e Terre di questo Regno di Sicilia, nell'anno 1575 et 1576*. Palermo: appresso Giovan Mattheo Mayda.

Jones, Colin. 1989. *The Charitable Imperative. Hospitals and Nursing in Ancien Régime and Revolutionary France*. London and New York: Routledge.

Muratori, Lodovico Antonio. 1714. *Del governo della peste, e delle maniere di guardarsene*. Modena: Per Bartolomeo Soliani.

Pastore, Alessandro. 1991. *Crimine e giustizia in tempo di peste nell'Europa moderna*. Rome and Bari: Laterza.

Pullan, Brian. 1992. Plague and Perceptions of the Poor in Early Modern Italy. In *Epidemics and Ideas. Essays on the Historical Perception of Pestilence*, ed. Terence Ranger and Paul Slack, 101–24. Cambridge: Cambridge University Press.

Quammen, David. 2020. The Warnings. Why We Should Have Known to Prepare for COVID-19. *The New Yorker*, May 11.

Ripa di San Nazzaro, Gianfrancesco. 1598. *Illustris de peste tractatus iuridicus ac politicus*. Lipsiae: imprimebat Michel Lantzemberger.

Roland, Charles G. 1992. *Courage Under Siege: Starvation, Disease, and Death in the Warsaw Ghetto*. New York and Oxford: Oxford University Press.

Roscio, Gregorio. 1665. *De Postrema Pestilentia Urbis Romae*. Rome: Excudebat Vitalis Mascardus.

Slack, Paul. 1988. Responses to Plague in Early Modern Europe: The Implications of Public Health. *Social Research* 55 (3): 433–53.

Snowden, Frank M. 2019. *Epidemics and Society. From the Black Death to the Present*. New Haven and London: Yale University Press.

Tadino, Alessandro. 1648. *Raguaglio dell'origine et giornali successi della gran peste contagiosa, venefica, & malefica seguita nella Città di Milano, & suo Ducato dall'anno 1629 sino all'anno 1632*. Milan: per Filippo Ghisolfi.

Thompson, Edward P. 1971. The Moral Economy of the English Crowd in the Eighteenth Century. *Past & Present* 50: 76–136.

———. 1974. Patrician Society, Plebeian Culture. *Journal of Social History* 7 (4): 382–405.

———. 1993. The Moral Economy Reviewed. In *Customs in Common*, 259–351. London: Penguin.

CHAPTER 8

Moral Economists: The Jesuit Mission in Paraguay and the Idea of Economic Growth in Early Modern Times

David Bete and Philip Knäble

The Catholic Ethic and the Spirit of Capitalism

Admittedly, it is not very original to begin an essay about the relationship between religion and economy with Max Weber, even though the 100th anniversary of Weber's death in 2020 does indeed lend it a certain legitimacy. In his search to identify the founding groups of capitalism, Weber analyzed the influence of puritan-Calvinist moral theology on economic ethics during the seventeenth and eighteenth centuries. Here he focused, in particular, on the ascetic lifestyle of the Calvinist doctrine of predeterminism, which led to a certain professional ethos and the "pursuit of profit in the ongoing, rational capitalistic activity" (Weber 1905, 4).

D. Bete · P. Knäble (✉)
Georg-August-Universität Göttingen, Göttingen, Germany
e-mail: philip.knaeble@phil.uni-goettingen.de

D. Bete
e-mail: david.bete@uni-goettingen.de

T. Skambraks and M. Lutz (eds.), *Reassessing the Moral Economy*, Palgrave Studies in Economic History,
https://doi.org/10.1007/978-3-031-29834-9_8

Even though Weber's theses have been critically discussed and partially refuted, the protestant Netherlands and Great Britain still often remain the starting point for modern-day narratives about the development of capitalism (Kypta et al. 2019, 24–32).

But Weber did not limit himself to Protestantism. He dealt with many other world religions in his studies on economic ethics without bringing his ideas on Catholicism to an end (Weber 1905, footnote 56; Hersche 2006, 442).

The world economic crisis of 1929 and its consequences brought new impetus to the study of capitalism, in which discussions focused on the possibility of its end. As a result, the question about the genesis of capitalism was raised again, this time by the economist Hector Robertson in 1933.

In Robertson's book "Aspects of the Rise of Economic Individualism" he dealt with Weber's "Protestant ethics." Weber's works had been made accessible to English-speaking readers through Talcott Parson's translation, published in 1930. For Robertson, it was not the Calvinists as Weber had seen it, but rather the Catholics who he believed to be the founders of modern capitalism. In particular, he viewed the Jesuit's economic ethics as central to this process, since their break from the medieval understanding of usury offered the internationally active merchants a hitherto unknown social prestige (Robertson 1933, XIV–XVI). Robertson's aim was to show, in analogy to Weber's method, that the catholic moral theories of the sixteenth and seventeenth centuries had been influenced strongly by the Jesuits. He states therefore: "Yet it would not be difficult to hold that the encouragement of economic rationalism was even stronger among the Catholics than among the Protestants" (Robertson 1933, 133.).

It would not take long for the Jesuit order to respond with criticism to Robertson's thesis. One year later, the Jesuit James Brodrick (1891–1973) published his monograph "The Economic Morals of the Jesuits" defending his order against Robertson's theses. Above all, Brodrick accused Robertson of negligent source analysis and was able to identify a number of errors and generalizations thus weakening Robertson's main thesis and thereby indirectly strengthening Weber's argumentation (Brodrick 1934, 88–117). In many cases, Brodrick provided clarifications to the examples offered by Robertson. Hence his conclusions were as follows:

> The answer to that is that the Jesuits, unlike the Calvinists, had not seized on the civil power in any country and so were in no position to secure restrictions on trade. In the one place where they were granted civil administration, namely the Reductions of Paraguay, they not only restricted the trade of outsiders with the Indians but stopped it altogether, and so made for themselves a host of bitter enemies. (Brodrick 1934, 16)

The "powerlessness" of the order, which dominated the educational landscape in many Catholic areas and had a far-reaching influence on kings and emperors via their Jesuit confessors, can certainly be questioned. In addition, the idea that the Jesuit order fought to stop trade, as claimed above, is not very convincing. Trade in Paraguay was, in fact, dominated by the local Jesuits, not impeded by them. This led to criticism by the regional merchants. In our contribution, we want to discuss this research question about the economic interactions of the Jesuits in Paraguay, which has been discussed for a long time but has not yet been solved.

This essay will investigate the role of the Society of Jesus, in particular in the Paraguayan province, in the development of semantics on economic growth that emerged in the early modern period. First, we will discuss the concept of moral economy and the benefits of using this approach to study the Jesuit's ideas of growth. The third and fourth chapters will present the connections between the concepts of mission and economic growth and will describe how the Jesuits in Paraguay implemented these ideas in their economic practices. Our article proposes that with their ideas of mission the Jesuits established a hitherto unknown concept of perpetual growth within the premodern economy.

The Jesuits as "Moral Economists"

The concept of moral economy in early modern studies is inseparable from E. P. Thompson's research on the English hunger riots in the eighteenth century. Against the mainstream of English social history with its focus in the 1960s and 1970s on statistics, Thompson had a more mentality-based approach. Instead of using the term "moral," he could have used the term "sociological economy" because of his interest in social institutions and discourses in economic processes, as he explained 20 years after coining his concept in an article. Such an understanding of moral economy analyzes the forms of demarcation between legitimate and illegitimate discourses and practices of the economy, associated power struggles, symbolic forms of communication and knowledge formations. Catholic clergymen like the Jesuits creatively used the semantics of different economies and thus actively contributed to the change in contemporary economic understanding. (Knäble 2019, 57–61, 75).

In a premodern context, religious discourses certainly played an important part in the formation of societies, including their economies. Research on the relationship between Christian ethics and capitalism did not stop with Max Weber and his recipients such as Robertson and Brodrick. We will mention just two approaches out of several that have focused on the relationship between Catholicism and the economy in recent years.

Peter Hersche confirmed *ex negativo* Weber's thesis with his book titled "Leisure and wastefulness" (2006). In his view, the economy of baroque Catholicism was mainly shaped by leisure and wastefulness instead of an investment in the (proto)industry. He describes the investment and innovation of catholic territories in agriculture and artisanry, often overlooked by studies focusing solely on industrial capitalism.

The contribution of Franciscans to the conception of the economy during the late Middle Ages and at the beginning of the early modern period has been shown by Giacomo Todeschini and Tanja Skambraks (Todeschini 2021; Skambraks 2023). Both underline the practical economical knowledge of mendicants, their role in the establishment of public credit institutions, and their significance in the creation of new economic terms. Also, Joseph Lemberg stresses (Lemberg 2019) in an essay the role that Franciscans in the late medieval period played in economic semantics by combining the ideas of economy and mission. He analyzes this connection on the basis of concepts of growth within the medieval society and focuses therein on the semantic field of sowing, which was used frequently in thirteenth-century Europe to describe biological, social and economic growth. The term "growth" is, originally, an agricultural one and so was strongly linked to the work of sowing and harvesting. Referring to Jürgen Link, Lemberg understands the metaphor of sowing as a "collective symbol" that integrates various contexts, in this case agriculture, theology and economy, into one discourse.

For the Paraguayan Jesuits, the use of this metaphor was quite common throughout the province's existence. In the provincial reports, the *Litterae Annuae* of 1609–1614, we see that Jesuit missionaries sent to "infidel" indigenous tribes are described as "the first grain of it, which has been sown in Puren, to expect from them a very plentiful fruit" (Universidad de Buenos Aires 1927, 237f). Some 120 years later, the *Litterae Annuae* mentioned this early evangelizing, saying that for the indigenous to sin meant to "suffocate the good seed, which has been sown in their souls in other times by the Fathers" (Salinas and Folkenland 2017, 201).

Even though the metaphor of growth had been applied in the thirteenth century to the economic sphere and despite the contemporaneous introduction of the term "capital" by the Franciscan Petrus Iohannis Olivi, ideas of growth remained limited to the micro-perspective and limited periods of time within the commercial-economic sphere (Lemberg 2019, 296). The metaphor of growth did not transport any ideas of a macro-level economy or of limitless growth, especially not within the writings by merchants in what is called the *ars mercatoria*. However, this macro-level understanding was present in the context of the Christian mission and has been discussed by theologians:

> The yield of missionary sowing was calculated on the aggregation of converted souls, which lasted until the end of times and culminated in the *plenitudo gentium*, a spatial-social all-embracing category. (Lemberg 2019, 297)

We can thus observe a link that already existed between growth and economy during the late Middle Ages, which, however, did not yet include any ideas of a kind of "national economy" or of the economy as an autonomous sphere. During the early modern period, which has been described in economic history as an epoch of early capitalism, this constellation began to change.

The Jesuits, as described earlier, established with their missionary zeal a paradigm of growth within the premodern economy. But the reference to older concepts of economic growth was not done to regulate the economy and to return to old familiar patterns, as was true for Thompson's hunger rioters. Instead, the integration of the medieval metaphor of growth into economic thinking resulted in a new impetus for economic semantics. By remaining subordinate to the mission, economics could be conceived of using the metaphor of mission and be translated into new practices, because the purpose of economic activity continued to be seen as a higher missionary one. In this context, Christian ethics were not based upon the concern to ensure predestination through economic success, rather they were based on the desire that missionary zeal should not be spatially or temporally limited.

Growth and Mission I: Harvesting the Souls

Missionary work as a primary field of activity was even more important to Jesuits than to Franciscans, whose founding documents do not emphasize it (Lemmens 1929, 3). The founder of the Society of Jesus, Ignatius of Loyola, impressed his fellow students in Paris and the first Jesuits in Italy with his idea of a spiritual pilgrimage. In the "spiritual exercises," which every aspirant to the Jesuit order was supposed to follow for four weeks, but also were conceived to be lifelong guidelines, Loyola asks the participant to imagine all places, where Jesus had acted and preached (Sievernich 2005, 9–11). Then, the participants are asked to imagine how great their readiness to follow would be, if a king called them to arms and how much greater this willingness must be, if Jesus himself calls them to arms.

> It is my will to conquer the universe and all the enemies, and therefore to enter the glory of my Father. Therefore, anyone who wants to accompany me in this enterprise must be determined to work with me, because by following me in exertion, one may follow me in glory. (Monumenta Historica Societatis Iesu (MHSI), vol 100, 219f)·

This exercise mentioned above and conceived by Ignatius of Loyola is influenced by the Bible passage of the great harvest in the Gospel of Matthew, where it says: "The harvest is plentiful, but the workers are few. Therefore ask the Lord of the harvest to send out workers into his harvest-ready fields" (Gospel of Matthew, 9, 37–38). This metaphor was also used by Francis Xavier, the first Jesuit missionary, when he described the need for more missionaries in Asia in a letter of 1543 (Coleridge 2009, 107).

Referring to this passage, Loyola demands: "Consider how the Lord of the World chooses so many persons, apostles and disciples etc., and sends them out into the whole world to sow his holy doctrine to all men of all states and conditions" (MHSI, vol. 100, 247).

Loyola's autobiography *A Pilgrim's Journey,* then, contributed to the development of the constitutions and rules of the Jesuit order. The rules consider an important—if not the most important—purpose of the Society of Jesus to be the mission, i.e. the spread of Christendom to "varias mundi parti" (Angeli 1616, 210). This centrality of the mission, both internal and external—of which aim was to deepen the faith of Catholics and convert non-Christians—had already been stated in the Jesuit's constitutions:

> The aim and end of this Society is, by traveling through the various parts of the world at the order of the supreme vicar of Christ our Lord or of the superior of the Society itself, to preach, hear confessions, and use all the other means it can [...] to help souls. Consequently, it has seemed to us necessary [...] that those who will enter the Society be persons of good life and sufficient learning for the aforementioned work. However, those who are both good and learned are relatively few, most are already seeking rest from their labors. [...] Therefore all of us [...] have thought it wise to take another path, that of admitting young men whose good habits of life and talent give hope that they will become both virtuous and learned in order to labor in the vineyard of Christ our Lord. We shall likewise accept colleges under the conditions stated in the apostolic bull. (Padberg 1996, 131)

These colleges, which were the only Jesuit institutions allowed to own worldly possessions in order to generate an income, had the purpose of training pastors and missionaries. Since the economic activities of the colleges were justified by the increased need for educating the missionaries (Friedrich 2016, 259), the direct relation between mission and economy was anchored within the constitution of the Society of Jesus.

However, the constitutions don't go into detail when it comes to economic semantics or practices. Even the topic of non-European missions is not regulated in detail here, which could be explained by the fact that when the founding documents of the order were being drawn up, there were very few missionaries preaching overseas.[1]

Therefore, the more general instructions and rules of the founding documents had to be adapted to the specific missionary contexts. José de Acosta formulated in 1588 in Salamanca a missionary guideline titled *De procuranda indorum salute* for the Jesuit provinces of South America,

[1] The short text *Constitutiones circa missiones* was written in 1544 and later included in the constitutions of the order. It focuses on the act of being sent out (by the Pope or the Superior General) but doesn't clarify the missionary institution itself. In 1550, when the first version of the society's constitutions was finished, a handful of Jesuits had established themselves very recently in Brazil. Shortly earlier, four Jesuit missionaries had begun their labor in Kongo. In Asia, there were around 50 Jesuits at that timer (Alden 1996, 46–75).

which, except for Brazil, belonged to the Spanish assistancy. Therein, the Provincial of the Peruvian province, which at that time still contained the later separated provinces of Paraguay and Chile, demanded that missionaries and future missionaries should focus on learning the languages and habits of their indigenous environment, in order to facilitate preaching. The work undertaken by the missionaries in this province received much attention, both within and beyond the Jesuit order (Dürr 2017, 216).

Acosta describes in the guide, apart from many other aspects of the American continent, the problems faced by the Jesuit missionaries. At the beginning of the missionary work, the "fruits harvested" still had, in his opinion, "an excessive flavor of old paganism," but nobody could deny "that later generations will sprout fruits, which are worthy enough to present to God, once the old taste has been eradicated" (Acosta 1954, 426).

Acosta therefore sees missionary work as yielding little success at the outset, but believes its efforts will be rewarded in the future. Due to the innumerable number of indigenous peoples with their own different rites, which had to be accounted for with specific missionary methods, Acosta saw himself to be confronted with a nigh-on insoluble problem: "and if I knew them all, it would still be an interminable task" (Acosta 1954, 391). Acosta thus describes the work of missionaries—at least for the Peruvian province—as endless, and therefore the need for missionaries is endless too. According to the constitutions, there should be no limit to the economic expansion of the province in order to facilitate the subsistence of an unlimited number of missionaries.

For the province of Paraguay, which separated from the Peruvian one in 1609, there are references to the harvest of souls in a book titled "Spiritual Conquest," written by the former head of the mission villages of the Guaraní, Antonio Ruiz de Montoya in 1639. The title itself takes up the Ignatian image of the Christian mission as an act of conquest. In his foreword, Ruiz de Montoya stressed the almost infinite size of the Paraguayan province with its impenetrable forests, mountains and deserts. The province extended around 2000 kilometers from east to west and nearly 3000 kilometers from north to south. Topography of almost infinite size was also to be found in other provinces in America or Asia, but the Paraguayan province had, unlike Peru or Mexico, no urban centers of the pre-Hispanic period. This leads Montoya to conclude in his book that Paraguay lacks any wealth or comfort compared to other provinces.

Because of that, the missionaries had to live in complete poverty, as Ruiz de Montoya describes it (Ruiz de Montoya et al. 2017, 14).

Following the example of ancient monks, Ruiz de Montoya sought the desert "where the spiritual seed is spread, strengthened and grown" (Ruiz de Montoya et al. 2017, 18). The Jesuits of that region had sown their seeds "in such glorious labors and services given to God and the church in the most distant parts of the world" (Ruiz de Montoya et al. 2017, 14) and thus had "harvested many souls" (Ruiz de Montoya et al. 2017, 38). Despite these successes and the sacrifices of the missionaries, the number of converts remained "few, for such a big harvest, which was offered by the well-nigh countless number of pagans" (Ruiz de Montoya et al. 2017, 38). For a land with a nearly unlimited number of (pagan) inhabitants, the number of missionaries had to grow endlessly.

This assessment that there was a need for more missionaries, in which Ruiz de Montoya and Acosta were in agreement, was also voiced in the Paraguayan province's official reports, the *Litterae Annuae* in its first years. Therein the Provincial writes about a region near Asunción, where Jesuits worked as missionaries:

> I have no other reports from there, other than demands of the Patres for more workers [which is: missionaries] [...] so that I, if it was possible, would divide myself in so many parts to fit the need for new masters of souls of the ever-increasing amount of indigenous people who ask for them. (Universidad de Buenos Aires 1927, 292f)

Successful missionary work, i.e. a successful harvest of souls, demanded therefore a steadily growing influx of missionaries.

Growth and Mission II: Harvesting the Fields

It was quite clear to the Paraguayan Jesuits that for a successful "harvesting of souls," the missionaries' earthly needs would need to be provided for, thus by the harvest of the fields. Unlike other religious orders, doing physical work was forbidden for the Jesuit priests. Only the lay brothers, the temporal coadjutors, were permitted to fulfill such duties. Even though the Jesuits were always seeking skilled craftsmen to join their order as coadjutors, their number was never enough to meet the needs. In the case of Paraguay, the number of priests was usually nearly double the number of coadjutors.[2] Therefore, the Jesuits used both a contracted and enslaved workforce in order to generate income for subsistence and to maintain their establishments, as the following section will show.

In 1627, Superior General Muzio Vitelleschi wrote the following to the Paraguayan provincial Nicolás Durán:

> According to what your reverence and others write to me, I take note that it is of great importance for the growth of the estates, that their rectors arrange to buy as many slaves as will serve the need of cultivating the land and to mind the cattle; and therefore I order [...] that the rectors shall not sell cows, sheep, mares, land or slaves, which are necessary for the subsistence and expenses of the order's members, without the knowledge and permission of the provincial. For since the lands are worthless if we have neither cattle nor slaves on them, [...] it is just to maintain and increase the number of cattle and the slaves, as if they were immobile goods. (Morales 2005, 361)

As it is evident from this letter: the desire for economic growth and efficient usage of the order's estates emanates from the Paraguayan Jesuits. Vitelleschi only responds here to the wish to legitimize these efforts. While we do not have the mentioned letters sent from Paraguay to the Superior General to refer to, it seems that there were qualms concerning the legitimacy of those economic practices, which were dispelled by Vitelleschi in his response. Growth of the estates and thus potential growth of personnel in the province seemed to outweigh any reservations the Jesuits may have had against seeking economic growth through the exploitation of slaves. Such requests, sent by letter to Rome, were often made not by individual Jesuits but by the provincial congregations. Usually every six years, Jesuit fathers gathered together to discuss local matters at a provincial level. Those congregations then raised requests

[2] Considering the *Catalogi* from 1620, 1660, 1710 and 1744, there were 1.8 priests on every coadjutor in a college making it impossible for the coadjutors to maintain the priest through their workforce (Archivum Romanum Societatis Iesu (ARSI)), Paraq. 4 and 6).

which were to be brought to the order's curia by the provincial procurators.[3] The congregations didn't just allow the congregationists to request guidance from Rome, but to also question controversial matters such as the legitimacy of certain economical practices on a provincial level, as indeed happened at a number of provincial congregations in Paraguay (Fechner 2015, 285–297; Fechner 2020, 277).

About 70 years later, the Paraguayan provincial Blas de Silva even declared that it was legitimate for procurators to order slaves to work on Sundays and church festivals "however it seems to him the most convenient for the college's profit" (Piana and Cansanello 2015, 40). The Sunday observance, nothing less than the third commandment, was apparently less important for the regional head of a Catholic order than the temporal benefit of the college—at least when it came to slaves. This obvious conflict between economic success and the goal of the whole operation, the spread of the Catholic doctrine, must have provoked disagreement. And just a few years later, the visitor Antonio Garriga banned Sunday work in a memorandum for the college of Buenos Aires. But it seemed to him more important to uphold this Commandment "for the good example that we should give to the outsiders" (Piana and Cansanello 2015, 50) than for abiding by Christian doctrine.

Although slaves were made to work on Sundays, this was not the case for the indigenous inhabitants of the mission villages. In 1723, the Provincial Luis de Roccafiorita ordered that the missionaries "shouldn't force the Indians to work on holidays, as if the commandment did not apply to them" (Piana and Cansanello 2015, 139). The first impression may be that the indigenous people, being the missionary target or "the gold and silver" (Morales 2005, 314) that the Jesuits were seeking there, as the Superior General Muzio Vitelleschi described it in 1624, had to be kept under the Christian doctrine and that the indoctrination of the slaves was of much less important because they were seen as a mere workforce. However, the Jesuits benefitted less from indigenous labor in the villages than from enslaved labor on their estates. So, in this case, it isn't quite clear if the different attitudes toward Sunday observance are derived from missionary or economic considerations.

[3] The provincial procurators were sent to Europe to report the local situation in the headquarters and—ideally—brought new missionaries and European items on their way back.

Some instructions to the estate of the Jesuit college in San Miguel del Tucumán by Pedro de Oñate, who was its Provincial between 1615 and 1623, may shed more light on this topic. Oñate ordered that

> the *yanaconas*[4] and other similar indios are to be treated and paid well; should be kept in moderate labor so that they are neither weighed down nor useless; catechize them two times a week [...] and pay great attention too that they are good Christians. (Piana and Cansanello 2015, 27)

Soon after issuing these instructions, he ordered that the estate should buy more African slaves "because it is the largest increase this estate could have" (Piana and Cansanello 2015, 27), without mentioning any care for their workload or lessons in Christian doctrine.

This case is different from the ones above, because here, the difference isn't made between African slaves and the inhabitants of mission villages, but between African slaves and the indigenous forced workforce at the order's estates. Therefore, in this case, the Jesuits benefitted from the labor of both groups in a very similar or the same way. The indigenous workers as primary target of the mission were of such importance to Oñate that he reduced their workload in order to make them "good Christians." Supposedly, the African slaves being good Christians was not important enough to offer them similar relief.

Another topic of Jesuit economic practice was the power of disposal of the Jesuit priests over the labor and goods of the missionary villages. In 1685 the Provincial Tomás Donvidas addressed the province's missionaries in a letter with his own qualms regarding this. Even though the indigenous new-Christians in the villages were formally the owners of the goods they produced, "one can impede the holy poverty with the absolute disposal, which the priest can have over the goods that are really and truly those of the Indians" (Biblioteca Nacional de España (BNE), MS 6976, 127). His reservations that the priests could be more concerned about harvesting the fields and too little about harvesting the souls, he expresses as follows:

[4] The term yanacona described an indigenous person who has been given to a Spanish or creole *encomendero*, to whom he had to give tribute in the form of labor. Yanaconas had to live on the *encomendero* 's property which made them even more vulnerable to any form of abuses such as "slavery-like" (Salinas 2008, 18) perpetual serfdom, which was forbidden by law but practiced in estates.

> It is laudable to turn towards the earthly and to care about its increase, because on this depends the spiritual to a high degree: therefore it can be obligatory to do that delicate task, which is carried out by those who care for the villages: but be careful not to reverse it, converting the means to the purpose and the purpose to the means. (BNE, MS 6976, 130)

Here, Donvidas stresses that the importance of the economy for the mission lies not in its role to supply the educational needs of the new missionaries, but in the subsistence of the people who are to be converted by the mission. The specific danger that a "too successful harvest of the fields" posed for the "harvest of the souls," had already been pointed out by the Superior General Vitelleschi: "they pull out so many plants from the field so zealously, with the danger so well known of losing the life of soul and body" (Morales 2005, 465).

This topic of the order's focus on economic concerns comes up regularly in both the correspondence within the province of Paraguay and between the province and the Roman headquarters. The often-mentioned priority of the earthly over the spiritual was handled quite differently by different actors. It ranged from a carte blanche-style liberality seen in Vitelleschi's letter of 1627 to vehement condemnation from some quarters. Earlier in 1624, the same Vitelleschi, however, had also condemned what in his view was an overly zealous attitude toward economic matters on the part of the colleges. He expressed these concerns in a letter to the same Francisco Vázquez, who at that time was the rector of the college of Buenos Aires:

> I admit that it was very painful for me to hear that the basis [for accusations of illegitimate economic practices made by Jesuits] was given by some of us, and the most complaints were made about this college [Buenos Aires]. If we really care about for what we went there to seek, which is to support the salvation of the poor Indians and to win many souls for God, we can surely trust in the divine Providence, that we won't lack the necessary to maintain the life, without the necessity of converting us into merchants of earthly goods, those who did go there to be [merchants] of the spiritual. (Morales 2005, 300)

But it was not just during the first decades of the Paraguayan province's existence that such controversies came up. In 1754, the Provincial José de Barreda wrote a letter to the head of the Guaraní mission, criticizing the economic practices in the mission villages. He accused some of his Jesuit brothers of being "merchants of souls" who "don't care for the earthly just to advance the spiritual, but who gave themselves completely to the means of industry of striving for more and more" (BNE, MS 6976, 308).

Some decades earlier, this same economic striving had resulted in the province having "the wealth and means to maintain the novices, pay for the expenses of the procurators and individuals who are brought from Europe etc." (ARSI, Paraq. 11, 500), as the Provincial Lauro Núñez quoted the Superior General Tirso González de Santalla. Therefore, González de Santalla ordered that his Paraguayan brothers should invest the surplus profit in an estate in Spain in order to use its rent to pay for the transportation costs of new missionaries sent over the Atlantic Ocean. Here, it is very obvious that for the Superior General, the economy had to serve the mission and that economic growth was to be aimed at missionary growth.

Interestingly, the Paraguayan Provincial and his advisors refused to do this in order to invest the surplus in a profitable office at the Mint of Potosí, arguing that their experience had shown that it was difficult to transfer profits from Spain to Paraguay. Therefore, Núñez wrote concerning the offices at the Mint of Potosí, "even though they don't have the convenience of having the silver in Spain, they have the safety and permanence" (ARSI, Paraq. 11, 500). The estate in Spain, which would have facilitated the payment for the transport of missionaries, seemed less attractive as an investment than a purchasable office in Potosí because its profits were to be sent directly to the Paraguayan province. The estate's profits would have been spent in Spain, sending returns just in the form of missionaries. The Peruvian silver seemed to appeal more.

This episode shows that engaging in economics was a very "delicate" task for the Jesuits, just as Donvidas had described it. The limits of legitimate economic practices were constantly debated and the reason why many letters were sent across the Atlantic Ocean.[5] But despite all differences, the assumption that a successful mission needed a successful economy was widely accepted. Or, to take the metaphor further: a successful harvest of souls had to be preceded by a successful harvest of the fields. The examples of this essay also show, that the Jesuits didn't just harvest their fields, but also looked for many other methods of getting returns on their investments.

[5] In North America the same problem keeps the Moravian Church busy in the late eighteenth century (Dorfner 2020, 40f).

Conclusions

Overseas, the Society of Jesus, as the prototype of a missionary order of the early modern era, was confronted by the problem of being unable to convert the masses of non-Christians with its comparatively few missionaries. To cope with its aim of converting nigh on unlimited numbers of "pagans" to Catholicism, they needed more and more missionaries. Hence, to supply those increasing numbers of missionaries, they increased their means of productions such as land, cattle and slaves.

As seen in many examples of this essay, it wasn't seen as always necessary to keep economical practices subordinate to the missionary goal. While the economical semantics were altered through the missionary idea of unlimited growth thus allowing changes in economic practices to take place in the colleges, some activities seemed to go beyond the purpose of solely serving the mission altogether, as we have seen mentioned in Provincial Barreda's criticism. The province's poverty and lack of attractiveness for missionaries in the early years may have been the catalyst for the newfound intense interest in economic growth, to maintain the order's establishments and to pay for the subsistence of the missionaries. This interest in economic growth helped the province to achieve financial stability, as the Superior General Tirso González de Santalla wrote it in 1687, making it possible for the province to increase its numbers of missionaries. According to González, this set Paraguay apart from all other Jesuit provinces.

At first glance, the connection of the economic practices of the Jesuits with the topic of moral economy might not seem very obvious, given the fact that they had nothing to do with hunger riots of the poorer sections of society. It would have been more fitting to analyze the reactions of both the indigenous population of the mission villages and the African slaves toward the Jesuit's economic ideas. Unfortunately, the consulted sources don't answer those questions and it is unlikely that there are sources that do so.

In the case of the Jesuits, we could refer to Hans Medick when he speaks of a "moral economy from above" (Medick 1985, 43), in which "older semantics were used by the authorities to impose particular interests or to influence subordinates" (Knäble 2019, 61). References to the common good and to fair prices, principles that were demanded by the rioters in Thompson's texts, can be found in Jesuit writings, too. This intersection is no coincidence, but the result of the close connection between religion and economics in the early modern period. At this time economic success and economic growth could hardly be formulated as the sole goals of economic practices, neither by merchants, let alone by religious orders. In this respect, the essay shows the close lexical and conceptual overlap between economic practice and missionary goals of the Jesuits in Paraguay.

Since their higher goal was—at least initially—the harvesting of souls, the concept of growth intrinsic to the mission, could also be transferred to the economic sphere as "the harvesting of the fields." By the semantics of mission the Jesuits established a new concept of perpetual growth within the premodern economy.

In recent years, the concept of moral economy has helped to show that in premodern but also contemporary societies there are political and social rights that are not determined by market mechanisms (Armstrong 2016, 28–31). At the same time, this approach makes it clearer that certain market mechanisms such as the concept of unlimited economic growth didn't arise outside of moral philosophy or moral theology, but instead were made possible by them. These ideas and semantics can contribute to our understanding of economic change has been postulated in recent years (Plumpe 2009, 28). While Plumpe emphasizes the role of political-economic relations, Giacomo Todeschini analyzes how religious semantics left their mark on economic terminology in the early modern period (Todeschini 2021).

To understand key concepts of capitalism, like the idea of economic growth (Kocka 2013, 10), it is furthermore necessary to expand the view beyond central Europe and North America and beyond well-known economic actors. The protestant entrepreneur is one such important actor who helps us understand how new investment strategies changed the economic system, but he could not have conceived of them without the ideas of the Jesuits in South America.

References

Acosta, José de. 1954. De procuranda Indorum salute. In *Obras del P. José de Acosta de la Compañia de Jesús*, ed. Francisco Mateos and José de Acosta, 387–608. Madrid: Ed. Atlas.

Alden, Dauril. 1996. *The Making of an Enterprise: The Society of Jesus in Portugal, Its Empire, and Beyond, 1540–1750*. Stanford: Stanford University Press.

Angeli, Bernardo d'. 1616. *Regvlae Societatis Iesv. Auctoritate Septimae Congregationis Generalis auctae. Collegium Romanum Societatis Jesu*. Rome: Collegio Romano eiusdem Societatis.

Armstrong, Lawrin. 2016. *The Idea of a Moral Economy. Gerard of Siena on Usury, Restitution, and Prescription*. Toronto: University of Toronto Press.

Brodrick, James. 1934. *The Economic Morals of the Jesuits: An Answer to Dr. H. M. Robertson*. London: Milford.

Coleridge, Henry James. 2009. *The Life and Letters of St. Francis Xavier*. Memphis: General Books.

Dorfner, Thomas. 2020. "Commercium nach dem Sinne Jesu". Überlegungen zum Marktverhalten der Herrnhuter Brüdergemeinde am Beispiel des Labradorhandels (1770–1815). *Jahrbuch für Wirtschaftsgeschichte* 61 (1): 39–66.

Dürr, Renate. 2017. Reflection on Language in Christian Mission. The Significance of Communication in the Linguistic Concepts of José de Acosta SJ and Antonio Ruiz de Montoya SJ. In *Translating Catechisms, Translating Cultures: The Expansion of Catholicism in the Early Modern World*, ed. Antje Flüchter and Rouven Wirbser, 50–91. Leiden: Brill.

Fechner, Fabian. 2015. *Entscheidungsprozesse vor Ort*. Regensburg: Schnell + Steiner.

Fechner, Fabian. 2020. Regulating the Forbidden. Local Rules and Debates on the Missionary Economy in the Jesuit Province of Paraguay (17th-18th Centuries). In *Trade and Finance in Global Missions (16th-18th centuries)*, ed. Hélène Vu Thanh and Ines G. Županov, 269–287. Leiden: Brill.

Friedrich, Markus. 2016. *Die Jesuiten: Aufstieg, Niedergang, Neubeginn: Mit 33 Abbildungen und 3 Karten*. Munich: Piper.

Hersche, Peter. 2006. *Muße und Verschwendung. Europäische Gesellschaft und Kultur im Barockzeitalter*. Freiburg im Breisgau: Herder.

Knäble, Philip. 2019. "Moralische Ökonomie"? - Zur Wirtschaftsethik der Schule von Salamanca am Beispiel von Martín de Azpilcueta und Leonardus Lessius. *Saeculum* 69 (1): 55–77.

Kocka, Jürgen. 2013. *Geschichte des Kapitalismus*. Munich: Beck.

Kypta, Ulla, Julia Bruch, Ulf Christian Ewert, Stefan Köhler, Christian Scholl, and Tanja Skambraks. 2019. Grand Narratives in Premodern Economic History. In *Methods in Premodern Economic History: Case Studies from the Holy Roman Empire, c.1300–c.1600*, eds. Ulla Kypta, Julia Bruch, and Tanja Skambraks, 11–45. Springer International Publishing.

Lemberg, Joseph. 2019. Wachstum denken im 13. Jahrhundert. Ökonomie, Mission und die sozionaturale Logik der Saatmetapher. *Saeculum* 69 (2): 271–303.

Lemmens, Leonhard. 1929. *Geschichte der Franziskanermissionen*. Münster.

Medick, Hans. 1985. Teuerung, Hunger und „moralische Ökonomie von oben". *Beiträge Zur Historischen Sozialkunde* 15: 39–44.
Morales, Martín María. 2005. *A mis manos han llegado. Cartas de los PP. Generales a la Antigua Provincia del Paraguay (1608–1639)*. Madrid: Univ. Pontificia Comillas.
Padberg, John W. 1996. *The Constitutions of The Society of Jesus and Their Complementary Norms: A Complete English Translation of the Official Latin Texts*. Saint Louis: Inst. of Jesuit Sources.
Piana, Josefina, and Pablo Cansanello. 2015. *Memoriales de la provincia Jesuitica del Paraguay (siglos XVII–XVIII)*. Córdoba: EDUCC Editorial de la Universidad Católica de Córdoba.
Plumpe, Werner. 2009. Ökonomisches Denken und wirtschaftliche Entwicklung. Zum Zusammenhang von Wirtschaftsgeschichte und historischer Semantik der Ökonomie. *Jahrbuch für Wirtschaftsgeschichte* 50 (1): 27–51.
Robertson, Hector Menteith. 1933. *Aspects of the Rise of Economic Individualism: A Criticism of Max Weber and His School*. Cambridge: Univ. Press.
Ruiz de Montoya, Antonio, Barbara Anne Ganson, and Clinia Saffi. 2017. *The Spiritual Conquest: Early Years of the Jesuit Missions in Paraguay = La conquista espiritual ; los primeros años de las misiones Jesuíticas en Paraguay*. Chestnut Hill: Institute of Jesuit Sources Boston College.
Salinas, María Laura. 2008. *Encomienda, trabajo y servidumbre indígena en Corrientes. Siglos XVII–XVIII*. Sevilla: Universidad Internacional de Andalucía.
Salinas, María Laura, and Julio Folkenand. 2017. *Cartas anuas de la Provincia Jesuítica del Paraguay: 1714–1720, 1720–1730, 1730–1735, 1735–1743, 1750–1756, 1756–1762*. Asunción: Centro de Estudios Antropológicos de la Universidad Católica (CEADUC).
Sievernich, Michael. 2005. Die Mission und die Missionen der Gesellschaft Jesu. In *Sendung, Eroberung, Begegnung. Franz Xaver, die Gesellschaft Jesu und die katholische Weltkirche im Zeitalter des Barock*, ed. Johannes Meier, 7–30. Wiesbaden: Harrassowitz.
Skambraks, Tanja. 2023. *Karitativer Kredit. Franziskanische Wirtschaftsethik, Monti di Pietà und städtische Sozialpolitik in Italien (15. und 16. Jahrhundert)*. Stuttgart: Steiner.
Todeschini, Giacomo. 2021. *Come l'acqua e il sangue. Le origini medievali del pensiero economico*. Rome: Frecce.
Universidad de Buenos Aires. 1927. *Cartas anuas de la provincia del Paraguay, Chile y Tucumán, de la compañía de Jesús (1609–1614)*. Buenos Aires: Peuser.
Weber, Max. 1905. Die protestantische Ethik und der "Geist" des Kapitalismus. *Archiv für Sozialwissenschaft und Sozialpolitik* 21: 1–110.

CHAPTER 9

Profit Due to Christian Behaviour: The Moral Economy of the Moravian Church in the Eighteenth Century

Thomas Dorfner

In memoriam Prof. Dr. Johannes Burkhardt (1943–2022)

Introduction

Did merchants of the eighteenth century operate without consideration of moral principles? A brief glance at contemporary handbooks for mercantile education seems to indicate this, as their writers dealt extensively with the concept of the "unchristian merchant" (Anonym 1745; Büsch 1799, 41). Even more recent academic publications emphasise that Christian norms would have held virtually no significance in context of the eighteenth century's trade practices. Economic historian Werner Plumpe, for

T. Dorfner (✉)
Department of History, RWTH Aachen University, Aachen, Germany
e-mail: dorfner@histinst.rwth-aachen.de

T. Skambraks and M. Lutz (eds.), *Reassessing the Moral Economy*, Palgrave Studies in Economic History,
https://doi.org/10.1007/978-3-031-29834-9_9

instance, assumes that the discourse about the common good and the (un-)christian merchant occurred in eighteenth-century merchant handbooks, primarily because "everyday practices were in opposition" (Plumpe 2009, 48). However, in this chapter, I intend to argue conversely in favour of the Pietistic Moravian Church: The Moravians were economically successful in the eighteenth century mainly because they strictly observed Christian norms in their trading activities. Thus, this chapter analyses the specific moral economy of the Moravians which tied Christian norms and Pietistic semantics to trade and production methods which were, at that time, "state of the art".

There are very few studies on the activities of Pietistic merchants. However, those publications that do exist, such as Anne Sophie Overkamp's monograph on the merchants of Wuppertal, provide clear evidence that together with Pietism, religion returned to commercial practice. Overkamp shows that the generation of merchants active between 1760 and 1800—many of whom demonstrated Pietistic influence—explicitly demanded "Christian conduct" from their business partners (Overkamp 2020, 196). Merchants in Wuppertal began engaging in this moralistic communication when they were unsatisfied with the prices set by their business partners or the quality of the goods.

The following chapter focuses on the trade activities of the Moravian Church during the latter half of the eighteenth century and aims to fill out the patchy and insufficient research on the subject. The Moravian Church is especially well suited to this type of analysis due to the specifics of how its traditions were passed down (Peucker 2000a). On the one hand, the governing bodies of the Moravians, based in the Holy Roman Empire, regularly deliberated on whether the trading activities practised were "in accordance with the mind of Jesus" (Circular Letter, 31.8.1783. The Unity Archives—Moravian Archives Herrnhut [UAH], R.3.B.27.III). Their resolutions were distributed among all their settlements and missions in the Atlantic World. The deliberations and results of these council discussions can be reconstructed through official records and letters preserved in the archives of the Moravian Church in Herrnhut and Bethlehem, PA. On the other hand, countless publicists and councillors trained in cameralistics monitored the Moravians' economic and trade activities (Dorfner 2018). These external observations are extremely useful for assessing the extent to which Moravian trade activities differed from their non-Pietistic competitors.

Upon the institutionalisation of global history as a field of research, the Moravian Church emerged as an internationally respected subject of research. The extraordinarily high mobility of the Moravians in the Atlantic World of the eighteenth and early nineteenth centuries has prompted numerous historians to research their transnational networks and diasporic way of life, as well as their diverse missionary activities (Sensbach 2005; Mettele 2009; Freist 2017). The moral economy of the Moravians, in contrast, has not often been considered so far. In the 1980s and 1990s, William R. Ward, Peter Zimmerling, and Gisela Mettele analysed the "economic ethics" of the founder of the Moravian Church, Count Nikolaus Ludwig von Zinzendorf (1700–1760), yet without further consideration of economic practices (Ward 1987; Zimmerling 1991; Mettele 2005). Not before the turn of the millennium, did a larger extend of historians begin to examine both, the economic practice and the "post-Zinzendorf period": two excellent examples for this are Katherine C. Engel's and Christina Petterson's studies on economic and religious life in the settlements of Bethlehem and Christiansfeld (Engel 2009; Petterson 2017).

The chapter is divided into three sections. It begins with a brief exploration of the origins of the Moravian Church during the first half of the eighteenth century. The second section focuses on the General Synod of 1764 and examines the regulatory efforts of their participants. In this context, I provide an analysis of how the participants made their decisions known to all Moravian settlements and how the Moravians in Bethlehem, PA implemented them. The third section demonstrates that the specific moral economy of the Moravians was often a competitive advantage in the second half of the eighteenth century. In the midst of an environment that increasingly labelled self-interest and profit maximisation as legitimate, or even desirable, many contemporaries considered Moravian merchants—as well as craftspeople in the settlements—to be unusually trustworthy.

Missionary Work as Main Task: A Short Introduction to the Moravian Church

The Moravian Church, with its roots in Herrnhut, Saxony, would not have come into being without its charismatic leader Imperial Count Nikolaus Ludwig von Zinzendorf (Meyer 2000, 19–29). From 1722 on, he allowed numerous Protestants and (radical) Pietists, who had fled the Hereditary Lands of the catholic House of Habsburg to settle on his estates in Saxony (Peper 2017). As tensions grew within this very heterogeneous group, Zinzendorf himself moved from Dresden to Herrnhut in 1727. On site, he issued two documents that were instrumental in easing tensions: the so-called "Manorial Commandments" regulated the civic affairs, whereas the "Brotherly Agreement" addressed spiritual matters. Zinzendorf's efforts to regulate coexistence in Herrnhut and his other villages eventually led to a "Pietist-style revival experience" on August 13, 1727 (Atwood 2010, 59). This day is considered as the actual date of foundation of the Church.

The Moravian Church of the eighteenth and early nineteenth centuries was characterised by a pronounced devotion to Jesus. In 1741, the Moravians officially appointed Jesus as their "general elder" ("Generalältester") and thus as the formal head of the church (Böß 2016, 156). As a result, Count Zinzendorf and, after his death, the governing bodies used lots to determine Jesus' will on all important issues (Homburg 1996, 203). The second major characteristic connects the Moravians to other Pietistic groups of the eighteenth century. They felt particularly bound by the great commission of the Gospel (Mt 28, 19–20) and considered proclaiming the gospel to all non-Christians, including Jews, and Muslims, to be one of their most important tasks. The Moravians started their very energetic missionary activities in the Atlantic World in 1732. They set up missionary stations for example in Greenland (1733), Georgia (1735), Suriname (1738), the Danish West Indies (1738), and Labrador (1770) (Dorfner 2020, 47–51). In addition, the Moravians established a larger number of settlements ("Ortsgemeinden"), exclusively inhabited by members of their faith, like Bethlehem in Pennsylvania or Christiansfeld in Denmark. This rapid expansion into the Atlantic World was, above all else, very expensive. As Heidrun Homburg has recently shown, the Moravian Church faced "uncovered debts" of around 1 million Guilders in 1750 (Homburg 2021, 303). Therefore, the Moravians urgently had to find reliable sources of income.

Abraham Dürninger, Jonas Paulus Weiß, and a few other Moravians who had grown up in renowned merchant families emphasised that new revenue opportunities had arisen with the rapid expansion into the Atlantic World. They pointed out what potential there was in their (transatlantic) networks for realising trade projects. Peter van Damnitz characterised this potential particularly succinctly in 1750:

> What potential we have for great undertakings by being at home in Silesia, in Saxony, in Holland, in England, in Ireland and in America, and by being able to communicate from one country to the other that which is least valid here and most valid there. (Hahn 1977, 326)

Damnitz's proposal to become (more) active in long-distance trade was anything but unproblematic, as both the New Testament and the Apocrypha consider trade critical in several passages. For example, Moravians who were in favour of trade were confronted with the wording of Jesus Sirach 26:29, according to which no merchant could remain innocent from sin. Set against this background, it is not surprising that in the 1730s and 1740s there were "strong reservations" in the Moravian Church against *any* kind of trading activity (Philipp 1975, 414). Count Zinzendorf did not completely reject trading activities but was critical of them almost his entire life. As Justus Nipperdey aptly points out, Zinzendorf's dismissive attitude derived from two different sources: First, he was concerned that trading activities could lead to sinful profiteering. Second, due to his aristocratic upbringing, he looked with disdain at trading activities (Nipperdey 2021, 536). Until the early 1750s, Zinzendorf argued that missionary activities should be financed primarily through donations from wealthy friends (Homburg 2021, 303). Only after the count had barely escaped debtors' prison in London in 1753, he began to successively revise his negative attitude towards trading activities (Podmore 1998, 272).

From the late 1750s onwards, the conviction became increasingly widespread within the Moravian Church that "trade itself was a noble thing" ("das Commercium ist an sich eine noble Sache") (UAH, R.2.B.44.1.c.1, 862). However, the Moravians were convinced that the way in which trade was carried out could be either sinful or beneficial (ibid.). The most visible expression of this change of conviction was the foundation of the so-called Commercial Society ("Commercien Societät") in 1758 (Engel 2007, 120). The company was initially based in Herrnhut and transferred to London in 1765. However, this transfer did not change the fact that the church leadership meticulously controlled the activities of the Commercial Society. The latter mainly exported textile fabrics to North America, the Caribbean, and Russia, drawing on the strong ties of the Moravian networks. For example, the fabrics made in Saxony were primarily sent to Moravians who then took care of sales, such as Henry van Vleck in New York. Their profits were divided annually according to the formula laid down in the Society's statutes: The shareholders received 50 per cent, the other 50 per cent was given as a "voluntary gift" ("ein freywilliges Present") to the Mission Diacony and was used for mission funding (12.8.1758. UAH, R.4.A.41).

As trading activities expanded, so did the efforts to ensure that these activities were carried out according to the will of Jesus. However, considering the geographical extension of Moravians in the Atlantic World, this was anything but an easy task. The following section therefore examines how the General Synods in the second half of the eighteenth century tried to bring commercial activities in line with biblical norms.

"Commerce that Jesus Could Approve". The Moral Economy of the Moravian Church

Debates on Profit and Sin at the General Synod of 1764

After the passing of Count Zinzendorf on 9th May 1760, the General Synod evolved into the "constitutional assembly" of the Moravian Church (Peucker 2000b, 51). By the end of the eighteenth century, five General Synods were held, each lasting about two to three months (1764, 1769, 1775, 1782, 1789). They were attended by members of the central governing bodies and by delegates from the Moravian settlements. The following analysis will focus on the General Synod of Marienborn in 1764. One of the most important tasks of this very first General Synod was to answer the question of who should lead the church in the time between two synods (Mettele 2009, 76). The delegates therefore created the so-called Unity Directorate ("Unitätsdirektorium"; after 1769 called "Unity Elders' Conference"), which took the lead after conclusion of the synod. At the same time, the delegates had to deal with numerous pressing problems in the field of economy.

From July 1st to August 27th in 1764, 90 delegates met in Marienborn, located about 30 kilometres northeast of Frankfurt/Main. Ahead of the Synod, some of the delegates concluded that more and more Moravians were striving too much for profit. The Minutes of the Synod therefore contain the delegates' complaint that especially merchants and craftsmen made "profit the main thing" in "commercium" ("daß [...] der Gewinnst zu einer Haupt-Sache gemacht wird") (UAH, R.2.B.44.1.c.1, 861). At the same time, the delegates recorded the excuse often used by merchants and craftsmen to justify high prices, emphasising that the more profit they would make, the more money they could give to the Church, for example, to finance missionary work (ibid. 861f.). In the eyes of the delegates, the pursuit of large profits was extremely dangerous in a twofold respect. Their main concern was that Jesus Christ might turn away from the Moravians if they continued to act like mundane merchants. If the Saviour were to turn away—the delegates were convinced—the result would undoubtedly be the failure of all commercial activities and the decline of the settlements. At the same time, the delegates were concerned about the reputation of the Moravians in the world. They noted the rumour, that in some countries people could no longer distinguish between Moravians and the Quakers, whom the delegates considered rapacious and degenerate (ibid. 867).

Given these perceptions, it is not surprising that the delegates decided on drastic measures: At the end of the General Synod, a Commercial Committee ("Commercien Committee") was to be set up in each settlement "to keep a close eye" on the activities of the respective merchants and craftsmen (ibid. 864). Furthermore, the delegates instructed the Unity Directorate to inform all settlements how to bring the "commercium" in line with the "heart of Jesus" (ibid. 869). The Directorate took both instructions very seriously and established a first Commercial Committee in Herrnhut, which discussed in several meetings how to harmonise biblical norms and trade practices. The resolutions were summarised in a circular letter that was sent to all settlements on 1st March 1766, almost two years after the synod began.

In this circular, the Unity Directorate emphatically recalls that all trading activities are to be understood as service to others:

> The basic idea of a brother-commercio should be a sincere, honest and as much as possible mutually beneficial service of the neighbour, which is based on the words of our Lord: 'What you want people to do to you, you do to them. (Moravian Archives Bethlehem [MAB], BethCong, 533)

In the perception of the Directors, the pursuit of large gains without moderation was incompatible with the Golden Rule of the Gospel of Matthew (7:12), which was quoted verbatim by them. Instead, Moravians should charge fair prices for their goods so that both they and the buyers could be satisfied with the deal. Moreover, the Directors did not fail to point out how much the pursuit of wealth endangered personal salvation. In their circular letter to all settlements, they quoted 1 Timothy

6:9, a passage also frequently used by Quakers to warn merchants against greed (Sahle 2015, 9): "They that WANT be rich, fall into temptation, and a snare, and into many foolish and hurtful lusts, which drown men in destruction and perdition" (MAB, BethCong, 533). By capitalising the word "WANT" ("WOLLEN") they made it clear that the pursuit of wealth was incompatible with membership in the Moravian Church.

Both quotations vividly demonstrate that the Moravians established a moral economy that without doubt had similarities with the old European economic concept of the fifteenth and early sixteenth centuries. As Winfried Schulze and Johannes Burkhardt have shown, for example, the selfish pursuit of wealth was considered a violation of the divine order and thus sinful in the sixteenth century (Schulze 1987, 15f.; Burkhardt 1993, 10f.). Above all, Martin Luther emphasised that merchants and traders should strive to earn their honest living without succumbing to profiteering (Luther 1524). Needless to say, the majority of merchants in the sixteenth century were striving for (large) profit. However, the discourses on the just price and the common good remained present, especially in the Holy Roman Empire, well into the eighteenth century (Hellmuth 1986). Thus, the Unity Directorate wanted to ensure with their circular letter that, sociologically speaking, there was no difference between "talk" and "action" among Moravians (Brunsson 1986, 170–173).

In addition, the Directors emphasised several times in their letter how much the principal reputation of the Moravian Church depended on satisfied customers. Once people would experience that the Moravians "provide them with good goods", the creditworthiness ("credit") of the Moravian Church in society would automatically increase (MAB, BethCong, 533). This concern for the reputation of the church becomes understandable when one considers what a negative reputation the Moravians had in the mid-eighteenth century. In the Holy Roman Empire, the Moravian Church faced a massive discourse in the 1740s in which they were branded as dangerous sectarians (Dorfner 2018, 283). This discourse was so dense that review journals printed omnibus reviews of the numerous anti-Moravian publications. In England, meanwhile, the above-mentioned debt crisis of the Moravians in 1753 had done serious damage to their reputation. When several English settlements could not pay their debts, the idea arose among merchants, publicists, and theologians that the Moravians were shady bankrupts (Whitefield 1753; Podmore, 1998, 271–273). It can thus be concluded that the moral economy of the Moravians was also intended to secure their acceptance in the Atlantic World. However, given the vast geographical distances between the governing bodies in Marienborn or Herrnhut and the settlements in, for example, North America, the question arises as to whether the Directors' circular was followed at all. In the next section, the focus will be on the implementation in Bethlehem, PA.

Watchmen for Bethlehem's Moral Economy. The Commerce Conference in Bethlehem (1766–1768)

It is not possible to determine when exactly the Unity Directors' circular letter arrived in Bethlehem. In fall of 1766, the local Elders Conference selected a total of seven men who would henceforth be the members of the Commerce Conference ("Commercien Conference") of Bethlehem. On December 11th 1766, the day had come: Ferdinand Detmers, Jasper Payne, Abraham Boemper, George Klein, Mathew Weis, Georg Huber, and Christian Christensen gathered for the constituent meeting of the Commerce Conference. They vowed to advice and oversee "everything that concerns the commerce" in Bethlehem in such a way that the Saviour's name "thro' it may be glorified" (MAB, BethCong, 533, December 11, 1766). In other words, from that day on, there were seven watchmen in Bethlehem who kept a close eye on the local Moravians' moral economy.

The Commerce Conference's Minute Book allows for a detailed reconstruction of its activities. The minutes also provide evidence that the letter of the Unity Directors of March 11th 1766 was the impetus for the founding of the Commerce Conference: One of the seven conference members copied the letter in its entirety on the first 14 pages of the Minute Book. Henceforth, in all cases of doubt, the members could refer to the Minute Book to see what guidance the Directors had given to ensure that Jesus approved of the trading activities.

In its first year of existence, the Commerce Conference met approximately once a month. Looking at the total of 12 meetings held in 1767, it becomes apparent that the members were primarily concerned with two challenges. First, they strove to ensure that all goods and services in Bethlehem were both of good quality and fairly priced. During the April 2nd meeting, for example, the members discussed the price setting of scrivener John Okely. Several of his customers had "complain'd off, that he takes too large a price for his writings" (Ibid, April 2, 1767). The Conference therefore decided to exhort Okely in a personal conversation to take less profit. The second major challenge of the Commerce Conference was to enforce the third of the Ten Commandments, contained in the Old Testament, that obliged Moravians to keep Sunday holy. The members of the Conference admonished several Moravians not to work on Sundays because they believed that breaking the Third Commandment would particularly anger the Lord (ibid. May 1, 1767).

At first glance, it seems that clear parallels existed between the regulatory efforts of the Commerce Conference and the guilds in, for example, the Holy Roman Empire. The latter also monitored the quality of goods and took measures against Sunday work (Ennen 1971, 59–61; Canzler 1999, 90). Their goals, however, differed fundamentally. While guilds restricted competition to ensure an honest living for their members, the goal of the Commerce Conference was to establish a godly moral economy which would raise the standing of Moravians both in Jesus's eyes and in the world.

How did the Moravians in Bethlehem react to interventions of the newly created Commerce Conference? There is some evidence in the Minute Book that the deviant but at the same time God-fearing Moravians reacted with great understanding to the exhortations. After being admonished by a member of the Commerce Conference, the deviant person usually promised to "do so no more" (MAB, BethCong, 533, April 2, 1767). The recalcitrant attitude of Brother Fischer, who was admonished not to work on Sundays, therefore, formed a clear exception. Accordingly, on May 1st, 1767, the members of the Commerce Conference noted with irritation, that Fischer "hath not promis'd to do so no more" (ibid. May 1, 1767).

In the second year of its existence, the Commerce Conference met less frequently. Between January 1st and November 20th, 1768, only seven meetings were held. The November 20th entry is also the last in the Minute Book. Why no more meetings were held after that cannot be explained with absolute certainty. It is striking, however, that the Commerce Conference in 1768 saw less need for action. For example, the members did meet on February 4th, 1768, only to note in the Minute Book that "no matters arose" that needed to be addressed (ibid. February 4, 1768). And the meeting on August 18, 1768 did not take too much time either. After two items on the agenda, the minute-taker noted that "nothing else occurred this time" ("sonst kam dieses mahl nichts vor"; Ibid. August 18, 1768).

Katherine Engel, who has extensively researched the North American Moravians, does not address the end of the Commerce Conference in her book (Engel 2009). However, she emphasises that "the church partially withdraw from the economic life of the town's residents" (ibid. 215). In the 1770s, Engel continues, "moral economic behaviour" became "primarily a question of individual choice" (ibid. 216).

This statement may be valid for Bethlehem and the local Elders' Conference. However, the central governing bodies of the Moravian Church, operating in the Holy Roman Empire, opposed an individualised economy. The Elders' Conference in particular was not willing to let individuals decide whether they were shaping their economic activities "according to the mind of Jesus". Accordingly, the Elders sent out circulars in the later years, for example in 1783, exhorting all Moravians to uphold the moral economy (UAH, R.3.B.27.III, "Circularia wegen Commercii in den Gemeinen"). However, further attempts by the Unity Elders' to shape and secure the Moravian moral economy will not be analysed in the following. Instead, the focus in the last section is on the external perception of the Moravian moral economy.

"... Brotherly Love and Honesty in All Their Dealings". Christian Behaviour as a Competitive Advantage

In the last third of the eighteenth century, the way the Moravians were perceived in Europe changed significantly. As outlined above, numerous theologians had branded the Moravians as dangerous sectarians in the mid-eighteenth century. However, after the deeply religious Moravians began transnational trade activities and successfully established manufactories, they garnered attention in a very different way from the 1760s onwards as cameralists, princely councillors, and publicists visited the settlements of the Moravians in large numbers (Dorfner 2018, 292–296). The latter addressed the Moravians' moral economy in their publications and thus ensured that they were henceforth perceived primarily as trustworthy trading partners and industrious subjects. These positive publications in turn led to more market participants entering business relations with the Moravians.

One of the publicists who promoted this change in perception was Johann Adolph Hildt (1734–1805). He published a six-page article about the Moravians in June 1787 in the renowned German "Handlungs-Zeitung" ("Merchant business Journal") which he edited (Hildt 1787, 169–171 and 177–179). Hildt, who was not only a publicist but also a merchant in Gotha and published his journal for a clearly defined target group, i.e. merchants and manufactory owners residing in the Holy Roman Empire (Middell 2002, 310). The journal was therefore specialised in news "from the trade sector" (Hildt 1784, preface) which is why Hildt does not inform his readers about the religious practices of the Moravians such as the use of lots to determine the will us Jesus. Instead, he tells his readers that the Moravians have chosen "trade and manufactures as their tools" ("wählten [...] Handel und Manufakturen zu ihrem Hülfsmittel") and then goes on to discuss their specific moral economy (Hildt 1787, 169). Life in the Moravian settlements, according to Hildt, was characterised by "industriousness, orderliness, brotherly love and honesty in all their dealings" ("Arbeitsamkeit, Ordnung, Bruderliebe und Redlichkeit in allen ihren Geschäften", ibid, 169). Following his general remarks about the moral economy of the Moravians, Hildt offered his readers a list of all the merchants and manufactory owners who were active in the Moravian settlement of Neudietendorf, 15 kilometres from Gotha. In addition, readers throughout the Holy Roman Empire learned that the Moravians produced goods in large numbers that were highly sought after by the emerging consumer society. Hildt mentioned, for example, the manufactory owner Jacob Lilienthal, who was born in what is now Oslo, (Hildt 1787, 171; Benneckenstein 2001, 32). Lilienthal and his employees processed whalebone, which was needed to produce corsets, among other things, and offered their products for sale in Neudietendorf as well as at the fairs in Frankfurt/Main, Braunschweig, and Kassel (Steele 2001, 6–16).

The moral economy of the Moravians generated a great deal of attention among publicists. At the same time, it proved to be a competitive advantage in practice, as becomes clear when considering the impact on the areas surrounding the Moravian settlements. The merchants and craftsmen in the neighbouring towns and villages suffered (significant) financial losses because the inhabitants of their communities often preferred to buy from the Moravians and even accepted much longer journeys to do so. The Christiansfeld settlement in the Kingdom of Denmark and the city of Haderslev (German: Hadersleben), about 11 kilometres away, are vivid examples.

The foundation of Christiansfeld on April 1st 1773 was preceded by an initiative of the Danish Minister of Finance Johann Friedrich Struensee (1737–1772). He had invited the Moravians in 1771 to find a settlement in the duchy of Schleswig (Fischer 2013, 175; Petterson 2017, 35). After the founding of Christiansfeld, it only took two decades for the Moravians to gain such a "good reputation" in trade matters, that they posed a serious threat to many merchants and craftsmen in Haderslev ("der gute Ruf", Lyna 1797, 725). Against this background, the journal "Lyna", published in Haderslev, advertised a prize question on how to eliminate or at least contain the competitive pressure from the Moravians (Lyna 1797, 31). The winning essay was printed on 20th October 1797 and brings into focus the interplay between moral economy and economic success (Fig. 9.1).

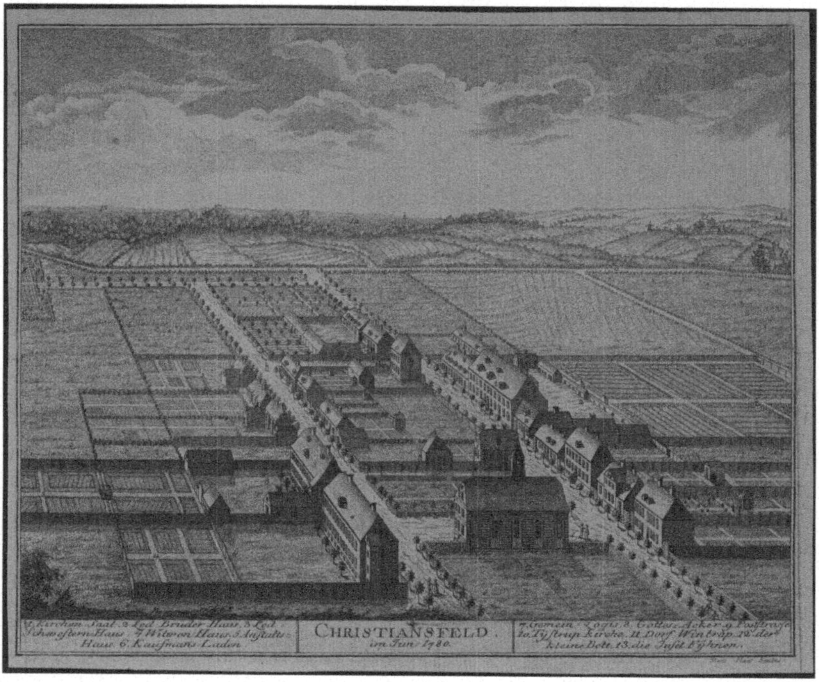

Fig. 9.1 "Christiansfeld in June 1780", engraving by Johann M. Haas (1752–1833) (Kgl. Bibliothek, MP001409)

The anonymous author with the initials F. J. M. frankly admits that many inhabitants of Haderslev visited Christiansfeld on a regular basis because they "get or believe to get better goods or easier prices there" ("weil sie entweder bessere Waaren oder leichtere Preise daselbst bekommen oder zu bekommen glauben", ibid. 722). The Moravians' efforts to find fair prices and their deep-rooted conviction that trade was a service to others thus created a distinct pull effect. The good reputation of the Moravians, the author continues, even resulted in some Haderslev residents being convinced that all goods, without exception, were better in Christiansfeld (ibid. 722). Another important factor contributing to this pull was the fact that prices in Christiansfeld were fixed prices. All customers, whether Moravian or foreigner, had to pay the same price for a good. In Haderslev, on the other hand, every interested party had to propose a price for the desired good and enter negotiations with the seller—a procedure that the author describes as not only ridiculous but also off-putting for potential customers (ibid. 725). With their system of fixed prices, the Moravians were pioneers not only in the Duchy of Schleswig, but—strictly speaking—throughout Europe (Philipp 1991, 71).

Finally, the good reputation and thus the pull effect was also promoted by the fact that the Moravians themselves were willing to pay higher prices, especially for food. The European Moravians did not engage in agriculture, partly because Count Zinzendorf was convinced that sedentary farmers would be less willing to become missionaries (Gollin 1967, 166). As a result, the Moravians living in Christiansfeld and the other European settlements had to buy most of their food in the neighbouring villages. In this regard, the author notes that Moravians "usually pay a little better for the products of the peasants than is done in Haderslev" ("daher sie auch die Produkte des Landmanns gewöhnlich etwas besser bezahlen als in Hadersleben geschieht" Lyna 1797, 725).

It is worth mentioning that there was one more reason for the people of Haderslev to shop in Christiansfeld, which had nothing to do with the moral economy of the Moravians. As a result of their transnational networks, the Moravians were able to offer goods in Christiansfeld "that could not be bought anywhere else" ("die sonst nicht zu haben sind", ibid. 724). These goods included, for example, tobacco from Herrnhut, English ceramics, etc. (Wagner 1940, 62). The presence of exclusive goods thus further strengthened Christiansfeld's attractiveness. But since the customers mainly bought everyday products in Christiansfeld that were also in stock in Haderslev, it can be assumed that it was primarily the moral economy that triggered the pull factor. This assumption is supported, among other things, by the F. J. M.'s statement that the postal service brings whole wagonloads of everyday products from Christiansfeld to Haderslev every week (ibid. 724).

Given these findings, sceptics might suggest that the Moravians in Christiansfeld and the other settlements deliberately used fair prices to make more profit on the bottom line. This anachronistic assumption, however, diametrically contradicts the mindset of the deeply religious Moravians of the eighteenth century. They considered the way non-Pietist people traded to be a "most dangerous thing" ("eine höchst gefährliche Sache") (Circular Letter, 31.8.1783. UAH, R.3.B.27.III). Accordingly, their own moral economy, aligned with the word of the Bible, seemed to them the only guarantee of securing the salvation of Moravian merchants and craftsmen.

Summary

Religious norms significantly informed and shaped the moral economy of the Moravian Church. In the eyes of the Moravians, the pursuit of large profits was wholly incompatible with the Golden Rule formulated in the Gospel of Matthew (7:12). Instead, they understood trading activities as a service to others, which is why a fair price had to be set for all goods and services. Given the geographic spread of the Moravians throughout the Atlantic World, ensuring adherence to religious norms in trade activities was anything but easy for the governing bodies that were in the Holy Roman Empire. The Unity Directorate sent circular letters to all settlements and mission stations, emphasising that commercial activities should always be carried out in a way that would please Jesus Christ. In addition Commerce Conferences were established in the settlements, whose members monitored whether the merchants and craftsmen complied with the instructions of the Unity Directors.

In the last third of the eighteenth century, the Moravians' moral economy proved to be a competitive advantage. In an environment where, for example, Lutherans and Puritans refused to regulate the market by means of biblical norms (Valeri 2010, 234–249), many market participants considered the Moravians to be particularly trustworthy. This competitive advantage becomes particularly visible when the interactions between Moravian settlements and the towns or villages in their surrounding areas are brought into focus. Many inhabitants of the Danish town of Haderslev regularly shopped in Christiansfeld, 11 kilometres away, because they were convinced that they would get better quality goods at better prices from the Moravians. The merchants and craftsmen in Haderslev, on the other hand, suffered massive losses in income at the end of the eighteenth century. In 1797, their situation was so precarious that the journal "Lyna" published the prize question on how to limit the competitive pressure from the deeply religious Moravians.

As the case study has shown, the Moravians contributed to the return of religious norms to eighteenth-century trade practices. However, the Moravians represent only one group, albeit a very important one, within the heterogeneous Pietist movement. Moreover, Pietism was by no means the only Christian renewal movement of the eighteenth century. In Catholicism, adherents of Jansenism considered the official church to be secularised and set themselves apart from it with "moral rigorism" (Hersche 2006, vol. 1, 137). Accordingly, it should prove very worthwhile for historians to study the moral economies of eighteenth-century religious renewal movements more intensively in the future.

References

Archival Sources

Moravian Archives Bethlehem (MAB)
BethCong, 533 (Minutes of the "Commercien Conferenz")
The Unity Archivs—Moravian Archives Herrnhut (UAH)
R.2.B.44.1.c.1
R.3.B.27.III
R.4.A.41.

Primary Sources

Anonym. 1745. *Der Christliche Kauffmann, oder Erweis, daß ein Kauffmann auch ein Christ seyn könne und müsse.* Berlin: Johann Gottfried Michaelis.

Büsch, Christian A. 1799. *Moral für Kaufleute.* Giessen: Stamm.

Hahn, Hans-Christoph (Ed.). 1977. *Zinzendorf und die Herrnhuter Brüder. Quellen zur Geschichte der Brüder-Unität von 1722 bis 1760*, Hamburg: Wittig.

Hildt, Johann A. 1784. *Handlungszeitung oder wöchentliche Nachrichten von Handel, Manufakturwesen, Künsten und neuen Erfindungen*, Gotha: Hildt.

Hildt, Johann A. 1787. *Handlungszeitung oder wöchentliche Nachrichten von Handel, Manufakturwesen, Künsten und neuen Erfindungen*, Gotha: Hildt.

Lyna. Eine Wochenschrift, 44 (1797).

Whitefield, George. 1753. *An Expostulatory Letter Addressed to Nicholas Lewis, Count Zinzendorff, and Lord Advocate of the Unitas Fratrum*, London: G. Keith.

Secondary Sources

Atwood, Craig D. 2010. *Community of the Cross. Moravian Piety in Colonial Bethlehem.* University Park, PA: Pennsylvania State University Press.

Benneckenstein, Horst. 2001. Wie der Sareptaner nach Neudietendorf kam. Oder wie durch Zuwanderer ein neuer Ort entstand. *In Heimat Thüringen* 8: 31–32.

Böß, Stephanie. 2016. *Gottesacker-Geschichten als Gedächtnis. Eine Ethnographie zur Herrnhuter Erinnerungskultur am Beispiel von Neudietendorfer Lebensläufen.* Münster: Waxmann.

Brunsson, Nils. 1986. Organizing for Inconsistencies. On Organizational Conflict, Depression and Hypocrisy as Substitutes for Action. *Scandinavian Journal of Management Studies* 2: 165–185.

Burkhardt, Johannes. 1993. Die Entdeckung des Handels. Die kommerzielle Welt in der Wissensordnung der Frühen Neuzeit In *Wirtschaft und Literatur. Drei Perspektiven aus historischer und literaturwissenschaftlicher Sicht*, ed. Rektor der Universität Augsburg, 5–28. Augsburg: Universitätsverlag.

Canzler, Gerhard. 1999. *Zünfte und Gilden in Ostfriesland bis 1744*, Weener (Ems): Risius.

Dorfner, Thomas. 2018. Von bösen Sektierern zu fleißigen Fabrikanten. Zum Wahrnehmungswandel der Herrnhuter Brüdergemeine im Kontext kameralistischer Peuplierungspolitik (ca. 1750–1800). *Zeitschrift für Historische Forschung* 45: 283–313. https://doi.org/10.3790/zhf.45.2.283.

Dorfner, Thomas. 2020. Commercium nach dem Sinn Jesu. Überlegungen zum Marktverhalten der Brüdergemeine am Beispiel des Labradorhandels (1770–1815). *Jahrbuch für Wirtschaftsgeschichte/Economic History Yearbook* 61: 39–66. https://doi.org/10.1515/jbwg-2020-0003.

Engel, Katherine C. 2007. Commerce that the Lord could Sanctify and Bless. Moravian Participation in Transatlantic Trade, 1740–1760. In *Pious Pursuits. German Moravians in the Atlantic World*, ed. Michele Gillespie and Robert Beachy, 113–127. New York and Oxford: Berghahn.

Engel, Katherine C. 2009. *Religion and Profit. Moravians in Early America*, Philadelphia: University of Pennsylvania Press.

Ennen, Reinald. 1971. *Zünfte und Wettbewerb. Möglichkeiten und Grenzen zünftlerischer Wettbewerbsbeschränkungen im städtischen Handel und Gewerbe des Spätmittelalters*, Köln and Wien: Böhlau.

Fischer, Ole. 2013. Wirtschaftliche Prosperität und religiöse Erweckung. Das Handwerk in der Herrnhutersiedlung Christiansfeld. In *Aus der Mitte des Landes. Klaus-Joachim Lorenzen-Schmidt zum 65. Geburtstag*, ed. Detlev Kraack and Martin Rheinheimer, 175–194. Neumünster and Hamburg: Wachholtz.

Freist, Dagmar. 2017. A Very Warm Surinam Kiss. Staying Connected, Getting Engaged—Interlacing Social Sites of the Moravian Diaspora. In *Connecting Worlds and People. Early Modern Diasporas*, ed. Dagmar Freist and Susanne Lachenicht, 62–80. London and New York: Routledge.

Gleixner, Ulrike. 2005. *Pietismus und Bürgertum. Eine historische Anthropologie der Frömmigkeit*. Göttingen: Vandenhoeck & Ruprecht.

Gollin, Gillian L. 1967. *Moravians in Two Worlds*. A Study of Changing Communities, New York and London: Columbia University Press.

Hellmuth, Eckart. 1986. Praktische Philosophie und Wirtschaftsgesinnung. Zur Reflexion über Wirtschaft, Erwerb und Gewinn in Deutschland des 18. *Jahrhunderts. Archiv Für Kulturgeschichte* 68: 135–149. https://doi.org/10.7788/akg.1986.68.1.135.

Hersche, Peter. 2006. *Muße und Verschwendung. Europäische Gesellschaft und Kultur im Barockzeitalter*, vol. 2. Freiburg im Breisgau: Herder.

Homburg, Heidrun. 1996. Ein kaufmännisches Unternehmen in der Oberlausitz: Abraham Dürninger & Co. *Jahrbuch für Wirtschaftsgeschichte* 37: 199–221. https://doi.org/10.1524/jbwg.1996.37.2.199.

Homburg, Heidrun. 2021. Gläubige und Gläubiger. Zum ‚Schuldenwesen' der Brüder-Unität um die Mitte des 18. Jahrhunderts. In *Pietismus und Ökonomie (1650–1750)*, ed. Wolfgang Breul, Benjamin Marschke and Alexander Schunka, 301–335. Göttingen: Vandenhoeck & Ruprecht.

Mettele, Gisela. 2005. Kommerz und fromme Demut. Wirtschaftsethik und Wirtschaftspraxis im “Gefühlspietismus”. *Vierteljahresschrift Für Sozial- Und Wirtschaftsgeschichte* 92: 301–321.

Mettele, Gisela. 2009. *Weltbürgertum oder Gottesreich. Die Herrnhuter Brüdergemeine als globale Gemeinschaft 1727–1857*. Göttingen: Vandenhoeck & Ruprecht.

Meyer, Dietrich. 2000. *Zinzendorf und die Herrnhuter Brüdergemeine: 1700–2000*. Göttingen: Vandenhoeck & Ruprecht.

Middell, Katharina. 2002. *Die Bertuchs müssen doch in dieser Welt überall Glück haben. Der Verleger Friedrich Justin Bertuch und sein Landes-Industrie-Comptoir um 1800*, Leipzig: Leipziger Universitäts-Verlag.

Nipperdey, Justus. 2021. Wirtschaft. In *Handbuch Pietismus*, ed. Wolfgang Breul, 535–541. Tübingen: Mohr Siebeck.

Overkamp, Anne S. 2020. *Fleiß, Glaube, Bildung. Kaufleute als gebildete Stände in Wuppertal 1760–1840*. Göttingen: Vandenhoeck & Ruprecht.

Peper, Ines. 2017. "Wir aber in der ganzen Gemeine durften einander trauen". Vom mährischen Geheimprotestantismus zur Herrnhuter Brüdergemeine. In *Maria Theresia? Neue Perspektiven der Forschung*, ed. Thomas Wallnig, Elisabeth Lobenwein and Stefan Seitschek, 67–86. Bochum: Verlag Dr. Dieter Winkler.

Petterson, Christina. 2017. From Communal Economy to Economic Community. Changes in Moravian Entrepreneurial Activities in the Eighteenth Century. *Journal for the History of the Reformed Pietism* 3: 25–48.

Peucker, Paul. 2000a. In Staub und Asche. Bewertung und Kassation im Unitätsarchiv 1760–1810. In *Alles ist euer, ihr aber seid Christi. Festschrift für Dietrich Meyer*, ed. Rudolf Mohr, 127–158. Köln: Rheinland-Verlag.

Peucker, Paul. 2000b. Synode. In *Herrnhuter Wörterbuch. Kleines Lexikon von brüderischen Begriffen*, ed. Paul Peucker. Herrnhut: Unitätsarchiv.

Peucker. Paul. 2022. *Herrnhut. The Formation of a Moravian Community, 1722–1732*. University Park, PA: Pennsylvania State University Press.

Philipp, Guntram. 1975. Wirtschaftsethik und Wirtschaftspraxis in der Geschichte der Herrnhuter Brüdergemeine. In *Unitas Fratrum. Herrnhuter Studien*, ed. Mari P. van Buijtenen, Cornelis Dekker and Huib Leeuwenberg, 401–463. Utrecht: Rijksarchief.

Philipp, Guntram. 1991. Die Sozial- und Wirtschaftsstruktur und die kulturellen Ausstrahlungen der Herrnhuter Brüdergemeine in Schlesien im 18. und 19. Jahrhundert. In *Kirchen und Bekenntnisgruppen im Osten des Deutschen Reiches. Ihre Beziehungen zu Staat und Gesellschaft. Zehn Beiträge*, ed. Jähnig, Bernhart and Silke Spieler, 71–130. Bonn: Kulturstiftung der Deutschen Vertriebenen.

Plumpe, Werner. 2009. Ökonomisches Denken und wirtschaftliche Entwicklung. Zum Zusammenhang von Wirtschaftsgeschichte und historischer Semantik der Ökonomie. *Jahrbuch Für Wirtschaftsgeschichte* 50: 27–52. https://doi.org/10.1524/jbwg.2009.50.1.27.

Plumpe, Werner. 2019. *Das kalte Herz. Kapitalismus. Die Geschichte einer andauernden Revolution*, Berlin: Rowohlt.

Podmore, Colin. 1998. *The Moravian Church in England, 1728–1760*. Oxford: Clarendon Press.

Sahle, Esther. 2015. An Investigation of Early Modern Quakers' Business Ethics. *Economic History Working Paper Series*, 216, 1–32.

Schulze, Winfried. 1987. *Vom Gemeinnutz zum Eigennutz. Über den Normenwandel in der ständischen Gesellschaft der Frühen Neuzeit*, München: Stiftung Historisches Kolleg.

Sensbach, Jon F. 2005. *Rebecca's Revival. Creating Black Christianity in the Atlantic World*, Cambridge, Mass: Harvard University Press.

Steele, Valerie. 2001. *The Corsette.* A Cultural History, New Haven: Yale University Press.
Valeri, Mark. 2010. *Heavenly Merchandize. How Religion Shaped Commerce in Puritan America*, Princeton: Princeton University Press.
Wagner, Hans. 1940. *Abraham Dürninger & Co. 1747–1939. Ein Buch von Herrnhutischem Kaufmanns- und Unternehmertum*, Herrnhut: Abraham Dürninger-Stiftung.
Ward, William R. 1987. Zinzendorf and Money. In *The Church and the Wealth*, ed. W. J. Sheils and D. Wood, 283–305. Oxford: Blackwell.
Zimmerling, Peter. 1991. Christliche Maßstäbe für das Wirtschaftsleben bei Zinzendorf und der Herrnhuter Brüdergemeine. In *Loving God and Keeping His Commandments*, ed. Markus Bockmuehl and Helmut Burkhardt, 107–121. Giessen: Brunnen-Verlag.

PART III

Modern Period

CHAPTER 10

Negotiating Religion, Moral Economy and Economic Ideas in the Late Ottoman Empire: Perspectives of Peasants and the Intelligentsia

E. Attila Aytekin

Introduction

There are various misconceptions about Ottoman economy, economic policies and economic thought for the later period (nineteenth century and early twentieth century) as well as earlier centuries. The most widespread argument about pre-modern Ottoman economy is that the state wanted to control all sectors and actors of the economy and employed various successful (at least until the eighteenth century) measures to that end. The classic formulation of this idea has been put forward by Mehmet Genç who has argued that the Ottoman

E. A. Aytekin (✉)
Department of Political Science and Public Administration, Middle East Technical University, Ankara, Turkey
e-mail: erdena@metu.edu.tr

T. Skambraks and M. Lutz (eds.), *Reassessing the Moral Economy*, Palgrave Studies in Economic History,
https://doi.org/10.1007/978-3-031-29834-9_10

state followed a comprehensive tripartite economic policy: provisionism (securing a cheap and high-quality supply of goods and services), traditionalism (desire to protect the status quo and the tendency to look to the past for models in case of change) and fiscalism (the systematic efforts to maximize revenue of the treasury) (1994, 60). Genç and his many followers (for example Çizakça 1985; Kuran 2004; for a nuanced formulation, see White 2008, 24–26) have underlined the tight grip of the state over economy through various measures such as market controls, tutelage over guilds and confiscation and stressed that the measures declined in efficacy as the eighteenth century progressed.

The conventional perspective has considered the nineteenth-century Ottoman economy in the context of decline and increasing foreign dominance (Issawi 1966). It has been argued that the Ottoman state did little to prevent the influx of imported goods into the empire, leading to the collapse of Ottoman manufacturing, long-term decline of the economy, abysmal situation of state finances and a late-developing capitalism. It has also been claimed that modern economic thinking found room in intellectual debates late and when it did, it was largely through importation of Western ideas by intellectuals and policy-makers (Kaynar 2014, par.6; Ş. Mardin 1985; Seyitdanlioğlu 1998). To sum up, the picture is extensive state control over the economy until the eighteenth century, weakening of such control in the eighteenth, and the influx of goods and ideas from abroad in the nineteenth, leading to an economic decline and a dearth of original ideas.

This picture is fraught with theoretical, methodological and empirical problems some of which have been clearly laid out in critical scholarship (Quataert 1993; 2003; Darling 2002) whereas others need further elaboration. First of all, the idea of a pre-modern state keeping the economy under strict control reflects the state- and dynasty-centred thinking that has dominated Ottomanist historiography for a long time. Instead of investigating the actual operation of the economy, such scholarship has focused on the agenda of the state and the mindset of those who rule it. A classical formulation of the state-centred approach can be found in Halil İnalcık, one of the foremost Ottomanist historians: "The Ottoman economic mind was closely related to the basic concept of state and society in the Middle East. It professed that the ultimate goal of a state was consolidation and extension of the ruler's power and the only way to reach it was to get rich sources of revenues. This in turn depended on the conditions making the productive classes prosperous. So the essential function of the state was to keep in force these conditions" (İnalcık 1970, 217). Secondly, the conventional perspective is highly anachronistic as it attributes to pre-modern state capabilities even modern states do not have and ignores the limitations pre-modern technology, infrastructure and communication channels put on the states (Aytekin 2021, 241).

At the empirical level, the conventional view of the nineteenth-century Ottoman economy is inaccurate as it, in conjunction with world economy, experienced an upturn (Özveren 2002, 130). The growth rates even indicate that the Ottoman economy did better than similar countries and areas such as Iran and Egypt and developing countries as a whole, although it lagged behind Latin America (Pamuk n.d.; 2018, 135–36). Moreover, manufacturing did not collapse and continued to evolve and grow (Quataert 1993). The steady expansion of domestic and international trade and the commercialization of agriculture ensured that there was significant accumulation of capital in the later Ottoman Empire. While political, military and economic foreign pressure was felt strongly, the development of Ottoman capitalism was also fuelled by internal dynamics. In parallel, the economic policies and ideas formulated and implemented were not completely imported; "home-grown" policies and thinking could be seen from the late eighteenth century onwards. The idea that all modern economic thinking was a product of foreign influence is a remnant of the modernization theory, which basically treats the entire Ottoman history from Selim III (1789–1807) onwards as one of Westernization. Indeed, there was hardly any foreign pressure or impact on the first laisser-faire policies implemented during the reign of this very sultan (Sayar 2000, 185) and the first modern original economic treatises of Ottoman authors dated from as early as the 1830s.

The piecemeal measures of economic liberalization and political and administrative centralization during the reigns of Selim III and Mahmud II (1808–1839) consolidated from 1839 onwards into a full-blown reform program generally known as the *Tanzimat*. While political and military pressure of the Great Powers gradually increased and Ottoman trade with the advanced capitalist countries became increasingly uneven, the reforms were largely a product of internal dynamics.

Different segments of the society related to the reforms in different ways; all, however, understood their depth and responded accordingly. Ottoman intelligentsia took varying positions regarding political and administrative reforms but the room for consensus was larger in the field of economics. From the last quarter of the nineteenth century, the free trade—protectionism competition dominated the debates; even then, the points on which Ottoman economic authors agreed remained sizable. A clear majority of the authors who wrote directly on economic issues were high-level bureaucrats who were also engaged in political and intellectual debates.[1] As the economy was being transformed along capitalist lines, these authors discussed the issues surrounding economy, culture and morality systematically. While the scientific study of economy was promoted in the empire starting from 1830s, religion remained an important component of the debate. Peasants, on their part, adopted the language of the reform program, protested its incomplete implementation and took radical steps when they deemed necessary. As they experienced the transformation of the economy unevenly, the relation they established between economy and morality diverged significantly from intellectual debates. In particular, the cultivators who worked in the large estates or who clashed with local notables over land conceived of a moral economy that was strikingly different from that of the Ottoman economic writers. As this chapter shows, one noticeable characteristic of their moral economy was the rarity of religious themes.

The paper starts with a brief theoretical discussion about the relation between the economic and the non-economic in capitalism. The next section concentrates on what moral economy meant for late Ottoman peasants and how that unfolded in different agrarian conflicts in the nineteenth century. The study then turns to the Ottoman intellectuals and bureaucrats who wrote about economy and economics, focusing especially on their views regarding the problems of Ottoman economy and society, market-state relations, the importance of hard work and the role of religion in all those debates.

Capitalism and Moral Economy

As various thinkers within the Marxist theoretical tradition have dwelt upon, capitalism is distinguished from previous modes of production by the separation of the economic from other spheres of human activity.

[1] They were usually prolific authors who wrote on a wide range of topics. The first thinker to treat economics as a separate field and to limit his interest to that field was Sakızlı Ohannes (d.1912) and the first academic department of economics was established in the Republic of Turkey in 1936 (Aslanmirza 2018, 4).

While exploitation of the direct producers by the appropriators of the surplus had previously taken place through extra-economic means, in capitalism "the social functions of production and distribution, surplus extraction and appropriation, and the allocation of social labour are, so to speak, privatized and they are achieved by non-authoritative, non-political means. In other words, the social allocation of resources and labour does not, on the whole, take place by means of political direction, communal deliberation, hereditary duty, custom, or religious obligation, but rather through the mechanisms of commodity exchange" (Wood 1995, 29).

One has to be cautious, however, when thinking about the separation of economy from politics, culture, morality, etc., in capitalist societies as two reservations are in order to understand this separation fully. First, there are historical conditions specific to capitalism that has made such demarcations of human activity possible and created an autonomous sphere of economy (Wood 1995 Chapter 1). Secondly, economy and other spheres such as politics, culture, law, etc., are not separate in reality from each other; they *appear* as such in capitalism. The non-economic fields of social relations are not external to production relations; instead, it is the peculiarity of capitalism that the social relations of production themselves take the forms of apparently exclusive economic and non-economic spheres (Corrigan and Sayer 1981). Not only are the coercive power of the state and the legal recognition and enforcement of private property necessary conditions for the existence of a system of capitalist accumulation, capitalism requires social norms and cultural values that sustain the processes and relation of production (Wood 1995, 62).

Andrew Sayer makes this point forcefully in the context of a discussion of moral economy. He first underlines that markets are not equal to capitalism; capitalism has always depended also on non-market modes of coordinating division of labour. While market forces tend to displace moral norms and traditional cultural values, the autonomy that market forces have from values and norms has necessary limits (A. Sayer 2006, 79). "Economic relations (...) are structured by moral-economic norms about rights, entitlements, responsibilities and appropriate behavior" (A. Sayer 2006, 80). Sayer also criticizes the Polanyian metaphor of "embeddedness" as it suggests the externality of norms, values and other social relations in general to economy. What is also important in his intervention for the present study is that it draws attention to the historical struggles waged around certain characteristics of capitalist economic relations that were intense in the past but we now take for granted (A. Sayer 2006,

82–83). In other words, the historical processes that gave rise to capitalist accumulation also involved changes in moral norms and values that enable such processes to take place. It is no coincidence that classical liberal thinkers have tried hard to deny the historicity of capitalist relations and stressed the compatibility of the domination of market forces with human nature. It is crucial, therefore, to look into the periods before capitalism and before the associated ways of organizing production and coordinating division of labour looked simply "natural" and without alternative.

Morality, therefore, has been an important part of the debates surrounding capitalism in its early stages. It is, as A. Sayer and Wood warn us, still relevant to economic activities as well as economic thinking; hence the significance of "moral economy" for our times as well as the past. Although there is a history of the term moral economy before E.P. Thompson (Götz 2015), it was his 1971 intervention (Thompson 1993) that made it an established social scientific concept. Many others have discussed the concept or applied it to different contexts since then. I have elsewhere (Aytekin 2012) critically discussed moral economy based on the perspective of Thompson and James C. Scott, who has applied the concept compellingly to rural contexts and peasants (Scott 1976). I have offered a conception of moral economy that is applicable to late Ottoman instances of peasant resistance and revolt, and used that conception to analyse peasant strategies of resistance in three cases. In the following section, I elaborate on peasant moral economy in the late Ottoman context without going into details about the specific cases of peasant resistance.

Peasants and Moral Economy

In the context of late nineteenth-century Ottoman peasant resistance, moral economy can be defined as a combination of three tendencies: subsistence ethics, a notion of justness and valourizing labour. In late Ottoman cases of peasant insurgency, the role of subsistence ethics was visible most as the attachment to land as the source of livelihood. It was possible to see the impact of the subsistence ethics of the cultivators in cases where the peasants were faced with maximal demands of the landlords or when the demands would be limited. In one case of peasant insurgency that fits the first situation, the cultivators made clear that they would not enter negotiations about the amount of dues, but desired to eliminate all claims by landlords on the land they cultivated.[2] In another region where the cultivators found themselves in a situation closer to the second one, and where peasants had meaningful control over land and the production process, the shortage of arable land, the small strips that peasant households controlled and the low productivity led to sustained peasant resistance to any claim on their surplus, be it small or big.[3]

A notion of justness—a sense of what is just and what is not—was the second component of peasant moral economy. This can be considered as a rather vague component of peasant economy, variably referring to legality, legitimacy or acceptability. The notion of justness was most relevant to issues of taxation or other forms of extraction. Peasants reacted particularly strongly when the lines that define the "just" regarding taxes and dues were systematically violated by the rural upper classes or the state. Tax strikes were a frequent method of protest as Ottoman cultivators often used it, withholding taxes and dues, in some cases for more than a decade.[4]

The third component of the moral economy of peasants was valourization of own labour. For example, the cultivators would argue that the land in question consisted of territory that had been rocky and rough but had been turned into arable land through the intensive labour and great expense of the villagers.[5] In a similar vein, one of the issues that came up frequently in many mid-century rural disturbances was *angarya* (corvée).[6] Cultivators in different parts of the empire complained of corvée and tried various means to end or limit the practice. Rather than being simply related to staying above the subsistence threshold, the peasant opposition to corvée stemmed from their attribution of high importance to hard labour performed in the past.

One of the most striking characteristics of nineteenth-century peasant movements was the lesser visibility of the religious elements in peasant moral economy. There were occasional references in peasant petitions and

[2] BOA (Republic of Turkey Presidential State Archives–Ottoman Archives), İ.DH 15,687.

[3] FO 336/2, 31.12.1840, from Stevens to Brant.

[4] BOA, HR.MKT 26/24; BOA, A.MKT.UM 18/46, 58/30, 137/69; BOA, A.MKT.MHM 33/13.

[5] BOA, HR.MKT 98/85.

[6] BOA, İ.DH 15,687 app.1; BOA A.MKT.MVL 37/47.

testimonies to concepts with religious connotations, such as *zulüm*.[7] Yet, sustained references to religious concepts or a systematic attempt on the part of the cultivators to justify their demands and actions on the basis of religion was conspicuously absent. In contrast, the *Tanzimat* reforms and the new polity they brought about was a frequent framework of reference. Below I discuss the infrequency of religious references and the prominence of the reforms in peasant moral economy as well as briefly describe the reform program.

In 1839, the Ottoman state initiated the *Tanzimat* reforms, which aimed at guaranteeing security of life and property, establishing the principle of equality before law regarding Muslim and non-Muslim Ottomans, radically reforming the taxation system and putting a regular system for military service in place. The reform program that lasted until the promulgation of the first constitution in 1876 brought about significant change through an enlargement and reorganization of the bureaucracy, gradual democratization of decision-making processes, enactment of a large number of modern laws, steps taken to institute equality before law and steps towards secularization (Aytekin 2012, 196–97). The trend of secularization proceeded more gradually than other trends as Islam remained a major pillar of legitimacy of the state throughout the century. The impact of this was also seen in the disadvantages non-Muslim cultivators could experience when they brought a conflict with Muslim notables to the attention of the state.

In different parts of the late Ottoman Empire there was a widespread pattern in which the owners of large estates were Muslim, and the cultivators were non-Muslim. Although there were certainly areas where the direct producers and the landowners belonged to the same ethno-religious group, more common was the model juxtaposing Muslim landowners and non-Muslim cultivators. Among the regions where non-Muslim cultivators found themselves in conflict with Muslim landowners/elite were Canik (present-day Turkey; see Şahin 2003), Vidin (present-day Bulgaria; see İnalcık 1943), Tırhala/Trikala (present-day Greece; see A. Y. Kaya 2012), İvranye/Vranje (present-day Serbia; see Kırlı 2015), Niş/Niš (present-day Serbia; see Uzun 2002), Bosnia (see Gelez 2016), Diyarbekir/Diyarbakır (present-day Turkey; see Özbek 2012) and

[7] *Zulüm* is a term meaning oppression and cruelty, which can be found in the Quran many times and which could refer to both rejecting the divine commandments and injustice committed by one person to another (see Çağrıcı n.d.).

Eflak/Wallachia (present-day Romania; see Yıldız and Kokdaş 2020). In regions where class and ethno-religious demarcations largely or fully overlapped, being non-Muslim was a structural basis of the exclusion of direct producers from landholding. As a result, in the agrarian disputes during the nineteenth-century religious difference played an accentuated role; many elements of the relation of exploitation between the direct producers and appropriators of surplus in various Ottoman provinces came to depend on the social, political, legal and cultural repercussions of religious difference.

In addition, religious difference resonated with the tensions that emanated from the imperfect implementation of reforms. The Ottoman state in the *Tanzimat* period had been metamorphosing in the direction of a modern state in terms of its laws, administrative structure, the development of the principle of representation, etc. At the same time, however, in times of rural unrest Ottoman authorities often defended practices and ideas that were blatantly against the new principles declared. In handling cases of agrarian conflict, the authorities often underlined the significance of religious difference, and did not hesitate to note it as a fundamental reason why the non-Muslim cultivators should not have the control of land. Religious difference thus acted as a structural constraint on direct producers whenever they attempted to modify the relations of production prevalent in the estates in their favour. Under these circumstances, it was only natural for Ottoman peasants who were involved in intensive agrarian conflicts to leave the religious element largely out of their moral economy. Instead, they opted for using the mid-century reforms as a window of opportunity and voiced their complaints and demands increasingly in a language of reform.

While there is a larger body of literature regarding the way non-Muslim peasants related to the *Tanzimat*, there is indication that the reaction of Muslim peasants was similar, as seen in the case of Palestinian peasants. In the second half of the nineteenth century, developing capitalism, increasing integration with the global economic networks and Ottoman reforms led to the creation of a new elite in Ottoman Palestine, which depended more on commercial success than traditional forms of legitimacy and was therefore concerned less about peasant demands and concerns (Freas 2010). Under pressure, the peasants turned to official channels, including the *kadi* (Islamic judge and notary) courts. It is significant that even when addressing these institutions which were Islamic in character, they did not make much use of religious notions and arguments. Instead, they appealed to a sense of justice and the principle of equality before law of the reformed polity (Doumani 1995, 175–76). In the petitions they addressed to local authorities it was possible to see that Muslim peasants did not make recourse to religious elements, instead complained of the violation of rules of decent behaviour and just regulations by the local elite (Doumani 1995, 172).

The conventional wisdom considers the reforms as a top-down project designed and implemented by the high-level and reform-minded bureaucrats, which was either not understood by or met with the hostility of different groups in Ottoman society (Ortaylı 1999; İnalcık 1985; Lewis 2002). This view has been challenged by more recent research which has shown that the reforms were implemented as a result of negotiation and accommodation with local forces (for example, Köksal 2002; Ueno 2013). The way both Muslim and non-Muslim peasants related to the reform also challenges the idea that the general populace was either indifferent or hostile to the Tanzimat. Cultivators across the empire were not against the reforms; instead, they protested the incomplete realization of the reform program in their provinces and the problems that created for them. As the tax reforms were implemented gradually in different provinces, some of them also pushed for the implementation of the reforms in their province immediately.[8] Moreover, "while struggling to avoid double taxation and ward off the extra pressure exerted by the upper classes during the transition to the new system of taxation, Ottoman peasants also adopted the language of reform, justice, and equality introduced by the Tanzimat" (Aytekin 2012, 227). Either by implicitly referring to the reformed polity by injecting phrases such as "from now on" or "the new law" to their petitions (Kırlı 2015, 18), or directly referring to constitutive texts (Chevallier 1959, 49), they endorsed the reform program and adopted its language, trying to make most of the window of opportunity the reforms opened for them.

[8] FO 195/296, 04.09.1850, from Bennett to Neale.

Intelligentsia, Economics and Religion

It is possible to roughly divide late Ottoman economic policies and thought into four periods. The first period started with the liberalization attempts including the weakening of market controls and steps to institutionalize security of property during the reign of Selim III (Sayar 2000, 182–85) and the formulation of matching ideas for economic reform (Kılınçoğlu 2015, 22). The second period more or less corresponds to the *Tanzimat* period, from 1830 to 1870s. During this period, the Ottoman state basically followed free-trade policies and the intellectual debate was dominated by laisser-faire economics. The earliest Ottoman study on economics in the modern sense dated from mid-1830s, which was an anonymous work called *Tedbir-i Ûmran-ı Mülkî* (Administration of Public Prosperity) (published in Kılınçoğlu 2018). There is indication that the Ottoman public was highly interested in economic debates as some of the economic treatises written by Ottoman intellectuals and statesmen were serialized in newspapers from 1860s onwards (Demir 2020, 264). In the last quarter of the century, which can be considered as the third period, parallel to the international trends, two rival theories, liberal economic tradition and protectionism competed at both policy and thought levels. Free-trade economics was represented by Sakızlı Ohannes, an Ottoman bureaucrat and intellectual, and the foremost representative of protectionism was Ahmet Mithat Efendi, arguably the most popular writer of the time. This debate lasted through the reign of Abdulhamid II (1876–1909) and the first years of the Committee of Union and Progress rule. The fourth period consists of the last years of the empire which witnessed the triumph of protectionist policies followed during the war years (1912–18), until the end of the empire following World War I.

Certain scholars have argued that free-trade policies and classical liberal economic principles were fully compatible with Islam (Sayar 2000, 185–86; Mardin 1985, 622). Some Ottoman authors such as Cevdet Pasha put forward that the ideas of free market and non-intervention by the state were not European inventions, but were first suggested by early Islamic scholars (Kılınçoğlu 2015, 40). For the majority of Ottoman economic authors, however, what mattered was not a purely theological discussion, but finding solutions to the burning practical problems of the empire. As such, they were not so much interested in proving the compatibility of Islam per se with liberal economics as of Islam practised in the Ottoman Empire. One can see this clearly in contrast with the political ideas of the Young Ottomans, a group of liberal intellectuals who opposed the *Tanzimat* regime on the grounds that the reforms did not go far enough and the *Tanzimat* statesmen caved too easily to foreign pressure.[9] In the 1860s the Young Ottomans built a powerful discourse that aimed to show that the liberal ideas of freedom, representation, constitution, etc., were not European ideas, but were necessary components of an Islamic understanding of politics. In defending "original" Islam, they were very critical of historical Islam and condemned, in the harshest words, despotic rulers in Islamic and Ottoman history. This assertive defence of liberal politics using Islamic idiom was not matched when it came to economics, neither by the Young Ottomans or other intellectuals of the time.

One factor that explains such hesitation could be their familiarity with the complexities of the relations between religious principles and prohibitions on the one hand, and exigencies of life, on the other. Throughout Ottoman history, there was always a degree of tension between shariah (religious law) on the one hand and *kanun* (sultan's law) and custom, on the other, and one area in which this was particularly visible was economy. In Islamicate societies in general, the shariah had to resign much to practise in the field of contracts and obligations (Schacht 1982, 77) and the Ottoman Empire was no exception. The institution of the cash *waqf* (Islamic pious foundation), for example, which was prohibited by religious law, were accommodated by Ottoman jurists on the basis of common usage, welfare of the people and common sense (Mandaville 1979, 298). Similarly, the issue of interest remained a "hot potato" for Ottoman jurists and bureaucrats throughout. Often the tensions between shariah and existing economic practices were solved through the use of *hiyal* (legal stratagems), which were frequently used creative devices based on legal fictions enabling Muslims to respect the letter of religious law while acting contrary to its spirit (Schacht 1982, 78–80; Kılınçoğlu 2015, 15).

Most Ottoman authors commenting upon economic issues strived to avoid thorny issues such as interest, although there were some exceptions. Ali Suavi, a rather eccentric member of the Young Ottomans, dealt with the issue of interest/usury directly, claiming that interest as part of the modern banking system was permissible in Islam (Günel 1993, 116–17, 333–34). Münif Pasha started his discussion of interest by saying that

[9] The classical work is (Mardin 1962). For more recent works on Young Ottomans, see (Çiçek 2010; Elfenbein 2017).

interest is not permitted in shariah and nowhere in the world usurers are welcome. But he also interjected that prohibiting interest completely will hinder the development of industry, commerce and crafts and render a banking system impossible (Münif Paşa 1884, 343–47). The author also adopted a minimal state attitude regarding the regulation of credits and interests, arguing that the state should not set the interest rates but try to create an environment in which both the creditors and the debtors could feel secure (Münif Paşa 1884, 349). Said Nursi, who is considered as one of the founders of political Islam in Turkey, took the opposite position and categorically rejected the Islamic permissibility of interest (Çamlı 2019, 74, 88). That most Ottoman authors were either silent on the issue of interest or implicitly approved it is not surprising as it became a significant point of contention in the Islamicate world only in the second half of the twentieth century (Kılınçoğlu 2018, 71). Only then did the Islamic intellectuals started trying to build a comprehensive critique of capitalism and interest played a central role in their religious and moral critique of capitalism (Tripp 2006, 126).

While Ottoman economic authors tried to avoid theological controversy, they did not discuss economics in ways that excluded religion or morality. In contrast, many authors of economic treatises made frequent references to Islamic ideas, sources and historical personalities. The anonymous author of the first Ottoman book of economics made several references to Quran and shariah, also explaining the concepts of goods and utility with reference to Islamic jurisprudence (Kılınçoğlu 2018, 68–69; p.4v in the transcription of the text). Süleyman Sudi's *Defter-i Muktesid* criticized European taxation practices and some Ottoman ones and praised in general the historical Ottoman system of taxation with respect to the superiority of Islam (Süleyman Sudi 1888, 20–21). The work also includes frequent references to Islamic figures, especially to Caliph Ömer ("Umar ibn al-Khattāb"), who is known in Islamic tradition for his sharp sense of justice. Nuri Bey tried to unearth an Islamic intellectual tradition of economics in his *Mebahis-i İlm-i Servet* (*Themes in the Science of Wealth*) (Kılınçoğlu 2015, 54–55). It was probably Münif Pasha who most directly linked morality to economy within a general religious framework. He argued that physical labour is not enough for creation of wealth; religious knowledge and an ethical disposition is also necessary for those who engage in economic activity (Münif Paşa 1884, 127, 169). He also claimed that morality in addition to religion influences the production of wealth in a society, using the French word *moral* in this context

(Münif Paşa 1884, 125). When commenting upon economic issues and ideas, therefore, Ottoman authors of the late period employed themes touching upon religion and morality; yet, they were quite selective when doing so.

"Backwardness" and Ethics of Hard Work

While the Ottoman public opinion in general recognized the superiority of the West vis-a-vis their own society, the intellectuals were careful to link it to recent developments, Ottoman failure to adapt to modern technology or oppressive sultans or bureaucrats and not to Islam. It was probably Namık Kemal, the archetypal Young Ottoman, who went farthest in accepting European advances as a fact and it is telling that he also forcefully underlined the advantages of adopting original Islamic values and institutions in order to restructure the empire. There were other authors such as Süleyman Sudi who preferred to imply the dominance of Western civilization but chose not to address the issue directly (Süleyman Sudi 1888, 18).

When the members of Ottoman intelligentsia delved into the reasons behind the backwardness of Ottoman economy, a popular theme was the domination of non-Muslims in economic life. A range of authors including Ali Suavi, Ahmet Mithat and Said Nursi complained that the commercial and industrial sectors of the economy were under the control of non-Muslims. In addition, as a corollary, many among them lamented the absence of an entrepreneurial spirit among Muslims (Kılınçoğlu 2015, 112; Çamlı 2019, 56). In fact, similar to economic texts, in the morality texts of the nineteenth century, Muslims were subject to a particularly harsh criticism for their alleged laziness and lack of entrepreneurialism (Hafez 2022, 27, 68). This idea of the absence of entrepreneurialism among Muslims is a by-product of a flawed argument that has been quite popular from the nineteenth century to the present day. It has been assumed that while Muslims were peasants, bureaucrats and soldiers, non-Muslims dominated the fields of arts and crafts, commerce, industry, finance and so on. It is now known that there was no ethnic division of labour in the Ottoman Empire. The majority of non-Muslim population were peasants, Muslims were also active in commerce (Çetinkaya 2015, 28–54) and domestic trade was actually dominated by Muslim merchants (Quataert 1994). The frequent complaints about non-Muslim dominance in economy, therefore, should be understood as a sign of a cleavage between Muslims and non-Muslims within the bourgeoisie and the former's attempts to dominate Ottoman economic life at a time it was metamorphosing in a capitalist direction.

As to the solutions that the authors offered to the economic woes of the empire, two points clearly stand out: avoiding wastefulness and extravagance and promoting diligence, both of which were supported by Islamic references. Mahmud Celaleddin Pasha's critique of mid-century Ottoman administration included repeated references to extravagance and wastefulness. He put forward that foreign credits were not spent on things that would boost commerce and increase wealth and the bureaucracy did not give up its habitual wastefulness (Mahmud Celaleddin Paşa 1907, 98–102). Said Nursi defended austerity within a more directly religious framework, pointing out that living a modest, austere life is an Islamic commandment (Çamlı 2019, 76). Some Ottoman authors condemned attempts to become rapidly rich, and in particular targeted practices such as gambling and lottery (Demir 2018); Namık Kemal opposed lottery on the basis of a combination of moral and economic principles. Münif Pasha similarly excluded lottery in addition to gambling and prostitution from legitimate, taxable fields of economic activity: "A tax should not be against moral norms and should not lead to moral deterioration" (1884, 375).

The most frequent idea held by Ottoman authors as a solution to Ottoman backwardness was diligence and the need to eliminate idleness in society. While some authors defended this on moral grounds rather detached from religion, referring to correct behaviour and duty towards one's fellow citizens, many sought direct support from Islam. It seems also that the laisser-faire supporters and protectionists united in underlying the value and necessity of hard work. Hardworking was stressed so much that one even gets a sense that in the writings of a large number of authors morality was reduced to being industrious. From Namık Kemal to Ahmet Mithat, from Said Nursi to Mizancı Murad,[10] a large number of Ottoman intellectuals lamented what they saw as the widespread laziness in Ottoman society and forcefully praised the importance of diligence. While the tone of such argumentation was often religious or quasi-religious, at times it took the form of summoning the help of foundational

[10] A *Jeune Turc* with Islamist inclinations. The Young Turks were a diverse group of intellectuals, activists and bureaucrats, mostly in exile, who opposed the absolutism of Abdulhamid II.

Islamic texts.[11] A typical example is the Quranic verse[12] often cited to support the importance of hard work. For example, Münif Pasha used that verse, which can be translated as "that each person will only have what they endeavoured towards" or "that man will only have what he has worked towards", to support the idea the human beings are obliged to work: "In sum, there is no other way than the sublime principle of "Leyse li'l-insân illâ mâ sa 'y'".[13] A person should strive to bring about a tangible or intangible product according to his devices in order to produce a fruit that is (religiously) permissible and acceptable. If he does not do so, it is obvious that he would be religiously and rationally shamed" (Münif Paşa 1884, 97–99). What is more interesting is that Kılınçoğlu argues that the verse has nothing to with economic activities; instead, it refers to humans being subject to divine judgement on the basis of their deeds (2015, 105). If this interpretation is correct, it means that these Ottoman authors wanted to stress the importance of diligence so much that they went as far as distorting a Quranic verse!

One could hardly resist relating the foregoing discussion to the Protestant Ethics argument of Max Weber. Weber's argument about the relations between ascetic Protestantism (Calvinism) and capitalism has been subject to a wide range of interpretations, of which Bryan S. Turner (1974) has identified four. While the simplistic and rather popular idea that Weber has claimed that Calvinism created capitalism is not sustainable (Weber 1930; Turner 1974, 232; D. Sayer 1991, 130), how he actually conceived the relation between the two is a highly complicated question. This and other questions such as Weber's understanding of Islam and his quest for the factors that hindered the development of capitalism in the Islamic world is out of the scope of the present study. The universalism of Christianity in general and Protestant Christianity in particular was part of the wider context in which Protestant Ethics was born and it is important to note that Islam is also emphatically universalist (Turner 2010). The main concern here is the Protestant stress on labour as this was also what

[11] Morality texts apparently went further than economic texts in attributing religious significance to terms related to work, diligence and laziness. Hafez calls these systematic attempts on the part of the authors of morality texts as "Islamization of work" (2022, 74).

[12] The Qur'an 53:39.

[13] The Arabic version of the verse.

united the Ottoman authors who commented upon economic matters in the nineteenth and early twentieth centuries.

Protestantism turned labour, once despised, into a duty and a calling (D. Sayer 1991, 129–31). We have seen how several Ottoman intellectuals quoted Quran in order to present work as a sacred duty, or as a natural inclination of humans which was ordained by God. Moreover, Protestantism treated ethics as a unified system, not inscribed in single acts but in the individual and his character (D. Sayer 1991, 121). Moving away from actions, therefore, Protestant Ethics required an ideal moral person who treated worldly affairs as he approached religious matters and lived in the world basically through his labour. Put as such, the similarity with Kılınçoğlu's portrayal of Ahmet Mithat Efendi's ideal Ottomans featuring in his novels is hard to miss: "modest, well-educated, thrifty, moral, and industrious. They start with modest means, as the sons of middle class families, but thanks to the modern education they receive in imperial colleges and their hard work, thrift, and systematic thinking, they succeed in accumulating significant amounts of wealth in the end. Besides, they marry ideal Ottoman women, who are also moral, modest, and educated; they thereby achieve happiness in private life in addition to material comfort" (2015, 169).

Conclusion

The Ottoman economy experienced growth and developed along capitalist lines in the long nineteenth century.[14] In parallel, the Ottoman state was restructured through a series of reforms. The two processes combined to bring about profound and extensive social change. Although there was significant influence and pressure of the Great Powers on the late Ottoman Empire, it was domestic factors and social pressure and demand that played the decisive role in the economic, political and social transformation of the Ottoman social formation. Contrary to the rather widespread conviction in the scholarly literature as well as popular level, in capitalist social formations non-economic fields of life in general, morality in particular, have continued to be internally related to economic

[14] The term "long nineteenth century" (1789–1914) is appropriate for the Ottoman Empire, as well. The liberalizing and centralizing reforms started under Selim III, who accessed to the throne in 1789; the empire entered World War I in 1914 and did not survive it.

relations. Echoing this, both Ottoman peasants and the intelligentsia developed solid conceptions of moral economy, whereas their conceptions considerably differed.

Peasant moral economy was characterized by subsistence ethics, a notion of justness and valourizing labour. Religion, in contrast, was mostly absent from their moral economy. This seems to have stemmed in part from religious difference between the cultivators and the upper classes in many cases of agrarian conflict and the fact that non-Muslim cultivators faced an extra disadvantage when the Ottoman state responded to such cases. On the other hand, Muslim as well as non-Muslim peasants endorsed the reformed polity, adopted the language of reform and strived to benefit from the reforms as much as possible.

The Ottoman Empire suffered serious territorial losses starting in the last quarter of the nineteenth century, and most of the cultivators who were engaged in intense agrarian conflicts found themselves in newly independent national states formed in Southeastern Europe. The empire's remaining Middle Eastern territories were lost during the Great War. The territories that would later become Turkey, on the other hand, underwent a major transformation in which the sizable Armenian and Greek communities were destroyed through war, deportation, massacres and forced population exchange. Most of the successor states of the Ottoman Empire have initiated some form of land reform scheme and followed certain policies that would favour peasant interests after independence (for Balkan states, see Palairet 1997), suggesting that peasant moral economy was a significant factor in the post-independence politics of those states. The Ottoman state itself followed wartime policies that put an immense burden on cultivators and entailed a massive transfer of wealth from lower to upper classes (Akyol 2022). While the Anatolian Muslim peasantry shouldered the bulk of the economic and manpower costs of the War of Independence (1919–1922), the Turkish government tried to alleviate the plight of cultivators through the abolition of the tithe in 1925 and some political steps as part of its populist ideological orientation. Peasants suffered from the post-depression economic policies and wartime policies during World War II, however, and despite decades-long intermittent debates, a comprehensive land reform program has never been implemented (S. Y. Kaya 2014). With fluctuating fortunes from 1919 onwards, Turkish peasants began to actively participate in representative system in Turkish politics only after 1946, with the onset of the multi-party politics (Yıldırmaz 2017).

Ottoman debates on economy, economics and economic policies began in 1830s within learned circles and continued until the end of the empire, producing both popular treatises and technical works. While the writings of well-known Western scholars were read, discussed and also adapted by Ottoman intellectuals interested in economics, a good deal of their writings presented original ideas to the public. While one observes an implicit trend of secularization during the late period of the empire, Islam remained a major pillar of legitimacy. The authors who engaged in economic debates, therefore, frequently included Islamic elements or references to religion in their writings. Most of them, however, avoided theological debates and directly addressing controversial issues such as usury and interest. Rather, they sought support from Islamic texts for a wide range of economic ideas such as free trade, protectionism or prudence. The most frequent moral and religious theme included in their writings was diligence and hard work. The authors stressed hard work so much and went to such lengths to vindicate it that it resembled an Islamic equivalent of the Protestant Ethics. While the Ottoman intelligentsia was divided on various aspects of economy such as the centrality of the market, the degree of state intervention and the factors that brought about the problems of Ottoman economy, it was united in holding hard work as the solution and glorifying labour, thus, discussing economic issues in moral terms.

The Ottoman legacy of the Turkish republic, the foremost successor state of the empire, is a highly complex issue with demographic, social, cultural, economic, political, diplomatic and biographical continuities and ruptures. Despite this complexity, one can argue that the multifaceted nation-building attempts of the young republic entailed a condemnation of laziness and celebration of industriousness (Hafez 2022, 250). The cadres that established the Republic of Turkey were in many ways a product of late Ottoman society, and the moral economy which was based on work ethics even instrumentalized Islam to promote industriousness and frugality, and vindicated by economic, moral and literary authors apparently influenced those cadres as well.

References

Akyol, Ayla Ezgi. 2022. Birinci Dünya Savaşı'nda Osmanlı İmparatorluğu'nda İlksel Birikim ve Kapitalist Devlet Oluşumu. PhD dissertation, İstanbul: İstanbul University.

Aslanmirza, Burak. 2018. The Evolution and Professionalization of Economic Thought from the Late Ottoman Empire to the Turkish Republic: The Case of İbrahim Fazıl Pelin. Master's thesis, Ankara: Middle East Technical University.

Aytekin, E. Attila. 2012. Peasant Protest in the Late Ottoman Empire: Moral Economy, Revolt, and the Tanzimat Reforms. *International Review of Social History* 57 (2): 191–227.

Aytekin, E. Attila. 2021. *Üretim, Düzenleme, İsyan: Osmanlı İmparatorlugu'nda Toprak Meselesi, Arazi Hukuku ve Köylülük*. Ankara: Dipnot.

Çağrıcı, Mustafa. n.d. Zulüm. In *TDV İslâm Ansiklopedisi*. Accessed June 14, 2022. https://islamansiklopedisi.org.tr/zulum#1.

Çamlı, Serdar. 2019. Osmanlı Devleti'nin Son Döneminde Müslüman Düşünürlerde İktisadi Gelişme Düşüncesi ve Bunun İktisat Politikalarıyla İktisadi Gelişmeye Etkisi. Master's thesis, Manisa: Celal Bayar University.

Çetinkaya, Y. Doğan. 2015. *Osmanlı'yı Müslümanlaştırmak: Kitle Siyaseti, Toplumsal Sınıflar, Boykotlar ve Milli Iktisat (1909–1914)*, trans. Özgür Bircan. İstanbul: İletişim.

Chevallier, Dominique. 1959. Aspects Sociaux de La Question d'Orient: Aux Origines Des Troubles Agraires Libanais En 1858. *Annales. Economies, Sociétés, Civilisations* 14: 35–64.

Çiçek, Nazan. 2010. *The Young Ottomans: Turkish Critics of the Eastern Question in the Late Nineteenth Century*. London: IB Tauris.

Çizakça, Murat. 1985. Incorporation of the Middle East into the European World-Economy. *Review (fernand Braudel Center)* 8 (3): 353–377.

Corrigan, Philip, and Derek Sayer. 1981. How the Law Rules. In *Law, State and Society*, ed. Bob Fryer, 21–53. London: Croom Helm.

Darling, Linda T. 2002. Another Look at Periodization in Ottoman History. *The Turkish Studies Association Journal* 26 (2): 190–228.

Demir, Kenan. 2018. Osmanlı'da Kalkınma Tartışmaları: İbret Gazetesindeki Ekonomi Yazıları. *Ekonomik Ve Sosyal Araştırmalar Dergisi* 14 (2): 281–300.

Demir, Kenan. 2020. Osmanlı Basınında İktisadi Tefrikacılık (Hazine-i Evrak Dergisi): Mahmud Celaleddin'in Ekonomi Politiği Ile Suphi Paşa'nın Layihası. *Karadeniz Teknik Üniversitesi Sosyal Bilimler Enstitüsü Sosyal Bilimler Dergisi*, 10 (20): 263–283.

Doumani, Beshara. 1995. *Rediscovering Palestine: Merchants and Peasants in Jabal Nablus*. Berkeley: University of California Press.

Elfenbein, Madeleine. 2017. No Empire for Old Men: The Young Ottomans and the World, 1856–1878. PhD dissertation, Chicago: The University of Chicago.

Freas, Erik Eliav. 2010. Ottoman Reform, Islam, and Palestine's Peasantry. *The Arab Studies Journal* 18 (1): 196–231.

Gelez, Philippe. 2016. Pauvreté et Modernité Dans Une Province Ottomane. La Question Agraire En Bosnie 1800–1918. Habilitation Thesis, Paris: EHESS.

Genç, Mehmet. 1994. Ottoman Industry in the Eighteenth Century: General Framework, Characteristics and Main Trends. In *Manufacturing in the Ottoman Empire and Turkey, 1500–1950*, ed. Donald Quataert, 59–86. Albany: State University of New York Press.

Götz, Norbert. 2015. 'Moral Economy': Its Conceptual History and Analytical Prospects. *Journal of Global Ethics* 11 (2): 147–162.

Günel, Necmi. 1993. II. Meşruiyet Öncesi Fikir Akımları ve Ali Suavi. Master's thesis, İstanbul: İstanbul University.

Hafez, Melis. 2022. *Inventing Laziness: The Culture of Productivity in Late Ottoman Society*. Cambridge: Cambridge University Press.

İnalcık, Halil. 1943. *Tanzimat ve Bulgar Meselesi*. Ankara: Türk Tarih Kurumu.

İnalcık, Halil. 1970. The Ottoman Economic Mind and Aspects of the Ottoman Economy. In *Studies in the Economic History of the Middle East from the Rise of Islam to the Present Day*, ed. M.A. Cook, 207–218. London: Oxford University Press.

İnalcık, Halil. 1985. Tanzimat'ın Uygulanması ve Sosyal Tepkiler. In *Tanzimat'tan Cumhuriyet'e Turkiye Ansiklopedisi*, 6: 1536–44. İstanbul: İletişim.

Issawi, Charles. 1966. *The Economic History of the Middle East, 1800–1914*. Chicago: University of Chicago Press.

Kaya, Alp Yücel. 2012. On the Çiftlik Regulation in Tırhala in the Mid Nineteenth Century: Economists, Pashas, Governors, Çiftlik-Holders, Subaşıs, and Sharecroppers. In *Ottoman Rural Societies and Economies*, ed. Elias Kolovos, 333–379. Rethymno: Crete University Press.

Kaya, Safiye Yelda. 2014. *Land Use, Peasants and the Republic: Debates on Land Reform in Turkey, 1923–1945*. PhD dissertation, Ankara: Middle East Technical University.

Kaynar, Erdal. 2014. Libéralisme et Protectionnisme: Ahmed Midhat et Les Questions Économiques de l'Empire Ottoman. *Anatoli* 5. https://doi.org/10.4000/anatoli.335.

Kılınçoğlu, Deniz T. 2015. *Economics and Capitalism in the Ottoman Empire*. Abingdon: Routledge.

Kılınçoğlu, Deniz T. 2018. *Islam, iktisat, ordu ve reform: Osmanlı İmparatorluğu'nda ilk iktisat eseri ve tarihsel bağlamı (Risale-i tedbir-i umran-ı mülki)*. İstanbul: İstanbul Bilgi üniversitesi.

Kırlı, Cengiz. 2015. Tyranny Illustrated: From Petition to Rebellion in Ottoman Vranje. *New Perspectives on Turkey*, 53: 3–36.

Köksal, Yonca. 2002. Imperial Center and Local Groups: Tanzimat Reforms in the Provinces of Edirne and Ankara. *New Perspectives on Turkey*, 27: 107–138.

Kuran, Timur. 2004. Why the Middle East Is Economically Underdeveloped: Historical Mechanisms of Institutional Stagnation. *Journal of Economic Perspectives* 18 (3): 71–90.

Lewis, Bernard. 2002. *The Emergence of Modern Turkey*, 3rd ed. New York: Oxford University Press.

Mahmud Celaleddin Paşa. 1907 [1979]. *Mirat-ı Hakikat*. İstanbul: Tercüman.

Mandaville, J.E. 1979. Usurious Piety: The Cash Waqf Controversy in the Ottoman Empire. *International Journal of Middle East Studies* 10 (3): 289–308.

Mardin, Şerif. 1962. *Genesis of Young Ottoman Thought*. Princeton Legacy Library. Princeton: Princeton University Press.

Mardin, Şerif. 1985. Tanzimat'tan Cumhuriyet'e İktisadi Düşüncenin Gelişmesi (1838–1918). In *Tanzimat'tan Cumhuriyet'e Türkiye Ansiklopedisi*, III: 618–34. İstanbul: İletişim.

Mirkova, Anna M. 2017. *Muslim Land, Christian Labor—Transforming Ottoman Imperial Subjects into Bulgarian National Citizens, 1878–1939*. Budapest: CEU Press.

Münif Paşa. 1884 [2021]. *İlm-i Servet*. ed. Gökhan Doğan. Ürgüp: Kapadokya Üniversitesi Yayınları.

Ortaylı, İlber. 1999. *İmparatorluğun En Uzun Yüzyılı*. İstanbul: İletişim.

Özbek, Nadir. 2012. The Politics of Taxation and the 'Armenian Question' during the Late Ottoman Empire, 1876–1908. *Comparative Studies in Society and History* 54 (4): 770–797.

Özveren, Eyüp. 2002. Ottoman Economic Thought and Economic Policy in Transition: Rethinking the Nineteenth Century. In *Economic Thought and Policy in Less Developed Europe: The Nineteenth Century*, ed. Michalis Psalidopoulos and Maria Eugenia Mata, 129–44.

Palairet, Michael. 1997. *The Balkan Economies, c.1800–1914. Evolution without Development*. Cambridge: Cambridge University Press.

Pamuk, Şevket. 2018. *Uneven Centuries: Economic Development of Turkey since 1820*. Princeton: Princeton University Press.

Pamuk, Şevket. n.d. Turkish Economic Development Since 1820. Ottoman History Podcast. Accessed June 1, 2020. https://www.ottomanhistorypodcast.com/2019/01/economicdevelopment.html.

Quataert, Donald. 1993. *Ottoman Manufacturing in the Age of the Industrial Revolution*. Cambridge: Cambridge University Press.

Quataert, Donald. 1994. The Age of Reforms, 1812–1914. In *An Economic and Social History of the Ottoman Empire, 1300–1914*, ed. Halil İnalcık and Donald Quataert. Cambridge: Cambridge University Press.

Quataert, Donald. 2003. Ottoman History Writing and Changing Attitudes Towards the Notion of 'Decline.' *History Compass* 1 (1): 1–9.

Şahin, Canay. 2003. The Rise and Fall of an Ayan Family in Eighteenth Century Anatolia: The Caniklizades (1737–1808). Unpublished PhD dissertation, Ankara: Bilkent University.

Sayar, Ahmed Güner. 2000. *Osmanli İktisat Düşüncesinin Çağdaşlaşması (Klasik Dönem'den II. Abdülhamid'e)*, 2nd ed. Istanbul: Ötüken.

Sayer, Andrew. 2006. Approaching Moral Economy. In *The Moralization of the Markets*, ed. Nico Stehr, Christopher Henning, and Bernd Weiler, 77–97. New Brunswick: Transaction Publishers.

Sayer, Derek. 1991. *Capitalism and modernity: An excursus on Marx and Weber*. London: Routledge.

Schacht, Joseph. 1982. *An Introduction to Islamic Law*. Oxford: Clarendon Press.

Scott, James C. 1976. *The Moral Economy of the Peasant: Rebellion and Subsistence in Southeast Asia*. New Haven: Yale University Press.

Seyitdanlioğlu, Mehmet. 1998. The Rise and Development of the Liberal Thought In Turkey. *H.Ü. Edebiyat Fakültesi Dergisi* Cumhuriyetimizin 75. Yılı Özel Sayısı: 151–62.

Süleyman Sudi. 1888 [2008]. *Defter-i Muktesid*. ed. Mehmet Ali Ünal. Isparta: Fakülte Kitabevi.

Thompson, E.P. 1993. *Customs in Common: Studies in Traditional Popular Culture*. New York: The New Press.

Tripp, Charles. 2006. *Islam and the Moral Economy: The Challenge of Capitalism*. Cambridge: Cambridge University Press.

Turner, Bryan S. 1974. Islam, Capitalism and the Weber Theses. *The British Journal of Sociology* 25 (2): 230–243.

Turner, Bryan S. 2010. Reflexive Traditionalism and Emergent Cosmopolitanism: Some Reflections on the Religious Imagination. *Soziale Welt* 61 (3/4): 313–318.

Ueno, Masayuki. 2013. 'For the Fatherland and the State': Armenians Negotiate The Tanzimat Reforms. *International Journal of Middle East Studies* 45 (1): 93–109.

Uzun, Ahmet. 2002. *Tanzimat ve Sosyal Direnişler : Niş Isyanı Üzerine Ayrıntılı Bir Inceleme, 1841*. Istanbul: Eren.

Weber, Max. 1930. *The Protestant Ethic and the Spirit of Capitalism*, trans. Talcott Parsons. Abingdon: Routledge.

White, Sam. 2008. Ecology, Climate, and Crisis in the Ottoman Near East. PhD dissertation, New York: Columbia University.

Wood, Ellen Meiksins. 1995. *Democracy Against Capitalism. Renewing Historical Materialism*. Cambridge: Cambridge University Press.

Yıldırmaz, Sinan. 2017. *Politics and the Peasantry in Post-War Turkey: Social History, Culture and Modernization*. London: I.B. Tauris.
Yıldız, Aysel, and İrfan Kokdaş. 2020. Peasantry in a Well-Protected Domain: Wallachian Peasantry and Muslim Çiftlik/Kışlaks under the Ottoman Rule. *Journal of Balkan and near Eastern Studies* 22 (1): 175–190.

CHAPTER 11

Leading a "Simple" Life in Modern Capitalism. The Moral Economy of Mennonite Consumption in Mid-twentieth-century America

Martin Lutz

Introduction

In January 1956, the authors of a "Nonconformity Study" presented their report to their Mennonite church in the state of Virginia. "Nonconformity" played a crucial role in the religious beliefs and identity of this Anabaptist-Mennonite religious community, related to the Biblical principle outlined in Romans 12:2 "And be not conformed to this world: but be ye transformed by the renewing of your mind, that ye may prove what is that good, and acceptable, and perfect, will of God." For Mennonites, nonconformity entailed distinct notions of a "good" daily conduct of life, notions that they intricately related also to consumption practices. As the

M. Lutz (✉)
Humboldt-University of Berlin, Berlin, Germany
e-mail: martin.lutz@hu-berlin.de

T. Skambraks and M. Lutz (eds.), *Reassessing the Moral Economy*, Palgrave Studies in Economic History,
https://doi.org/10.1007/978-3-031-29834-9_11

study report stated with regard to clothing, "[t]he nonconformed Christian has a simplicity of attire that is not only beautiful and enduring but that also draws attention to Christ."[1]

This chapter shows how Mennonite religious interpretations of what they considered "good, acceptable, and perfect" before God translated into moral valuations of simplicity that in turn shaped consumption choices. These notions increasingly came into tension with a rapidly changing environment as American society as a whole embarked on a journey to mass consumerism from the 1920s on. Mennonites were exposed to a secular trend toward materialistic consumption, challenging traditional notions of a "simple" life and necessitating a communal process of re-aligning Christian values with contemporary consumer culture. I argue in this chapter that despite partial adaption to a changing environment, the communal moral economy continued to shape ideas, institutions and practices of what Mennonites considered "simple" or unnecessarily "luxurious" consumption in modern capitalism.

The recent historiography of consumption has shown the accelerated growth of mass consumerism in the United States from the 1920s onward (Logemann 2019; Cross 2000). Yet, this literature largely neglects the role of religious ethic in consumption, or emphasizes the role of evangelicalism in promoting consumer culture (Balbier 2014). As Horowitz argues in *The Morality of Spending*, by the late nineteenth-century American consumer culture replaced "the sanctions of religion" with an individualistic "identification of happiness with pleasure" (Horowitz, xxvii).

The Mennonite case points in a different direction, as the church community scrambled to defend traditional boundaries of a "simple" life in response to societal change. Mennonites, as their Anabaptist coreligionists the Amish and Hutterites, present an intriguing counter-example of "simple" consumption practices that differed from ostentatious presentations of wealth and luxury that played a prominent role in the prosperity gospel of evangelical churches (Freudenberg et al. 2020). Moreover, Mennonites exemplify long-term continuities as twentieth-century Anabaptists stand in line of century-old debates on luxury and simplicity, going back to Medieval and early modern central European

[1] Report of the Findings Committee on the Nonconformity Conference, p. 3, I-F-5c Box 3, Virginia Mennonite Conference Archives, Harrisonburg, Virginia.

sumptuary regulations. The historiography of Mennonites lacks a systematic assessment of consumption in Mennonite history but it inhibits a strong focus on attire as this issue is so central in Anabaptist culture (Gingerich 1970).

The first section provides a brief overview of Mennonite religious values concerning consumption and their long-term evolution through the early modern period. I will then address the challenge to simplicity in a changing environment, and the discursive reflections of what Mennonite considered "good" consumption in the mid-twentieth century. The following section then explores how these normative reflections were included in the church community's institutional fabric, as new guidelines for "good" behavior in modern consumerism entered the rulebook. These included attire, architecture, interior design and automotive mobility.

The chapter focuses on acculturating Mennonites as one segment of this Anabaptist population as opposed the vastly more conservative Old Order and Old Colony Mennonites. Primary sources include published materials of Mennonite church bodies as well as committee records such as the Proceedings of the Annual Conferences on Mennonite Cultural Problems, a conference series that ran between 1942 and 1967, and the files of a "Nonconformity Study Conference" at the Virginia Mennonite Conference church archive. The conclusion summarizes how the Mennonite church members were tightly embedded in a communal moral economy that limited individual choices in consumption.

What Does It Mean to Lead a Simple Life?

Mennonites are a Christian community in the Anabaptist religious tradition that emerged in Reformation-era central Europe in the 1520s. Due to religious persecution, the first groups began immigrating to the British colonies in North America as early as in the late seventeenth century (MacMaster 1985). By the time of United States independence, they formed stable communities along the Eastern seaboard. Westward migration and new waves of European immigration then added new locations to the Mennonite landscape in the United States and Canada. "Mennonites" is an umbrella term for a diverse population that is not organized in one organizational entity. Mennonites form a plethora of independent or semi-autonomous church bodies or "Conferences" along traditional and regional lines. Today, a wide range of "acculturated," "Plain," "Old

Order" or "Old Colony" Mennonite groups occupy a spectrum from liberal to ultra-conservative, a "mosaic" (Kauffman and Driedger 1991) reflecting also ethnic traditions in clothing, language and communal culture. By the mid-nineteenth century, a rift emerged between Mennonites who followed the traditional church regulations (*Mennoniten alter Ordnung* or Old Order Mennonites) and acculturating groups who gradually transitioned from German to English as the primary language, updated their religious rituals and communal rules as to general conduct of life (Schlabach 1988).

Simplicity played a crucial role in the emerging Anabaptist movement from the 1520s onward (Goertz 1988). It was tied to the Biblical interpretations of nonconformity, that in turn necessitated a clear distinction between the believers' church and the evil, potentially hostile world. The Schleitheim confession of 1527, one of the most prominent early Anabaptist documents, outlined this principle in article four as follows:

> A separation shall be made from the evil and from the wickedness which the devil planted in the world; in this manner, simply that we shall not have fellowship with them [the wicked] and not run with them in the multitude of their abominations. (Wenger 1945, 249)

To be a nonconformed Mennonite Christian, one had to be separated from the world also in the sense of forgoing of luxury and refraining from indulgence. As Menno Simons (1496–1561), a Dutch Anabaptist leader and namesake of the Mennonites, stated "[w]e acknowledge, teach and seek no other kingdom than that of Christ which shall endure for ever, in which there is no pomp, splendor, gold, silver, meat and drink, but righteousness, peace and joy in the Holy Ghost" (Wenger 1952, 57). Simplicity in this Mennonite interpretation referred to food and clothing, architecture and general conduct of life. It was not an abstract principle but incorporated into everyday life and even non-Anabaptist observers noted the "simple" character of Mennonitism (Gingerich 1970, 14).

Early Anabaptism thus established simplicity as a Christian virtue with an impetus to reject the material temptations of the world (Klaassen 2001). Simplicity, however, was not a static principle but subject to constant reassessment, reinterpretation and internal conflict. By the late nineteenth century, the pressure of change increased through industrialization and the availability of cheap, pre-fabricated goods. Mennonite and Amish sources show how an increasing critique of perceived luxury items in this period. In 1867, the prominent bishop John M. Brenneman from Pennsylvania outlined this critique in his pamphlet Pride and Humility (*Hoffart und Demut*).[2] In equating humbleness with simplicity, Brenneman starkly warned of the material dangers in a sinful world, that "manifest[s] itself very plainly in the manner of dress and in the costly array with which poor dying mortals strive, frequently beyond their means, to decorate themselves, in order to gain the respect and esteem of a proud and wicked world" (Brenneman 1866). While giving dress as one example, Brenneman also emphasized that the Mennonite moral impetus of simplicity went far beyond attire.

By the early twentieth century, new consumer goods then provided a new battleground for assessments of simplicity in a consumer culture. Automotive transportation became a particularly contested issue as the car not only stood for enhanced mobility but also reflected individualism and was regarded as a status symbol of "worldly pride." While acculturating Mennonites embraced the new car culture with few limitations, the more conservative Old Order Mennonites inherently struggled with this issue. Whether or not one Old Order Mennonite church allowed the car became an issue of discontent and led to schisms (Scott 1996).

The evolution of the Old Order Mennonite Weaverland Conference church in Pennsylvania exemplifies this process on a microscopic level. This church was founded in 1893 by a conservative bishop in splitting from the pre-existing Lancaster Mennonite Conference church over diverging notions of progressiveness. Two decades later, the Weaverland Conference was in turn shaken to the core in a conflict between conservatives and ultra-conservatives over car ownership. At this point, the car had become a symbol of vanity and luxury (Hoover 1982, 813). In the course of the 1920s, the internal rift widened and led to a schism between the Weaverland Conference church and the newly emerging Groffdale Old Order Conference church. The latter entirely prohibited the car, while the Weaverland Conference allowed car ownership, albeit within tight constraints established in the church regulations. A church resolution from 1930 held that "no member is allowed to have an up-to-date automobile. Only touring cars, black in color, are to be used" (Muddy

[2] The pamphlet originated in three articles published by Brenneman in English and German in the Mennonite periodical Herold of Truth between June and August 1866. Anabaptist Mennonite Biblical Seminary Library, Digital Mennonite Periodicals, https://libraryguides.ambs.edu/digital_mennonite_periodicals, accessed December 5, 2022.

Creek Farm Library 2006, 232). Five years later, another church ordinance specified the rules for Weaverland Conference church members as follows:

> Conference having sanctioned the use of the automobile under certain restrictions as follows. The touring or phaeton. The roadster, if the rear seat is removed and not used. Closed cars that are out of style models. All cars in black in color, no stripes, nor flashy trimmings. Conference disapproves to make a display by folding tops. It being understood that the automobile be used for necessary use only. (Hoover 1982, 698)

Old Order Mennonites have continued to rely on these instructions concerning simple life consumption, similar to their Amish cousins (Kraybill et al. 2013). Change was slow and a carefully administered process that results in frequent schisms between "progressive" and "conservative" factions.

From the early twentieth century on, the framing of "simple" life led to increasingly diverse regulations across the Mennonite spectrum, ranging from acculturating communities to conservatives and ultra-conservative Old Order churches. Even as acculturating Mennonites gradually eased restrictions on attire, new technologies and consumption, their conservative cousins served as constant reminder of how related religious groups came to strikingly different outcomes in establishing boundaries toward the perceived threat of consumerism. It was thus not a coincidence that Mennonites by the mid-twentieth century engaged in an intense effort to reflect on the meaning of simplicity in a society of mass consumerism.

Simplicity Challenged

In August 1942, a group of Mennonite scholars, church leaders and laypeople assembled in Winona Lake, Indiana for the first "Conference on Mennonite Cultural Problems." This conference series eventually encompassed sixteen events addressing a plethora of themes—not just cultural, but also economic, social and political—that Mennonites considered as major contemporary challenges. Simplicity was one of them. Already in the first conference, George Stoneback, pastor of the Eight Street Mennonite Church in Goshen, Indiana gave a talk on "Mennonite

Church Architecture and the Simple Life,"[3] emphasizing the historically plain character of Anabaptist meetinghouses for church service, a stark contrast to the splendor inhibited in other denominations' religious buildings. Stoneback fervently argued against stained glass windows, church towers and pulpit platforms, and for a functional layout with lasting furnishing. This pastor's admonishments were not taken from thin air but a response to change creeping into Mennonite communities, change that went far beyond church building architecture and interior design. In calling for a renewed effort to retain simplicity, Stoneback speech in 1942 reflected widespread Mennonite concerns about changing lifestyles that affected every aspect of community life.

Change had been coming for decades. Mennonites were a predominantly agricultural people, but from the early twentieth century on increasingly left their farms to obtain higher education, get a professional job and move to an urban environment. This social and economic transition provoked deep concern among church leaders and Mennonite academics, as notions of traditional simplicity were tightly intertwined with an ideal of a simple, rural lifestyle (Gingerich 1942). As Mennonites gradually were drawn into mainstream society, the church frantically struggled to draw new boundaries to members' simplicity in an often urban, industrial and academic environment.

In the following years, a plethora of topics concerning a "simple" life in all its shapes and forms were addressed in the conference proceedings. As Menno Harder of the Mennonite Tabor College in Kansas stated, "Mennonites follow a simple interpretation of the Holy Scriptures. [...] They accept the Bible as the Word of God and attempt to apply its teachings in all simplicity in their daily lives."[4] This quote reflected an ideal depiction of Mennonite simplicity that stood in stark contrast with a vastly different reality.

Church leaders and academics played a prominent role in the "Conference on Mennonite Cultural Problems" series. They also used other

[3] George Stoneback: Mennonite Church Architecture and Its Influence on Mennonites Today, in: Proceedings of the first Conference on Mennonite cultural problems, pp. 12–19, Mennonite Historical Library, Goshen College, Indiana.

[4] Menno S. Harder: Contributions of the Russian Mennonites to the Culture of Kansas, in: Proceedings of the third Conference on Mennonite cultural problems, pp. 99–108, Mennonite Historical Library, Goshen College, Indiana.

forums to address their concern to a wider church audience. The prominent historian Melvin Gingerich, for example, published an article titled "Rural Life Problems and the Mennonites" in the Mennonite Quarterly Review journal in 1942. In this article, Gingerich lamented that "[o]ur former rural security is disappearing, we are becoming secularised, our community life is breaking down, and our culture is losing its distinctive qualities" (Gingerich 1942, 169). Yet, not all was lost for the Mennonite cause according to Gingerich. He outlined an agenda of church renewal to inspire new confidence in the ethical foundations and real-life applications in a modern society as

> [T]here must be new explorations in the possibilities of the simple life. As we receive increasing satisfaction from our own devotion to the ideals of a new, better, more co-operative community life, we will learn to depend less upon *things* for our pleasures. [...] We should learn [...] that it is possible to produce on the farm many things of the articles and services we now purchase. As we buy fewer things, our economic life will become more secure than it has been. Furthermore, as children are trained to help in the production of a variety of goods they cease to be economic liabilities and the familistic type of life is encouraged. (Gingerich 1942, 173)

Ten years after Gingerich's publication, the Mennonite theologian John C. Wenger systematized the religious tenets and contemporary challenges in the book *The Doctrines of the Mennonites* (Wenger 1952). Wenger devoted one entire chapter on the "Biblical Simplicity of Life," an indication of this aspect's prominent role in Mennonite theology. In drawing on Biblical examples and early Anabaptist writings, this chapter made a strong case for a renewed emphasis on a simple life in the face of countless temptations in a consumer society catering to "human desires that are not spiritual" (Wenger 1952, 42). Evoking the sixteenth-century writings of Menno Simons, the chapter warned of false Christians who have "no limits nor bounds to their accursed wantonness, foolish pomp, show of silks, velvet, costly clothes, gold rings, chains, silver belts, pins, buttons, curiously adorned shirts, handkerchiefs, collars, veils, aprons, velvet shoes, slippers and such like foolish finery" (Wenger 1952, 42).

Three years after *The Doctrines of the Mennonites*, Wenger published another book entirely dedicated on the meaning of Anabaptist simplicity in a modern society. The book *Separated unto God. A Plea for Christian Simplicity of Life and for a Scriptural Nonconformity of the World* was published by Herald Press, a Mennonite publishing house, in 1955. It was commissioned by the Mennonite Church to address contemporary challenges to the principle of nonconformity in a radically changing world as expressed in a church resolution from 1944 that stressed a continuous effort to maintain simplicity in attire. Wenger emphasized in the introduction that this principle was paramount in the Anabaptist-Mennonite religious faith as a "Biblical principle, and not mere social approval, [that] must govern his daily living" (Wenger 1955, xii). In the following, Wenger first outlined the theological and historical origins of Anabaptist simplicity in a broad perspective and then addressed issues that he considered crucial to a simple Mennonite life in mid-twentieth-century American society. These included various aspects in the daily conduct of life such as "Speech" (Chapter 4), "Recreation and Culture" (Chapter 5), "Worship" (Chapter 9) and the relationship with the State (Chapter 11).

In Chapter 12, Wenger focused on "The Life of Love in the Industrial World," addressing the tremendous challenges that modern capitalism had brought to a Mennonite lifestyle based on Biblical interpretation. These included urbanization, growing economic inequality, and the sometimes violent class struggle between organized workers and management. Mennonites had been exposed to this structural transformation in the American economy in the preceding decades, and Wenger considered it a vital problem for the traditional stance of Mennonite nonconformity. As a potential solution, he painted a somewhat romonantisized picture of an ideal world, saying that

> It is necessary to state again that it is impossible to regenerate completely the economic life of America apart from the conversion to Christian faith of the individual men and women of both labor and management. The most desirable solution to the whole problem therefore is the establishment of strong Christian communities which emphasize rural life and a simplicity of life which evades the class struggle described above. (Wenger 1955, 301)

These stark warnings of Gingerich, Wenger and other prominent Mennonites were not ignored by their church constituency. Mennonite reflections on simplicity played a vital role in the communal discourse of the mid-twentieth century. Problematizing contemporary challenges to a simple life, however, was not confined to a discursive level. While thinking and talking about the moral impetus to lead a simple life, Mennonite church bodies undertook new measures to restrain extravagance and unnecessary luxury among their membership.

Discerning New Arrangements

The doctrinal norms of what Mennonites considered a "simple" life were not merely prominent topos in the communal discourse but formed an integral part of the church's institutional fabric. The Anabaptist *Ordnung* or church regulations entailed detailed instructions for members' conduct of life, such as attire and hairstyle. As historian Leonard Gross conceptualizes the term, it formed an overarching "Brotherhood code; a social-economic-political set of Brotherhood regulations" (Gross 1980, 229). It was designed to regulate social behavior and it imposed formal constraints on individual action for it to comply with church doctrine. The Anabaptist *Ordnung* entailed potentially powerful sanction mechanisms that could lead to the expulsion of a member in case of deviant behavior. Conservative groups such as the Old Order Mennonites and Old Order Amish continued to employ these strict sanctions in the twentieth century (Kraybill et al. 2013, 165–68). For example, the Old Order Mennonite Weaverland Conference church expelled a member in 1910 for buying a car (Hoover 1982, 812). Less severe offenses, for example violating dresscodes, were punished in other ways. Acculturating Mennonites, on the other hand, did soften the harsh sanctions. Institutional constraints were adopted in constitutions and bylaws as Mennonites churches gradually shifted to a bureaucratic organizational structure (Juhnke 1989, 186). One of these was the Mennonite Church, an umbrella organization consisting of several regional church bodies in the United States and Canada.

In the face of perceived challenges and problems to Mennonitism in a capitalist society, the Mennonite Church issued its General Problems Committee (Toews 2010, 75) to compile a "Book of Standards" in 1940 to ascertain the membership of the role of the Gospel in contemporary life. It included one paragraph on the dangers of "worldly amusements," warning of the dangers posed by the entertainment industry in cinemas, theaters and resorts. In another publication provided by the General Problems Committee on "Worldly Amusements and Pleasures," these were considered a sinful activity as "the agencies of Satan whose business it is to destroy souls."[5] As the opportunities of recreational activities rapidly expanded in the course of the early twentieth century, these "amusements" became one of the most frequently addressed challenges for Mennonite nonconformity in the intra-church discourse.

The "Book of Standards" under another heading on "Christian Apparel" then outlined the following Biblical principles inherent in Mennonite religion:

> The Bible upholds the following standards with reference to clothing for God's people: (1) Substantial (Gen. 3:7, 21), as distinguished from clothing that is fragile or transparent; (2) modest (1 Tim. 1:9, 10; I Pet. 3:3, 4), as distinguished from vain display, superfluities, or partial nudeness; (3) sex distinction (Deut. 22:5), as distinguished from sex appeal; (4) economical (I Tim. 2:9; I Pet. 3:3), as distinguished from the wearing of jewelry and expensive ornamentation; (5) "not conformed to this world" (Rom. 12:1, 2; I Pet. 1:14) as distinguished from following the fashions of the world. There is no Bible teaching on dress that is not violated continually by the fashions of this world.[6]

The Mennonite Church's "Book of Standards" was distributed in the regional church organizations. One of these was the Virginia Mennonite Conference body that serves as a case in point in how these instructions on "Christian apparel" were further discussed and developed. This church was the regional organization representing a segment of Mennonites that had been migrating to Virginia from the eighteenth century on (Brunk 1972, 1959).[7] By the 1830s, these began forming their own regional church organization that became affiliated with the Mennonite Church of

[5] Pamphlet Worldly Amusements and Pleasures, Ten Reasons Why Christians Should Have no Part in Them Together with Rules for Guidance Concerning Recreation, Prepared and Distributed by the General Problems Committee of the Mennonite General Conference, III-A-7 General Problems Committee, Virginia Mennonite Conference Archives, Harrisonburg, Virginia.

[6] A Book of Standards, Published by Order of Mennonite General Conference, prepared by General Problems Committee, 1940, p. 9, III-A-7 General Problems Committee, Virginia Mennonite Conference Archives, Harrisonburg, Virginia.

[7] Virginia Mennonite Conference, History and Current Size, undated manuscript; Glendon Blosser and James O. Lehman: Virginia Mennonite Conference Historical Timeline, 2007, I-G-2 Box 1 Historical Commission, Virginia Mennonite Conference Archives, Harrisonburg, Virginia.

North America. The first constitution of the Virginia Mennonite Conference was drafted in 1919. Its article X "Non Conformity to the World" included a plethora of detailed rules for members including the prohibition to participate in warfare and to hold political offices. Moreover, this article X listed several items concerning a "simple" conduct of life. In social activities, it warned "members from indulging in any form of entertainment or amusement that is inconsistent with our faith," including swimming pools, games, dancing, the movies or theaters. One paragraph emphasized "plain" dress and hairstyle, and another one called for modesty in marriage ceremonies and "[o]ccasions of this kind shall be characterised by a symplicity [sic] that is in harmony with the principles of non-conformity to the world as believed by the Mennonite Church. The exercises shall be devoid of superfluities and vain display, while all attire shall be in harmony with our profession of faith."[8] A revised version of the "Rules and Discipline of the Virginia Mennonite Conference" from 1948 gave similar instructions for church membership in its Article VI on Nonconformity. It warned against social and recreational activities and stressed that "Brethren shall be consistent with our profession of godliness and simplicity" in attire.[9]

These doctrinal statements, however, must not be taken at face value. As recent historiography has pointed out, setting norms in the Mennonite and more general the Anabaptist context not necessarily reflects actual practice but an attempt to instill order in the face of ongoing deviance from church rules (Schlachta 2003, 98–102). The emphasis on "simple" conduct of weddings in the Virginia Mennonite Conference constitution might thus indicate that in fact such ceremonies were more extravagant than church doctrine required.

It was thus likely for good reasons that the Virginia Mennonite Conference church organized a "Nonconformity Study Conference" on November 18, 1955. In his invitation letter, the church's secretary Linden M. Wenger emphasized, the "importance of the issues involved and the great need for our church to give a united and consistent witness before

[8] Virginia Mennonite Conference (Hg.): Doctrinal State Constitution Rules and Discipline Adopted by the Virginia Mennonite Conference 1930. Menno Simons Historical Library, Eastern Mennonite University, Harrisonburg, Virginia.

[9] Rules and Discipline of the Virginia Mennonite Conference, revised version of 1948, p. 15. I-A-4 Miscellaneous, Virginia Mennonite Conference Archives, Harrisonburg, Virginia.

the world of true Biblical nonconformity",[10] urging every member to join the event. The conference's afternoon program included a "Panel Discussion on Attire," dealing with the principles of ornamentation, modesty, simplicity and economy in Mennonite attitudes toward clothing. One panelist, Harold Eshleman, reflected on the concept of simplicity itself. While contending that it "is not an easy term to define," Eshleman strongly advocated for an ongoing adherence of Mennonites to simple attire, while allowing for adjustments in a changing world, saying that "[t]here is nothing wrong with our attire resembling that worn by the culture of society around us so long as it does not violate scriptural principles and become a medium of expression for the lust of the flesh."[11] Another speaker, Lloyd Horst, was deeply concerned with the growing income of Mennonites in the mid-twentieth century, leading to disposable money that they could spent on fashionable clothing and luxury items such as jewelry. Horst called for his fellow church members to follow an economical life style "in our homes, and furnishings, and automobiles."[12]

Emphasizing home fashion, home furnishings, recreational activities, jewelry and cars was not a coincidence, but reflected some of the most prominent items in American consumer culture by the mid-twentieth century. These Mennonites speakers at the 1955 nonconformity conference were inherently concerned that church members might succumb to new temptations in consumption, thereby neglecting their moral duty to follow a simple life as part of their Mennonite religious tradition.

The finding committee picked up on these discussions in its final report from January 1955. The report first summarized general comments on the overall meeting, emphasizing the overarching role of Biblical principles in Mennonite doctrines of nonconformity. Crucially, it also established that where the Bible gave no specific instructions, the church and its agents possessed the authority to issue ordinances to regulate

[10] Letter Linden M. Wenger to all members of the Virginia Mennonite Conference, November 9, 1955, I-F-5c Box 3, Virginia Mennonite Conference Archives, Harrisonburg, Virginia.

[11] Harold Eshleman: Simplicity, Program and stenographic notes of the Nonconformity Study Conference, p. 8, I-F-5c Box 3, Virginia Mennonite Conference Archives, Harrisonburg, Virginia.

[12] Lloyd Horst: Economy, Program and stenographic notes of the Nonconformity Study Conference, p. 9, I-F-5c Box 3, Virginia Mennonite Conference Archives, Harrisonburg, Virginia.

members' behavior: "The church has the right to regulate attire, to say what the norm shall be. The church has the responsibility of directing and approving changes in the area of nonconformity."[13] The report then went on to outline specific features of nonconformity concerning "Personal Attitudes and Social Relations," "In Relation to Prosperity and Property," "In Attire" and "In Recreation." In the face of growing material prosperity of Mennonites, it called for a renewed effort to uphold religious values of nonconformity and a "simple" way of life. In this regard, the report went farther than traditional perceptions of Mennonite simplicity that were primarily focused on plain attire.

> There is danger of a lopsided practice because of stressing specific applications in certain areas and ignoring applications in other areas. For example, expensive homes, big cars and luxurious living are as real violations of the principle of simplicity as violations in the area of attire.[14]

In the end, the report stressed the ongoing notion that "under God's guidance the church find the best way to preserve the doctrine of nonconformity" and its various applications for a simple conduct of life.

The Virginia Mennonite Conference was not the only Mennonite church body wrestling with the intertwined issues of nonconformity and simplicity in the context of rapid change in the mid-twentieth century (Hess 2004). By the mid-twentieth century, several if not most Mennonite church bodies instituted committees under various names devoted to the challenges of church life in modern capitalism. Perceived threats were manifold. They included urbanization, industrialization, growing inequality in line with growing prosperity and the temptations offered by a world of mass consumption. In an attempt to restrain these temptations, Mennonite churches emphasized pre-existing and instituted new regulations concerning the question of what was perceived to be appropriate or too much for the Mennonite believer.

As the Virginia Mennonite Conference shows, the applications of "simplicity" as a moral concept were widened over time. While earlier

[13] Report of the Findings Committee on the Nonconformity Conference, p. 2, I-F-5c Box 3, Virginia Mennonite Conference Archives, Harrisonburg, Virginia

[14] Report of the Findings Committee on the Nonconformity Conference, p. 3, I-F-5c Box 3, Virginia Mennonite Conference Archives, Harrisonburg, Virginia.

restrictions as in the 1940 "Book of Standards" were limited to entertainment and clothing, the Virginia Mennonites deliberately addressed a broader spectrum of "worldly" temptations. For good reasons they included the car as a status symbol in their list of concerns, as well as expensive furnishings of a membership that had increasing disposable income. The "worldly fashions" that the 1940 Book of Standards warned off in relation to apparel thus inhibited a new meaning to encompass fashions and trends across a wider spectrum of consumer goods.

In contrast to Old Order Mennonites, acculturating Mennonites such as the Virginia Conference church did not produce specific details as not what exactly constituted a luxurious car or a luxurious home, and only some general guidelines as to what was considered too fashionable clothing. However, the impetus to lead a simple life continued to play a prominent role in Mennonite conceptualizations of nonconformity in a modern world.

Conclusions

This chapter showed how one Christian denomination, the Anabaptist Mennonites, discussed, refined and institutionalized notions of simplicity, a moral norm derived from Biblical interpretation. In the face of rapid societal change and the emergence of a consumer culture in a capitalist economy, these Mennonites drew on earlier notions of a simple life that were inherent in the Anabaptist religious tradition. As a response to societal change, new items were addressed in the communal discourse, such as the car as a new status symbol and sign of "worldly pride." In an attempt to constrain church members' temptations, the Mennonite church bodies then included these new items in their institutional fabric, i.e. the regulations that governed the church community. These regulations must not be interpreted as an indicator of actual practice, but as a normative statement of how the church wanted its members to behave vis-á-vis the "fashions of the world." Further research still needs to be done in order to explore to what extent Mennonite church members complied with church regulations and how that shaped consumption choices and expenses. Tentative evidence suggests that at least in some contexts, Mennonites were indeed leading a simple life compared to the non-Anabaptist population, with statistical effects for example in household expenses (Dawson 1936).

Simplicity, of course, has not been unique to Mennonites but it is an important tenet also in other religious groups such as the Quakers

(Lapsansky 2018). More recently, it was included in critiques of capitalism such as in the tiny house movement (Hennigan 2021). Yet, Mennonites—in particular the conservative and Old Order churches—stand out as they deliberately attempted to adjust traditional notions of a simple life to a modern consumer culture. Even acculturating Mennonites who gradually shifted away from their traditional "separation from the world" through attire and other expressions of nonconformity, retained the moral impetus to lead a simple life. Simplicity and nonconformity remained paramount in strengthening church boundaries toward a consumer society, leading to new institutional arrangements in church regulations. The relatively small Mennonite population—currently the Mennonite Church USA counts just a little above 62,000 members[15]—is certainly not representative for other Christian churches, but rather points to stark contrasts in the way consumption and consumerism has been employed particularly in the prosperity gospel of Pentecostal and Evangelical churches.

Mennonites exemplify one form of critique of consumerism that points to inherent discrepancies in modern capitalism. Redefining and recalibrating the church's moral expectations of what was considered a simple life is an ongoing process. In its most recent Confession of Faith, the Mennonite Church USA—a successor organization to the Mennonite Church—stated in article 17 on "Discipleship and the Christian Life" that

> Conformity to Christ necessarily implies nonconformity to the world. True faith in Christ means willingness to do the will of God, rather than willful pursuit of individual happiness. True faith means seeking first the reign of God in simplicity, rather than pursuing materialism.[16]

While this confession of faith rather vaguely addresses the ongoing relevance of nonconformity for the Anabaptist Christian in the twenty-first century, it becomes clear that leading a simple life still constitutes on pillar in the Mennonite Church's moral economy.

[15] https://www.mennoniteusa.org/who-are-mennonites/, accessed December 6, 2022.

[16] Confession of Faith in a Mennonite Perspective, Article 17 Discipleship and the Christian Life, adopted 1995 by Mennonite Church USA and Mennonite Church Canada, https://www.mennoniteusa.org/who-are-mennonites/what-we-believe/confession-of-faith/, accessed December 6, 2022.

References

Balbier, Uta Andrea. 2014. 'Selling Soap and Salvation': Billy Graham's Consumer Rhetoric in Germany and the United States in the 1950s. *Amerikastudien/ American Studies* 59 (2): 137–152.

Brenneman, John M. 1866. Pride and Humility (I). *The Herald of Truth* 3 (6): 44–47.

Brunk, Harry A. 1959. *The History of Mennonites in Virginia 1727–1900: Volume I*.

Brunk, Harry A. 1972. *The History of Mennonites in Virginia 1900–1960: Volume II*.

Cross, Gary S. 2000. *An All-Consuming Century: Why Commercialism Won in Modern America*. New York: Columbia University Press.

Dawson, C. A. 1936. *Group Settlement: Ethnic Communities in Western Canada*. Canadian Frontiers of Settlement 7. Toronto: Macmillan of Canada.

Freudenberg, Maren, Martin Lutz, and Martin Radermacher. 2020. "Gospels of Prosperity and Simplicity: Assessing Variation in the Protestant Moral Economy." *Interdisciplinary Journal of Research on Religion* 16 (Article 8): 1–47.

Gingerich, Melvin. 1942. Rural Life Problems and the Mennonites. *Mennonite Quarterly Review* 16 (3): 167–173.

Gingerich, Melvin. 1970. *Mennonite Attire Through Four Centuries*. Breinigsville: Pennsylvania German Society.

Goertz, Hans-Jürgen. 1988. *Die Täufer: Geschichte und Deutung*. Berlin: Evangelische Verlags-Anstalt.

Gross, Leonard. 1980. *The Golden Years of the Hutterites: The Witness and Thought of the Communal Moravian Anabaptists During the Walpot Era; 1565–1578*. Studies and Mennonite History 23. Scottdale: Herald Press.

Hennigan, Brian. 2021. "The Poverty of Simplicity. Austerity, Alienation, and Tiny Houses." Dissertation (PhD), Syracuse University.

Hess, H. Jean. 2004. "Addressing One Another on the Changing Demands of Culture and Economy: The Mennonite Church Doctrine of Nonconformity, 1930–1959." Thesis, Associated Mennonite Biblical Seminary.

Hoover, Amos, ed. 1982. *The Jonas Martin Era: Presented in a Collection of Essays, Letters, and Documents That Shed Light on the Mennonite Churches During the 50 Year Ministry (1875–1925) of Bishop Jonas H. Martin*. Farmersville: Muddy Creek Farm Library.

Horowitz, Daniel. *The Morality of Spending: Attitudes Toward the Consumer Society in America, 1875–1940*. Baltimore: Johns Hopkins University Press.

Juhnke, James C. 1989. *Vision, Doctrine, War: Mennonite Identity and Organization in America, 1890–1930*. The Mennonite Experience in America 3. Scottdale: Herald Press.

Kauffman, J. Howard., and Leo Driedger. 1991. *The Mennonite Mosaic: Identity and Modernization*. Scottdale: Herald Press.

Klaassen, Walter. 2001. *Anabaptism: Neither Catholic nor Protestant*. Kitchener: Pandora Press.

Kraybill, Donald B., Karen Johnson-Weiner, and Steven M. Nolt. 2013. *The Amish*. Baltimore: Johns Hopkins University Press.

Lapsansky, Emma Jones. 2018. "The Changing World of Quaker Material Culture." In *The Cambridge Companion to Quakerism*, ed. Stephen W. Angell and Pink Dandelion, 147–58. Cambridge Companions to Religion. Cambridge: Cambridge University Press.

Logemann, Jan L. 2019. *Engineered to Sell: European Émigrés and the Making of Consumer Capitalism*. Chicago: University of Chicago Press.

MacMaster, Richard K. 1985. *Land, Piety, Peoplehood: The Establishment of Mennonite Communities in America 1683–1790*. The Mennonite Experience in America 1. Scottdale: Herald Press.

Muddy Creek Farm Library, ed. 2006. *Whether by Word or Epistle: Letters of Frank W. Hurst and Other Weaverland Conference Mennonites of Pennsylvania to Thomas Reesor of Ontario, 1920–1948*. Sugarcreek: Carlisle Printing.

Schlabach, Theron F. 1988. *Peace, Faith, Nation: Mennonites and Amish in Nineteenth-Century America*. The Mennonite Experience in America 2. Scottdale: Herald Press.

Schlachta, Astrid von. 2003. *Hutterische Konfession und Tradition (1578–1619): Etabliertes Leben zwischen Ordnung und Ambivalenz*. Veröffentlichungen des Instituts für Europäische Geschichte Mainz. Abteilung für abendländische Religionsgeschichte 198. Mainz: Philipp von Zabern.

Scott, Stephen. 1996. *An Introduction to Old Order and Conservative Mennonite Groups*. Intercourse: Good Books.

Toews, Paul. 2010. *Mennonites in American Society, 1930–1970: Modernity and the Persistence of Religious Community*. The Mennonite Experience in America 4. Scottdale: Herald Press.

Wenger, John C. 1945. "The Schleitheim Confession of Faith: Translated by J. C. Wenger." *The Mennonite Quarterly Review* XIX (4): 247–53.

Wenger, John C. 1952. *The Doctrines of the Mennonites*. Scottdale: Mennonite Publishing House.

Wenger, John C. 1955. *Separated Unto God: A Plea for Christian Simplicity of Life and for a Scriptural Nonconformity of the World*. Scottdale: Herald Press.

CHAPTER 12

Tax Morale and the Church: How Catholic Clergies Adapted Norms of Paying Taxes to Secular Institutions (1940s–1950s)

Korinna Schönhärl

Tax Morale in History

The term tax morale says it all. Paying taxes as an economic act is so strongly morally encoded that almost all languages have a special term for it: the German *Steuermoral*, the Spanish *moral fiscal*, the Swedish *skattemoral* and the Greek *forologiko ithos* [φορολογικό ήθος], to name just a few examples. Transepochal studies show that the moralisation of taxpaying is not a temporary phenomenon, but has been recurrent from antiquity to the present day in very different regions of the world and in completely different cultural contexts (Schönhärl et al. 2023; Guex and Buclin 2023). Taxes were to be paid honestly despite a lack of regulation because they were an expression of solidarity with the weaker members of the community; because they were supposed to make a more just society

K. Schönhärl (✉)
Paderborn University, Paderborn, Germany
e-mail: korinna.schoenhaerl@uni-paderborn.de

T. Skambraks and M. Lutz (eds.), *Reassessing the Moral Economy*, Palgrave Studies in Economic History,
https://doi.org/10.1007/978-3-031-29834-9_12

possible; or because they were used to finance public goods that were essential for survival, in the sense of the "fiscal contract". Or they were *not to be* paid because such a refusal was a lever of resistance against an occupying regime or an autocracy. In all these cases, tax (non)payment was about much more than the transfer of money from citizens or subjects to their state or ruler. Rather, it was about negotiating social hierarchies, social power relations and norms of society that were used to legitimise paying or not paying. These norms differed according to space and time. They had to and still have to be renegotiated again and again in discourse: What is allowed and what is forbidden? Which practices of tax saving are sanctioned and how? From this perspective, tax morale appears as the set of norms on which a particular group agrees, and which serves the purpose of preventing (or allowing) deviant behaviour by group members.

This process of negotiating norms is a starting point for historians analysing the discourse on honest tax payment (Schönhärl 2019a). Who were the actors who have a say in this discourse and moralise about taxpaying, what norms did they refer to, how and with what motives did they do so? Many voices were involved. As we move into the modern era, these voices could emanate from actors as diverse as the press, politicians, authors of tax guides, etc. Time and again, however, faith communities and churches also spoke out as moral authorities in the discourse on honest tax payment, referring to a higher authority, to God, in the propagation of norms. Because they understood the discourse on honest tax payment as a field of negotiation for a fair, God-ordained social order, the religious communities felt called upon to take a stand.[1] So did the Catholic Church. The dogmatic history of tax morality in Catholic theology has been sufficiently studied by theologians (Hamm 1908; for a very helpful overview see Furger 1995), but the topic has received little attention from modern historiography, although it is very suitable for a study of the connection between morality and economics. The interventions of the Catholic Church in the discourse on honest tax payment are at the centre of the following analysis, focusing on the 1940s and 1950s as a period of rapid social changes which particularly challenged all the voices involved in this discourse.

[1] For historiographical approaches concerning US Protestantism and public finances see Jones (2002); concerning Judaism see Likhovski (2017); concerning Islam e.g. Nienhaus (2007), Cizakca (2013, 55–77).

Within the Catholic Church, it was not the pope that set the tone in tax issues. On the contrary, the central institution in Rome rather retreated to very general positions and left plenty of room for interpretation. What did Catholic theologians make of this in the diverse national contexts in which they operated? The following study is devoted to the question of how three Catholic theologians wrote about taxpaying in the 1940s and 1950s, what norms they propagated and how they justified their norm-setting in a range of very different texts including a dissertation in moral theology (Crowe), a journal and an encyclopedia article, a public speech (Nell-Breuning) and a seminar textbook (Azipazu). After describing the position of the Catholic Church and the popes concerning the payment of taxes in general, the chapter investigates the three aforementioned Catholic theologians as case studies in the USA, the Federal Republic of Germany and Spain, focusing on the norms they propagated to influence the tax payment behaviour of members of the Catholic Church.[2] The conclusion summarises the way in which theologians in the highly centralised Catholic Church nonetheless greatly adapted their moral teaching concerning taxes to the institutional framework of their various nations.

Tax Payment and the Catholic Church

There are remarks about paying taxes ("Give therefore to Caesar the things that are Caesar's and to God the things that are God's"[3]) in the Bible as well as in works of the early church fathers and the theologians of the Middle Ages (Hamm 1908; Crowe 1944). The central question concerning moral theologians was whether tax laws were to be understood as so-called penal laws, i.e. whether Christians should comply with

[2] The sample of case studies covers three different types of tax systems described by Uwe Wagschal: the liberal-conservative (USA), the Christian democratic and continental European (FRG) and the peripheral-residual type (Spain), see Wagschal (2005). The sample also covers three different positions of the Catholic Church in society: Catholics as a minority of ca. 25% of the population in the USA, as nearly half (46%) of the population in the FRG and as a majority of 96% in Spain. Nevertheless, we must not overestimate the weight of these figures: In the young FRG, e.g. although Catholics were mathematically a minority, the Catholic Church had a strong position due to the power of "Rhenish Catholicism" with Chancellor Konrad Adenauer as its representative.

[3] Matthew 22, 21.

them merely in order to avoid punishment, or whether tax laws were actually a matter of conscience.[4]

Until the second third of the nineteenth century, the predominant voices in the Catholic Church wanted to understand tax laws as penal laws that did not oblige the Christian in conscience, an interpretation which opened the door to the legitimisation of evasion. This argument, however, was challenged twofold in the times of the modern state: Firstly, the traditional argument that some laws were not necessarily binding in conscience because the legislator (e.g. an absolutist monarch) would not even expect all subjects to observe them, lost persuasiveness: such laws became fragile in modern states (be they democratic or autocratic) which claimed to enact universally valid laws for the benefit of their citizens. Secondly, the positioning of the Catholic Church with regard to the social question made the traditional approach questionable. This reached its first culmination with Leo XIII's encyclical *Rerum Novarum* in 1891. The pope here rejected socialist solutions and defended the right to property, which precluded communalisation as well as excessive taxation. At the same time, however, he called for state social policy to promote the common good, thus laying the foundation for the development of Catholic social teaching (Curran 1985, 115). It went without saying that the expanded tasks assigned to the state by Leo XIII had to be financed, even if the pope did not go into such details.

In many Christian and non-Christian countries where early forms of social policy started to be implemented in the last decades of the nineteenth century, income tax was introduced in parallel or shortly afterwards to meet governments' increasing financial needs. Compared to the previously widespread indirect taxes on consumption which burdened the poorer population in particular, income tax as a public finance tool was supposed to lead to a more socially just distribution of income through its progressivity (the more individuals earn, the higher the taxes that they have to pay) (Buggeln 2022, 92–124). Direct taxation was thus introduced in the USA in 1913 (after initial attempts during the Civil War in 1861) and in Germany as part of Miquel's tax reform in 1891 (then in

[4] This distinction goes back to the Letter to the Romans: Political authority is "God's servant, an avenger of punishment on him who does evil. Therefore, it is necessary to be subject, not only for the sake of punishment, but for the sake of conscience" (Rom. 13, 3–5), quoted in Bennett (1964, 12f).

a more systematised form in Erzberger's tax reform of 1919).[5] In Spain, where direct taxes already played a role after a major tax reform in 1845, income tax was introduced in 1932 during the Second Republic.

Spain, like most other countries worldwide, was then greatly impacted by the Great Depression from 1929 on, which caused unemployment, poverty and social unrest among workers. The worldwide crisis and its social consequences motivated the Catholic Church to take another explicit stand vis-à-vis economic and social policy. Thus, Pius XI echoed the forty-year-old approaches of his predecessor in his 1931 encyclical *Quadragesimo Anno*. He called for the responsible use of property, the reconciliation of capital and labour, and the development of a strong welfare state that protects the interests of the poor. On the subject of taxation, however, the encyclical only reiterates that the state should not overtax the unassailable property of the individual (Pius XI 1931, 13). Further statements of the popes on taxes are rare. When Pius XII reflected in 1948 on "Moral Principles of a Sound Financial and Fiscal Policy", he again primarily addressed questions of tax legislation: "financial transactions of the state are becoming more and more opaque" for the taxpayers and negatively impacting their morals (Pius XII 1954, 1797, translation by author). The pope did not address the norms of taxpaying, leaving further room for interpretation within the Catholic Church.

Catholic Theologians and Taxes Since World War II: Three Case Studies

The US Redemptorist Martin Timothy Crowe (1944)

In the USA, a highly progressive income tax was introduced in 1916 and became even more progressive during the New Deal years from 1935 onwards (Brownlee 1996, 109ff.). In 1941, the basis of income tax was significantly broadened to finance the war effort: the number of individual taxpayers soared from 3.9 (1939) to 42.6 (1945) million, and annual federal income-tax collections leaped from \$2.2 to \$30.1 billion (Brownlee and Boyer 2004). Vast numbers of US-Americans had to pay taxes in 1941 for the very first time in their lives. The Treasury Department took various measures to convince Americans to pay their

[5] Johannes Franz Miquel, Prussian Finance Minister 1890–1901; Matthias Erzberger, German Finance Minister 1919–1920.

taxes voluntarily and honestly. Tax education was conducted via newspaper coverage, radio addresses, the purchase of saving stamps and the education of schoolteachers (Jones 1996, 111, 117) but also by works of art and culture. Tax education campaigns addressed taxpaying as a patriotic act through which each citizen could enable America to win the war against the Nazi aggressors and to defend the American way of life. After the war, taxes were continued on the basis of a bi-partisan consensus.

In the following years, major topics among US theologians concerned the relationship between state and citizens and the question of whether the existing political and economic order was in accordance with Christianity. James T. Fisher speaks of an overwhelming comeback of religiosity in the USA (Fisher 2006, 44–46). Especially within Protestantism, debates about the advantages and disadvantages of collectivism or individualism were conducted with great commitment, e.g. by Protestant professor Reinhold Niebuhr (Niebuhr 1953; Jones 2002, 112), who believed that politics should lead people to consider ethical standards in economic matters as well. At the beginning of the Cold War under the administration of President Truman, various interest groups endeavoured to educate clergymen about economic topics, in order to win them as a voice against socialism (Jones 2002, 96–86).

Remarkably, in this extensive Protestant literature on the state–citizen relationship, tax morale was a much-neglected sideline in explorations of the rights and duties of state and citizen and the relationship between voluntarism and coercion in society. At times, a just tax system and the principles of taxation were considered, but the tax morale of citizens was not an issue. This was equally true of Catholic theologians in the USA who addressed economic issues, e.g. Sulpician John Francis Cronin, who was concerned with the practical application of Catholic social teaching to American economic life, criticising in particular the growing company concentration with its tendency towards monopolies (Cronin 1950). Neo-Thomist[6] Herbert Johnston, who taught *business ethics* (Mees 2020, 70) at the University of Notre Dame du Lac in Indiana, also only touched on the subject of tax morality in passing in his 1956 morality textbook for business practitioners (Johnston 1956). One of the few works that dealt specifically with the Catholic Church's position on taxation was the

[6] From the mid-nineteenth century, neo-Thomism was an intellectual current in Catholic theology that called for the revival of Thomas Aquinas' philosophy.

moral theology dissertation of the Redemptorist[7] Martin Timothy Crowe (1914–2007), which appeared during World War II (Crowe 1944).

A native of Johnsonburg, Pennsylvania, Crowe studied philosophy, dogmatic and moral theology at St. Mary's Seminary of the Missionary Order of Redemptorists in North East. A subsequent novitiate prepared him for practical missionary work (Erie Times-News 2007). In 1935 he entered the Redemptorist Order and was ordained to the priesthood on June 23, 1940 at Mount St. Alphonsus Seminary in Esopus, New York. He then entered doctoral studies at the Faculty of the School of Sacred Theology at the private Catholic University of America in Washington, graduating in 1944 with a doctorate in moral theology. He seems to have enjoyed a certain proximity to the progressive *Catholic Theological Society of America*, which, in the spirit of Catholic social teaching, was committed to linking theological scholarship with current social problems (Fenton 1946, 8). One can only speculate about the possibility of Crowe having had a positive attitude towards the New Deal, like most Catholic priests (e.g. on Crowe's positive attitude towards the minimum wage, see Crowe 1944, 8). After completing his doctorate, he served as a Catholic chaplain in the US Infantry from 1944 to 1947. After the war, he was a priest in various parishes in New York (Erie Times-News 2007).

In his 1944 dissertation "Moral obligation of paying just taxes", Crowe was explicitly *not* concerned with the question of whether the current tax law was just, but rather wanted to analyse the moral-theological question concerning "to what extent and under what virtue does it bind in conscience?" (Crowe 1944, 9). The Redemptorist proceeded systematically. After a brief overview of the various aspects of a just tax, he systematically worked through various doctrines of tax morale. He concluded that tax laws in modern democracies were not penal laws because the legislator did not envision them as such: "There is no evidence that such an intention [to make the laws purely penal] exists regarding tax laws" (Crowe 1944, 107). The legislator intended to make the laws binding in conscience and therefore they were just that, and were thus an obligation of legal justice.

But how is their binding force as "civic duty" (Crowe 1944, 151) legitimated? Crowe rejected legitimisation based on exchange, because

[7] The Redemptorist Congregation of the Most Holy Redeemer was founded in Italy in 1732 as a missionary society, conducting primarily so-called "home missions" geared towards Catholics.

he could not identify a fully valid, freely concluded contract between the state and the citizen: "The fact [is] that normally a man enters the state by way of the family, not by way of contract" (Crowe 1944, 127). Additionally, public services financed by the state through taxes could not be transferred into private ownership of the individuum (Crowe 1944, 135). But how else can the notion of taxation as binding in conscience be legitimatised? Crowe argued after careful consideration that "the immediate obligation is probably one of piety". Piety, which Crowe understood in St. Thomas's sense of "*pietas erga patriam*", he thought could best be translated as *patriotism*: "[F]or 'patriotism' has come to mean 'fulfillment of civic duties through *love of* country'" (Crowe 1944, 151, emphasis in the original). Thus, in his conclusion Crowe did not deviate very far from the patriotic narrative of the US government's tax education campaigns during World War II already mentioned above.

The West German Jesuit Oswald Von Nell-Breuning (1930, 1954, 1962)

After World War II, not much changed in the German tax system. The ideological and anti-Semitic excesses of the Nazi era were eliminated, but otherwise the design of the 1919 Erzberger tax reform remained largely intact. The legal basis was provided by the February Laws of 1946, in which the Allied Control Council established a uniform tax law for all four occupation zones. However, tax concessions were abolished and tax rates were drastically increased. The top rate of income tax was 95 per cent, and all other taxes also rose sharply (Ullmann 2005, 180; Muscheid 1986, 27; Buggeln 2022, 571–647). The goals were to de-nazify the tax code, to skim off the surplus money caused by inflation and to raise more revenue to cover the costs of occupation. This rigorous tax policy reflected the efforts of the Allies to make the "*beati possidentes*", who had been able to save their property from the turmoil of war, bear the expenses of the national economy, which was heavily burdened by refugees, war veterans, uprooted people and the destitute (Wehler 2008, 955). It was necessary to equalise the situation of war losers and war winners (or those who had suffered less), and in the view of the Allies, this was to be realised primarily through tax policy redistribution. Accordingly, they rejected the proposal of the tax relief put forward by the Economic Council, which was primarily interested in promoting investment.

While the Soviet-occupied zone went its own way in terms of tax policy (Ullmann 2005, 179), the Allies in the Western occupation zones prevented tax cuts on the basis of the Control Council laws even after the convening of the Parliamentary Council (in which the balance of power between the Social democrats and the conservatives was almost even). The Second Tax Reorganisation Act of April 1949 and the Deutsche Mark (DM) Opening Balance Sheet Act of August 1949 therefore failed to reduce taxes, but they did open up many possibilities for evasion, e.g. by allowing great leeway in the valuation of corporate capital in DM, favouring non-withdrawn profits and various possibilities for depreciation. Thus, while capital accumulation was encouraged, the original tax rates were eroded (Muscheid 1986, 44). The goal of these pre-Federal Republic tax laws was to promote investment and growth; combating social inequality remained a secondary objective. After the Bundestag took up its work in September 1949, the Allies initially continued to resist open tax cuts and long negotiations were necessary to gain agreement to an Income Tax Amendment Act (April 29, 1950), in which rates were "pulled apart" and reduced by an average of 17 per cent. In addition, the Allies tolerated the fact that tax concessions, such as depreciation allowances, were not reduced but rather further expanded, i.e. increasing the options for tax savings that were (just about) on the right side of the law (Muscheid 1986, 48).

Immediately after the end of the war, tax morale in Germany was already described as decidedly unsatisfactory by the media, who had gradually taken up their work, and there were also many complaints in the political realm about poor taxpaying behaviour (Schönhärl 2019b). This applied not only to the flourishing black market, but also to the payment of direct taxes. Press reports told of tax evasion on a large scale. After the currency reform (June 1948), there was apparently no increase in honest taxpaying by the Germans at all. Figures were rarely cited in the discourse; an exception was made by Ludwig Ellinger, Chief Finance President of Württemberg-Baden, who estimated that DM 4.5 billion of taxes were evaded in West Germany in 1950 (though without naming the method of measurement used),[8] which corresponded to more than a quarter of the budget of DM 16.3 billion. Otherwise, the discourse was largely devoid

[8] Quoted from Willi Lausen (SPD) in Bundestag (BT), 145th session, May 31, 1951, 5741. The Bundestag minutes are available at: http://pdok.bundestag.de/.

of a numerical basis. While conservatives and liberals proposed a reduction in the tax burden as an antidote, the Social Democrats called for stricter controls and higher penalties.

Oswald von Nell-Breuning (1890–1991) was born into a wealthy noble family in Trier. After schooling in Trier, he took up the study of theology in Innsbruck in 1910, entered the Jesuit order a year later, and was ordained as a priest in 1921. In 1928, he received his doctorate in Münster for a thesis on stock market morality (Nell-Breuning 1928), a work in which his Catholic-based anti-capitalism was clearly evident. He was then appointed professor of moral theology, canon law, economics and social theory at the philosophical–theological University St. Georgen in Frankfurt on the Main, founded in 1926 (Hengsbach 2010). Pope Pius XI commissioned him to prepare a draft for *Quadragesimo Anno,* into which Nell-Breuning, building on the key concepts of the forty-year-old encyclical *Rerum Novarum*, introduced his ideas for just distribution in society. The passages on professional organisation, which Nell-Breuning wanted to be understood as a "plea for the institutionalisation of economic-democratic and social-partnership forms of cross-corporate co-determination", were often misinterpreted at the time as "advocacy of authoritarian corporative models of order" (Süss 2015, 232, translation by author).

During the Second World War, Nell-Breuning was entrusted with the financial administration of the Lower German Province of the Jesuits. After the war, he taught not only at St. Georgen, but also at the Goethe University Frankfurt and at the Frankfurt Academy of Labour. From 1948 to 1965, he was a member of the influential Scientific Advisory Board of the Federal Ministry of Economics. He welcomed the founding of the German Confederation of Trade Unions in 1959 and contributed decisively to improvements in the relationship between the Catholic Church and the Social Democrats. In the 1980s, he participated in discussions on reducing mass unemployment, shortening working hours, reforming social security and an environmentally sound economy. "He called the economic form practised in the Federal Republic 'socially tempered capitalism' because it was still far from a fair distribution of purchasing power, adequate social security and forward-looking cost allocation" (Hengsbach 1999, translation by author).

Nell-Breuning was perhaps the most prominent, but he was not the only Catholic scholar in West Germany who took up the highly topical subject of tax morality (e.g. Höffner 1952). However, he probably did so most intensively. His reflections on tax morale were first published in 1930 in an article in the magazine "Voices of the Times" ("Stimmen der Zeit", Nell-Breuning 1930). His second publication on the topic was in 1954 (a speech held in 1952 at the Academy of the Diocese of Rottenburg, Nell-Breuning 1954). Finally, he published once again in an encyclopedia article (Nell-Breuning 1962). He remained largely faithful to his argumentation, but supplemented it with aspects of current research.

His first article from 1930 was published during the Great Depression, when Nell-Breuning had already worked out his ideas for *Quadragesimo Anno*, but supported Brüning's austerity policies (Suess 2015, 233). The Jesuit introduced his text by quoting the demands of business representatives and politicians to reduce tax rates, because keeping them at current rates was said to strain the morale of taxpayers. Lowering them would, in contrast, allow a return to fiscal honesty. Nell-Breuning decisively rejected this argument, because here tax dishonesty and tax losses were "regarded, so to speak, as a function of the level of tax rates", so that it would only be a matter of determining the "tax optimum" by means of a differential calculation (Nell-Breuning 1930, 254, translation by author). He considered this "idea of a maximum capacity existing somewhere on the tax scale, up to which point the tax conscience can remain steadfast" to be "unbearable"; it had nothing to do with morality. He believed that it was the tax system's inner logic and legitimacy and not the amount of taxes that was decisive for tax conscience, for the question of whether it was possible to generate an objective and binding obligation in the conscience. Nell-Breuning rejected the position of older theologians that while direct taxes were obligatory in conscience, indirect taxes were merely penal laws. In a tax constitution in which different types of taxes intertwine to ensure a just equalisation of burdens, this distinction would be nonsensical, so both types of taxes must be obligatory in conscience.

Decisive for the emergence of a genuine obligation in conscience was, first, the use of the tax money: the taxpayer "does not want to have paid the tax for nothing, it should not be money that is thrown away for him" (Nell-Breuning 1930, 256, translation by author). Instead of giving the taxpayer the feeling of "standing in front of an opaque, mysterious smokescreen" (Nell-Breuning 1930, 259, translation by author), tax collection must be bounded by necessity, and spending must be thoughtful, frugal and relevant, he said. Nell-Breuning clearly rejected the notion that evasion could be justified with the argument that everyone else was evading taxes too, particularly in times when deduction at source deprived most wage earners of any possibility of evasion. He pleaded for clear boundaries between what is permitted and what is prohibited and urged the closing of any loopholes that could endanger the fairness of burden sharing.

In his 1954 speech, Nell-Breuning remained true to his 1930 assessment on many points. He once again rebuked the "laxity" of older moral theology on the subject of tax honesty and emphasised the obligation of conscience to pay taxes. Since the church was responsible for the morals of the faithful, it would have to urgently adapt its principles to a modern, complex society in which it was not monarchs but a democratically legitimised parliament that decided on taxes.

> [A]s a member of the community, I have to contribute to the burdens of the community according to the position I occupy in the community and according to the powers and means I have at my disposal, whether by personal achievement or by material contributions I make to the community. (Nell-Breuning 1954, 11, translation by author)

Tax evasion involved a distortion of competition and thus burdened the conscience towards God. Again, he pointed out that in times when tax was deducted at source, any reference to widespread evasion practices no longer made sense. And he added that the church, which is financed by church tax, is called upon to be particularly conscientious here:

> It is not acceptable that one side finds these taxes so irreproachable and so blameless that they attach their own taxes unquestioningly to them, while the other side declares that these taxes are so unwarranted and so unjust in their distribution, and, moreover, so excessive, that we can do nothing better than avoid them as much as possible. (Nell-Breuning 1954, 15, translation by author)

In his 1962 publication (plans for a major "organic" tax reform that would have created a tax system "from a single mould" had largely failed by the mid-1950s), he first pointed out the ambiguity of the term tax morale, which could refer either to the duties of the state in terms of tax design or to the duties of the taxpayer.[9] With reference to the latter, he

[9] Following e.g. Adolph Wagner. Tipke later distinguishes between "morality of taxation" and "tax morale", cf. Tipke (2000).

drew attention to the now available results of the empirical social sciences, which understood tax morality as the *attitude of* taxpayers towards their tax obligations and attempted to capture this attitude using opinion polling methods (Schmölders 1960). He then referred to the importance of the legitimacy of rule, which is central to the obligation to pay taxes. But even in dictatorships, taxes should not simply be evaded, as this would impose a heavier burden on citizens with no means of evasion. A thorough examination of the unreasonableness of the demand would have to precede an evasion in any case. While Nell-Breuning did not quote the Spaniard Joaquin Azpiazu's writings, he discusses the conditions of tax morale in dictatorship, which indicates that this problem came to his attention in the early 1960s.

The Spanish Jesuit Joaquín Azpiazu Zulaica (1944/1952)

After Franco's victory in the Civil War in 1939, Spaniards had to deal with a tax system which mainly continued the structures of the nineteenth-century system, going back beyond the 1932 reform. The dictator and his supporters were not interested in modernisation in terms of fairer burden sharing within society. Thus, the tax rate was a very low 10%, indirect taxes were the most important source of revenue, and direct taxes (e.g. of wealth or income) were not progressive. Collection of the sparse direct taxes was organised via professional associations, which were responsible for parcelling out their designated tax duty among their members, a proceeding that provides a great deal of scope to the powerful. Where there was direct contact between taxpayers and the tax administration, the tax was determined not according to profit, but according to "objective" attributes like the number of staff or the technical equipment (Comín Comín 1995, 2007, 2015). The profits of the growing industrial sector thus could not be skimmed off by the exchequer, which caused an extraordinarily unequal society. For everybody apart from wageworkers and workers in agriculture, tax evasion or avoidance was very easy, and it was neither considered to be a crime nor punished as such. There were very few tax inspectors, and tax management was deficient (Comín Comín 2007). In the literature, the tax system of the autocratic regime is considered to be an instrument of remuneration for the elites that had supported Franco during the Civil War (1936–1939) and continued to do so after the war ended: the powerful landowners and the business elites, especially in the financial and banking sectors, and the Catholic Church (Comín

Comín 1994). But already in the 1950s, scholars and the administration recognised that tax evasion was a major problem, as the government painfully lacked investment funds and discontent among the population was growing (Torres Martínez 1950; Sánchez Asiain 1952; Torres López 1961). The tax reforms of 1957 and 1964 were intended to distribute the tax burden more fairly, but these attempts failed.

Joaquín Azpiazu Zulaica (1887–1953) was initially among the supporters of Franco's coup. Born in 1887 in San Sebastián (Guipúzcoa), he attended the Jesuit school *San Francisco Javier de Tudela* in Navarre and began his theological studies at the *Compañía de Jesús (Society of Jesus)* in Loyola in 1903. There he was ordained as a priest in 1915 and then sent to study at the traditional Jesuit University of Deusto in Bilbao. In 1921, he received his doctorate from the Faculty of Law of the University of Madrid with the dissertation *El derecho de propiedad* (*Property Rights*, Azpiazu 1930) before being appointed professor of political economy and finance at the University of Deusto, the only place in Spain where business administration was offered as a subject (Fernández Riquelme 2009; Velasco Sánchez s.t.).

Azpiazu, in the spirit of *Quadragesimo Anno,* professed Catholic social teaching and social work, defending the right of workers to property and work. Imitating the French Jesuits' *L'Action Populaire (People's Action),*[10] he and his fellow Jesuit Sisinio Nevares founded the *Fomento Social (Social Promotion)* as early as 1926. It was dedicated to spreading social Catholicism and Christian democracy among workers and peasants, to enable them to found their own trade unions, and to keep them away from socialism. The just redistribution of social wealth, also with the instrument of taxation, was an important goal. Azpiazu can thus be assigned to the left wing of the Jesuit order, much like Nell-Breuning in Germany. Accordingly, the clergyman welcomed the papal encyclical of 1931 euphorically. Under the socialist government, the *Compañía de Jesús* was banned in Spain in 1932 (Velasco Sánchez s.t.). However, teaching at the Faculty of Economics in Deusto could continue because it was not owned by the Jesuits, and so Azpiazu does not seem to have left Spain.

[10] The French Catholic social action movement was founded by two Jesuit priests in 1903. It aimed to give guidance to clergy directly engaged in social activities and to defend the rights of workingmen to establish their own trade unions in a Christian spirit, see Droulers (1969).

In 1934, the Jesuit published one of his major works on the corporate state, which went through a total of five editions (Azpiazu 1934).

With the beginning of the Civil War in 1936, Azpiazu sided with the putschists, as did most other Spanish clergy and most of the episcopate.[11] Bilbao was conquered by the putschists as early as 1937, allowing the Jesuits here to resume all their previous fields of activity. Azpiazu supported Franco's party, for example, with anti-communist articles in which he praised the authoritarian state as the founder of national unity and the protector of the Church, whose rights the state had to safeguard and protect (Azpiazu 1937b). The idea of the Francoist uprising being a crusade was also not foreign to him (Azpiazu 1937a). Azpiazu fervently hoped that a nationalist victory would enable a just society through the implementation of the corporate state. Martínez and Ramos mention, without further evidence, that he already enjoyed great prestige in conservative circles during the Civil War (Martínez Vara and Ramos Gorostiza 2018, 115).

In 1938, Franco officially allowed the Jesuits to return to Spain, and the activities of the *Fomento Social* were intensified. Support for the poor was sorely needed, as Bilbao was in dire need in the post-war period, and it was only thanks to the Jesuits' good relations with the new government that teaching could be maintained. Azpiazu contributed intensively to Franco's *Fuero del Trabajo (Labour Law)* of 1938, which he understood as an attempt to put into practice the Catholic corporate state envisioned in *Quadragesimo Anno*. Azpiazu's aim was to watch over the rights of the popular classes and help them achieve greater prosperity without interfering too much with their self-government (Azpiazu 1938, 147f.; Azpiazu 1949, 389).

As a basis for university teaching, the Jesuit wrote a book on the morality of the businessman (first edition 1944, second 1952) (Azpiazu 1952), in which he promoted the re-Christianisation of society, whose purpose should be the common good and the elimination of misery. From 1946 he additionally started directing the journal *Revista de Fomento Social (Social Promotion Magazine)*, where he published more than 50 articles. He also promoted Catholic social teaching and work in a large number of lectures in Spain, Argentina and Uruguay. However, Azpiazu was not uncritical even under the dictatorship: he belonged to those

[11] See e.g. the Carta colectiva de los obispos españoles con motivo de la guerra en España of 1937, cf. Ruiz Rico (1977, 50).

Basque clergy who protested so vehemently against the surveillance and restraints of the Franco regime that the ecclesiastical Basque province was divided in 1948 (Egido et al. 2004, 378f.). After 1950, Azpiazu was a member of the *Real Academia de Ciencias Morales y Políticas (Royal Academy of Moral and Political Sciences)* and the *Unión internacional de Estudios Sociales* (*International Union of Social Studies*, see Fernández Riquelme 2009). Azpiazu died on April 30, 1953 and so did not live to see the Concordat between Spain and the Vatican of August 1953.

In his 1944/1952 "The morale of the businessman", Azpiazu commented on the question of paying taxes in the chapter "The obligatory nature of tax laws" (Azpiazu 1952, 499–517, translation by author). He began by stating the responsibility of the individual to society, because humans, as social beings, could only exist in interaction and communication with others. The state, as the embodiment of this society, needs tax revenues to administer its business and to ensure the welfare of its citizens: schools, police protection and courts were the state's quid pro quo for taxes, and could not be maintained in any other way. Azpiazu argued here with *justicia conmutativa*, the justice of exchange, that also underlies the modern notion of the "fiscal contract". He described "a certain quasi-contractual requirement between the State and the subjects" (Azpiazu 1952, 505, translation by author). Quibbling exercises in logic, with which Crowe invalidated the obligation to pay taxes in terms of exchange justice, were as far from Azpiazu's mind as from Nell-Breuning's. Without further recourse to the history of dogma, he argued that just taxes that correspond to the individual's ability to pay are not simply penal laws, but are binding in conscience for the believer. This applied to both direct and indirect taxes, he said, regardless of whether or not the legislator was Catholic. In particular, it also applied to extraordinarily high profits, which were only possible within the framework of society and should therefore flow back to it for the most part. Here Azpiazu strictly demarcated himself from the older positions mentioned by all three theologians, according to which tax laws only possessed the status of penal laws. He emphasised that deficiencies in or even the corruption of the administration were no justification for tax evasion (Azpiazu 1952, 499f.).

But what if taxes were unjust? Crowe had explicitly excluded this case from his considerations and Nell-Breuning did not take up the problem until 1962. For Azipazu, however, it was central, because as a follower of Catholic social teaching he was not able to close his eyes to the obviously unfair distribution of burdens in the Spanish tax system. First of all, he argued that even corruption or unfairness in the tax system did not remove the principle of an obligation to pay. However, he conceded:

> And let it be supposed that the good must always pay for the frauds of the bad, then the good may also conceal their wealth. At least to an extent in keeping with the injustice of the tax. (Azpiazu 1952, 511, translation by author)

Not the letter, but the spirit of the legislation was to be followed in this case. In order to determine this, an exact study of the laws on the one hand and the opinion of the scholars on the other hand was necessary. For those who could not make the great effort required to determine exactly the just amount from case to case, the Jesuit gave a figure: a tax equal to about 4% of the income was just. If the demands of the tax authorities exceeded this percentage, then it was justified to disguise one's true income, e.g. by falsified accounting, in order to pay less—but not nothing at all! If the tax authority were to require an oath, it could be taken "under mental reservation" which would nullify its binding force. "This constitutes the merchant's defence against injustice" (Azpiazu 1952, 514, translation by author). With these concessions to Spanish realities, Azpiazu distanced himself considerably from the positions of his two brothers in faith in the USA and the FRG.

Conclusion

There are commonalities in the writings of the three theologians on (honest) tax payment. None of the theologians viewed the tax laws of modernity as penal laws, but all three argued that they bound taxpayers in conscience—in clear distinction to the older dogmatics, as these positions no longer suited the rapidly changing societies of the mid-twentieth century. The traditional dogmatic argumentation that state laws could not always claim to be binding on citizens because the legislator sometimes did not even expect them to be observed, no longer made sense for the *modern* state. But how was this binding force in conscience legitimated by the three theologians? Nell-Breuning and Azpiazu emphasised that citizens received from the state, even from the authoritarian or corrupt state, more or less adequate and satisfactory returns for their money and thus were obliged to pay in the sense of a “fiscal contract”. Crowe, however, did not see the obligation as stemming from *justitia commutativa*, exchange justice, (because no explicit, free will contract between citizen and state can be proven), but traced it back to patriotism.

The conclusions the three drew for practical taxpaying behaviour differed fundamentally. Crowe did not draw any such conclusions in his dissertation, but left it at the reader’s discretion—even though his characterisation of tax duty as a patriotic duty during WWII speaks a very clear language. Nell-Breuning argued strongly that taxpayers were not allowed to withdraw from their service to the community despite all the shortcomings of tax laws and tax administration, which in turn had to be improved in democratic processes. Azpiazu, however, in view of the widespread evasion practices and corruption in Spain, advised his audience of prospective businessmen to forge their tax returns so that the amount to be paid was a fair contribution, as determined by themselves but guided by his own notion of an appropriate percentage. In his opinion, this was the only way to ensure a kind of social justice, which the laws themselves failed to guarantee or even aspire to.

Starting from the same premises of Catholic social teaching, the three theologians arrived at different advice for economic practice—and thus show paradigmatically that theological norm-setting has never taken place in a social vacuum, but always occurs in the interplay between ideological positions and institutional, legal, economic and political frameworks that differ greatly in different states. Further analysis is required to determine the extent to which the three theologians succeeded in norm-setting concerning honest tax payment by occupying a powerful position in the public discourse or even by managing to lead public opinion. Their impact was certainly not primarily determined by the quality of their argumentation, but also by the strong or weak discursive position of the Catholic Church in general in their home states.

This chapter started from the concept of tax morale, highlighting that the very existence of the term in many languages shows that paying taxes is a field of economic action which is per se morally charged. Talking about taxes always involves balancing the tension between individual and collective needs, between the social, common benefit and the option of “moral hazard” of the individuum. Analysis of the emergence and changes of norms of taxpaying in societies is thus only possible through adopting a perspective that links economics and morality.

References

Azpiazu, Joaquín. 1930. *El derecho de propiedad: Estudio jurídico y económico.* Madrid: Razón y Fe.

Azpiazu, Joaquín. 1934. *El Estado corporativo.* Pamplona: Ed. Navarra.

Azpiazu, Joaquín. 1937a. ¡Por Dios y por la patria! *Razón y Fe: Revista Mensual Hispanoamericana* 112: 40–54.

Azpiazu, Joaquín. 1937b. Estado tradicional y Estado totalitario. *Razón y fe: Revista hispanoamericana de cultura* 112 (Sep-Dic): 181–192.

Azpiazu, Joaquín. 1938. *El estado corporativo*, 3rd ed. Zaragoza: Editorial Navarra.

Azpiazu, Joaquin. 1949. *Fundamentos de Sociología económico-cristiana.* Madrid: Compañía Bibliográfica Española.

Azpiazu, Joaquin. 1952. *La moral del hombre de negocios*, 2nd ed. Madrid.

Bennett, John Coleman. 1964. *Auch Christen sind Staatsbürger. Fragen aus der Praxis der Demokratie.* Gütersloh: Gütersloher Verl.-Haus Mohn.

Brownlee, W. Elliot. 1996. *Federal Taxation in America: A Brief History.* Washington, DC: Woodrow Wilson Center Press.

Brownlee, W. Elliot, and Paul S. Boyer. 2004. Taxation. In *The Oxford Companion to United States History*, ed. Paul S. Boyer.

Buggeln, Marc. 2022. *Das Versprechen der Gleichheit: Progressive Steuern und die Reduktion sozialer Ungleichheit 1871 bis 1945.* Berlin: Surkamp.

Cizakca, Murat. 2013. *Islamic Capitalism and Finance: Origins, Evolution and the Future.* Cheltenham: Edward Elgar.

Comín Comín, Francisco. 1994. El fraude fiscal en la Historia: un planteamiento de sus fases. In *El fraude fiscal en la historia de España*, ed. Instituto de Estudios Fiscales, 31–46. Madrid: Instituto de Estudios Fiscales.

Comín Comín, Francisco. 1995. Public Finance in Spain During the 19th and 20th Century: Fundación Empresa Pública, Working Paper. In *The economic development of Spain since 1870,* ed. Pablo Martín-Aceña and James Simpson, 521–560. Aldershot, UK: Elgar.

Comín, Comín, Francisco. 2007. Reforma tributaria y reforma de la inspección durante la transición a la democracia en España. In *Los Inspectores de Hacienda en España: Una mirada histórica*, ed. Juan Pan-Montojo, 85–124. Madrid: Centro de Estudios Financieros.

Comín Comín, Francisco. 2015. La Hacienda Pública durante el Franquismo: el retroceso en la modernización del Estado (1936–1975). In *La evolución de la hacienda pública en Italia y España (siglos XVIII-XXI)*, ed. Carlos Barciela López, Antonio Di Vittorio and Joaquín Melgarejo Moreno, 325–352. Alicante: Universitat d'Alacant.

Cronin, John F. 1950. *Catholic Social Principles: The Social Teaching of the Catholic Church Applied to American Economic Life.* Milwaukee: The Bruc Publishing Company.

Crowe, Martin Timothy. 1944. *Moral Obligation of Paying Just Taxes*. Washington, D.C.: The Catholic university of America press.

Curran, Charles E. 1985. Just Taxation in the Roman Catholic Tradition. *The Journal of Religious Ethics* 13 (1): 113–133.

Droulers, Paul. 1969. *Politique sociale et christianisme. Le Père Desbuquois et l'Action Populaire. Débuts, Syndicalism et intégristes 1903–1918*. Paris: Edition ouvrières.

Egido, Teofanes, Javier Burrieza Sánchez, and Manuel Revuelta González. 2004. *Los jesuítas en España y en el mundo hispánico*. Madrid: Marcial Pons Historia.

Fenton, Joseph C. 1946. The Foundation and Progress of the Society. *Proceedings of the Catholic Theological Society of America* 5–12.

Fernández Riquelme, Sergio. 2009. Joaquín Azpiazu y la Sociología cristiana. Nota biográfica e intelectual. *Revista La razón histórica. Revista hispanoamericana de Historia de las Ideas* 6: 42–49.

Fisher, James T. 2006. American Religion Since 1945. In *A companion to post-1945 America*, ed. Jean-Christophe Agnew and Roy Rosenzweig, 44–63. Malden, MA: Blackwell Pub.

Furger, Franz. 1995. Fehlt es an Steuermoral? In *Steuergerechtigkeit*, ed. Anton Rauscher, 37–50. Köln: Bachem.

Guex, Sébastien, and Hadrien Buclin, eds. 2023. *Tax Evasion and Tax Havens since the Nineteenth Century*. Cham: Springer International Publishing.

Hamm, Franz. 1908. *Zur Grundlegung und Geschichte der Steuermoral*. Trier: Paulinus.

Hengsbach SJ, Friedhelm. 1999. Nell-Breuning, Oswald von in *Neue Deutsche Biographie* 19: 56–58. https://www.deutsche-biographie.de/pnd118586920.html#ndbcontent.

Hengsbach SJ, Friedhelm. 2010. *Kapitalismuskritik bei Joseph Höffner und Oswald von Nell-Breuning*. https://nbi.sankt-georgen.de/assets/documents/2010/07_10Kapitalismuskritikfh.pdf.

Höffner, Joseph. 1952. Eigentumsbegriff und heutige Besteuerungsgrundsätze vom Standpunkt der Moral. *Steuer und Wirtschaft* 29: 137–149.

Johnston, Herbert. 1956. *Business Ethics*. New York: Pitman.

Jones, Carolyn C. 1996. Mass-based Income Taxation: Creating a Taxpaying Culture, 1940–1952. In *Funding the modern American State, 1941–1995: The Rise and Fall of the Era of easy Finance*, ed. W. Elliot Brownlee, 107–147. Cambridge: Woodrow Wilson Center Press.

Jones, Carolyn C. 2002. Hard Shells of Community: Tax Equity Debates within the National Council of Churches after World War II. In *Tax Justice: The Ongoing Debate*, ed. Joseph J. Thorndike and Denis J. Ventry, 95–122. Urban Institute Press.

Jones, Carolyn C. 2018. Seeing Taxation in the Mid-Twentieth Century: US Tax Compliance. In *The Leap of Faith. The Fiscal Foundations of Successful*

Government in Europe and America, ed. Sven Steinmo, 198–222. Oxford: Oxford University Press.
Likhovski, Assaf. 2017. *Tax Law and Social Norms in Mandatory Palestine and Israel*. New York, NY: Cambridge University Press.
Martínez Vara, Tomás, and José Luis Ramos Gorostiza. 2018. El catolicismo social y la recepción de la escuela de relaciones humanas en españa. *Historia Social* (90): 107–130.
Mees, Bernard. 2020. *The Rise of Business Ethics*. New York, NY: Routledge.
Muscheid, Jutta. 1986. *Die Steuerpolitik der Bundesrepublik Deutschland: 1949–1982*. Berlin: Dunckler & Humblot.
N. N. 2007. Rev. Martin Timothy Crowe. *Erie Times-News,* July 3 to July 5.
Nell-Breuning, Oswald von. 1928. *Grundzüge der Börsenmoral*. Freiburg im Breisgau: Herder.
Nell-Breuning, Oswald von. 1930. Steuerverfassung und Steuergewissen. *Stimmen der Zeit* 118: 254–268.
Nell-Breuning, Oswald von. 1954. *Sittliche Grundsätze zu Steuerrecht und Steuermoral*. Stuttgart: Akad. d. Diöz. Rottenburg.
Nell-Breuning, Oswald von. 1962. Steuermoral. In *Staatslexikon: Recht Wirtschaft Gesellschaft,* 6th ed, ed. Görres-Gesellschaft, 698–700. Freiburg: Herder.
Niebuhr, Reinhold, ed. 1953. *Christian Realism and Political Problems,* 5th ed. New York: Scribner.
Nienhaus, Volker. 2007. Zakat, Taxes, and Public Finance in Islam. In *Islam and the Everyday World: Public Policy Dilemmas*, ed. Sohrab Behdad and Farhād Nu'mānī, 165–192. London: Routledge.
Pius XI. 1931. *Quadragesimo Anno* (German). https://www.iupax.at/dl/MKNkJmoJOLmJqx4KJKJmMJmNMn/1931-pius-xi-quadragesimo-anno.pdf.
Pius XII. 1954, Sittliche Grundsätze einer gesunden Finanz- und Steuerpolitik. In *Aufbau und Entfaltung des gesellschaftlichen Lebens: Soziale Summe Pius XII*, ed. Arthur Fridolin Utz and Josef Groner, 1796–1798. Fribourg, Switzerland: Paulusverl.
Rico Ruiz, Juan José. 1977. *El papel político de la iglesia católica en la España de Franco: 1936–1971*. Madrid: Editorial Tecnos.
Sánchez Asiain, José Angel. 1952. El problema de la evasión fiscal en España. *Boletín de estudios económicos* 153–159.
Schmölders, Günter. 1960. *Das Irrationale in der öffentlichen Finanzwirtschaft: Probleme der Finanzpsychologie*. Reinbek bei Hamburg.
Schönhärl, Korinna. 2019a. "Der Imperativ des Nassauerns, Durchmogelns und Absahnens". Debatten um Steuermoral in der Bundesrepublik Deutschland Anfang der 1980er Jahre. *GWU* 70 (11/12): 678–694.
Schönhärl, Korinna. 2019b. Steuermoral in Westdeutschland nach dem Zweiten Weltkrieg. Eine diskursanalytische Rekonstruktion. *Leviathan* 47:169–191.

Schönhärl, Korinna, Gisela Hürlimann, and Dorothea Rohde, eds. 2023. *Histories of Tax Evasion, Avoidance and Resistance.* London, New York: Routledge.

Süss, Winfried. 2015. Die Arbeitsgesellschaft ordnen: Oswald von Nell-Breuning zu Grundfragen der Sozialpolitik. In *Den Kapitalismus bändigen: Oswald von Nell-Breunings Impulse für die Sozialpolitik*, ed. Bernhard Emunds and Hans Günter Hockerts, 225–240. Paderborn: Verlag Ferdinand Schöningh.

Tipke, Klaus. 2000. *Besteuerungsmoral und Steuermoral.* Wiesbaden: Westdt. Verl.

Torres López, Vicente. 1961. Las causas de las infracciones tributarias. *Semana de Estudios de Derecho Financiero* IX: 301–306.

Torres Martínez, Manuel. 1950. La distribución de la riqueza dentro de la Renta Nacional Española. Realidades y perspectivas. In *Hacia una más justa distribución de la riqueza. IX Semana Madrid 1949*, 139–154. Madrid: Secretariado de la Junta Nacional de Semanas Sociales.

Ullmann, Hans-Peter. 2005. *Der deutsche Steuerstaat: Geschichte der öffentlichen Finanzen vom 18. Jahrhundert bis heute.* Munich: Beck.

Velasco Sánchez, José Tomás. S.t. Joaquín Azpiazu Zulaica. In *Diccionario biográfico español: Online Biographical Dictionary*, ed. Real Academia de la Historia.

Wagschal, Uwe. 2005. Steuerpolitik und Steuerreformen im internationalen Vergleich: Eine Analyse der Ursachen und Blockaden. Münster: Lit-Verl.

Wehler, Hans-Ulrich. 2008. *Vom Beginn des Ersten Weltkriegs bis zur Gründung der beiden deutschen Staaten: 1914–1949 (Deutsche Gesellschaftsgeschichte 4).* München: C.H. Beck.

CHAPTER 13

"Resort City? Why What Happened to Las Vegas, Sin City?": Suburban America, Religious Groups, and the Moral Economy of Gambling in Las Vegas, 1945–1969

Paul Franke

Introduction—"A Seeming Cloak of Respectability"

In 1951, Democratic Senator Estes Kefauver, who served as the head of the Special Committee on Organized Crime in Interstate Commerce, the so-called "Kefauver Committee", declared that "gambling produces nothing and adds nothing to the economy or society of our nation" (Kefauver 1968, 132). His committee had investigated organized crime activities since 1950, and while it had dealt with a plethora of issues from corrupt officials to narcotic trafficking, gambling in general and the city of Las Vegas in particular had emerged as a focal point of Kefauver's attention. He and his colleagues reached a damning verdict: "It seems clear to

P. Franke (✉)
Philipps University, Marburg, Germany
e-mail: paul.franke@uni-marburg.de

T. Skambraks and M. Lutz (eds.), *Reassessing the Moral Economy*, Palgrave Studies in Economic History,
https://doi.org/10.1007/978-3-031-29834-9_13

the committee that too many of the men running gambling operations in Nevada are either members of existing out-of-state gambling syndicates or have had a history of close association with underworld characters who operate those syndicates. The licensing system which is in effect in this state [Nevada] has not resulted in excluding the undesirables from the state but has merely served to give their activities a seeming cloak of respectability" (Kefauver 1968, 236–37).

For the committee, gambling represented both an economic and a moral failure. It drained financial and economic resources from other enterprises, it preyed on honest and hardworking citizens and as a business it was run by criminals who used it to infiltrate the legitimate economy. Kefauver, and his allies thus made not simply an argument against legalized gambling as a vice, they argued it was economically damaging. To them, legalized gambling was, despite its lawful status, the entry point for the so-called "Mafia" into US society. The committee united traditional moralist arguments against gambling, with economic arguments and the US-American fear that an international, hidden power would infiltrate the nation's economy, society, and politics (Schwartz 2003, 73–74). The "Mafia" was just the latest example in a long list of such hidden, foreign, and diabolical forces, like "New Dealers", "Big Business", or "Wall Street" (Bell 1992, 24).

15 years later, however, Las Vegas was still thriving. Moreover, Billboard Magazine, running a special on the town in 1966, asked almost disappointed "Resort City? Why, what's happened to Las Vegas, the so-called 'sin city,' gambling capital of the world, swinger's paradise?"[1] Rather than gamblers rubbing shoulders with gangsters, Billboard only spotted families at the pool, married couples going to bed before midnight, and child care services for toddlers and kids. A casino sales manager addressed this supposed shift in perception: "Now we don't want to lose the image of a gambling town, If we lose that we're dead!"[2]

Gambling had not lost its controversial character, yet in Las Vegas, casinos and their political allies had succeeded in creating and maintaining a moral economy of gambling. This moral economy was localized and bound to specific spaces, as well as specific demographics who engaged in

[1] "Las Vegas…changed its image," *Billboard*, August 27, 1966, 14.

[2] "Las Vegas…changed its image," *Billboard*, August 27, 1966, 14.

it. Both altered the perception of games locally, moralizing both casinos and those who ran and operated them.

The chapter will focus on how the Las Vegas casinos between 1945 and 1969 constituted this localized moral economy of gambling. Using letters from gamblers to the casino executives, internal memos of the casinos, press articles, and archived oral history interviews, the chapter will show how the mostly white, Protestant, suburban middle class American visitors reconciled their socially conservative views and their faith with gambling and how religious organizations participated in moralizing Las Vegas. At the same time gambling entrepreneurs, many from marginalized religious and ethnic backgrounds, claimed their citizenship by running casinos as successful, legitimate businesses. While the concept of moral economy is often addressed as a set of intellectual arguments and discursive patterns, casinos on the Las Vegas Strip point towards the importance of spatial arrangements, consumption practices, and social interactions in moralizing economic conduct. It also exemplifies how religion and religious communities played a key role concerning the morality of consumption and economics, despite a general loss of influence in the twentieth century. To this end, the chapter will first introduce its usage of moral economy, before showing how spatial setups could be used to moralize consumption and economic conduct. In a next step, it considers that a moral economy of gambling could also legitimise gambling entrepreneurs, who often came from marginalized backgrounds, closely tied to religious prejudice. Although both Nevada and Las Vegas feature a large and diverse religious landscape, the chapter will primarily focus on Jewish, Catholic, and Mormon groups and individuals. As minorities of different economic and social standing, these groups had stakes in the casino business and its moralization, either to gain access to US citizenship or in order to use economic gains from the casino business to strengthen their own community.

Moral(izing) Economies

The gambling industry was, in the words of Kefauver committee member Senator Charles W. Tobey, unproductive and did not contribute to "human happiness" (Schwartz 2003, 70). Its promises of getting rich quickly, lack of a real product, as well as its transformation of money into something to be played with seem to mock the moral values that capitalism derives its legitimacy from: efficiency, personal responsibility, and focus on monetary gain through ingenuity and hard work (Reith, 5–7; Frevert 2019, 20–25).

These values themselves were highly contested products of shifting historical processes. The assumption that a capitalist economy is in inherent opposition to a moral economy ignores the embeddedness of economic systems within a broader range of social arrangements, often shaped by cultural factors, like religious beliefs. Economic exchanges remain social interactions, and are thus embedded in societal structures, judged according to established systems of morality (Sayer 2006, 79, 92–93; Frevert 2019, 23–26; Trentmann 2008, 266–69). British social historian E.P. Thompson introduced the notion of the moral economy as an analytical concept to show how morals and values structured the ways in which people engaged within the market place (Thompson 1971, 76–79; Thompson 2010, 260–63). He showed how traditional practices of buying and selling grain and food supplies were challenged by the advance of a market economy and how peasants tried to preserve their "moral" economy in the face of such challenges. While Thompson argued that food riots were more than just outbursts of senseless violence, but rather forceful corrections of the economy, he also showed how the poor reproduced and conserved their economic practices vis-á-vis these riots. They did not just loot the grain transports, but recreated their traditional way of buying and selling food. The lower classes used riots to reinstate what they considered a proper way of buying and selling grain (Thompson 1971, 76–79).

In other words, their moral economy had spatial and praxeological components. The spaces and the economic practices affiliated with them mattered, as they were an integral part of what historical actors considered "moral". This is not limited to food: consumption is heavily connected to spaces and practices, which in turn shape its perception and experience. Gambling is, as other forms of consumption, tied to specific spatial arrangements and practices as well (Reith 2002, 74–75; Schwartz 2003, 28–32).

In the case of the Las Vegas Strip, it might be more appropriate to speak of "moralizing economy" in which historical actors like entrepreneurs moralized gambling for the middle class (Ruppert 2006, 10–11, 191–198). By providing gambling in spatial settings and alongside morally accepted leisure activities, casinos in Las Vegas reshaped the perception of games of chance by their visitors. The "moralizing economy" did more than legitimise gambling in the eyes of players, it also gave casino entrepreneurs the chance to integrate themselves into US society.

Many of these entrepreneurs had been active in the bootlegging business, or illegal gambling during the interwar period, both on the West- and East Coast, as well as the Mid-West. In Las Vegas, they now could pursue legal business interests and use their economic success to "moralize" themselves. Religious groups played a key role here: First, many gambling entrepreneurs came from Jewish or Catholic backgrounds, as they were from immigrant families from Eastern Europe, Ireland or Italy. Their national identity was thus contested, because they had no ties to the White-Anglo-Saxon-Protestant (WASP) group that dominated US politics and society. The term itself already alludes to the strong alignment of religious and national identities in the twentieth-century US (Bell 1992, 25–31; Haller 1992, 315–19).

Local religious groups also played a key role in supporting and moralizing the gambling economy. Mormons, for example, who held significant political and economic influence in Nevada, often functioned as facilitators of casino businesses, despite rejecting gambling itself as sinful. In an effort to strengthen their community and participate in the economic growth of the region through the gambling industry, they supported the casino business without getting directly involved during the 1950s and 60s. Their indirect help, however, by securing loans, offers of political assistance, or shaping gambling regulations signalled that casinos were seen as legitimate businesses. The Catholic Church cooperated with casinos in some matters that were not gambling related: They supported the boycott of nude dancing shows influential casinos organized, lending legitimacy to "respectable casinos" and the people who ran them.

The "moralizing economy" of gambling was thus twofold: it shaped the experience and perception of gambling by grounding it locally and temporally in spatial contexts and practices that integrated it into already established leisure patterns. Additionally, it also served to moralize the activities of the entrepreneurs who offered it. Despite their marginalized backgrounds, they could present themselves as successful American businessmen.

Moralizing Gambling: Reimagining Gambling Through Spatial Arrangements

It was by no means certain that gambling would be one of the driving forces behind Nevada's or Las Vegas's development. Both had been largely defined by the westward expansion of Americans, especially the Church of Jesus Christ of the Latter-day Saints, or Mormons, who rejected gambling on moral and religious grounds (Moehring and Green 2005, 4–9). As part of the "American West", the city was dominated by the Mormon community and outside economic interest in the form of land speculation and investment of the federal government (Butler and Lansing 2008, 154, 161–177; Rothman 2010, 82–101).

With the Great Depression and a decline of the mining industries and cattle breeding, the state government decided to pursue a new policy to attract the needed out-of-state investments: A number of liberal laws in 1931 made Nevada a so-called "wide open state" without narrow restrictions on a number of activities. This included the legalization of gambling, price boxing, convenient divorces, and prostitution (Abt 1996, 192–94; Haller 1992, 304; 333–34).

From now on, the state was open to potential gamblers and those who wanted to run casinos in the open rather than underground. Since legal investors were hard to come by, either because of the uncertainty of the future of legal gambling, its disputed moral nature, or restrictive licencing regulations by the state of Nevada, many casinos on the Strip had to rely on organized crime to secure financial resources (Munting 1996, 144–47; Schwartz 2003, 103). Following the end of Prohibition, many former bootlegging and gambling entrepreneurs came to the city either to invest in existing or newly built casino-hotels, continuing their previous activities under the protection of Nevada's laws. Men and women, from the East Coast and the Mid-West, many with connections to networks of organized crime, were thus able to build legitimate careers in Vegas (Bell 1992, 17–21; Bubb 2012, 19–20).

The casino industry they built in Las Vegas followed some general patterns. As consumption spaces, they were designed to diffuse gambling throughout their whole space, making it an inseparable part of all leisure activities. The bar, the showroom, the pool, and the hotel were to be distinct, yet also not cloistered off from the gambling spaces. This was meant to normalize gambling, making it a natural extension of all activities within the casino-hotel. Strip casinos also mimicked suburban living conditions, architectural forms, and vacation practices. This was key for the moral economy of Las Vegas. The focus on the WASP suburban middle classes transformed gambling from a vice into leisure and made it feel like it did not pose a danger to the economic and moral cohesion of society (Dombrink 1996, 49; Schwartz 2003, 49).

Already in the 1940s, local elites had eyed this demographic as a potential market for gambling. For example, the Chamber of Commerce wanted to attract suburban families rather than Hollywood VIPs and professional gamblers. In an internal strategy paper the chamber stated that

> What Las Vegas needs is a brand NEW crop of vacationers who will come, have a good time at a cost they can easily afford, and then who will return for more fun, season after. [...] After this war the entire family is going to travel. The kids will be brought along and should assume as much importance in the resort operators' eyes as the adults who actually spend the money.[3]

Casinos on the Strip diverged from the image of the Wild West, or the saloon as the spaces associated with frontier gambling. They rather imitated suburban living conditions (Al 2010, 29–30; Bubb 2012, 36–37).

One of the most influential casinos on the Strip, The Desert Inn, is a great example of how spaces were laid out to legitimize gambling by fusing it with all other aspects of the hotel. The casino proper was located just behind the lobby of the main building, so that patrons had to cross it in order to get to the other facilities of the hotel. Gambling was virtually everywhere, even when people did not approach the tables (Spencer 2009, 49). The Desert Inn combined legal gambling with a focus on family vacations. For example, it offered a childcare service near the main casino complex (Jakle et al. 2002, 17–19, 150; Schwartz 2003, 87). The hotel rooms were built for families, with a separate bed for children and

[3] Las Vegas, Nevada Frontier Playground by Monrow Manning Treatment Outline. Box 11 Folder Correspondence Advertisement publicity 1949. Las Vegas Chamber of Commerce Records, 1911–2020. MS-00366. Special Collections and Archives, University Libraries, University of Nevada, Las Vegas. Las Vegas, Nevada.

individual bathrooms. Most of the private spaces within the casino-hotel were oriented around the idea of the suburban living experience.[4]

The Sands, a casino opened in December of 1952, featured similar elements of fusing gambling and suburbia. With its bungalow homes for hotel rooms, green lawns in front of them, and convenient parking, the casino combined suburban living conditions with a leisure infrastructure and a focus on consumption (Nichols 2007, 137–44). Casino managers and architects wanted to present all games as if there were a logical extension of a family trip.[5] The showroom and bar were only accessible through the casino floor. The casino and the bar were themselves indistinguishable since there was no physical wall separating them. The lights on the ceiling were not only designed to resemble giant roulette wheels, but projected streams of light onto the blackjack and roulette tables. As in most casinos, the room was otherwise only dimly lit (Jakle et al. 2002, 51–53; Schwartz 2003, 123–24). The space wanted people to "be a sport and gamble a little" (Schwartz 2003, 40).

One of the most prominent features of the Sands illustrates this well: Slot machines were placed at the edge of the swimming pool and a craps table on the water, allowing patrons to play while using the pool.[6] The floating craps table physically removed patrons from their everyday surroundings and put them into a space, the pool, which was traditionally associated with leisure and touristic activities. The pool signified the Sands

[4] "Desert inn's 3000 rooms each entity in itself". Oversized Box 2,misc. Press Clippings. Wilbur & Toni Clark Papers 1944–1991, MS-00361, Special Collections & Archives, University Libraries, University of Nevada, Las Vegas; "Plush Local Spa Introduces Latest Innovations for Patrons". Oversized Box 2, misc. Press Clippings. Wilbur & Toni Clark Papers 1944–1991, MS-00361, Special Collections & Archives, University Libraries, University of Nevada, Las Vegas.; Desert Inn Scrapbooks and Oversize Magazine misc. Press Clippings Oversized Box 2. Wilbur & Toni Clark Papers 1944–1991, MS-00361 Special Collections & Archives, University Libraries, University of Nevada, Las Vegas. Las Vegas, Nevada.; Al, *The Strip*, 53.

[5] Ann Geracimos, "In Las Vegas Women and Children are Loser," *Herald Tribune*, May 10, 1963; Riddle, Major: scrapbook, 1970s-1980s. Box 4, Folder 23. Dunes Hotel and Casino Records, 1954–1992. MS-00328. Special Collections and Archives, University Libraries, University of Nevada, Las Vegas. Las Vegas, Nevada.

[6] Tanned and Faded Suggested Picture Layout, Box 8, Folder 1. Sands Hotel Public Relations Records, 1952–1977. MS-00417. Special Collections, University Libraries, University of Nevada, Las Vegas. Las Vegas, Nevada.; Al Freeman Letter from September 16, 1955. Box 5 Folder 2. Sands Hotel Public Relations Records, 1952–1977. MS-00417. Special Collections, University Libraries, University of Nevada, Las Vegas. Las Vegas, Nevada.

as a space for suburbanites and WASP Americans. In the 1950s the pool had become a largely white suburban phenomenon and marker of class (Wiltse 2007, 154–156, 180–183). Patrons identified it as safe and appropriate, yet it also allowed for gambling while swimming, and ordering a drink from waiters in tuxedo tops and speedo bottoms.

Las Vegas and the Strip remained a unique casino setting between 1945 and 1969, but they also emerged as a moral economy and legitimate gambling experience that was emulated: All over the US during the 1950s and '60 s, church groups and charity organizations hosted events dubbed "Las Vegas Nights". Americans gambled for a good cause, using either play money or real cash, which they then donated. To recreate an atmosphere reminiscent of Las Vegas, they wrote to the city's casinos asking for objects like, decks of cards, dice, or cocktail napkins.[7]

Spatial arrangement within casinos played a huge role in this shift and superseded design and marketing decisions. They point towards a general effort to moralize gambling by grounding it into spatial arrangements that were closely associated with middle class, suburban families and their leisure practices. Spaces shaped the perception and experience of consumption and its supposed moral character. Gambling on the Strip could thus be normalized and legitimized for middle class patrons, because of the spaces it was done in.

Moralizing Gamblers: Economic Success in the Gambling Industry as a Path to Society for Marginalized Entrepreneurs

The executives planning and building casinos had thus constructed spaces for a social class they themselves sought access to: WASPs. Their ethnic-religious backgrounds had however been a hurdle in this regard. They were Italian or Irish Catholics and Eastern European Jews, many second generation immigrants. For these marginalized religious-ethnic groups, the illegal economy of Prohibition offered a path to success and a chance to climb the social ladder. Making money from bootlegging and illegal

[7] Veda Heinze to Al Freeman, July 5,1957. Box 7, Folder 4. Sands Hotel Public Relations Records, 1952–1977. MS-00417. Special Collections, University Libraries, University of Nevada, Las Vegas. Las Vegas, Nevada; Joe Brandeis to Al Freeman April 3, 1956. Box 7, Folder 4. Sands Hotel Public Relations Records, 1952–1977. MS-00417. Special Collections, University Libraries, University of Nevada, Las Vegas. Las Vegas, Nevada.

gambling during the 1920s and 1930s, turned a generation with few ties to WASP-dominated America into successful entrepreneurs of capitalism. Illegal entrepreneurs of the Prohibition had learned similar lessons as American mainstream business: they applied the logic of market supply, competition and demand, understood the importance of consumption businesses, competition, and used political corruption to their advantage (Bell 1992, 296–297, 308–310; Haller 1992, 301–4).

The presence of former criminals in the Las Vegas gambling economy was no grand conspiracy, as Kefauver had warned about, but the result of Nevada's efforts to legalize casinos and finding entrepreneurs to run them. As historian David Schwartz points out: "In the 1950s, there were no formal professional schools to churn out fresh-faced young casinos executives. Indeed, virtually anyone who was qualified to run a casinos resort on the Las Vegas Strip was, technically, a criminal" (Schwartz, 2003, 111).

One of them was Moe Dalitz of the Desert Inn. Born in 1899 in Boston to a conservative Jewish family,[8] Dalitzled the so-called Mansfield Park Gang, a criminal syndicate operating in Cleveland and outside of Chicago. A bootlegger, gambler, and real-estate entrepreneur, he represented the societal aspirations of religious minority entrepreneurs, who used their success in casino gambling to moralize themselves in the eyes of American society. Together with long time gambler and casino entrepreneur Wilbur Clark, he headed the syndicate that effectively ran the Desert Inn (Schwartz 2003, 102–7). In 1976, he made a revealing statement that illustrates how many illegal entrepreneurs saw themselves after almost 20 years in Las Vegas:

> For 30 years now I have lived in Nevada. I am considered a good citizen of Nevada. I have done all the things a good citizen should do. I have been charitable. I have been honest. I have raised a family. My life has been just as good as anyone's in this room ... I have very candidly told you that I was in the liquor business when it was considered illegal. I told you that I was in the casino business... In none of these businesses is moral turpitude involved. These are things that if people didn't patronize a casino we couldn't have one. If people didn't drink liquor it wouldn't have been

[8] Moe Dalitz oral history interview transcript, 2014 December 18. OH-02067. [Transcript]. Oral History Research Center, Special Collections and Archives, University Libraries, University of Nevada, Las Vegas. Las Vegas, Nevada, 1–3.

> necessary to bring it over.[...] We didn't regard this as a hideous affair. I don't think you do either in your heart. (Haller 1992, 294–312)

Other members of the Jewish community also had a big influence on the gambling industry: Carl Cohen, who effectively headed the gambling operations at the Sands, and the casino's entertainment director Jack Entratter were also born into Jewish families. They too made a career in affiliation with organized crime which helped them to manage casino operations in a legal context (Bell 1992, 17–21; Nichols 2007, 137–44). Besides being successful businessmen, Cohen, Entratter, and Dalitz used charity and engaged in community organizations in order to present themselves as respectable citizens. They did so deliberately in Jewish organizations and religious institutions, despite their gambling careers. Entratter served as president of the Sands casinos and the Beth Sholom Temple between 1959–1963 and again from 1966–67 (Fleeko 2000, 144). Dalitz and the Beth Sholom Temple were particularly active in the support for Israel, organizing fundraisers and solidarity events together with Zionist organizations (Fleeko 2000, 60–62).

Charity work and the fulfilment of civic duties played a huge role in the construction of the self-image gambling entrepreneurs had of themselves and their quest to moralize their gambling business. In 1966, one unnamed casino executive resented the Sin City label, pointing out that: "Percentagewise [sic] the major hotels in this city give more money to recreation and charity than any comparable business in the world. These people (civic do-gooders), who curse us, would be starving to death of it weren't for us."[9] These activities were also grounded in the social-conservatism of casino entrepreneurs. Until the 1970s, the Jewish organizations of Las Vegas were staunchly conservative. The Temple Beth Sholom was associated with the United Synagogue of America, rather than the Reform-Judaism that dominated most other Jewish communities in the state (Davis 2010, 38; Fleeko 2000, 56–57).

For these men, religious activism in conservative communities was complementary to their economic success. It mirrored their goal to participate in the success story that was American capitalism. They wore nice suits, went to cocktail parties, and presented themselves as businessmen, successful, capitalist entrepreneurs embodying America's promise of wealth through hard work. In other words their economic

[9] "Las Vegas...changed its image," *Billboard*, August 27, 1966, 14.

success also served to legitimize them as Americans, an identity linked to similar values which were ascribed to capitalism (Balboni 2006, 53, 93; Welskopp 2010, 319–338, 368–397).

But the truce between the largely WASP establishment and casino entrepreneurs remained uneasy: In Nevada's white, Protestant administration, religious stereotypes about Catholics and Jews blended seamlessly with xenophobia. For many middle class Americans, illegal gambling in the urban centres was associated with Jewish immigrants, African-Americans, and street gangs. The overwhelmingly WASP, or Mormon political authorities, including the members of the Gaming Control Board, charged with giving out gambling licences, also regarded illegal gambling as a largely Italo-American and Catholic affaire. These assumptions were based on the general view of organized crime, and bootlegging in the urban centres of the East Coast: Recent and second generation immigrants from Southern and Eastern Europe, meaning Jews, Catholics, and other religious-national minorities, were regarded as the driving force behind both. Confronted with these accusations, entrepreneurs had to make sure their casinos remained appealing to the white-protestant middle classes of America and a worthwhile venture for the protestant and Mormon politicians (Farrell and Case 1995, 5, 24–29; Schwartz 2003, 49, 81–82 Sallaz 2009, 167–171).

Preserving the Moral Economy: Preserving Casinos as Leisure Spaces for the Suburban Middle Class

The efforts to moralize gambling on the Strip and the entrepreneurs who offered it was a continuous endeavour and part of a constant process. Religious communities and values played a significant role in this ongoing struggle to make gambling on the Strip acceptable for often social conservative suburban middle classes. The conflict around burlesque shows on the Strip between 1956 and 1958 offers insight into the inherent tension between gambling, conservative values, and the moral economy in Las Vegas. It began with the Dunes in 1956. Harold Minsky, a successful producer from New York, started bringing burlesque and topless shows to a number of casinos, the Dunes among others.[10] This triggered a harsh response from visitors, executives, and

[10] The Issue Stardust, Nude Dancers Controversy. Box 3, Folder 7. Sands Hotel Public Relations Records, 1952–1977. MS-00417. Special Collections, University Libraries,

public figures alike. Entratter was one of them. His staff issued a memo in which they compiled the basic arguments against nude dancing shows, as well as listing Entratter's allies: Las Vegas religious community leaders. Entratters's arguments included economic and moral ones, although the distinction remained fluid. The town would lose its appeal to middle class tourists and families as well as the great entertainers it attracted if the practice continued. The Sands clearly seemed to have felt the pressure to confirm to the moral standards of the local population and its religious communities, despite being a gambling house. As the memo points out:

> Las Vegas is a privileged phenomenon—it exits thru the will of the people of Nevada [...] You don't ask your neighbors to let you comeinto [sic] their home, then turn their house into a freak burlesque and gaudy, freaky burlesque spectacle [...]. Ethically, it's stupid—morally, it's bad—but rather than preach morals and ethics on one hand , and still operate gambling, even though on a clean, high-class, and public level—it's important to look at it from the common decency and courtesy angle, too.[11]

The tension of offering gambling yet trying to ban nude dancing shows was not lost on Entratter and the Sands staff. Yet, in order to appeal to their target audience as well as not to endanger their privileged position, they argued against this sort of entertainment. They saw themselves as outsiders in the state and their business as a privilege depending on the goodwill of the local elites, and religious authorities, which seemed to have increased the pressure to act in accordance to the present moral and religious sentiments.

Banning the nude shows yielded results: John J. Ryan of the St. Anne's Catholic Church, Adam Yacenda the Catholic Managing Editor of the SUN Newspaper, and Al Cahlan the Protestant publisher of the

University of Nevada, Las Vegas. Las Vegas, Nevada; Freeman to Jim Bacon March 28, 1955. Box 4 Folder 1. Sands Hotel Public Relations Records, 1952–1977. MS-00417. Special Collections, University Libraries, University of Nevada, Las Vegas. Las Vegas, Nevada.

[11] Points of Disscussion on Bare Bosom Shows Box 3, Folder 7. Sands Hotel Public Relations Records, 1952–1977. MS-00417. Special Collections, University Libraries, University of Nevada, Las Vegas. Las Vegas, Nevada.

Review Journal became staunch allies of the casino.[12] Local businesses and visiting gamblers agreed with the Sands' decision. Religious narratives of morality were often used to show this. For example, the Rose de Lima Hotel in Henderson congratulated the Sands on its stance concluding its letter with "God bless you and be assured of my prayers for your continued success."[13] Supports of the ban on nude dancing shows saw the Sands as part of a whole religious movement against the perceived indecencies of nude shows. The letter from a woman called Amy de Voot to the Sands from August 1958 reads: "It is commonly known by law-abiding citizens, and religious groups that the Dunes today is nothing more than a house of ill-repute, frequented by thieves, con-men, gangsters, and husbands without wives looking for a stray."[14] De Voot's letter showed how it was possible for a casino to satisfy demands by religious patrons in terms of morality, while still offering gambling.

In August 1958, the Catholic Church did get involved: Robert J. Dwyer, Catholic Bishop of Reno, published a pastoral letter calling for unity against the shows and consequences for those who presented and attend them. The bishop acknowledged that he was not part of the law enforcement, yet asserted his role as "guardian of the morals". As such he issued his orders: "Let it be clearly stated that all Catholics are strictly forbidden by the divine law itself to have any part in entertainment which is of its nature indecent, suggestive, or calculated to excite thoughts or actions contrary to the Sixth Commandment. [...] There is no vacations form the Ten Commandments."[15] He banned Catholics, to participate in the management, direction, production, or even the advertisement of such entertainment. The bishop urged his flock to protect Nevada as

[12] Points of Discussion on Bare Bosom Shows Box 3, Folder 7. Sands Hotel Public Relations Records, 1952–1977. MS-00417. Special Collections, University Libraries, University of Nevada, Las Vegas. Las Vegas, Nevada.

[13] Rose de Lima Hospital to Jack Enttratter August 1 1958, Box 3, Folder 7. Sands Hotel Public Relations Records, 1952–1977. MS-00417. Special Collections, University Libraries, University of Nevada, Las Vegas. Las Vegas, Nevada.

[14] Amy de Voot to Jack Enttratter August 1 1958, Box 3, Folder 7. Sands Hotel Public Relations Records, 1952–1977. MS-00417. Special Collections, University Libraries, University of Nevada, Las Vegas. Las Vegas, Nevada.

[15] Pastoral Letter by Bishop Robert J Dwyer, Box 3, Folder 7. Sands Hotel Public Relations Records, 1952–1977. MS-00417. Special Collections, University Libraries, University of Nevada, Las Vegas. Las Vegas, Nevada.

a tourist destination and join forces with Protestants and Jews for the cause.[16]

That the bishop did not mention gambling, yet acknowledged the fact that Vegas was a prime tourist destination points towards the fact that the local religious communities had arranged themselves with the casino business. Moreover, a casino like the Sands had now a believable claim to be a legitimate, morally upstanding leisure space, even in the eyes of religious leaders and visitors, who were usually critical of gambling. One of the most important religious groups, the Mormons, went a step further and actively facilitated the growth of the gambling business.

Mormons as Facilitators of the Moral Economy: "How Can Good Mormons Be Involved Indirectly in Gaming?"

The Pew Forum U.S. Religious Landscape Survey in 2008 revealed how much Nevada's religious make-up differed from the US national average: Protestants were a majority, but it was much slimmer than in the rest of the country. Catholics made up 27% of people that stated to adhere to some kind of faith, in contrast to the national average of 24%, for example. The greatest difference is found in the strong presence of Mormons, which constituted 11% (national average 2%) (Mitchum and Borer 2012, 6).

Mormons were among the first to settle the territory of Nevada and acted as a driving force behind the state formation, building the first fortified settlement and mission in the Las Vegas area in the 1850s (Findlay 1986, 111). These historical ties between the Silver State and the Latter Day Saints had consequences for the moralization of the gambling economy. Outside of the Catholic and Jewish organizations, local religious communities had different approaches to the gambling industry of their home town. For example, the First Southern Baptist Church emphasized that they believed gambling to be sin, yet were much more against alcohol than games of chance. Reverend E. Darell Eveenson pointed out, that "since gambling is legal in Nevada, we have to live with it, although we don't approve or condone it" (Wagner 1972, 91). The Southern Baptist Church had originally banned any church member from gambling

[16] Pastoral Letter by Bishop Robert J Dwyer, Box 3, Folder 7. Sands Hotel Public Relations Records, 1952–1977. MS-00417. Special Collections, University Libraries, University of Nevada, Las Vegas. Las Vegas, Nevada.

or working in the gambling industry, yet discontinued this restriction in their efforts to attract more people in joining the church (Wagner 1972, 93).

The Mormons, however, despite being anti-gambling and banning people from directly running casinos, took on the role of facilitators of the luck business. Las Vegas offered entrepreneurial Mormons the chance of a somewhat urban lifestyle away from the family farms in Utah and the chance to build up communities to live in accordance to their beliefs (Ward 2002, 35–37). Since the westward expansion of their church, Mormons had occupied influential positions in Nevadan politics and economy. They were part of the gambling regulation and licencing institutions, as well as state government (Farrell and Case 1995, 12–20). While Jewish and Catholic groups organized themselves around and with men from the gambling business, the Mormons sought to profit from gambling without taking part in it. Gambling's legal status in Nevada and a pro-growth, pro-economic attitude seemed to have prevailed over concerns over a still indirect involvement in the luck business. Mormons cooperated with other religious groups for the sake of building up the community, which they saw as a quintessential task of their own spiritual calling. This is reflected in their choice of involvement: while Jewish and catholic newcomers to Las Vegas distinguished themselves as casino entrepreneurs, Mormons took on civil and political duties early on, like County and City Commissioner or Justices of Peace, or even Senator (Steward 2003, 16–17, Rothman 1998, 299, Moehring and Green 2005, 243).

They also took on an active role in casino financing, for example. The Bank of Las Vegas, for example, was headed by Parry Thomas, a Mormon from Nevada married to a descendant from Mormon leader Brigham Young. Thomas and his partners were the only bank granting large scale loans to casinos entrepreneurs so they could build or expand their gambling houses (Davis 2010, 62). The Bank of Las Vegas financed expansions of the Sands, Dunes, Hacienda, Stardust, and other casinos, but also offered a boost to the legitimacy of casinos: led by Mormons and WASP Americans, it could not be linked to Jewish, or catholic institutions and thus could not be accused of being involved in organized crime. Thomas also encouraged investments by large Pension Funds, like the Teamster Pension Fund and (as a staunch Republican) lobbied for the possibility for large companies to be able to invest in casinos as well. He and other Mormons served as advisers to Howard Hughes. The eccentric billionaire who had made a fortune with his aviation company in 1967, had bought multiple casinos in Las Vegas, opening the Strip up to investments outside the traditional networks of organized crime, or the Bank of Las Vegas. He nonetheless depended on the advice of established casino managers and local Mormons (Schwartz 2003, 107–11; Steward 2003, 185).

Mormons never built their own casino, yet their strong sense of community and building up Nevada as an economical strong state, as well as their extensive networks, made them valuable partners for the casino industry (Davis 2010, 67). The casino business thus constituted not a point of contention between religious groups in Las Vegas, but rather a field of cooperation. The acceptance of legal casino gambling and its integration into Mormon economic activity strengthened the bonds between the various religious groups and served to moralize the gambling business. Casinos could count on the support of the Latter Day Saints in the political conflicts that frequently erupted with the federal government and other political forces pressuring Nevada to pursue a less favourable policy concerning games of chance. Nevada constituted a peripheral and young state, which led to less entrenched communities, willing and able to cooperate to some degree. As Jewish and catholic casino entrepreneurs acted as real-estate developers, charity patrons, and gambling entrepreneurs, Mormons took on the role of facilitators, thus helping to moralize the gambling industry locally (Davis 2010, 63). Ashely Hall PR director of the Las Vegas Mormons pointed out: "You can ask the questions of 'How can good Mormons be involved indirectly in gaming?" Hall said. "But to us, business is business. Gaming is not illegal in Nevada."[17] She echoed Thomas sentiment that Mormons were community builders and bankers, and thus free to support any legal enterprise.

Strip casinos could offer gambling to socially conservative middle class patrons, as they could present themselves as compatible with religious beliefs outside the traditional stigma games of chance were placated with. It was a narrow line to walk: Appealing to religious sentiments without losing the hedonistic and leisure focused atmosphere casinos were built to produce. The moralizing economy was established by spaces that felt acceptable to the suburban WASP Americans and by casinos championing selected moral causes, like the banning of nude dancing and the support

[17] Willis, Stacy J. 1998. Mormons knit LV's fabric. Las Vegas Sun, October 7.

for religious institutions. In that sense E.P. Thompson's argument, that a moral economy is a set of traditional beliefs, anchored in economic spaces and practices, but also grounded in the law, can be observed in Las Vegas as well.

Conclusion

In 1976, New Jersey legalized casinos in Atlantic City. The legalization was the result of a referendum, in which the electorate of the state was called to the polls to support or deny the expansion of casino gambling. Las Vegas, the former Sin City, was now referenced as the prime example of a legitimate, economically viable, and community rejuvenating casino industry. Gambling, as long as it adhered to the established Las Vegas model, was now compatible with the American mainstream economy. This did not mean gambling at large was normalized: Hispanic and African-American gambling entrepreneurs in large cities, who "ran the numbers" were still specifically targeted by police in an effort to police minorities and gambling (Vaz 2014, 71–80).

Las Vegas thus stands out as an example of how a moral economy was not only bound to specific cultural, social, and religious groups, but also to locally confined spatial arrangements and practices that shaped the perception and character of economic endeavours and behaviours. Strip casinos fused gambling with well-established leisure opportunities of the WASP, suburban middle class, making it indistinguishable from them. Gambling entrepreneurs, often belonging to religious, discriminated against minorities and with a chequered past in organized crime, used economic success to moralize themselves in the eyes of WASP society. More and more Americans were willing to accept Las Vegas as an extravagant, yet in the end legitimate, gambling town, as groups, like the Mormons aligned themselves with the gambling business, pointing towards its legality, in order to justify their indirect involvement.

Vegas' shift from Sin City to role model for Atlantic City happened not only on a discursive level, it was grounded in spaces and practices, in temporary and stable alliances between different religious and social groups. It depended on the lawful status of gambling, which allowed religious minority businessmen to run casinos in the open. Similar to E.P. Thompson's moral economy of the poor, the moral economy of gambling was embedded in local laws and regulations, cultural, social, and religious contexts, spaces, and practices that shaped its perception and moral evaluation. Economic exchanges, activities, and actions remain social interactions and can thus not be boiled down to formal transactions. Their embeddedness in local, and broader contexts, as well as the ways they are performed matters immensely as they shape the individual and societal experience of them. The concept of moral economy seems uniquely suited to capture this if used in an analytical, rather than normative way.

References

Primary Sources

Billboard Magazine
Las Vegas Sun

Archival Sources

Dunes Hotel and Casino Records, 1954–1992. MS-00328. Special Collections and Archives, University Libraries, University of Nevada, Las Vegas. Las Vegas, Nevada.

Las Vegas Chamber of Commerce Records, 1911–2020. MS-00366. Special Collections and Archives, University Libraries, University of Nevada, Las Vegas. Las Vegas, Nevada.

Sands Hotel Public Relations Records, 1952–1977. MS-00417. Special Collections and Archives, University Libraries, University of Nevada, Las Vegas. Las Vegas, Nevada.

Wilbur & Toni Clark Papers, 1944–1991. MS-00361. Special Collections and Archives, University Libraries, University of Nevada, Las Vegas. Las Vegas, Nevada.

Oral History

Moe, Dalitz. 2014. Oral History Interview Transcript, December 18. OH-02067. [Transcript]. Oral History Research Center, Special Collections and Archives, University Libraries, University of Nevada, Las Vegas. Las Vegas, Nevada

Literature

Abt, Vicki. 1996. The Role of the State in the Expansion and Growth of the Commercial Gambling in the USA. In *Gambling Cultures: Studies in History and Interpretation*, ed. Jan McMillen, 179–198. London: Routledge.

Al, Johannes S. 2010. *The Strip: Las Vegas and the Symbolic Destruction of Spectacle*. Dissertation, University of California, Berkeley.

Balboni, Alan R. 2006. *Beyond the Mafia: Italian Americans and the Development of Las Vegas*. Reno: University of Nevada Press.

Bell, Daniel. 1992. Crime as an American Way of Life: A Queer Ladder of Social Mobility. In *Crime & Justice in American History: Historical Articles on the Origins and Evolution of American Criminal Justice*, ed. Eric H. Monkkonen, 12–33. Westport: Meckler, 1992.

Bubb, Daniel K. 2012. *Landing in Las Vegas: Commercial Aviation and the Making of a Tourist City*. Reno: University of Nevada Press.

Butler, Anne M., and Michael J. Lansing. 2008. *The American West: A Concise History*. Malden, Mass: Blackwell.

Davis, Matthew R. August, 2010. Saints in Sin City: Religion and Community Building in Twentieth Century Las Vegas. DIssertation, University of Nevada Las Vegas.

Dombrink, John. 1996. Gambling and the Legalisation of Vice: Social Movements, Public Health and Public Policy in the United States. In *Gambling Cultures: Studies in History and Interpretation*, ed. Jan McMillen, 43–64. London: Routledge.

Farrell, Ronald A., and Carole Case. 1995. *The Black Book and the Mob: The Untold Story of Control of Nevada's Casinos*. Madison: Blackwell.

Findlay, John M. 1986. *People of Chance. Gambling in American Society from Jamestown to Las Vegas*. Oxford: Oxford University Press.

Fleeko, Joel. 2000, 1 May. Jews Wandering in the Desert: A History of the Jewish Community of Las Vegas. Brandeis University.

Frevert, Ute. 2019. Moral Economies, Present and Past. In *Moral Economies*, ed. Ute Frevert et al., 13–44. Geschichte und Gesellschaft Sonderheft 26. Göttingen: Vandenhoeck & Ruprecht.

Haller, Mark H. 1992. Bootleggers as Businessmen: From City Slums to City Builders. In *Crime & Justice in American History: Historical Articles on the Origins and Evolution of American Criminal Justice*, ed. Eric H. Monkkonen, 294–312. Westport: Meckler.

———. The Changing Structure of American Gambling in the Twentieth Century. In *Crime & Justice in American History: Historical Articles on the Origins and Evolution of American Criminal Justice*. ed. Eric H. Monkkonen, 313–41. Westport: Meckler.

Jakle, John A., Keith A. Sculle, and Jefferson S. Rogers. 2002. *The Motel in America*. Baltimore, Md., London: Johns Hopkins University Press.

Kefauver, Estes. 1968. *Crime in America*. New York: Greenwood Press.

Mitchum, Ariane G. and Michael Ian Borer. 2012. Religion and Spirituality in Nevada, In Dmitri N. Shalin, *The Social Health of Nevada: Leading Indicators and Quality of Life in the Silver State*, 1–27.

Moehring, Eugene P., and Michael S. Green. 2005. *Las Vegas: A Centennial History*. Reno: University of Nevada Press.

Munting, Roger. 1996. *An Economic and Social History of Gambling in Britain and the USA*. Manchester, New York: Manchester University Press.

Nichols, Chris. 2007. *The Leisure Architecture of Wayne McAllister*. Salt Lake City: Gibbs Smith.

Reith, Gerda. 2002. *The Age of Chance: Gambling in Western Culture*. London, New York: Routledge.

Rothman, Hal. 1998. *Devil's Bargains–Tourism in the Twentieth-Century American West*. Lawrence, KA. University Press of Kansas.

Rothman, Hal. 2010. *The Making of Modern Nevada*. Reno: University of Nevada Press.

Ruppert, Evelyn S. 2006. *The Moral Economy of Cities: Shaping Good Citizens*. Toronto, Buffalo: University of Toronto Press.

Sallaz, Jeffrey J. 2009. *The Labor of Luck: Casino Capitalism in the United States and South Africa*. Berkeley: University of California Press.

Sayer, Andrew. 2006. Approaching Moral Economy. In *The Moralization of the Markets*, ed. Nico Stehr, Christoph Henning, and Bernd Weiler, 77–97. New Brunswick, NJ: Transaction Publishers.

Schwartz, David G. 2003. *Suburban Xanadu. The Casino Resort on the Las Vegas Strip and Beyond*. New York, London: Routledge.

Spencer, Donald D. 2009. *Mid Century Vegas: 1930s to 1960s*. Atglen, Pa: Schiffer Publ.

Steward, Stanley A. 2003, 1 January. *Where Sin Abounds: A Religious History of Las Vegas*. Dissertation, University of Nevada Las Vegas.

Thompson, Edward P. 1971. The Moral Economy of the English Crowd in the Eighteenth Century. *Past & Present* 50: 76–136.

Thompson, Edward P. 2010. *Customs in Common*. Pontypool, Wales: Merlin Press.

Trentmann, Frank. 2008. Before Fair Trade: Empire, Free Trade and the Moral Economies of Food in the Modern World. In *Food and Globalization: Consumption, markets and politics in the Modern World*, ed. Alexander Nützenadel and Frank Trentmann. English ed, 253–76. Cultures of Consumption Series. Oxford, New York: Berg.

Vaz, Matthew. 2014. We Intend to Run It: Racial Politics, Illegal Gambling, and the Rise of Government Lotteries in the United States, 1960–1985. *The Journal of American History* 101 (1): 71–96.

Wagner, Walter. 1972. *To Gamble, or Not to Gamble*. St. Louis: Dunaway Books.

Ward, Kenric F. 2022. Saints in Babylon: Mormons and Las Vegas 1st Book Library.

Welskopp, Thomas. 2010. *Amerikas Große Ernüchterung: Eine Kulturgeschichte der Prohibition*. Paderborn: Ferdinand Schöningh.
Wiltse, Jeff. 2007. *Contested Waters: A Social History of Swimming Pools in America*. Chapel Hill: University of North Carolina Press.

PART IV

Conclusion

CHAPTER 14

Reassessing Moral Economies. Concluding Thoughts

Benjamin Möckel

"Maybe the trouble lies with the word 'moral'" (Thompson 1991, 271), speculated E.P. Thompson in his 1991 reflection on his then 20-year-old article on the "Moral Economy of the English Crowd in the 18th Century" (Thompson 1971). One might agree and only be tempted to add: "…or maybe with the word 'economy'". Bringing both concepts together could indeed seem counterintuitive or even provocative, especially in the early 1970s as a time when the economy became more and more associated with the supposedly neutral mechanisms of "free" markets. Despite these conceptual challenges, "moral economy" has become one of the key concepts in recent attempts to bridge the gap between cultural history and economic history and to think in a new way about economic structures and practices.

This text has nothing new to say about the concept of "moral economy". It is well-known that the term was originally coined to describe

B. Möckel (✉)
Department of Modern History, University of Cologne, Cologne, Germany
e-mail: bmoeckel@uni-koeln.de

T. Skambraks and M. Lutz (eds.), *Reassessing the Moral Economy*, Palgrave Studies in Economic History,
https://doi.org/10.1007/978-3-031-29834-9_14

a concrete historical situation: A time in which a set of customs and assumptions about social obligations came under threat from a new principle—the market, a political economy, capitalism—and in these conflicts produced forms of dissent, protest, and outrage, which could be used by historians to analyze those "traditional" assumptions about social justice and reciprocity that normally remained hidden and implicit until they were challenged or drastically violated.

However, in recent appropriations of the concept, a consensus has emerged that Thompson's term can be fruitfully applied to other times and social contexts. We can ask for the moral economies of modern capitalism, as well as for the moral norms and assumptions that regulate ancient and premodern societies and economic practices. In this way, one can indeed argue that "all economies are moral economies" (Sayer 2006, 78), although this might provoke the question of why we need the prefix at all.

I generally adhere to this argument. I don't interpret "moral economy" as a descriptive term, but rather as a perspective with which we can look at different economic systems. I take for granted that all economic systems are in some way embedded in social systems, norms, and collective expectations, and thus it makes sense to ask for those social frames. In this way, the question is not whether some economic system *is* a moral economy, but rather what we can learn about a certain economy when we ask for the—often implicit—norms and social expectations by which it is tacitly governed.

This is how I have read the articles in this volume. I have posed myself a simple question: What exactly did people do in these very different economies? What practices were seen as essential for the economies and why were they deemed morally precarious or relevant? Revisiting the articles of this volume from such a praxeological perspective will, I hope, shed new light on the very different contexts in which the authors of this volume think about and conceptualize "moral economies".

There are two reasons why I think this approach is helpful for our understanding of moral economies: On the one hand, asking what people actually do in a specific economic setting avoids postulating a priori certain criteria of moral economies but rather looks inductively at the norms and expectations that govern these economies. More importantly, I also think that it does justice to the original concept of E.P. Thompson. I read his argument about the "moral economy" primarily as an argument about agency. His key argument, both in the "Making of the English

Working Class" and in the "Moral Economy of the British Crowd" was to show that common people of the time had a certain sense of justice and moral norms and that they acted collectively and with a sense of rationality when they thought that these norms had been violated.

The way Thompson emphasized the notion of rationality might sound a bit out-of-date after 50 years, but his general argument still holds. Analytically, this perspective highlights the subjective dimension of moral economies: The concept of "moral economy" can help us to ask about the norms and expectations people have about economic ideas and practices and how these ideas influence their behavior. What amount of inequality are people in a given society ready to accept and how are these inequalities morally justified? What do people expect from state institutions? And how do ideas of "justice", "wealth", and "community" influence the everyday economic behavior of individuals? All these questions can be fruitfully asked without necessarily assuming "a" moral economy that we can reconstruct.

I. From these preliminary considerations, this chapter asks what kind of economic practices can be found in the approximately 2500 years that are covered in this volume, and how these practices were perceived and debated. Although it is self-evident that the concepts of the economy—if they existed at all—have changed dramatically through the ages, and even though we can assume that many people in the past would not have understood terms like "the economy" or "economic practices", we can still distinguish some human actions that were part of social life throughout the broad timespan of this volume. People buy and sell things, own and inherit property, make profits or go bankrupt, give loans and pay them back (or don't), give alms or receive them, produce and consume goods, and work or let work. None of these practices are per se morally charged, but as the case studies in this volume show: most of them could be in some way or the other. Buying things might prima facie be morally neutral, but buying luxuries in times of scarcity might prompt moral outrage. Possessing things might be morally neutral, but if we say someone is "hoarding", the possession of goods automatically becomes embedded into a moral narrative.

Referring to the contributions of this volume, one can distinguish at least three ways in which economic practices were linked to moral claims, doubts, and narratives. First, some practices were in itself deemed morally dubious or contested. These are often the most widely discussed examples. The debates about the legitimacy of credit and interest rates might be the most famous example of such moral and religious reservations toward an economic practice. The concept of usury made this conflict explicit, but as the contributions in this volume show, debates about the legitimacy or illegitimacy of interest and credit were much more complex and could not be resolved by referring to an indisputable religious ban (*Skambraks*, *Doron*, *Lizzul*). In a different setting, gambling can be seen as a practice that was morally contested through the ages, in late medieval merchant textbooks (*Skambraks*), in intellectual discourses in the nineteenth-century Ottoman Empire (*Aytekin*) and in 1950s and 1960s Las Vegas (*Franke*). Generally speaking, all societies seem to have some norms and expectations about economic and social practices that are deemed inappropriate, even when they are not legally forbidden. It is in this grey zone that moral narratives become particularly important and widespread. Moral arguments about the duty of citizens to pay their taxes, to take another example, were particularly widespread at a time when modern states were not yet able to efficiently control taxpayers and thus depended on the cooperation of their citizenry (*Schönhärl*).

Second, some practices only became morally dubious when they were attached to money or economic rationales. This has been an important theme in thinking about the "moral limits of markets" in modern capitalism, asking for example if it is legitimate to buy kidneys, political offices, or the right to emit CO2 (Satz 2010; Sandel 2012). This theme also recurs in this volume, for example, when an inheritance is donated to the church in exchange for prayer services after death (*Quaas*). In general, it is a recurring theme in this volume that economic practices became morally suspicious when they appeared to become ends in themselves, for example making profits (*Drofner*, *Bete/Knäble*), but also acts of consumption (*Lutz*). Thus, a recurring strategy by contemporaries was to explicitly downplay the economic aspect of their activities and to frame them as a means to achieve a higher—social or religious—goal: for example earning enough money only to lead a peaceful life in leisure and contemplation (*Hinsch*), to build a community of missions and convert people to Christianity (*Bete/Knäble*), or to serve the community (*Dorfner*). Even gambling in Las Vegas only became morally accepted by framing it as a pure leisure activity, with winning (and losing) money only as a negligible side effect (*Franke*).

Finally, the case studies also show that morality is not only a restrictive force that limits or prohibits certain economic practices, but could also become an enabling and supporting factor that could be used strategically by economic actors. Many economic practices—especially in premodern societies, but also in modern capitalism—relied on some degree of mutual trust. Buying things depended on the assumption that goods had a reasonable quality and were not adulterated, giving credit relied on the assumption that creditors had at least the intention to pay back their loans, and long-distance trade was only possible with a certain degree of trust in the reliability of people in faraway places. Being seen as "moral" and "trustable" could thus be an important asset or "moral capital" that helped to be successful in business (*Hinsch*, *Dorfner*).

This classification is far from complete, and from a praxeological point of view, things become even more complicated, pointing to the fact that the meaning of any practice always depends on the social context in which it is performed. The case studies show this in many details: Giving and receiving credit had different meanings depending on whether Jews or Christians were involved and whether money was lent to peers or people outside of one's religious community (*Doron*); speculating with government bonds was generally considered problematic, but moral panics seemed to get even more widespread when women were involved (*Lizzul*); demanding state support in times of crisis was evaluated completely different depending on whether plaintiffs were seen as deserving or underserving poor (*Coccoli*).

Even more importantly—and also much more challenging from the historian's perspective—is the fact that the moral meaning of any economic practice was often directly related not only to the question of *who* did something but also to speculations about *why* people behaved in a certain way. Reading through the pages of this volume, it almost seemed like an obsession of all observers of "moral economies" to ask for the reasons and motivations of people to pursue certain economic practices: Was an inheritance given to the church out of religious zeal or to protect one's property from state seizures (*Quaas*)? Did people invest in small-scale credit schemes or government loans out of feelings of responsibility and patriotism or as a profit-seeking investment (*Skambraks*, *Lizzul*)? Were taxes paid as a "matter of conscience" or out of fear of punishment (*Schönhärl*)? And were those people at the roulette table playing for the fun of it or did they look for an easy way to make money (*Franke*)?

Such speculations about legitimate and illegitimate motives emphasize that there is another thing that people do in "moral economies": namely, to talk, write, and argue about economic aspects and their social and moral significance. This brings in new historical actors like religious experts (*Skambraks*, *Doron*, *Schönhärl*), philosophers (*Hinsch*), or a new social group of intellectuals (*Aytekin*), and also new text genres like canonical law, sermons, or merchant handbooks. These debates outline a wide spectrum of topics and concepts that were used to delineate "good" and "bad" economic practices. They show how some of these norms remained surprisingly stable over time while others lost their moral significance. Some key concepts that are used to delineate a just "moral economy" were picked up in many different contexts: ideas of reciprocity, balance, justice, moderation, and charity were used as guiding principles for a "moral economy". Other concepts were much more contested, such as wealth, work, growth, or competition.

These theoretical concepts are often put at the center when thinking about concepts of "moral economies". But from a praxeological point of view, we might again ask a slightly different question: namely, what people are actually doing when they refer to these concepts? Concerning the concept of "moral economy", the question would then be: What are the different ways in which "morality" was invoked in debates about economic matters?

At first sight, the answer to this question might seem straightforward: External observers—often religious authorities—used moral arguments primarily to criticize economic actors in an attempt to uphold moral and religious norms against economic practices that they deemed inappropriate. But if we look closer at the detailed descriptions in this volume, it becomes evident that individual motives and strategies were much more complex and heterogeneous. To be sure, moral arguments were often used to regulate, forbid, and punish certain economic practices, but there were also other dimensions. We can, for example, read the responses of Jewish authorities on economic and moral queries (*Doron*), the decisions of the Moravian "commerce committees" (*Dorfner*), or the statements of Catholic thinkers about the duty to pay taxes (*Schönhärl*) also as attempts to educate people about the "right" kind of economic behavior. In other cases, moral arguments were also used to justify and legitimize economic practices. This often happened by transforming the moral framework in which a certain economic practice was embedded: providing credit from profit to charity (*Skambraks*), economic growth from material gains to spiritual accomplishments (*Bete/Knäble*), and gambling from vice to leisure (*Franke*). Apart from this, moral arguments could also be used to explain economic developments, such as in the Ottoman empire of the nineteenth century, where a supposed "economic backwardness" was explained by morally charged arguments about a lack of entrepreneurial spirit and work ethic, pointing at the same time to an equally morally charged solution of work spirit, diligence, and modest lifestyles (*Aytekin*).

Finally, moral arguments did not only come "from above", but were also applied "from below". People demanded action and claimed material provisions or securities, especially in times of crisis (*Coccoli*), they could accuse authorities if they did not live up to such demands, and they used moral narratives to justify their behavior, often against other morally charged accusations. Such explicit references to moral arguments are very common and they are often at the center of historical analyses of "moral economies" because they leave explicit traces in historical sources. But often another practice seemed even more pervasive, even though it is more difficult to detect in historical accounts: That is, to ignore or circumvent certain political, moral, or religious demands, be in the complex architectures to circumvent medieval credit laws (*Doron*) or in the passive resistance to economic reforms (*Aytekin*). And, of course, if moral arguments about specific economic practices recur throughout the centuries, we can be quite sure that the moral reach of these arguments remained at least sketchy. In short: We should also remain aware of the limits of any "moral economy".

II. I have tried to look at the concept of "moral economy" through the economic practices and moral arguments that can be found in the case studies of this volume. The heterogeneity of these practices shows something trivial, yet important: in premodern and modern societies alike, we find a plurality of moral concepts and ideas that are used to describe economic practices. Thus, talking of "moral economies" in the plural does not only refer to the fact that there are different moral perspectives on economic matters at different times and in different social contexts, but also within any given society. It would also be too simple to clearly distinguish a "moral economy from above", in which moral arguments were used to legitimize an economic order and to discipline and educate citizens, from a "moral economy from below" that "the crowd" used to protect themselves against the political and economic pressures of the day. Instead, the case studies of this volume regularly point to the intersection of both perspectives and the transformation of moral and religious arguments in different social contexts.

Secondly, the examples in this volume show that we can think about the concept of "moral economy" in two ways: on the one hand, it can refer to economic practices that became attached to moral meanings and restrictions. On the other hand, we can also see how moral or religious doctrines became confronted and partly challenged by economic practices and realities. The fact that the term "moral economy" seems so plausible today could partly stem from the fact that we have a strong sense that economic practices have moral significance, but also from the fact that we interpret moral questions increasingly within the realm and the logic of economic questions and conceptualizations. Historical debates and conflicts about "moral economies" are often so interesting, because they not only apply moral doctrines to the realm of the economy, but because these very doctrines were always influenced by everyday economic encounters and practices.

Looking for these conflicts and intersections might be an interesting starting point to pick up the initial challenge of E.P. Thompson's 1971 article. Even after more than 50 years, the text still resonates with today's questions about the relationship between economy and morality, in particular, because Thompson goes such a long way in trying to adequately describe what the "English Crowd" actually did in the social conflicts of the eighteenth century. His key argument was that they did not just riot. Instead, he elaborates a rich vocabulary to describe what he called a "highly-complex form of direct popular action, disciplined and with clear objectives" (Thompson 1971, 78). Based on their practical knowledge of their local economy, these people acted in very different ways: They looked suspiciously at the quality of goods and the measures used by vendors and demanded action to ensure that products were not adulterated and measured correctly. They complained to authorities, but also informally spread accusations and rumors about malpractices. In times of crisis, they tried to prevent the export of corn and flour to other regions, for example, by threatening to destroy ships or canals. They used collective protests and marches through towns to win public support, and they also used violence, but often in a rather reflective and strategic way, for example, to "set the price" of products in a way that they deemed appropriate, or to force vendors to bring their products to local markets. There was also looting and window-smashing, but more characteristically debates and attempts to reach an agreement with authorities or local merchants.

Thompson describes these practices very meticulously and with the attempt to do justice to the complexity of motives, norms, and expectations that influence human agency. It is this detailed and multifaceted description—at least as much as his conceptual terminology—that can be seen as the most important legacy for any historical thinking about moral economies.

References

Sayer, Andrew. 2006. Approaching Moral Economy. In *The Moralization of Markets*, ed. Nico Stehr, Christoph Henning, and Bernd Weiler, 77–97. London: Transaction Publ.

Satz, Debra. 2010. *Why Some Things Should Not Be for Sale: The Moral Limits of Markets*. New York: Oxford University Press.

Sandel, Michael. 2012. *What Money Can't Buy: The Moral Limits of Markets*. New York: Farrar, Straus and Giroux.

Thompson, E. P. 1971. The Moral Economy of the English Crowd in the Eighteenth Century. *Past and Present* 50: 76–136.

Thompson, E. P. 1991. The Moral Economy Reviewed. In *Customs in Common*, 259–351. London: New Press.

Index

T. Skambraks and M. Lutz (eds.), *Reassessing the Moral Economy*, Palgrave Studies in Economic History,
https://doi.org/10.1007/978-3-031-29834-9

The manufacturer's authorised representative in the EU is Springer Nature Customer Service Centre GmbH, Europaplatz 3, 69115 Heidelberg, Germany. If you have any concerns regarding our products, please contact ProductSafety@springernature.com

Printed and bound by CPI Group (UK) Ltd, Croydon, CR0 4YY
01/10/2026
02225894-0009